Human Relationships

Third Edition

Steve Duck

SAGE Publications

London • Thousand Oaks • New Delhi

© Steve Duck, 1986, 1992, 1998

First published 1986
Second edition 1992
Reprinted 1992, 1994, 1996
Third edition 1998
Reprinted 1999, 2000, 2003

 SAGE Publications Ltd
6 Bonhill Street
London EC2A 4PU

SAGE Publications Inc.
2455 Teller Road
Thousand Oaks, California 91320

SAGE Publications India Pvt Ltd
32, M-Block Market
Greater Kailash – I
New Delhi 110 048

British Library Cataloguing in Publication data

A catalogue record for this book is available
from the British Library

ISBN 0 7619 5710 3
ISBN 0 7619 5711 1 (pbk)

Library of Congress catalog card number 97–061789

Typeset by Mayhew Typesetting, Rhayader, Powys
Printed in Great Britain by Athenæum Press Ltd.,
Gateshead, Tyne & Wear

For the loving, kind associates
who taught me to appreciate human relationships

Contents

Preface

When I finish reading a social science textbook I always regret that I learned so little about so much that is a familiar part of the real everyday social life of myself and my students. Whereas liking and disliking, falling in and out of love, shyness, jealousy and embarrassment, loneliness, friendship and romance are now routinely included in chapter 5 of most general textbooks in social psychology and interpersonal communication studies, the coverage still feels to me incomplete. Much of the material on relationships is covered in a dry way that is remote from my life and my students' personal experience of everyday living in a society, in a set of networks of other people, and in a system of language that all constrain our freedom to have relationships in any old way we might like. I therefore wanted to write this book as an account of the communicational and social processes with which we actually live because the research descriptions are, on their own, incomplete accounts of the living personal experiences of our daily lives. Therefore, my aim is to supplement available introductory texts by covering some important elements of life which they do not.

I focus upon the essence and substructure of interpersonal behaviour, the long-term and the short-term relationships which we have with other people and which so strongly influence our thoughts and behaviour and vice versa. The influence of relationships runs deep through the fabric of social behaviour and interpersonal communication. Relationships have real effects on our behaviour and the ways in which we spend our time. Equally, the groups, communities and societies which we talk about in the abstract are actually composed of real people and the personal and social relationships that bind them and bring them together. When we speak or write of 'students' or 'communication scholars' or 'social psychologists' or 'society' we are actually referring to real human beings with real personal ties and real relationships with one another. These relationships affect the ways in which information is transmitted. They exert pressures on individuals to act in certain ways (e.g. in their dress or even their responses to fashionable attitudes) in order to be accepted and liked. They influence the sorts of social behaviour that we choose from our repertoire on a given occasion, for instance, whether we treat someone in a special way because we know him or her or merely as 'yet another person in a hurry who is claiming special treatment'.

For these reasons I believe that everyday life and everyday relationships should be the starting points for the exploration of interpersonal behaviour.

The first edition of this book started with a chapter on emotions and cognition, because it is often felt that emotion and cognition are the bases of relationships. The second edition argued otherwise and found the basis of relationships in routine behaviours and everyday communication. The third edition focuses on the ways in which those routines are reflections of people's efforts to make sense of their world in a cultural and linguistic context. Not only relationships but also emotions themselves are based in routine and in social and linguistic frameworks for understanding and expressing our feelings. We could sit and love someone desperately, but if we do not let them know, or if they do not work it out for themselves from our behaviour – in short if the emotion were not communicated to them – then they might as well inhabit a different universe as far as relation-shipping is concerned. Furthermore any expression of emotions and any working out of relationships takes place in a set of contexts that give sense to those expressions – people know how the culture expects them to express love, for example.

Emotions are as much founded in the routine knowledge that we have about our partners and their regular styles of behaviour as they are to be found in our own particular styles of feeling. More than this, however, they are founded also in cultural knowledge, shared and commonly understood language and terminology, and ways of expressing ourselves. Thus a proper starting place for exploration of relationships is not in abstract thought or in emotion but in the cultural basis of knowledge and the ways in which behaviour is systematized as a context for relationships.

Given the title of this book, it is obvious that I will be writing about relationships and their influences, both hidden and declared, on people's behaviour. But I am not as able as many authors before me have been to think of a way of doing this without focusing explicitly on the communi-cation that goes on in relationships. I find it hard to think about 'inter-action' in the abstract, or 'social participation' without talk, for example, so I have made communication the topic of the first chapter in this edition of the book. This term is used somewhat loosely and in one form or another we cover many forms of such communication where we see our normal behaviours coming into view. For example, language usage, metaphors, everyday nicknames, coded relational words, everyday speech, friendly chat, gossip, discussing, asking, requesting, offering, persuading, pleading, influencing, arguing, are all familiar ways in which our subjects – human beings just like us – use speech and discourse every day to relate to other people in their interpersonal behaviour. Such crucial timbers of the structure of relationships are too often ignored.

Talk is inextricably linked in to human social interaction and underlies human relationships. To write about relating is actually to imply and assume a continuous and routine basis for interaction, but also to imply a language and communication system that provides the daily basis for our relation-ships. This system contains the things we say to each other to conduct and maintain the relationship, the terms that we use to describe our relationships or our feelings, the way we comfort a miserable friend, the way we present ourselves, the means or strategies we select to ask someone out on a date, the chosen ways in which we try to persuade someone else into or out of a relationship, or the subtle manner in which we convey our feelings about someone else by our choice of words and names for them.

Therefore, I begin the book with interpersonal communication and go on from there to emotion and the growth of personal relationships, influencing strangers, and social relationships in childhood. I look at the development of courtship, at sexual decision making in dating, and at the family. I discuss problems in relationships and how to put them right, deal with gossip and persuasion, and apply research on relationships to behaviour in the courtroom and the psychology of health.

(Mainly for the instructor) A psychology of human concerns

My intent is not to write a non-standard version of the familiar attack on laboratory research, to criticize the old for the sake of it, but instead to point in some new directions. The status of laboratory research is prematurely attacked, since we cannot properly claim that it is 'artificial' until we know exactly how daily life is made up.

Whereas textbooks often contain an implicit model of a daily life that is populated by young people who get together to do important things in cognitively sophisticated ways, our own daily lives are likely to consist of quite humdrum experiences with the same people we have known for years, whom we meet for insignificant social, emotional, or relational purposes, in a special context where we have plans about the future. Furthermore, some of these people will be colleagues with whom we have a long-standing relationship, be it friendship, formality, or feud. We often see people squabble and make stupid, irrational mistakes; we have meetings where no-one acts like a scientist; and we may deal with deans and tenure committees to whom none of our kindly textbook assumptions can possibly be applied. In short, our real social lives are based on complex but routine relationships which we do not emphasize in the textbooks, and we go around believing 'It's not what you know but who you know' and writing as if we didn't. Routines and relationships run through the fabric of our lives, too, and pattern the experience of those lives.

I began to notice some time ago that my students were often wise enough to know what really mattered in life. Whenever I asked them to pick a topic from a journal and evaluate the important research on it in the last five years, using tools such as *Current Contents* and *SSCI* (see the exercises in the Afterword, pages 212–14), I gave them a list of topics derived from the adopted text, but did not restrict them to that list. Not one of them picked a 'pure' research topic. Instead, all chose personally relevant research that, broadly speaking, focused on everyday experiences in relationships. Those people who were noticeably shy tended to research shyness; students from broken homes followed research on the effects of parental divorce on children; unattractive students wrote about self-fulfilling prophecies and Pygmalion effects. Moreover, the answers invariably were better than those for the usual class assignments and often were thoughtful and even exciting to read. I realized not only how much more effectively students learn from being personally involved but also the great potential of relationship research for illuminating their personal involvements.

I believe that, for all the preceding obvious and unobvious reasons, everyday relationships are significant subject matter and consequently I have structured this book around the theme of personal relationships. They are simultaneously the most personally important part of most people's lives, a potentially cohesive force in theories of interpersonal behaviour, and a recently booming area of research. Not least of my reasons for taking that position, however, is the belief that social science lacks substance when it addresses only the large-scale societal issues of the day. Social science has a supplementary and equally significant role: to be informative about the familiar; to explain the everyday; and to understand life as it is lived by the individual relating to other people in the street.

Acknowledgements

I am grateful to many people for their help, both witting and unwitting, in preparing me for the writing of this book. These include Jesse C. Stickler, Miss Jordan, Miss Burt, Robin Ovens, F.C.G. Langford, John Radford, Michael Booker, Lynda Cox, Mike Gardner, J.C.B. Glover, my late father and my mother, Carole Wade, Brian Little, Chris Spencer, George Kelly, Sanchez and John Davies, Linda Acitelli, Pembroke College (Oxford), Sheri Meserow Scott, Diane Lowenstein-Pattison, Sandra, Christina, Jamie, and Joanna, Ben and Gabriel.

Also, I thank those who helped and supported me during my guest professorship in the University of Connecticut, Storrs, when the first edition was prepared: Carol Masheter, Reuben Baron, Barbara Montgomery, Ross Buck, Bob Ryder, Jeff Fisher, Dave Kenny, Steve Anderson, and, above all, Linda Harris who fixed it all up. I thank also Peter Collett, David Clarke, Jill Crosland, Robert McHenry, and Michael Argyle at Oxford University for their hospitality whilst I was a visiting scholar during the preparation of the first edition of the book.

David Watson, Mark Leary, and Andrew Colman made extensive and careful comments about various drafts of the first edition, and Roz Burnett, Kathryn Dindia, Sue Jones, and Paul Wright made detailed and insightful comments on the draft of the second edition. Robin Gilmour provided prolonged discussion of some of the key ideas in the first edition. Michael Saks, Peter Blanck, and Zick Rubin gave me extensive advice and guidance for the chapter, new to the second edition, on relationships and the law, and Christina Duck read and advised on the revision of that chapter for the third edition. Joanna Lawson read several drafts of the whole manuscript for the first and second editions and provided many excellent critiques and case examples. For the third edition I thank Lee West for her careful reading and commentary on the book and her suggestions for the changes in emphasis and design that were needed. I also thank Linda Acitelli again for her thoughtful suggestions and very specific recommendations about ways to develop the project and incorporate new material. Those discussions helped me to focus some of the newer arguments that I offer in this edition. I am grateful to them all. I am also grateful to Farrell Burnett, formerly of Sage, whose attentive editing of the first edition contributed substantially to those parts of the book that attracted praise.

1

Meaning as a Context for Human Relationships . . . and Vice Versa

'Attention to the ways in which contexts influence relationships is the exception to the trend to investigate relationships as if they were private preserves immune to the overall social order.' (Wood, 1995: 114)

'Interpersonal relationships and communication are always developed in a specific cultural context that has its own values, norms and even institutions to cope with different types and levels of interpersonal relationships.' (Mamali, 1996: 217)

When those of us from a Western culture first think about human relationships we tend to assume that they are simply composed and constructed from the emotions that two people have for one another. You like someone, so you become friends; you love someone so you become romantically attached. More often we think the converse: we are friends with someone because we like them; we get romantic because we love someone.

In these first thoughts, we overlook the many contexts that modify expression and interpretation of such preferences, even if they are the real basis for relationships, and the real life practical constraints that limit our ability to act on our emotions. The present book takes a look at the research on relationships with a new contextual lens and teaches that even individual liking or attraction is not so individualistic as we may sometimes think and that desire is only infrequently the origin of actual relational behaviour. I will emphasize the roles of culture, of personal meaning systems, of communication, of 'audiences' for our behaviour, of nonverbal communication – and of several other contexts (the things we read in the papers or see on TV, for instance) that both facilitate and limit what we do. Human relationships are not simply created by liking or by an individual's attitudes about another person. They are based on many other features that we tend to overlook and which a rich and growing field of research in social and personal relationships has uncovered in the last few years. To explore this better, and to try to understand human relationships better, I shall weave together research and scholarship from communication, social psychology, family studies, sociology, and developmental psychology.

Begin by thinking about the humdrum activities and structures of social experience that bring people together whether they like one another or not. Some relationships – perhaps most relationships – are composed and constructed by circumstances over which partners have little emotional control, yet which bring us together. The workplace, the living place and the

social environment are all made out of passages, offices, rooms and buildings that are close to other buildings, offices, rooms and passages where
other people live and work. These environmental contexts shape our relationships, influence the kinds of people we meet, and constrain or facilitate
relationships: we are likely to know people we meet a lot, yet even those we
love deeply may never be real partners if we live in different countries
(Rohlfing, 1995).

We perhaps also overlook the fact that our society contains blueprints for
relationships both openly and implicitly and that these shape our thoughts
about relationships and how to do them. For example, we all know what a
'mother' is and what a 'friend' is, but we would not perhaps understand
relationships of obligation that are familiar in Japan such as the 'amae'
relationship where each partner identifies with the self-interest of the partner
and sees a direct connection between the outcomes of the other and the self.
Also we probably wouldn't assume that a relationship like 'son of a second
wife' could be more important in some cultures than 'sister' or that in some
cultures it is impolite or disrespectful to address an older brother by his first
name – rather the *title* 'brother' should be used (Valdez, 1996). We may
also not appreciate that in a society which stresses individualism we very
readily assume that relationships are formed from individual choice and
preference whereas other cultures (e.g. Colombia) emphasize that relationships are based on the interconnectedness of all persons in the network, who
do favours for one another and exercise 'palanca' (or 'leverage') on one
another's behalf as a part of everyday life (Fitch, forthcoming). Yet other
cultures look at relationships in terms of the overall good that accrues to the
family as a whole rather than to the individual (Gaines and Ickes, 1997). In
such a culture two people might get married because it would be a good
match for the two families, not because they fall uncontrollably in love with
one another in the way in which our Western culture approves or expects.

Although we are often intrigued by these 'odd' (from our perspective)
ways of relating, we simply do not realize how much of our own relating is
influenced by our own culture. We are so fully soaked in our own culture
that we assume it is normal and we take it for granted. Part of the reason
that we do not think about such cultural underpinnings of our own relationships is because they are hidden parts of the cultural ideology to which
we all unwittingly subscribe (Billig, 1991) and which will become even
clearer as you proceed to read through this book and challenge some of
your existing assumptions about human relationships.

We might not stop and ponder the ways in which our views of relationships are shaped by ideological influences such as media, yet magazines
and TV shows regularly depict 'the right way' to have marriages, conduct
romances, or be friends. Some magazines run quizzes along the lines of '10
ways to improve your marriage', 'Intimacy: the five steps' and other kinds of
articles that effectively shape a reader's expectations and judgements about
relationship conduct. Duran and Prusank (1997), for example, looked at the
advice about 'relationships' contained in men's and women's magazines and

found not only that there was a great deal of it but that it concerned a large range of relationships (e.g. marriage, dating, friendship), relational issues (e.g. conflict, sexual relations, initiating relationships), and rhetorical presentations of how they *should* be conducted. They concluded: 'Given the various configurations of relationships and the ambiguity they generate, it is logical to assume that men and women are turning to the media as one source of information concerning relational issues. Researchers interested in the study of interpersonal dynamics cannot ignore the influence of media messages which overtly and covertly make their way into the public consciousness and serve to (re)shape and (re)frame relationships' (Duran and Prusank, 1997: 186).

OK, you may feel that these are just magazine articles and they are quite interesting but they do not really influence anyone . . . but if they do not have any effect then why do people keep reading them and why do people compare their relationship experiences with the magazines' recommendations and buy millions of self help books that tell them how to do relating or how to win friends and influence people? And can you honestly say that you have never read such an article nor been influenced by the portrayal of relationships in films and TV or compared your way of doing relating with the way other people in such sources do them? What, never? Gimme a break! It will be worthwhile for you to discuss this matter with your classmates and see the extent to which there is conformity in the class concerning the ways in which relationships could be conducted. Think of the number of times other people have commented about whether someone should have treated a friend the way they did. Consider how many times someone has given you advice about the sorts of ways to carry on with your relationships (if they have not then your in-laws will!). All these things feel normal and usual, but in fact as the rest of this book will show, they are the places where an ideology about relationships is put into effect, the place where cultural stereotypes of relating are enacted in everyday life. They are where we are influenced by social norms concerning the emotions that (we may have assumed at first) are purely personal experiences.

While these kinds of subtle influence and gender stereotypes are familiar parts of everyday life experience, researchers, too, operate with prototypes of relationships. Davis and Todd (1985) listed the characteristics of 'true friendship' and distinguished them from other forms of relationships using scientific techniques. Such lists contain the implicit notion that there is a *right* way to do relating and that it can be articulated and written down, as Montgomery (1988) points out. Few of us would immediately recognize this as a means of social control or an ideology, and yet in subtle ways it lays the ground for a kind of social influence that sets a standard for other people to use in commenting on the ways in which we conduct relationships: 'It's not right', 'He should not treat his friends that way', 'She was disloyal to her parents', 'He betrayed her and friends don't do that.' Such comments come from the contexts available in any society for people to judge relationship conduct (Klein and Milardo, 1993). Comment and criticism based on social expectations are also available to every one of us as we conduct our own relationships ('I felt like hugging him but it would have looked bad'). The little person inside our heads tells us when we are doing something that we would find hard to justify to other people, even if that 'something' is the conduct of personal relationships. These feelings arise because sociological context, structural factors and social forces are ever-present houseguests in the ways in which we decide what is 'appropriate' in human relationships – for instance, society forbids even married couples to have sexual intercourse in the street; politeness rules encourage us often to conceal our true emotions in public ('Be nice even if you don't really feel it'); we may exaggerate or misrepresent expression of our interest in someone or our relational feelings about them, as when we smile at boring strangers at parties or kiss embarrassing relatives at Christmas time. Furthermore, even the highly positive expression, 'I love you', can be judged inappropriate if it comes from the 'wrong person' or at the 'wrong time'. Thus, it is clear that simply *having* emotions (or simply *expressing* them naked and raw) is not all that we need to understand in learning about human relationships: we need to think more about contexts.

But there is a deeper aspect of contexts for relationships also. Wood (1995) observes that women assume a disproportionate share of responsibilities for home-making in a marriage and childcare in parent–child relationships. She indicates that if we explain such observations only in terms of individual attitudes or beliefs and values then we mistake the degree to which attitudes are constructed by cultural views of 'a woman's place', views that are represented in literature, TV shows, talk, use of language and even video games (where women are often depicted as objects to be chased while men get on with the really important business of decapitating fighting lizards). J. West (1995) further points out that many social organizations, such as the priesthood or the police, reinforce particular views of relationships – e.g. by telling battered women that they should 'tough it out' because marriage is a relationship that 'requires that a woman obeys her husband'. For this reason, many battered women stay in abusive relationships because they receive no support from cultural institutions like the Church, which takes the view that a wife's duty is to oblige her husband, come what may.

Lastly, we may not realize that language itself provides a context for discussion of relationships. It structures our ways of thinking about relationships along culturally normative lines. Obviously, most of the forces mentioned above (magazines, norms, friends, 'others') use language to shape up our views of acceptable relationship practices. Yet, even when people do not explicitly say things that accord with cultural norms, like 'Be loyal to your friends', the choice of terms in which to tell stories about our friends can play in tune with cultural norms anyway. For example, friends' accounts of their behaviour toward one another can point out their loyalty, and hence endorse the cultural norm of loyalty in friendship. As we gossip with friends so we select out descriptions of people's behaviour that record our approval or disapproval as compared to cultural norms ('Sure, I'll help you. What are friends for?'), or decide whether a person was being good or bad ('He's so reliable', 'No he's just boringly predictable'). In such subtle ways as the selection of points to include in a story or the ways to gossip about others' behaviour, people use language to reinforce social norms, but also language embodies some of the norms for us. Furthermore in ways that we will explore further later, language, communication and everyday talk serve to present our choices about the ways in which the world *should* be viewed and our hopes that other people will accept and endorse those views. Language – or more broadly, communication and all that is culturally encoded within it – is thus a crucial basis for establishing ways in which we conduct human relationships and judge their quality.

Obvious, too, but often overlooked, is the fact that language is the medium through which many relationship activities are conducted. We talk, write, call or email to friends, lovers, parents, children, neighbours, or colleagues – and we obviously use language to do that. Language is not neutral, however, and not merely a slack medium of transmission. Language serves to *structure* meanings about the human relationships that we seek to understand or perform (Duck, 1994a) and it is important to recognize the ways in which language and meaning seep into all our experiences of relating. For example, we are used to explaining relationships in terms of emotion, feeling, love and attraction, but language sets up a context that 'takes a view' about the ways in which independent entities are supposed to progress in building a relationship (Allan, 1993). The way in which we describe the development of a relationship is really a story or narrative imposed on a number of events and occurrences perceived within a particular social context as a *reasonable* path in a particular culture (Duck et al., 1997). Think about it. Duck et al. suggest that 'We met, fell in love, and got married' is more acceptable in Western culture than 'I ate some ground almond paste and the relationship just developed from there', or 'We sacrificed some sheep and therefore we became closer', or 'Our parents picked our partners from a catalogue and naturally we got married the next day.' By subscribing to certain kinds of stories, cultures provide contexts for individuals not only to view the way relationships are *supposed* to develop, but also to speak with culturally-shared vocabularies for representing relationship growth. 'We fell in love' is a commonly accepted explanation for romantic involvement in most Western cultures; 'It is a good match for both families' is more acceptable in many other parts of the world. What we should not overlook are the subtler influences on relationship conduct that are created by these contexts of talk, topics thought fit for discussion, and communicative guides that enact social norms or invite moral judgements about relational behaviour.

Judgements about acceptability of relationship behaviour and form will ultimately be made by a group outside the relationship itself or individuals alone (Simmel, 1950). The conduct of a person in a relationship and of relationships themselves will ultimately be judged by social communities

rather than by self and relational partner alone. In that knowledge, relationship partners reflect on the ways in which their behaviour may be
judged by others (e.g. 'What will the neighbours think?' and 'What do we
tell the kids?' are common thoughts in couples considering divorce – see
Chapter 4 here). Klein and Milardo (1993) discuss the ways in which third
parties comment on – or even 'referee' – conflicts within couples, and
although Klein and Milardo studied the ways in which relatives made such
comments, there are other wider social sources for comment, too, and those
reference points are built into our familiar language. J. West (1995) notes
that when we talk of relationships breaking up our cultural reference point
is placed within a language of 'failure' and it is a very powerful language
that makes partners think carefully about their relational skills. Many
people stay in bad relationships because they do not want other people to
think of them as failures.

Thus a book about human relationships has to recognize that even relationship behaviours do not mean much without being placed in some larger
conceptual contexts (Duck, 1993). An individual's own personal meaning
system creates a personal context for interpreting other people's behaviour
(Duck, 1994a). Socially and culturally shared meaning systems are built into
a person's views of the world (Mead, 1934). A part of the human experience
of life is the effort after meaning that derives from membership of a society
and networks of relationships whose judgements one must take into account
(Duck, 1994a). Attempts to focus explanations for relationship processes
only on the inside of the relationship or the individual partners' choices and
emotions are therefore incomplete and limiting because they overlook such
important social, sociological, and cultural contexts (Berscheid, 1995; Duck,
1993). As we shall see later in the book, ideology enters into the examination of relationships just as it does elsewhere (Billig et al., 1988);
whenever we talk about relationship quality or assess relationships as 'good'
or 'bad' or partners as 'skilled' or 'unskilled', or evaluate people as 'good
friends', or see divorce as a relational failure rather than a bold or realistic
move, then we are essentially backing into an ideology that sets a standard
and also has set criteria for 'quality' (Montgomery, 1988, 1993; Spitzberg,
1993).

We can and should start a study of relationships therefore by looking not
just at the individual *per se* but at the ways in which an individual's
understanding and practices of relationships are influenced by the magic of
language and the practicalities of a person's membership of a culture and
society. Culture and society are systems of meaning that filter into
individuals' psyches in very interesting and complicated ways (Duck,
1994a). These individual systems of meaning inevitably provide the schemes
that must be interleaved when two people come together to make their
relationship within a culture that has definitions of what is appropriate,
what behaviour is expected, what may be said and not said – and where
you can do it. Thus we start examining human relationships by looking first
at language and talk, since these are broad public contexts for relating.

Contexts for talk

Two scholars once wrote that 'We converse our way through life' (Berger and Kellner, 1975), and in the case of human relationships, it is clear that this is so. If you were to sit and list the things that you do with friends, one of the top items on the list would surely have to be 'talking'. Talking is fundamental to relationships – whether they are starting, getting better, getting worse, or just carrying on. Also such talk is one obvious vehicle for creating change in relationships, for expressing emotion, for handling conflict, and for indicating love and affection. We talk to share attitudes; we express our personalities through talk, we declare love through talk; we talk about our desires, goals and relational fantasies; in short, we talk to relate, whether well or badly. We also talk to handle conflicts, resolve disputes, manage irritations, get out of relationships and deal with daily relationship hassles (Duck, 1994a). We talk to exact revenge, deal with enemies, forgive, complain, and manage the light and dark sides of relationships in general (Duck and Wood, 1995).

In carrying out these activities we choose the words to use and the descriptions to employ, and the preferences and judgements that they implicate. Even casual talk selects out such descriptive preferences or registers a decision to stay silent. Silences and words both record our views of the world and the people in it. Communication registers these views and offers them to other people. In this subtle way our talk presents to the world and our audiences our own way of looking at the world and it attempts to persuade others to endorse that view. All talk is persuasive in ways that we shall explore further (Duck, 1994a).

There is more to human relationships than talk, though. It is rather the broader context of *communication* as a whole that is the basis for relating in the real world – communication that includes not only talk but 'para-language' (such things as tones of voice that communicate emotions or feelings about another person). One recent development in human com-munication – email – provides an interesting instance here. There are some rules of etiquette developing (such as 'Do not write in all capital letters without explaining why or people will think you are angry and shouting') and a whole range of special keystrokes intended to show nonverbally that the speaker is joking, teasing or surprised, such as :-) :-{ and :-o (Lea and Spears, 1995). Indeed there are those who claim that every verbal message contains not one but two elements (Watzlawick et al., 1967): the *content* and a *message about the relationship* between the speaker and the listener. In other words, you can barely utter a word to another person without also simultaneously indicating how you feel about the other person.

Communication is thus not merely the passing of messages from one person to another but the whole context of processes by which meaning is created and managed (Krauss and Fussell, 1996). This context thus also includes NVC (i.e. nonverbal communication), the silent messages of touch, smiles, warm and tender eyes, and bodily postures that convey culturally

accepted messages of invitation, approval or rejection. Through usage of
spacing (closeness or distance, for example), messages of intimacy or dislike
can be conveyed in a given culture, just as they are by words. From the
nonverbal accompaniments of speech, human beings tend to deduce
important overtones about relationship messages, as when a sensitive
comment is made more comforting by a tender touch or a supportive
embrace.

Much of this sort of communication in relationships – whether it is
verbal, paralinguistic or nonverbal — is extremely familiar to us. Yet just as
a child may be able to ride a bicycle without being able to explain anything
about balance or the physics of motion, so too we may be unaware of the
complex system of rules and meanings that underlies such routine
behaviours as conversing with friends. To begin our broader comprehension
of communication in human relationship and for understanding the contexts for talk and for inferences about other people we will start with the
silent behavioural context for talk in relationships. Then we can go on to
explore, in Chapter 2, the ways in which emotions are given meaning in that
context.

Silent language: nonverbal communication

Bodies talk. Whenever we sit, stand, walk, position ourselves next to
someone, or look at someone else, we give off messages, some of which we
may not have intended to make public. Equally, we can learn that someone
dislikes us when they have not even said a word, that he or she is deliberately lying to us, or that a person finds us sexually attractive. We can do all
this by understanding the hidden languages of social behaviour which we
understand by assimilating it in socialization or by seeing it reinforced in
media or by the commentary of third parties (Klein and Johnson, 1997).

Our human relationships with one another are based not on one language
but on two. Spoken language is the one that we recognize more easily, but
there is an unspoken language of nonverbal communication that provides
context for talk. Nonverbal communication (NVC) is made up of, for
instance, the spacing between people when we interact, the gestures, eye
movements and facial expressions that provide context for but also supplement our speech, and a range of other cues (Keeley and Hart, 1994). We
never speak without adding to the message by body language, such as
frowning or smiling or looking interested, impressed, or bored. These
messages are at least as powerful as speech itself. They also have considerable relational relevance. Guerrero (1997) showed that close proximity,
touch and gaze, along with reduced verbal fluency, longer times between the
end of one person's speech and another's starting, and more silence,
distinguished romantic relationships from friendships. Frequent nonverbal
cues such as nodding and vocal interest were more prevalent in friendships
than in romantic relationships. There were even relational differences

---

Box 1.1 Nonverbal behaviour, cultural meaning and context

- Is social behaviour a skill, like riding a bicycle, with certain, almost automatic abilities, that we have to know how to use properly in order to get along with other people?
- How does an apparently 'unrelational' factor, like the usage of space in social interaction or decoration of territory, have any impact on relationships or on 'atmosphere' in interpersonal interaction?
- Nonverbal communication (NVC) is less susceptible to conscious control than is speech, so we can readily 'leak' our real feelings unintentionally.
- How can we tell when other people are lying? What cues give them away to us?
- We can also add important emphasis or context to our words through socially meaningful messages like accent, humorous sarcasm and winks, significant stares, gestures, and loudness/softness of voice.
- NVC also conveys attitudes to relationships, through formality and informality in messages, by 'leaking' or openly showing that we like or dislike someone, creating status differences and by showing who is in charge.
- NVC is a system with culturally specific meaning, and different cultures manage space in different ways, some retaining a relatively formal distance in order to hold conversations and some preferring to be close enough to touch each other on the arm while conversing.
- NVC conveys great meaning and is generally (and often incorrectly) regarded as giving us better evidence about someone's feelings or intentions than are other sorts of communication.

---

between the ways in which bodies were arranged in the complementary ways ('postural congruence'); postural congruence occurred more in same-sex than in opposite-sex dyads. More than this, women displayed more direct body orientation and gaze, but men engaged in more forward lean and postural congruence. In other words, there are important dimensions of nonverbal behaviours that are different as a result of relationship type. Yet it is important to recognize that such findings about relationships emerge against the background of the profound importance of nonverbal communication in general interactions and the inappropriateness that is indicated when nonverbal behaviour mismatches the words spoken. If someone spoke to you saying that he or she was interested but looked bored or was reading the newspaper, which would you believe – the verbal or the nonverbal message? However, before we look at studies that show the effects of combining nonverbal communication and talk, we need to learn a little about each of them on its own first and we can start with something important yet subtle: use of space.

Are there social rules about space?

A large number of messages about status and liking are structured into interactions and a great deal of influence on social encounters is exerted by space and its management. These factors position people both literally and metaphorically in relationship to one another. Space carries forceful messages about relationships and is a powerful ingredient in the mix of nonverbal and verbal indicators of liking.

Space even gets into our language and so contextualizes our talk about relationships. For example, isn't it interesting that we talk about being 'close' to someone? 'Close' is a word that literally refers to space and to physical distance or nearness, and yet we use it metaphorically to apply to relationships, almost unthinkingly. We can even talk about 'growing further apart' when we mean that our liking for someone is decreasing or our relationship with them is getting more difficult. In fact spatial metaphors run through much of our thinking about relationships and there is a reason for that: space influences the way in which we relate to others and it communicates messages of power, liking and attitudes towards others. Just think for a moment about the rich array of metaphorical statements about power and position that are made in spatial terminology. For example, we talk of people being 'high and mighty', they can be 'head and shoulders above the rest', 'the tops', 'way above the competition', 'the greatest'. Good experiences are 'highs' or 'high-points'. We have *high* moral principles and are *above* doing anything mean such as showing *low* cunning.

Spatial metaphors are also used to refer to 'inferiority' (which is derived from the Latin word *inferus*, meaning 'lower'): people are of low status, lowly, lowdown no-goods, beneath (rather than above, beyond, or outside) contempt. A bad experience is a 'downer', and we feel low. In doing something bad, we may be accused of stooping low, or letting others down. When we assert ourselves, on the other hand, we stand up for ourselves or stand up to someone powerful. In short, our language equates spatial position with moral or social or relational position, with 'up' being 'good' (Lakoff and Johnson, 1980). As evidence of a general human tendency to prefer 'up' to 'down', consider that even words like despise ('look down on'), deride ('laugh down at'), superior ('above') and prefer ('to put higher up') contain the same metaphor directly in their original Latin roots from 2000 years ago.

There are also powerful social rules governing the actual rather than metaphorical use of space in social situations and movements through space. These work nonverbally, by means of bodily cues to do with posture, gesture, orientation (i.e. the way our body is facing) and various other subtleties like eye movements (Keeley and Hart, 1994). Unfortunately, the very discussion of it is something that is embarrassing and hard to do. We hardly ever refer directly to someone's nonverbal behaviour and to do so is usually rude or aggressive ('Wipe that smile off your face', 'Look at me when I'm talking to you', 'Don't stand so close to me'). The rarity of such comments is testament to the power of NVC and emphasizes that the competent use of NVC is a prerequisite to relating to other people. The dynamic rule system for NVC makes six basic assumptions: (1) the use of nonverbal cues is identifiable and recognizable; (2) the operation of non-verbal cues is essentially systematic, even if occasionally ambiguous; (3) we all translate our feelings and intentions into nonverbal messages (i.e. we *encode*); (4) observers are able to interpret (or *decode*) it; (5) whether or not we intend it, observers may decode our behaviour systematically and as relationally relevant, even attending to signals that we thought we had successfully concealed; (6) NVC is judged in cultural context, such that a behaviour that is appropriate (or carries one meaning) in one culture may not be appropriate (or may carry another meaning) in another cultural context (for instance, the placing of the thumb and forefinger together to form a circle means 'Perfect!' in the USA but is a crude sexual insult in Sicily).

As Patterson (1988) has shown, nonverbal communication is not only systematic in the above ways but also serves five functions for us, some of which I will explore here. These functions are: (1) to provide information to others about ourselves, especially our feelings or our relational attitudes; (2) to regulate interaction (e.g. by enabling us to see when someone has said all that they intend to say and it is our turn to talk); (3) to express intimacy and emotional closeness in relationships; (4) to attempt social control (e.g. by dominating others); (5) to engage in a service-task function (i.e. to depersonalize certain contacts that would otherwise be 'intimate'. For example, think of the parts of your body that physicians can touch but which other people may not – unless they are remarkably close friends). Also note that some parts can be touched in private meetings but not in public (Davis, 1983), or in informal settings but not, say, when you are in the audience of a classical music concert.

Territories in space   Let us begin with a large context for behaviour: the space in which it occurs. At first sight space and 'territory' may seem irrelevant to everyday human relationships, even though animals and governments use the concept a lot. Some birds fight other birds that come into their 'patch', baboons control space and attack invaders, dogs and cats mark out their territorial boundaries with body products, and governments put up their flags on their territory. Yet humans use space in relationships, too, in a systematic way that has territorial and relational overtones (i.e. we use space as if it is invisibly 'attached' to us or under our control). This occurs both in fixed settings, like offices, and in dynamic settings, during conversations.

The study of human spatial behaviour is known as 'proxemics' (Keeley and Hart, 1994). Hall (1966) differentiated space into *intimate* (i.e. from direct contact to around 18 inches [46cm] away from another person – obviously used with someone we know and like); *personal* (from around 18 inches [46cm] to about four feet [1.4m] apart – usually used when talking to casual friends or acquaintances); *social* (from around four feet [1.4m] to around 12 feet [4.2m] apart – usually used for business transactions and impersonal encounters), or *public* (from around 12 feet [4.2m] or more apart

– e.g. think how a speaker at public events stands away from the rest of the group or audience).

As long as we can breathe comfortably and our basic physiological needs are met (e.g. we are not too hot or too cold) then sociocultural and relational rules for distribution of space will be the ones that we follow. In different relational contexts we are comfortable with different distances; imagine talking to friends, to a teacher, and going to a lecture – you would not sit as close to a teacher giving a lecture as you would to a friend telling a story. Another thing to notice is that as we get to know someone better so we indicate this by holding conversations standing at smaller distances from each other. The more intimate we become emotionally, the more intimate we get spatially; we get closer in two senses (Duck, 1994a; Rubin, 1973).

Claiming space is claiming power Space rules carry extra information about status, ownership, and the social or personal relationship between participants (see Box 1.2). Human beings decorate their rooms, houses, cars, other possessions and themselves and do so in a way that indicates these things. For instance, furniture in offices is arranged in ways that indicate who owns what, who is superior to whom, and how much of the space is 'public'. Desks and tables can be arranged to show power relationships between people, in addition to any reasons to do with lighting or ease of communication. For example, bank managers usually make you sit across the desk from them as a distancing device to indicate their power and importance. By contrast, therapists tend to have their desks off to the side, or to sit with nothing but a low table in between clients and themselves. This reduces both physical and psychological barriers and promotes a context for a less formal and more relaxing relationship.

Furniture is used in this way to make implicit statements about relative power in a relationship, who is in charge and how far you can go. For example, receptionists' desks are usually placed in your path and so communicate the receptionist's power to control your entry further into the office or your access to the boss. It is physically possible to break the rules, but is a social offence. For example, moving your chair round the barrier so that you sit next to the bank manager, moving round to the other side of the table, opening a door marked 'Private', or sitting on a receptionist's desk, all violate a social rule. Such violations would most probably lead to comment or discomfort or possibly to the other person becoming angry. Someone who habitually violates such rules in conducting relationships will obviously be rather difficult to deal with.

Symbolic decoration also indicates ownership of space and so it affirms control and power. The most obvious example is clothing: physically, I could put my hand in your pocket, but socially . . . The placing of posters or decorations on a wall can also indicate that the person claims that space as under personal control, too. Furthermore, if, in a library or refectory, we observe an empty seat with a coat hanging over the back, we know it is a meaningful symbol laying claim to the space: the coat owner is indicating that he or she will return and use the chair. If we see sets of books arranged on library tables in such a way that someone could read them, when no-one is in fact doing so, then we would probably go somewhere else to seat ourselves. You might like to consider whether the same sort of principle is implicit in relational 'decoration' such as wedding rings.

A further way of claiming space is achieved through self-extension. Placing your feet on a coffee table or desk, sprawling across an otherwise empty bench, and leaning across a doorway are all ways of claiming control over the space. Claiming space is claiming power, ownership and, above all, status. As people are promoted in an organization, so this is symbolically recognized by the award of larger offices, longer desks, broader areas of carpet, taller chairs and wider blotter pads. Space is a metaphor for status.

Most often, a spatial claim is horizontal and concerns the amount of floor space allocated to a person. Status claims, however, are often related to vertical space too, as in 'higher' or 'lower' status. Kings, queens, judges, and professors sit on raised platforms. Popes are carried round at shoulder height when they are elected. Equally, temporary changes in status can be acknowledged by height changes as when a scoring footballer jumps up in the air or is lifted up in triumph by team-mates. More subtly, persons sometimes bow or curtsey (thus reducing their height) when they are introduced to someone of much higher status, and in ancient China persons introduced to the emperor had to reduce their height to the extent of hurling themselves to the floor and banging their foreheads on the ground. Nowadays, only assistant professors seeking tenure do this.

Space and conversation   Space matters also in the dynamic flux of conversations and social encounters (Keeley and Hart, 1994). To lean across someone's desk more than about halfway is a threat to them personally. To lean beside someone with your hand on the wall behind his or her shoulder at a party is to 'claim' the person so enclosed: you are telling other people to 'Keep out'. The other person in these circumstances can obviously escape physically by brushing past, but to do so would violate a social rule about the relational 'meaning' of space. It would be rude, explicit and offensive too. Likewise, invasion of someone's space by touching them can be a statement about intimacy, as can moving closer, or crossing over the table to sit next to one another rather than opposite, though these may also be seen as just as invasive. Guerrero and Andersen (1991) showed that the level of public touch between partners was actually curvilinear – lower for couples at early or late/stable stages of relationships, highest for those at middle or developing stages. They found that public touch increased primarily in the hand and waist areas during the intermediate stage of relationships. In short, a dynamic use of space carries relational messages that affect the tone of an interaction and can lead to judgements of disliking/liking or hostility/friendliness, or can publicly display the level of relationship.

Box 1.2   Some research findings about space usage

People find it more appropriate to sit opposite others with whom they will have an argument and to sit next to someone with whom they agree (Keeley and Hart, 1994). Conversely it is 'harder' to disagree with someone who is sitting next to us, and Warner et al. (1987) found that there are increases in rhythm and patterning of NVC as positive feelings increase.

There are cultural differences in tolerance for closeness in conversation. Watson and Graves (1966) observe that Arabs habitually stand close to partners and touch them during conversations whilst Americans stand further apart. Legend reports that if you put an Arab and an Englishman in a room to stand and converse, you get fascinating results. The comfortable distance for the Arab is too close for the Englishman, who will therefore edge back. This makes things uncomfortably distant for the Arab, who edges forward. But, for the Englishman, this is now too close . . . a slow but definite movement around the room then occurs! The same 'dance' can be created when you talk to other people. If you edge slightly forward, they will edge slightly back and vice versa.

Violent prisoners overreact negatively to spatial invasion (Kane, 1971), particularly to someone entering the 'body buffer zone' that we all perceive around ourselves. Such body buffer zones are the area that we regard as 'ours' immediately around our body. Since the body buffer zones for violent prisoners have been found to be larger than normal ones, they are more easily invaded and violated. That is, normal people have smaller body buffer zones than the violent prisoners did and people can therefore get closer to the normal people without violating the zone. For the violent prisoners, the body buffer zone was larger than normal and so the 'owners' more easily and frequently became upset when other people got physically close. A negative reaction was particularly likely in response to invasion from behind.

Space is used in relationships in important ways. People typically have romantic meetings in 'appropriate' places (not in the office for example, but somewhere arranged in a way that is intimate and private and permits physical closeness; Duck, 1991).

Space is also used symbolically in relational celebrations (Werner et al., 1993). For example it is decorated for birthdays or weddings; key players in such celebrations are given more space for the occasion (being moved 'up' to the head of the table, for instance).

Space is allocated for relational purposes or to particular members of a family (e.g. the playroom) and parts of a house are allotted to specific relational members (Altman and Ginat, 1996). This turns out to be a particular problem for Mormon polygamists who have more than one wife or household (one man complained that he could never find his socks because different wives put them in different places!).

Nonverbal systems of meaning

You may be starting to see a problem here. What exactly is 'the' meaning of proximity and space in social encounters? At some times, proximity (or physical closeness) indicates intimacy (e.g. when we sit next to people whom we like) but at other times closeness can indicate exactly the opposite: invasion and personal threat. When a stranger stands close to us we can experience threat, irritation, fear or even a rise in blood pressure (Clore, 1977). The two kinds of meaning are attached to eye movements as well as to proximity. Gazing at a person's eyes is often, but not always, an indication of intense liking; we look at people more often if we like them. In the West, eye contact (i.e. when two people look one another in the eye) indicates interest, liking and acceptance (Keeley and Hart, 1994), but in the East it is contextualized by hierarchy: inferiors may not look superiors in the eye because it is regarded as a disrespectful or challenging gesture. Pupil size marginally increases when we see someone or something that we like, and we prefer faces in which the pupils are dilated – presumably because it signals that the face likes us (Walker and Trimboli, 1989). Yet, as with proximity, staring and gazing can be threatening also. An intense stare can be used as a threatening cue both in animals and in humans. The stare is a stimulus to flight, and persons who are stared at when they stop at traffic lights will move away faster from the junction when the lights go green (Ellsworth et al., 1972). Like physical closeness, eye contact thus can indicate either threat or dominance, as well as liking.

How do people decide the intended meaning then? As indicated at the start of the chapter the interpretation of space rules is something we learn to do within a specific culture. Space both provides a context for interaction and takes its meaning from broader cultural contexts and rules, as does eye contact. The cultural system basically guides us not only on the interpretation of individual cues but also on how to put different cues together and add sense to the whole context. This happens because the verbal–nonverbal communication system is a system of parts (like space, eye contact) that provides a context to help us to decode people's meaning (see below) but also is a system within a cultural system of meaning (Patterson, 1992). The parts work together to help us to clarify meanings in particular cases but they do so within a cultural context that 'explains' how they work together. For one thing, the individual cues, like proximity, hardly ever happen in isolation. A complex interrelationship exists between space and other nonverbal cues, such as eye movements. The way in which we can learn the full relational message is by attending to the system of cues, not to just one in isolation. We work out relational meaning from eye-contact-plus-context or from proximity-plus-words. When someone stares and smiles, then we know we are favoured; if someone stares and frowns, then we are in trouble.

If we add two positive messages together, what do we get? For example, does eye contact plus closeness take the intimacy level beyond what people can bear? Argyle and Dean (1965) proposed an equilibrium model (later modified by Patterson, 1992), namely, that the appropriate intimacy level of an interaction is held steady by a balancing of proximity and eye contact. As proximity increases so eye contact will decrease (unless the two are lovers where the two cues are 'appropriate' together); that way, the total level of signalling for intimacy will stay about right. If proximity decreases then eye contact should increase to maintain the equilibrium of the encounter. This works with other signals for intimacy, too. For example, as an interviewer's questions become more personal, so the interviewee reduces eye contact when giving answers (Carr and Dabbs, 1974). Also, Ickes et al. (1982) found that a person who expected a partner to be unpleasant used greater positive patterns of NVC to compensate and to encourage the partner to balance his or her attitude. (At this point you may like to think how, then, people *develop* intimacy. If the intimacy level is kept at an appropriate equilibrium, how can it ever change? We will return to this question later.)

Nonverbal signals as interaction regulators   Simple nonverbal cues, such as spatial positioning or eye contact, serve to communicate liking and disliking and attraction to a relationship, but NVC serves another important function, too. It smoothes out and regulates social behaviour. There are social rules about speakers' turn-taking, for instance, and interactions do not run smoothly if one or both partners violate(s) the rule. Think briefly whether you could state precisely what the rules of social behaviour are. (You could even try to list them for yourself before reading on and then check your list against mine.) The behaviours are termed 'social skills' and the teaching of such behaviours is called 'Social Skills Training' or SST for short.

Interactions have to be started, sustained and ended in culturally appropriate ways, and this is usually managed by nonverbal means. Two nonverbal signals are generally used to start typical interactions: one is eye contact (in this case, 'catching someone's eye'); the other is orientation (i.e. we need to face the right way and have our body oriented openly towards the other person). It is inappropriate, rude and extremely difficult to open up a conversation without looking at the person and having them look back. It is also hard to continue an interaction when one is wrongly oriented; for instance, try sitting back-to-back with a friend and having a cosy chat. You will certainly be physically able to hear what your friend is chatting about, but you will soon become socially uncomfortable with this form of communication.

A person can decline to engage in a conversation merely by refusing to establish eye contact or orientation. Busy waiters and bartenders do it all the time. However, eye contact conjoins with many other cues to serve a regulatory function in interactions also (Keeley and Hart, 1994; Patterson, 1992). Eye contact, gaze, looking and eye movements are associated with 'floor-sharing' (i.e. turn-taking in conversation) and with power and dominance of interactions. Speakers look at listeners less than listeners look at speakers, but speakers start to signal that they have come to the end of their 'speech' by looking at the listener and establishing eye contact; this lets the listener 'take over the floor', if desired (Kendon, 1967). Socially anxious people tend to avert their eyes too frequently and so disrupt the flow of the interaction by breaking the rules (Patterson, 1988). High power, on the other hand, is associated with high levels of looking at a listener whilst you are talking whereas less powerful or less expert people tend to look only when listening (Dovidio et al., 1988).

Our conversations are regulated also by other factors, some to do with the general rewardingness that is expected in social encounters (Burgoon et al., 1986), and some to do with the general rules about turn-taking (Cappella, 1991). Specifically, we alter our speech patterns and conversational turns as a result of the 'reinforcements' that we receive. Reinforcements here are nonverbal cues that reinforce, encourage or lead us to increase whatever behaviours they positively reinforce or seemingly approve. Several forms of reinforcement for speaking are available. Smiling, nodding and gazing at other persons in an interaction have historically been shown to be reinforcers that will induce other people to continue talking (Gatewood and Rosenwein, 1981). This can be generalized: the same nonverbal cues will encourage and reinforce quite subtle parts of behaviour. One can influence the production of plural nouns, use of abstract concepts, or particular kinds of topic, each of which can be reinforced and increased by specific nonverbal encouragements from a listener (Argyle, 1967).

However, there are also social expectations about amount of gaze, and people who do not gaze enough are violating such an expectation. Without such reinforcements, speakers will often stop, under the impression that the listener is bored, is becoming less involved in the conversation or else, perhaps, wants to intervene (Coker and Burgoon, 1987). One way of 'taking the floor' (or getting a word in edgeways) is to stop being reinforcing and to signal one's disinterest. The listener sends a strong signal by this: 'Please stop talking. It's my turn now.'

Does nonverbal communication show how we really feel?   An important role of nonverbal communication is to convey attitudes (Keeley and Hart, 1994; Patterson, 1992). These may be attitudes about self (e.g. conceited, diffident, mousey, shy, humble); attitudes towards the other person (e.g. dominant, submissive, attracted, disliking, hostile, aggressive); or attitudes about the interaction (e.g. affability, comfortableness, relaxation, intimacy, nervousness).

Some findings (Box 1.3) indicate that we tend to assume nervousness and anxiety just by detecting the presence or absence of certain nonverbal behaviours. This is not surprising, given that increased body movement tends to occur in association with speech dysfluencies or errors (Hadar, 1989). Several studies find that such cues are the ones used by police or customs officers in detecting criminality or smuggling (Miller and Stiff, 1994; Stiff and Miller, 1984). However, there are many reasons for nervousness apart from criminality (such as embarrassment, low self-esteem, shyness).

Let us consider the issue of whether such nonverbal cues actually indicate anxiety, deceit and the like, or whether people just continue to believe that they do. In a provocative paper, Stiff and Miller (1984) looked at the behaviours that people show when they lie and the behaviours that people use to determine when someone else is lying to them. The crucial behaviours that we use are response latency (i.e. the time the person takes before

---

Box 1.3   Functions of nonverbal communication

Mutual gaze (when two people gaze or stare at one another) is used to signal that two persons wish to 'engage' or start a social encounter (Keeley and Hart, 1994). It is also used at the correct distance – during the 'salutation' or greeting phase at the start of an encounter. Sometimes if people see each other from too far away, they will move towards one another but will look away (or look down) until they are closer, when they will start mutual gaze again (Kendon, 1967).

Speakers begin long glances at the listener just before the end of an utterance (Keeley and Hart, 1994), and increases in rhythmicity or patterning of NVC are associated with increased liking (Warner et al., 1987); decreases are associated with increased anxiety or deception (R. Miller, 1996).

In couples of equal power, female–female pairs exhibit higher amounts of mutual gaze than either male–male or male–female dyads (Mulac et al., 1987), and King (1993) showed that partners' ratings of each other's expressiveness correlated with marital satisfaction.

Eye contact relates to 'floor-sharing' and the patterning of speech in an encounter (Cappella, 1991), but staring at someone else will cause him or her to make more frequent speech errors (Beattie, 1981).

Gaze and eye contact are reduced when a person is embarrassed or when a partner makes unsuitable self-disclosures to the other person (R. Miller, 1996).

Cappella (1991) notes that patterns of interaction are important to the proper functioning of the psychological and social life of the adult – and the infant. Infants whose NVC is synchronized with their mothers' are more securely attached emotionally at one year old.

Gaze and eye contact also serve to indicate:

- warmth, interest, and involvement in the interaction (Duck, 1991);
- liking for one's conversational partner (Patterson, 1992);
- dominance of or involvement with the other person (Burgoon et al., 1989);
- degree of honesty and absence of intent to deceive (Keeley and Hart, 1994).

Hooley and Hiller (1997) discuss various ways in which the nonverbal and other interpersonal communicative behaviours of depressed or schizophrenic persons are abnormal and make it difficult for their marital partners to relate to and deal with them.

NVC can be explicit and straightforward. Captain Cook (famous for revealing Australia and New Zealand to the European world) noted in 1774 that when he first met the Maoris, 'One fellow showed us his backside in such a manner that it was not necessary to have an interpreter' (Hughes, 1991: 258).

---

starting to answer a question) and speech errors (i.e. interruptions to the flow of speech). Facial expressions are generally less useful for detecting deception, but they do indicate nervousness.

In a pair of studies where people were filmed telling real lies (i.e. concealing the fact that they had cheated on a test to earn $50), judges relied heavily on the stereotypical vocal and visual cues, but these are not actually related to deception (Stiff and Miller, 1984). Evidently, observers tend (foolishly) to interpret any unsystematic, awkward or nonfluent behaviours as indicating deception, and may sometimes remark on a person's 'smoothness' and fluency as a sign of their plausibility. Obviously this is very relevant to relationships – particularly beginning ones – since people who appear shy or nervous may be unfairly distrusted or disliked.

One feature of real lying is that it involves some concentration ('cognitive load'). We do not merely have to say yes or no to some experimental question that we care nothing about: we are involved, so we experience emotional stress. In fact, lying as normally understood (i.e. saying something that is deliberately false) seems to be quite rare in close relationships, but rather deception is commonly practised in relationships in the form of withholding of information. Indeed, L. West (1994) has shown that deception occurring in conversation between relational partners appears most commonly to involve withholding a thought or feeling, either positive or negative, with the intention of maintaining the current level of relational intimacy. In other words relational deception is normally done with the hope of sparing a partner's feelings and is done by omission of information rather than by expression of false information accompanied by NVC. Naturally enough, what is omitted cannot be accompanied by nonverbal cues, though hesitancy in speech can indicate that something else more important is being omitted.

We also all know that if we are talking to someone we know, then they may know us well enough to spot behaviours that give us away – so we pay close attention to our behaviour and try hard to control anything that might 'give us away', or 'leak' our true meaning or feelings or the true state of affairs. The whole experience is therefore arousing for us. In a clever study looking at these factors Greene et al. (1985) had subjects lie (about where they had been on holiday) to a confederate of the experimenter. That was the easy part; many people can lie that they have been to Puerto Rico, as some of the subjects were asked to do. It's particularly easy if you have been told some time in advance that the question will be asked and what you should say. The difficult part – which the subjects were not actually expecting – was what to do when the confederate became intensely interested in the trip and asked all sorts of details about it. Greene et al. (1985) found that subjects can control leakage of the fact that they are lying up until the point when they suddenly have to think hard and carefully about what they are saying.

These results are interesting in themselves, but let us apply the principles directly to relationships. Miller et al. (1986) suggested that in real-life relationships we have other cues that are operative in our assessment of others' deceptiveness, such as the coherence of what they say relative to what else we know about them. We are unlikely in an established relationship suddenly to surprise our partner with an unexpected question that will make him or her sweat. L. West (1996) noted further that deception is often a socially contextualized activity and confidence tricksters or relational deceivers often manipulate the *context* of their deception as well as the act itself. For example, confidence tricksters wear business clothes that convey an impression of (or create a relational context for) trustworthiness; relational deceivers may make extra efforts to appear happy and relaxed or to relax their partner by smiling. Such setting of a scene will influence the interpretation of specific acts, since acts do not occur without contexts that aid in their interpretation and even sometimes steer that interpretation (Dixson and Duck, 1993). The above literature tends to look at deception as if it were placed inside and done by the individual alone, and as such, deception is (implicitly) conceptualized as involving strictly personal intentionality. However L. West (1996) points out that deceptive actions may involve socially constructed intentionality, that is, social rules and expectations which guide not only behaviour (deceptive actions) but also interpretations of behaviour (orientation to detect deception). If we view deception through a social lens then we start to notice that it is not a singular act of an individual person in isolation but is partly an action that responds to others, to expectations of others, and to the social context in which all communicative actions, including deception, occur.

Skilful use of nonverbal cues

Nonverbal communication is relevant to relationships in another way also. Some shy, lonely or psychologically disturbed or depressed people have very poor NVC skills (Guerrero, 1997; Hooley and Hiller, 1997; Patterson, 1992). They are nervous, embarrassed or socially incompetent and their NVC communicates unflattering attitudes about themselves or their awkward feelings in the encounter. Persistently lonely people have poorly adapted eye movement, smiles, gestures, nods and the like (Duck, 1991), but this is often because they have essentially disengaged from the social world and stopped trying. They become passive in encounters and have a poor view of themselves and their own social performance (Duck et al., 1994).

Such poor quality of social skills could take two forms: poor encoding or poor decoding. *Encoding* refers to the ability to put our feelings into practice, to 'do what we mean' (e.g. to act assertively if we want to assert, to look friendly if we feel friendly). Conversely, *decoding* refers to the ability to work out what other people mean, by observing their nonverbal communication and correctly working out their intent. Some people are inept at this. For example, sometimes you may read in the papers that a fight began in a bar because someone was staring 'provocatively' at someone else. Perhaps one person really was staring inappropriately (poor encoding), or perhaps the other just thought he or she was doing so (which would be poor decoding on this thinker's part), or perhaps drink caused their respective social psychological judgements to decline in validity.

People with poor social skills   Many people have poor social skills, and this, in particular, is true of depressives and schizophrenics (Hooley and Hiller,

1997). Such skills deficits not only are symptoms of their problems but may be partial causes (or, perhaps, may exacerbate and increase their problems). Also, Noller and Gallois (1988) show that partners in distressed marriages (especially the husbands) are poor at decoding one another's meaning and/ or poor at encoding their own feelings, often communicating feelings as negative ones when they are not intended to be negative. McCabe and Gotlib (1993) also showed that depressed wives became increasingly negative in verbal behaviour over the course of an interaction.

The list of people who show social skills deficits is well established. At the extreme end, patients with schizophrenia are very poor at decoding nonverbal signals (Hooley and Hiller, 1997), as are some violent prisoners (Howells, 1981), and depressed patients (Gotlib and Hooley, 1988), particularly when describing themselves (Segrin, 1991). In less extreme ways, the same has been found to be true of alcoholics (before they became alcoholics – afterwards they are even harder to relate to, of course; Orford and O'Reilly, 1981) and children who are unpopular at school (Asher and Parker, 1989) or who become bullies or victims of bullying (Smith et al., 1993). By contrast, those who are successful in their careers are better at social skills than those who are failures (Argyle, 1987), and physicians can improve their success in healing patients by improving their social skills (Hays and DiMatteo, 1984). Clearly, then, such socially skilled communication cannot be underestimated in importance. Although it usually occurs in the context of verbal behaviour also (see following sections), it has been found that nonverbal cues exert 4.3 times more effect than does verbal behaviour on the impressions formed of a speaker (Argyle et al., 1970), and also found that people consider NVC (especially negative NVC) carries more relational meaning than does verbal disclosure (Pike and Sillars, 1985). Even when such results have been challenged on the grounds that the studies were poorly carried out (Walker and Trimboli, 1989), the dominance of NVC is still accepted. It is important, however, to pay attention to the context in which the cues are shown and which provides 'relational meaning' for people. For these reasons, correction of social skill problems is often attempted in training programmes (Duck, 1991). Such social skills training brings about improved social functioning in relationships and also improves the person's feelings about himself or herself, as Box 1.4 shows.

We have plenty of evidence, now, that NVC provides an important context for relationships and represents a significant context for relational communication. NVC affects the way in which other behaviours and styles are interpreted, provides a context for comprehending emotions, sincerity, dominance and feelings towards someone else, and has a significant impact on relational feelings and conduct. NVC not only conveys important relational meanings but also serves to control and moderate the conduct of relationships. Having established this basic context for relationships we can now go on to language itself and the context that it provides for the conduct of relationships.

Box 1.4   Social Skills Training (SST)

Some examples of successful social skills training are:

- General 'pepping up' of depressives' responsivity in social encounters is shown in several mental health contexts to contribute to patient recovery and improvement (Dunkel-Schetter and Skokan, 1990).
- Lonely and shy people can be trained to adopt new styles of social behaviour that enhance the skill of their performance (Jones et al., 1984). Such training can also be directed at conversational turn-taking or topic management and general interpersonal communication competence (Spitzberg and Cupach, 1985).
- Nonassertive persons benefit from training related to posture as well as to other behaviours more obviously related to request-making (Wilkinson and Canter, 1982).
- Muehlenhard et al. (1986) developed ideas for SST to help women convey their (lack of) interest in dating a particular man and to help men to grasp that meaning.
- Curran (1977) successfully trained young people to make dates with members of the opposite sex by use of social skills training and related techniques.
- Social skills training can be used to train managers to take the chair effectively at meetings, deal with disruptive employees and sell products (Rackham and Morgan, 1977).

Speaking up for yourself: using words

It ain't what you say. . . : the role of paralanguage

As I noted at the start of this book, words are important in relationships not only in themselves but also because they are used metaphorically to provide context. The ways in which we use words are just as important as the words themselves. If I shout 'Fire!', then it means more than just 'I can see pretty dancing flames': it means there is an emergency. Following on from the preceding discussion of the nonverbal context for relating, I will first look at the structure, use, and form of language rather than content. Such structure and form carry messages over and above the content or meaning of the actual words that are spoken. Researchers use the term *paralanguage* to refer to such features of speech as accent, speed, volume, error rate and tone of voice. Rather like NVC in the paragraphs above, however, paralanguage has meanings in relationships but also occurs within a system of meanings that sometimes clarify what is intended. For instance, persons who shout 'Fire!' in an emergency probably also have some accompanying NVC that indicates at least urgency and possibly even panic and so distinguishes them from someone shouting it out as a joke. Also notice that the way a person does the shouting could convey messages about their credibility: someone who screams while looking distraught is likely to be believed;

someone who shouts 'Yoo . . . oo . . . oo . . . hooo! . . . Fi . . . i . . . re!' may be disregarded.

These observations create two issues for us to think about. First, how do people use language so that it conveys messages for (and about) speakers? Second, how does language interface with NVC to affect human relationships? We want to know how accent, speed, volume, error rate, tone of voice and 'speech style' affect the relational impact of messages. We shall see that power is indicated by a communication's tone and shall learn how to structure messages to maximize their persuasiveness. Language style conveys more information than is merely contained in the sentence. For example, different actors can give different character to the same passage of Shakespeare just by speaking it differently. Thus a 'message' is more than the content of speech and is significantly embossed by a number of elements of speech not contained in the content alone, and so it is an out-of-date and inadequate idea to see 'communication' as simply equivalent to message content or to simple transfer of content from one person to another (Duck, 1994a).

Amount of speech   A measure of leadership in small group discussions is the amount of speech that a person contributes to discussion: the more often someone 'holds the floor' the more will observers assume that the person was leading the group's activities (Stang, 1973). In Stang's study, subjects listened to tape-recorded group discussions which had been arranged so that one person spoke 50 per cent of the time, another person 33 per cent of the time, and a third spoke only 17 per cent of the time. The most talkative person was seen as the leader, irrespective of what was said, and the second most frequent contributor was rated the most popular. This is further confirmed and extended by Palmer (1990) who showed that management of 'floor time' (or amount of time spent 'holding the floor' by speaking) is used as an important indication of someone's control of, and contribution to, the conversation.

Amount of speech is also affected by communication apprehension and social anxiety (Ayres, 1989), with highly anxious males talking less (and also using smaller amounts of reinforcing head nods) than less anxious subjects. This is probably because the anxious people tend to withdraw from interpersonal interaction somewhat and to say very little. When they do speak, however, it is probably planned out and hangs together well because they have thought about it and it is important to them! Thus there is some truth to the common belief that fluency means something about expertise, mastery, competence and truthfulness. From a person's verbal fluency, we deduce information about the kind of person that he or she is, how that feels inside, and whether anxiety is felt in the present setting. The other side to this belief is the assumption that persons' views of themselves, the kind of person they (think they) are, actually does affect fluency. Competent people simply do speak fluently: they know what they are doing and their fluency is a signal of that (a fact used by lawyers examining expert witnesses, see

Chapter 6). Hence we are likely to deduce a person's competence from the *appearance* that they are composed and self-possessed, whether or not that is how they feel inside.

Rules about speech   How does language change as a result of the situation or relationship in which the conversation takes place, and what are the influences of language and 'speech style' on social evaluation or on the impressions that observers form? Where a linguist would be interested in the purely grammatical rules in a given society (the so-called *langue*), a communication scientist, social psychologist, or sociolinguist is more likely to be concerned with the ways in which people actually use the language (the *parole*). Social uses of language do not always follow the strict rules of grammar (e.g. on the radio this morning I heard an interviewee say 'I reckon there's lotsa workers as thinks the same like what I does' – and yet everyone could have a stab at knowing roughly what he meant to convey by this).

Language is 'situated' in various ways according to the goals of the interactants. As people's goals change, so does their speech. For instance, in a social setting, conversation is frequent and almost any topic of conversation is permissible in a chat with close friends. By contrast, when concentration is required, it seems perfectly natural that people converse less and speech acts will decline or, at least, that speech will be task-oriented. Similarly, competent university lectures are supposed to contain information about the course, and competent professors do not normally just show holiday slides and talk about their vacation.

Just as in nonverbal communication, a most significant aspect of verbal communication is an appreciation of the social rules that apply. Actors in a conversation must be polite and recognize when it is appropriate to raise particular topics and when it is not. They must know when to match their speech acts to the rules, since evaluation of their competence depends upon it. Daly et al. (1987) indicate that especially competent conversationalists are excellent at picking up social cues of appropriateness, sensing the hidden messages in others' speech, and noting unspoken power dynamics in conversational settings.

Such sensitivity can apply to issues surrounding the goals of the actors. In task-oriented discussions, people are happy with a language system containing technical jargon-based forms. By contrast, a conversation between friends is usually not task-oriented but socio-emotionally oriented. Because it is focused on feelings, 'atmosphere' and informality, a different speech style is appropriate – one where grammatical rules may be broken and where the transfer of information is less significant than is the aim of keeping people happy and relaxed. Of course, such 'atmosphere' is important in human relationships, and 'atmosphere' is another word for context, the underlying theme that I am developing in this chapter.

Most cultures have two forms of language code available, a so-called *high form* and a *low form*. The high form is planned, formal, careful, precise, complex, full of jargon, and a little pompous. It appears in educational settings, religion, courtrooms and on official notices: for instance, 'I was proceeding in a northeasterly direction towards my domestic establishment' and 'Kindly extinguish all illumination prior to vacating the premises.' The low form is informal, casual, direct and simple. It is the most familiar form of everyday speech. For example, 'I was going home' and 'Kill the lights when you go.'

The two forms are used in different settings in appropriate ways. However, there are occasions when this causes difficulties and we deliberately break the rules to communicate a social message, like a joke or a distancing from someone. An example of the conveyance of social messages through use of codes is use of a high form in a casual setting to deflate someone, for instance when a close friend abruptly addresses you as Ms or Mr and starts to use formal language. This calculated misjudgement of the circumstances conveys a social message over and above the grammatical content. In a formal setting, however, if the message form or structure is made inappropriate to the form or structure of the encounter (e.g. informal language in a formal setting) the social result is negative (e.g. a judge called by his or her first name by a witness might fine the witness for contempt of court).

One other message is conveyed by differences in use of high and low forms of code, and that is knowledge and hence power. Powerful and knowledgeable persons use jargon-based high code, while the rest use low code translations. One reason why do-it-yourself motor car repairers are usually 'one down' in going to buy spare parts is because they do not know the proper terminology. Asking for 'one of those round things with the bent bit at one end' is a betrayal of low status in such situations. Use of technical terms is a way of claiming status, particularly if it is done deliberately to someone who does not know the terminology. Car mechanics could perfectly well talk about 'round things with the bent bit at one end', but they instead talk about 'modified CJ47s' and so on. Social scientists could write about chatting and conversation, but instead they write about 'socially situated speech acts' and 'interacts' (Knapp and Vangelisti, 1994).

More about content

The content of speech carries two important social messages, one of which is power and the other is relationship between speaker and listener. Brown (1965) refers to these dimensions as status and solidarity. These two dimensions are very similar to two 'messages' conveyed by nonverbal cues also: dominance and liking.

Relationships between speaker and listener In some languages (e.g. French, German, Spanish), there are two words that can be translated as 'you' in English, and in times gone by there were also two choices in English (thee/ thou, ye/you). The so-called V-form (*vos* in Latin, *vous* in French, *sie* in

German, *usted* in Spanish) is actually plural, just as ye/you used to be in English, where the T-form (*tu, du,* thee/thou) is actually singular. Where the two forms still coexist, intimate friends and relatives are addressed with one pronoun (*tu, du*) and the other is used for people whom one does not know or whom one treats with respect and deference (*vous, sie, usted*). Thus the French say *tu* when talking to a friend, to someone younger, or to a person of lower status, but use *vous* for talking to a stranger, to an elder, or a parent-in-law. Use of the T-form therefore conveys implicit messages of solidarity and intimacy, while the V-form implicitly conveys messages of formality, respect and distance (Fitch, forthcoming). Brown (1965) also notes that a status norm has evolved in countries which still use the two forms of address. The choice of just one single word (*tu* or *vous*) tells everyone about the speaker's status and familiarity relative to the other person and communicates something about the closeness or social distance of relationship between speaker and addressee. The V-form is thus used to address a person superior to oneself in status. The T-form is reserved for those of status lower than oneself. Persons who are of equal status both use the T-form to each other if they are close personally, but the V-form if they are not. German and French each contain special verbs (*dusagen, tutoyer*) to describe the switch from one form to another (i.e. to indicate that it is acceptable to be more intimate). The form of address carries a message about the power relationship between the speakers. The message can be a personal one ('I am superior to you'), a solidarity one ('We are both equals'), or a political one ('All persons are equal; there is no hierarchical structure in society'). During the French Revolution, the peasant revolutionaries purposely addressed the toppled aristocrats as *tu* in order to reinforce by language the social and political changes that had taken place. It was meant to stress the new-found equality. In more recent times the switch from Miss/Mrs to Ms conveys a similar message about social status and equality.

In the seventeenth and eighteenth centuries, the Quakers also decided to adopt the style of calling everyone 'thou' in order to indicate the equality of all people. As in present-day French (*tu*) or German (*du*), this pronoun had previously been reserved for use only to close intimates, lower- or equal-status family members, and 'inferiors' like servants, children and pet animals. This style caused considerable amounts of abuse to be heaped on Quakers; indeed, in 1714 Thomas Ellwood found that it led to trouble between himself and his father, who evidently felt disrespected: 'But whenever I had occasion to speak to my father . . . my language did [offend him]: for I [did] not say YOU to him but THEE or THOU, as the occasion required, and then he would be sure to fall on me with his fists!' 'Thou' was also used as an insult indicating moral distance or inferiority when two persons were otherwise socially equal. At the trial of Sir Walter Raleigh for treason, the prosecutor (Sir Edward Coke) berated Raleigh with the words 'All that Lord Cobham did was by Thy instigation, Thou viper; for I 'thou' Thee, Thou traitor' (Hughes, 1991: 98).

Fitch (forthcoming) analyses some interesting examples of the same linguistic style in present day Colombia where not only is there a recognized status message conveyed by the use of *tu* or *usted* but the distinction is built into other forms of address that are used, such as the use of first names. First names are used to address equals or social inferiors but never social superiors, except in a teasing or playful way, and, as already noted, in some cultures first names may be used within a family by people of greater age to address younger people but not vice versa, even when the two people are brother and sister (Valdez, personal communication). The same signifi-cance of personal names is not, however, simply a quaint circumstance of historically or geographically distant cultures. Our culture also knowingly distinguishes respectful forms and informal ones. Do you call your professor 'Professor Surname', or 'Chris'? What do colleagues call the same person? Do you call your father by a title (Dad, Father, Pop or even 'sir') or by his first name? What does he call you? Whenever I discuss this with my students in class it is obvious that the difference is a very real one. Those people who use a title would feel uncomfortable using a first name and vice versa. As with all cases of 'in-law relations' the problem is even more acute for people in deciding how to address the parents of their romantic partner, as you may be able to testify yourself. (Try it and see.) Mamali (1996) notes that a reification of political control can also be achieved by names and titles, since in some formerly Soviet countries the custom was to address a person by his or her communist party title, thus subtly reinforcing the remem-brance of the party and its control over social life.

In some cases, a fictitious first name is used when one person does not know the proper name, but does not want to accept a lower status by using a general polite form like 'sir' or 'madam'. Thus, New York taxi drivers call male passengers 'Mac', Londoners call men 'John' and many Scotsmen call other men 'Jimmy', and – unfortunately for me – many people in northern England call one another 'duck' (the North Yorkshire dialect nickname for a hunchback, as it turns out). Interestingly, when talking to other women or when women talk to either sex, a term of endearment is often used in England, such as 'luv' or 'dear', which are terms seen to be extremely patronizing if used by men to women. These points and obser-vations may seem quaint and unreal until you actually try to break the rules. Try calling some of your professors by their first names without permission and see what reaction you get. More interestingly, see how it feels to you personally. If you really want an experience then try calling them 'Mac'.

Speech style, power and relationships   Speech style can also be classified as representing a relationship of speaker to audience in terms of whether the speech is structurally powerful or powerless (Lakoff, 1973). Powerless speech uses a high proportion of *intensifiers* (very, extremely, absolutely, totally, really); *empty adjectives and adverbs* (wonderful, incredibly, amaz-ingly); *deferential forms* (would you please? may I?); *tag questions* (isn't it? don't you? *n'est ce pas?*); *hedges* or *lack of commitment* (I suppose, I guess, maybe, it was . . . like); *hypercorrect grammar* (to whom is it that you wish to speak?); overuse of *gestures* during speech (suggesting lack of emphasis in the speech itself); *intonational patterns* that seem to 'fuss' and 'whine'; *lack of perseverance* during interruptions and *acquiescence in simultaneous speech.* Note that since many of these forms are 'polite' in our culture, polite speech can seem powerless. The problem that I see here however is that speech, whether 'powerless' or not, rarely occurs without a context of other cues, such as accent, sex, position in a hierarchy or familiarity of listener to speaker. It is likely to be the whole package rather than one single element that creates the picture.

Using language to relate to other people

Content and types of talk   You already know that you do some types of talk with some people and not others. Goldsmith and Baxter (1996) discovered that everyday relating 'appears to be dominated by six kinds of talk event: gossip, making plans, joking around, catching up, small talk, and recapping the day's events'. The types of talk in which people are engaged appear to be organized in their speech as well as relationally and there is a taxonomy of types of talk arranged on three dimensions: formal/ goal directed, important/deep/involving, and positive valance. Goldsmith and Baxter suggest that changes in speech are not simply strategies by which people change their relationships but are in fact ways in which they embody the very nature of the relationship and make it what it is. Even the small talk of everyday relating is making the relationship (Duck and Pond, 1989) and we have already seen in this chapter some subtleties of expression that make relationships work differently. Thus instead of seeing communication as something that is used by people in a relationship merely to achieve some desired goal or express a cognitive state or attitude, Goldsmith and Baxter see it instead as 'an *embodiment* of a particular kind of relationship constructed jointly by the parties (Duck, 1994a)' (emphasis added).

The advantage of such a way of looking at the connection of communication to relationships is that it notes the ways in which communication *is* relational and is not simply an instrument for making relationships. Communication generally, both verbal and nonverbal, involves relational activity – my whole point in this chapter – and the use of language is relational in and of itself.

I have provided several familiar examples of this so let us try a less obvious but still familiar example of talk that shows the relationship between the speaker and audience: the profanity that is found in everyday speech (some estimates indicate that 13 per cent of everyday talk is profane; Winters, 1993). Most of us probably think that when someone curses or swears at us they are simply being vulgar or inappropriate and indeed that is one way to look at swearing. People tend to swear when they are angry or have very strong feelings about something and the use of cursing or swearing words is a strong way to indicate that level of emotion. However, such a view of swearing is limited and superficial as Hughes (1991) has very clearly shown. When one starts to look at the sorts of swearing that take place and have taken place over the course of history, the sorts of slurs that are chosen for people, and the history of changes in the uses of such words, it is easy to show that swearing is not only relational but also subtly about power. It involves social structure, hierarchy, rights, social position, the marginalization of groups and the endorsement of, or persuasion against endorsement of, certain attitudes and beliefs. Let's think a bit about that and connect it to the topic of this chapter and the endorsement or enforcement of particular ways of viewing the world (which is what 'context' is about).

Remember that I have taken the position that speech is rhetorically persuasive and endorses (cultural) visions of the world, that is to say it proposes and embodies ways of seeing things about the world in socially guided ways. Words are not idly chosen but express personality, attitudes and a person's total view of the nature of the world and their self-identity within the culture. The same is true of swearing and cursing, which represent ways of seeing other people, ways of categorizing other people, ways of denigrating other people and ways of enforcing particular interpretations of the central features of life and of a present situation. Try to recall the last time you called someone a 'blackguard' (which your fifteenth-century ancestors would have felt to be a terrible personal insult). How recently did you wish 'a pox on you' to someone, which your seventeenth-century ancestors would have found deeply offensive?

Hughes (1991) traces the changes in swearing and profanity that have taken place through history. Those words which we use as swear words – the 'F-word' for example – were once regarded as simple descriptions of activity and were perfectly acceptable as an ordinary language word with no vulgar overtones. Instead in fifteenth-century England the words that people used to bully and belittle one another were more likely to do with social position: a 'blackguard' was the lowest kitchen servant who washed the blackened pots and pans, a 'villain' was a lowly member of the feudal system; a 'bastard' was an illegitimate child without legal rights; and like their modern counterparts, our ancestors often called one another the names of lowly regarded farm animals like 'pigs'.

Hughes (1991) indicates that such words then were used as *relational* insults, conveying messages of status discrimination or implying that the other person was the social or moral inferior of the speaker. In much the same way modern swearing applies names that refer to parts of the body that are regarded as particularly unappealing. You can probably think of several examples of such names associated with undelightful bodily functions, and even the phrase 'the pits' (as applied to a place of little value) is short for 'armpits'. (Insults and 'swearing' can also be observed in NVC insofar as actions like 'flipping the bird' (raising the middle finger while clenching the rest of the fist), sticking out one's tongue, or 'mooning'

Box 1.5   Language as a means of differentiation of relationships: inclusion and exclusion from relationships

The Romans had several styles of address just as we do (see text). When talking to the mass of private citizens in the forum at Rome, orators would address them as 'Quirites' ('(Ladies and) Gentlemen'); serving legionaries in the field were hailed 'Milites' ('Soldiers'). Once when Julius Caesar's legionaries mutinied, he began his speech to them with 'Quirites' rather than 'Milites', thus implying that they were not acting like trained soldiers but like a crowd of private citizens in Rome. Caesar's own account of this event is that this single word was enough to shame the troops and quell the mutiny.

We may see cursing and swearing as simply foul-mouthed, but Hughes (1991) goes deeper and shows how they were used to marginalize and stratify social orders. For example, a word like 'knave', 'beggar', or 'blackguard' was originally a simple description of a person's social rank ('knave' originally meant 'male child', 'beggar' and 'rascal' described common soldiers and camp followers, and a 'black-guard' was the kitchen servant who guarded or kept the blackened pots and pans). By metaphorical extension, however, they all came to acquire moral overtones and indicated not simply social lowliness but general unworthiness.

Hatred and rejection for others is conveyed by nicknames just as are endearment and closeness. Whereas a lover may be 'Honey', 'Sweetie' or 'Sugar' – all meta-phors to do with consumption of food, obviously – many nicknames of rejection are associated with the opposite end of the alimentary canal, such as 'he's a shit' 'an arsehole' or even a 'septic' (septic tank = Yank, in Cockney rhyming slang) which was current in World War II in Europe.

Gossip might seem like a casual way to spend one's time, but Bergmann (1993) shows its social and relational force. For example, gossip serves as a form of relational control – we gossip about other people's relational activity ('I hear they're having an affair . . .') or their treatment of one another ('He is really mean to her'). Such comments act out a social control of others' behaviour by moralizing about it and supporting a view of what is 'right' in relationships or how conflict should be handled (Klein and Milardo, 1993). Yet gossip also structures our social world. Think for a minute: (a) to whom, and (b) in what order you would break the news that you had just found out that you (or your partner) were expecting a baby or when you discovered that one of your close friends had committed suicide. The release of such information is not random but rather is ordered in a way that shows the relationship between people and their placement in a person's social network and relational structure.

(showing the naked buttocks), though often a prank or taunt, are also an insult – see Box 1.3).

As Hughes has documented, then, many swear words convey relational or hierarchical position, but are moulded by a culture's concerns at the moment. When disease was especially threatening and disfiguring (as was smallpox), our culture used many disease-based terms as curses or profanity ('A plague on both your houses' in *Romeo and Juliet*, for example). Many of our profane phrases these days involve associating the target with morally debased activity (e.g. 'motherfucker') and hence with morally tainted evaluation. The use of such terms in everyday life functions rather like gossip in that it comments negatively on the moral character and hence the social status of a target. The implicit message of such a label is an invitation for the person to adjust his or her behaviour or position by taking a different and morally better-rated pathway, and so the use of profanity makes moral judgements in a cultural context of relationships (as we shall see gossip doing in Chapter 3).

Structure of talk   One most intriguing aspect of language is thus the way in which it can be used subtly to indicate the relationship between the speaker and the listener. We have already learned that power and solidarity can be conveyed by such a simple cue as the choice of pronoun used to address persons (whether the T- or the V-form). There are, however, other ways in which the immediacy of language can indicate closeness, intimacy, or acceptance (Mehrabian, 1971). 'Immediacy' refers to the amount of positive feeling or inclusion of the other person in the message and to the amount of distance implied in the message. Consider the differences in 'Ms Jones and I have just been for a walk', 'We two have just been for a walk', and 'Jonesey and I have just been for a walk'. What about 'X is my neighbour' and 'X and I live in the same neighbourhood'? And, what of 'I hope your career is successful' as distinct from 'I hope you are successful'? These subtly different phrasings convey different degrees of interest and involvement.

Such messages also help to create and hold together our relationships with other people. We are all sensitive to the different relational messages conveyed by our forms of speech, and we change them as relationships develop. Processes of growth in a relationship are managed through communication; we can indicate to a partner and to the world at large that we have grown closer simply by subtly changing the way in which we address the person (Premo and Stiles, 1983). To become noticeably more immediate is to become noticeably more intimate; to start talking of 'us' is to claim that a relationship exists or is coming into existence; to encourage greater intimacy in language is simultaneously to instigate greater intimacy in relationship (Morton et al., 1976), since relationships are often constituted in talk (Duck et al., 1991; Goldsmith and Baxter, 1996).

Such internal features of speech can convey messages of connectedness that are evident to outsiders as signals of the relationship between two speakers. Planalp and Benson (1992); Planalp (1993) and Planalp and Garvin-Doxas (1994) have accumulated evidence that judges can discriminate between conversations of friends and of acquaintances on the basis of the coherence and internal structure of the conversation. They have shown that indeed there are systematically observable differences in the conversations of friends and acquaintances, typically evidence of mutual knowledge and content intimacy, and that the level of accuracy in discriminating such conversations is about 80 per cent. In other words, there are structured aspects of speech, forms and contents of language, and features of conversations that give off cues to everyone that a conversation is between intimates as distinct from between simple acquaintances. Thus language not only indicates amount of relaxation and competency in an interaction but it also shows degrees of relationship, like NVC does. Thus even coherence of speech creates an embodiment of relationships. For one thing, the speech of friends usually includes reference to 'taken for granted' aspects of their relationship, such as their mutual knowledge of one another or their common understanding of specific events or places. For instance, if we hear a conversation between two people swapping their names and addresses we'd be likely to assume that the people are not friends but have just met; if we hear them discussing 'Joe's new date' we are likely to assume that they know one another and have mutual friends.

Equally, partners develop private languages and personal idioms to personalize their relationship (Hopper et al., 1981) and there are eight types (nicknames for the partners; expressions of affection and terms of endearment; labels for other people outside of the relationship; confrontations; requests and routines; sexual references and euphemisms; sexual invitations; and teasing insults). Even long-term married partners use nicknames for one another (Bruess and Pearson, 1993), such as 'sweet pea' and 'pussycat', and it turns out that greater marital satisfaction is associated with greater numbers of idioms in the relationship. Couples without children use the most nicknames and those later in life use the fewest. Also, some partners use such single words as 'jellybeans' to mean 'He's talking over my head and I don't understand'. Such terms may be used in public to make comments about others without them even knowing that they are being mentioned. The use of such idioms thus serves to create coherence between relational partners but simultaneously to exclude other people and so to draw boundaries around the relationship. In short, language conveys degrees of intimacy, is a powerful developer and definer of relationships, and is used to indicate many privacies in relationships. It conveys relational messages by its structure as well as by its content.

Since there are public and private languages, both high and low forms, informal and formal styles and so on, we need to explore the social and relational functions of 'switching' between styles during a single conversation. What social messages are conveyed by a sudden switch in immediacy or a switch from high to low or from low to high forms of speech? Low form is typically associated with informal, friendly settings whilst a high form goes with formality and emotional distance. A switch from low to high is a distancing strategy that shows disapproval, aloofness, dislike and hostility. By contrast, a high–low switch is an affiliative strategy that indicates liking, approval and a desire to become less formal and more friendly. For several years, Giles (e.g. Giles et al., 1973) has been showing that we 'accommodate' our language (whether language style, speech style, accent, code or content) to our interaction partner if we feel attracted. We play down the distinctiveness of our own individual style of speaking and accommodate, or move towards, that of the other person ('convergence'). For instance, parents frequently accommodate the style of their language and talk 'baby talk' to young children, whereas adults adopt the code form preferred by the powerful actor in a given setting (e.g. they talk formally to their boss). Also, speakers often adapt their speech to be more similar to that of their conversational partner, particularly when they wish to relax that person or ingratiate themselves (Giles et al., 1973). Such 'convergence' occurs at various linguistic levels, involving speech rate, silences, choice of language (where the speakers are bilingual), regional accents, or vocal intensity and loudness (Giles and Powesland, 1975). The higher prestige language is usually adopted in a bilingual community as long as partners like one another (Giles, 1978). Divergence is equally powerful (Bourhis and Giles, 1977). When speakers dislike their partner or the ethnic group from which he or she comes, they will adopt extremely different speech styles, occasionally refusing to speak in the partner's adopted language (e.g. persisting in speaking Welsh to disliked English weekend-holidaymakers in Wales).

It is thus quite clear that language itself indirectly and directly conveys important relational messages. However, it does not do it on its own in the course of normal everyday interactions. It is a part of a system. We can be both verbally immediate and nonverbally intimate, for instance, and this could be important in indicating relational intimacy – yet it could be problematic if the two 'channels' (verbal and nonverbal) do not match up, as we'll see below.

Putting verbal and nonverbal together

So far, I have been looking at the components of communication separately as linguistic and nonverbal forms; but obviously, in real life they occur together most of the time. In relationships especially, they most often go together and amplify one another. When we say angry things, we usually look angry; when we say 'I love you', we usually look as if we mean it. Thus NVC can complement verbal messages. However, verbal and nonverbal messages can be put together in interesting and conflicting as well as complementary ways. Some research has shown that use of NVC can help in the production of speech (Hadar, 1989). This might explain why people gesture vigorously when they are on the telephone and the person at the other end of the line cannot see any of it! However, researchers have been interested for a long time in looking at the inconsistencies between the two channels (verbal and nonverbal). For instance when I say nice things but frown, or when I shout 'I'm NOT ANGRY!', how do observers interpret such inconsistencies?

Facial messages are long established as the most powerful components of such contradictions (Zaidel and Mehrabian, 1969). They are seen as conveying the real messages and as giving the true evaluation of the person. Words, on the other hand, are assumed to relate to the person's acts or deeds. That is, we tend to assume that the facial expression indicates the speaker's evaluation of the person as a person, while the words evaluate the person's behaviour. 'Well done,' said with a scowl for instance, indicates grudging praise for someone who is disliked. Young children have particular difficulty with such inconsistent messages and tend to treat all such messages as if they were negative, whichever channel conveyed the negativity (Cappella, 1991). Walker and Trimboli (1989) point out that laboratory or experimental work on such inconsistencies very often strips it from all the important embedding context in which it is always placed in real life. Such a context, which is created by the human relationships in which the communication occurs, gives people very strong cues about the overall 'meaning' of the inconsistency. While the NV channel is usually seen as the more important ('Actions speak louder than words', after all), the most likely thing is that an observer will actually work out the 'true meaning' from the context – and that is usually built into the relationship between hearer and speaker as much as anything.

In sum, the evidence shows the importance of nonverbal cues in social behaviour and the extreme subtlety of some influences upon impressions, social judgements and relationships. We know that impression management can depend upon our nonverbal performance, and we have learned that judgements of ingratiation, liking, intention and sincerity can depend on the way we move our eyes or distribute our limbs, as well as on what we say in speech. Both ordinary language and the silent language of nonverbal cues convey messages about liking, strength of feelings towards someone, trust, liking, status differences and power. Most of these are relational messages, so in Chapter 2 we shall look at the ways in which we express and communicate emotions in relationships, while Chapter 3 will look at relationships, their growth, decline, and repair.

Summary

Language and nonverbal communication (even down at the level of usage of space) both convey implicit as well as explicit messages about power, control and liking, many of them based in cultural and social expectations and norms about human relationships. Every time we speak to someone we can convey social messages about how much we like them and what we think is our relationship to them – not just by explicitly saying so in the content of our talk but also by the style of the language that we use and the accompanying nonverbal communications that we make. Identity management is achieved by both verbal and nonverbal means, and the form of speech is as important as are the minute movements of face, eyes and body that make up the whole nonverbal system. In Chapter 6, we shall see that there are some extremely powerful applications of such work in the law courts, and in Chapter 7 also applications to health.

Further reading

Burgoon J.K., Buller, D.B. and Woodall, W.G. (1989) *Nonverbal Communication: The Unspoken Dialogue*. New York: Harper and Row.

Duck, S.W. (1993) *Social Context of Relationships.* (Vol. 3) *Understanding Relationship Processes.* Newbury Park, CA: Sage.

Giles, H. and Powesland, P.F. (1990) *Handbook of Language and Social Behaviour.* Chichester: Wiley.

Keeley, M. and Hart, A. (1994) 'Nonverbal behaviors in dyadic interaction', in S.W. Duck (ed.), *Dynamics of Relationships.* (Vol. 4) *Understanding Relationship Processes.* Thousand Oaks, CA: Sage. pp. 133–62.

Leathers, D.G. (1997) *Successful Nonverbal Communication: Principles and Applications.* Boston, MA: Allyn and Bacon.

2

Social Emotions: Communication and Feelings about Other People

'A consensus is building that romantic jealousy is best defined in terms of a situation and is not itself an emotion.' (Sharpsteen, 1993: 69)

Although we usually think of emotions as feelings that happen to us or which we experience, recent theory, as the opening quotation indicates, is taking the view that many of our feelings in relationships are contextually and situationally driven rather than being 'pure feelings'. In short the feelings that we think we have in relationships are partly the result of context in many different ways. As indicated in the preceding chapter, one significant context for the practical conduct of relationships is the use of language. We can recognize the force of language in expression of emotions (e.g. in expression of anger, hurt, or declarations of love), but communication is also something that takes place directly *about* relationships as well as *in* relationships. Not only do people talk about how their relationship is going (Dindia, 1994), but they may talk in order to express deeper emotion in relationships or to start a relationship in the first place (Sprecher and Duck, 1993). Partners also often show relationship awareness and convey their thoughts about the relationship to one another in talk (Acitelli, 1988, 1993, 1997). Finally, emotion may be both generated and discussed during conflict itself or dealing with daily hassles (Bolger and Kelleher, 1993), or in confronting various relationship challenges, such as dealing with long-distance relationships, temporary separation, or the declaration of the relationship to friends or family (Baxter and Widenmann, 1993; Duck and Wood, 1995; Huston and Schwartz, 1995; Rohlfing, 1995).

Emotions are often represented as the stuff of which the peaks and troughs of life are made, as when, for example, we feel exhilarated, depressed, shy, lonely, jealous or in love. Those selected emotions are particularly powerful (for example, love and jealousy – which some countries accept as legitimate excuses and legal justifications for 'crimes of passion'). However, the emotional experiences that create and sustain relationships are not necessarily so consistently dramatic and are certainly not limited to the dramatic or the turbulent emotions. Clearly in daily relationships we experience regret, disappointment, sadness, guilt, anxiety, contentment, joy, satisfaction, irritation, admiration, disgust – and most important, and most of the time, not very much at all except a sense that things are pretty much where they were last time we checked. What is true of relationships is one simple fact: they are not composed of universally strong nor universally positive emotions (Duck and Wood, 1995). Most of what we do in daily life is to *manage*. We manage and balance our own feelings as against those of a partner; we manage the good and the bad in a relationship; we handle daily 'stuff' (Duck and Wood, 1995; Levitt et al., 1996). The present chapter explores some of the emotions that we instantly – and perhaps superficially – think of as 'relational'; the next chapter relates them to actual experiences of living relatively mundane daily life in human relationships. My point is that to focus only on dramatic emotional upheavals and to use them as the focus of research on emotions in relationships is unbalanced. It is important to understand that strong emotions may be relatively rare experiences in the daily conduct of human relationships and that a focus on such things takes our attention away from the huge amount of routine relational and emotional work that we do at other times and in rather trivial ways.

Secondly, it is important to recognize that the topic of 'emotion' is in any case one surrounded by much controversy. Our automatic approach is to represent emotion as a strong, internal, individual feeling of some kind. We may even think about how it is that people represent emotions to other people and we may recognize that whatever they are, emotions are not just internal subconscious disturbances that never get out into the real world. Indeed, as cheating lovers may well find, jealousy can be expressed in some intriguing, and occasionally fatal, ways. All the same, just as we saw in Chapter 1, and can see from the opening quotation above, the feelings about other people occur, or come into being, as part of contexts that are outside the individual *per se*, such as the culture, society, family and workplace. Therefore the exploration of emotion in relationships should not stop short at the point where the feeling is felt, nor rest satisfied with explanations in terms of the cognitive or social structures that 'produce' it. Rather we must understand the ways in which emotions have impact on relationships in their everyday working contexts and vice versa. Such a goal will entail us understanding the ways in which human beings have been socialized to express (or limit their expression of) emotions about relationships and relational partners within a particular social and relational context. That goal will also entail us realizing the extent to which emotions are exacerbated by contexts for expression and the ways in which a culture judges emotions as appropriate to a given context or set of circumstances. For instance, one interesting and recurrent observation in jury trials is that defendants who appear calm and collected when told about a spouse's death are often catapulted into first place as prime suspects because that sort of emotional (non)reaction is not regarded as 'appropriate' to the receiving of tragic news.

Labelling and expressing feelings

The emotions that are expressed in a given society are a mixture of apparently universal human feelings and cultural prescriptions that define the form and appropriateness of the expression of those emotions. For example, we assume that all humans experience fear and joy; indeed Darwin did some work not only suggesting that such emotions are common to all societies and to some animal species also, but that there is a certain amount of 'cross-species' recognition of major emotional expressions. Some societies, however, emphasize such emotions as shame while others recognize it but give it little weight (Retzinger, 1995). Some societies expect grief to be borne with quiet, stoic dignity and reserve, and others expect loud wailing expressions accompanied by energetic physical demonstrations of distress (Duck, 1991). There is some discussion by scholars on whether communication of emotion *is* the emotion (for example, some argue that we can never know more than the expression of emotion; some people get angry just by shouting), or whether communication is a component of emotion (some people feel worse when they *express* anxiety than when they do not), or whether emotional expression is simply the externalizing of some inner state that is ascribed by socially accepted labels. For example, Schachter and Singer (1962) showed that people who were emotionally aroused could be enticed to describe their feelings as either anger or joy depending on the label that fitted their social surroundings best. In other words, the 'emotion' they were feeling was steered towards the label presented by the social setting and was not simply felt as a pure emotion. This analysis was even applied to the emotion of love by Berscheid and Hatfield [Walster] (1974) and held some currency for a while as researchers showed that high arousal led to descriptions of 'appropriate' emotions if people were presented with the right cues to pin their feelings upon. The discussion of emotion is thus complicated by some important cultural contexts for emotion and is not simply a question of looking at the feelings that people 'naturally' have.

First, the strong social imperatives about the need for, and means of, communication of emotion spoil some people's relationships; relationship problems, like shyness, often show up as culturally unusual or inappropriate ways of communicating feeling. Second, when we report or describe emotions, we frequently edit our accounts of them so that they make sense to other people, not just to ourselves. Therefore we use culturally accepted language, reference points and narrative form for describing emotions (Duck et al., 1997). Typically these describe emotions and relational behaviours in ways that are accepted in our culture as valid ones (for example, our culture accepts that someone 'falls in love' rather than 'gets bitten by the love god's mosquito').

Usually our language for describing emotions in relationships also means that we summarize them as future-oriented, enduring or continuous states rather than momentary or fleeting micromomentary feelings (Duck and Sants, 1983). For instance, we are more likely to say 'I am in love with you' or 'I will love you for ever' or 'I am friends with you', rather than 'I felt a twinge of love for you at the particular moment when you looked at me', or 'I felt friendship towards you just for the moment when you shared that secret with me.' This characteristic of language – that it labels and stabilizes or perpetuates an appearance that life is made up of 'states' and transitions between states – is crucial to the conduct of relationships, which we also tend to describe as continuous states rather than turbulent, or at least variable, experiences (Duck, 1994a). All the same, much of our emotional life is based on the long-term organization of the variabilities and inconsistencies of daily experience or the creation of uniform labels for muddled and diversiform experiences.

The summary of emotions and translation of them into state language in this way make it hard to pinpoint the true initial causes of emotions or love and friendship. Perhaps we can explain it as 'love at first sight', but usually we prefer to look back over a whole range of experiences and events to 'explain' emotional states. We would feel foolish saying that we loved someone only at a particular few seconds a week or only when we thought of it or merely for the shape of the nose. Our culture prefers to believe that it takes time to fall in love, and that love is a complete emotion constructed from many cues and causes all rolled together over periods of time, particularly due to something uplifting, like expanding one's awareness by including the other's perspectives as part of one's self (Aron and Aron, 1997). Yet considerations of the role of language and communication in relation to love are becoming more common. Beall and Sternberg (1995) noted that the depiction of love draws on a large arsenal of social expectations such as those created in novels concerning the ways in which love *should* proceed. Kidd (1975) and Prusank et al. (1993) have documented the ways in which popular magazines influence and also reflect people's experiences of romance and marriage by providing guidelines and advice about how relationships 'should' be conducted (see Box 2.1).

Rephrasing the above in more technical language, statements about social emotions use dispositional or continuous language to provide 'summary affect statements' about our partner and these are socially appropriate to the culture in which we happen to find ourselves. They summarize our feelings about someone using culturally approved terminology and culturally accepted explanations for the basis of relationships. They are not simple descriptions of short-term emotional peaks or troughs; instead they reverberate to social norms. They emphasize implicit continuity in relationships and prepare partners and others to expect a certain shape to the future – a future that still has the relationship in it! In fact, much of the construction of relationships is based on various ways of manipulating our expectations about the future in this way, since relationships involve unfinished business that continues throughout the life of the relationship itself (Duck, 1990, 1994a). Much of the basis of emotion is founded in the organization of routines of behaviour that make up the day-to-day conduct of this unfinished business. In short, social emotions are not just fleeting physiological experiences but are organized, long-term *behavioural* creations that find their form and shape in the behaviour and routines of everyday conduct of relationships, expressed in ways that carry symbolic force in a given society (Fitch, forthcoming).

Box 2.1 On magazine advice and cultural expectations about relationships

Kidd (1975) showed that popular magazines have presented advice on relationships for at least several decades and that the nature of the advice appears to reflect cultural values at the time; hence the advice changes over time. In the 1950s the advice about relationships, especially marriage, often took the form that the women should obey husbands in all circumstances, but the advice was also presented as the agreed advice of experts (and hence created the impression that there really was one right way to do things). In the 1960s the advice became more varied and was often focused on the need to 'communicate' and do what you thought 'was right for you' or 'being more your real self'.

Prusank, Duran and DeLillo (1993) followed up on Kidd's work and explored more recent advice in magazines. They found that in the 1970s and 1980s the nature of advice changed again, though was still focused on the use of one's own personal standard. In more recent advice the focus falls on the importance of knowledge of self and other, equality, and appropriateness of behaviour to the stage of relationship and time of life (Duran and Prusank, 1997).

Less obvious influences on our standard views of relationships are general cultural models for quality in relationships such as are drawn from conversations with others and from general exposure to the stories, values, literature, films, media or discourse of a given culture (Montgomery, 1988).

Klein and Milardo (1993) also note that the other people we know well will often be called upon (or will invite themselves) to give advice, commentary or evaluation of relationship conduct and so provide a sounding board for relational action as well as a 'court of opinion' to which accounts for relational action must ultimately be given.

As a matter of fact there is some evidence that the symbolic values of emotion and relationships have changed somewhat through history, even in our own culture. In a fascinating report, Contarello and Volpato (1991) have explored both the similarities and the differences in literary descriptions of friendship over the last 1000 years. They found that friendship has always involved intimacy, respect and mutual help, plus the likelihood of the friend confronting one's own weaknesses honestly. By contrast, in the passage from the sixteenth to the seventeenth century, friendship went through a profound change, with conflict emerging as a common element. Also although all the texts examined in this study were written by female authors, female friendship was hardly ever mentioned in the early texts. Werking (1997) gives close discussion to another often overlooked relationship, cross-sex platonic relationships. Although Harry (*When Harry Met Sally*) felt that 'Men and women can never be friends; the sex thing always gets in the way', West et al. (1996) and Werking (1997) discuss at length the fact that such friendships are increasingly commonplace. Yet cross-sex friends always face cultural constraints on the relationship, must contend with disbelief that their friendship is not really a secret sexual one, and have to battle scepticism that there really is 'just' friendship. Indeed for many reasons, cross-sex friendship is one of the hottest understudied relationships in the research literature (Werking, 1997; West et al., 1996; Wood and Duck, 1995), partly because it points so clearly to the fact that relationships are not the result of pure emotion but take on a life (and form of life) that is shaped by response to the prevailing opinion in the cultural context.

Heterosexual and homosexual love

Love is blamed for a lot of things from the Trojan War to various crimes of passion that appear in the tabloid newspapers. It is called 'a temporary insanity' (Bierce, 1985. He went on to add that it is 'curable by marriage'). So what is it? 'It is difficult, if not impossible, to answer the question "What is love?" because any answer must reflect its time period and place and in particular the functions that romantic love serves there' (Beall and Sternberg, 1995: 417). In attempting to answer the question, however, several lines of work have been developed. Their focus has been almost exclusively on heterosexual romantic love until quite recently when Huston and Schwartz (1995) extended the discussion to exploration of homosexual love.

Love is a juicier topic than friendship, and could be seen as the primary relational emotion. If we were Contarello and Volpato, mentioned above, we'd immediately note that love was not 'big' in marriages in the twelfth century. It was not even expected to be there – at least not in the sense that we expect it to be the basis of marriage nowadays. Marriage, especially between noble persons, was politically arranged and served the needs of strengthening the ties between different groups, families, or 'houses'. If the partners liked each other then that was a bonus, but all that was *necessary* was loyalty, with fidelity. Nowadays we do things differently and, in America and the UK, we have a divorce rate at 50 per cent.

Also important is the fact that the 'experience' of love is tied in important ways to the manner in which it may be expressed in a given society. Kovecses (1991) notes that we communicate about love in many different ways, using some very obscure and some very complex metaphors and cultural meaning systems. For example, love is often likened to food or eating ('sugar', 'honey', 'feast your eyes upon . . .', 'good enough to eat . . .') but also to consumption of other types ('all aflame with passion . . .', 'burning desire', 's/he sets my heart on fire'). The extensive system of meaning and communication through metaphors and other linguistic devices shows us, through Kovecses's analysis, the power of the system of description. This perhaps points to common threads of experience for us all in trying to understand and communicate our feelings of love to other people. For instance, we can readily understand and sympathize with someone who claims to be displaced (for example, 'head over heels in love' – rather a curious phrase when you think that the head normally is over the heels anyway) or distracted (for example, 'I'm mad with love for you', 'They are nuts about each other').

Does such a finding of regular and systematic use of specifically vivid metaphors about love indicate that we typically experience it in culturally 'agreed' ways? Marston et al. (1987) looked at the subjective experience of love and the ways in which people communicate about it. From interviews and questionnaire data they found that there are essentially six ways in which people communicate about love. The subjective experience of love has at least three components: (1) relational labels/constructs, like commitment and security; (2) physiological labels, such as feelings of nervousness and warmth; (3) behaviour and NVC, such as doing things with the other person or ways of looking at one another (Marston et al., 1987). Given that love-smitten subjects conceptualized love in terms of *different mixes* of these elements, rather than in terms of different strengths of the same mix, Marston et al. found evidence for six types of experience of love. These are: collaborative love (supportiveness); active love (joint activities and 'erratic rhythms' such as changes to the pace of daily routines); intuitive love (NVC ability to communicate feelings); committed love (togetherness); traditional romantic love (future commitment and feeling good); and expressive love (telling the other person about one's feelings). Hecht et al. (1994) found that people experiencing committed love have higher quality relationships. However, the relationship labels themselves are *cultural provisions*, as are the criteria for deciding whether a relationship is of high quality: cultures have norms that help individuals decide what is a relationship and whether it is 'good'.

Another interesting question is the extent to which love is felt in later life in a way that is strictly influenced by the way in which it was experienced in infancy and childhood. This has mostly been addressed in terms of connections between the infant's 'attachment' to mother and the influence of such a relationship on the person's general style in relationships as an adult (see Box 2.2). More interesting than such an implicitly fatalistic or deterministic approach is the work of Putallaz et al. (1993), who have shown that mothers' remembrances of their own childhoods indirectly affect their own parenting styles when they have children, in particular the tendency to try and ensure that their own child does not suffer the nasty things that happened to them, but experiences the good things that they enjoyed as a child. Well, that's one version. Another is 'I suffered this so why shouldn't you?' The point, however, is that the parent's meanings for certain childhood experiences are recalled and used as guides in deciding the manner in which to bring up the child. This way is different from that suggested by approaches based on attachment in that the *meaning* of past relationships affect the future ones. Also coming closer to home you can find almost anyone who will say at the end of a romantic relationship, 'I want someone completely different next time. I learned a lot/I learned my lesson last time.' The same principle is at work, and this again shows that 'pure emotions' are felt and expressed in ways that are guided by other forces and influences than just the emotion itself.

Box 2.2 *Past relationships as influences on present ones*

Hazan and Shaver (1987) suggested that adult styles of loving represent processes similar to, and based on, those found in attachments between infants and their parents. *Secure attachment* is based in a sense of confidence and security in intimacy. By contrast, *anxious/ambivalent attachment* is characterized by dependency, lack of confidence in attachment and a sense of lack of appreciation by others. Finally, *avoidant attachment* is characterized by lack of acceptance of others, avoidance of closeness and discomfort in intimate situations.

Bartholomew (1990, 1993) extends Hazan and Shaver's (1987) three-part system to a four-part one. She distinguishes two types of 'avoidant': a *fearful avoidant style* when the person feels a desire to obtain social contact but is fearful of its consequences; and a *dismissive avoidant style*, when the person defensively denies the need for social contact. People who are fearfully avoidant tend to regard themselves as undeserving of the love and support of others, whereas dismissively avoidant people view themselves positively but just do not regard the presence and support of other people as necessary.

By contrast, the reverse is also partly true. Miller (1993) has shown that individuals have a tendency to remember their childhoods in ways that are consistent with their adult styles of handling conflict, and aggressive people recall their childhood as filled with aggression towards themselves, for instance.

Putallaz et al. (1993) point out the bi-directionality of socialization forces, with kids influencing parental behaviour as much as the opposite. However, parents have more formal power and physical strength than children and parents also are more likely to attempt to instil beliefs and values. In the everyday context of parent–child interaction, parents no doubt communicate ideologies of relating that influence (but do not determine) a child's experiences of childhood, of relationships and of social reality.

Some parents recall their own childhood with strong repugnance (or with strong affection) and so avoid (or try to reproduce) the opportunity for their own children to experience childhood similarly (Putallaz et al., 1991).

Latty-Mann and Davis (1996) found a tendency for secure adults to see their own partners as secure whereas those who were insecure tend to see their partners as insecure.

Dresner and Grolnick (1996) found that women who saw their fathers as accepting were more likely (than women whose fathers were distant) to experience later adult relationships as intimate.

Are there different type of love?

Several scholarly approaches to understanding love are based on the idea that we can distinguish different sorts of the same basic emotion. For example, there are some differences (though there are also many similarities) between the ways in which women and men respond to love. For one thing, although men and women report experiencing the same levels of intensity of love (Rubin, 1973), men 'fall in love' at an earlier point in a relationship than women do, whereas women fall out of love sooner than men do (Walster and Walster, 1978). This has led to men being called 'FILOs' (First In, Last Out) and women 'LIFOs' (Last In, First Out). On the other hand, women say that they have been infatuated more often than men (on average, 5.6 times for women and 4.5 times for men), but both sexes report being in loving relationships about as often – around 1.25 times (Kephart, 1967).

Such findings raise the possibility that love is not a simple single emotion but a complex mix of many different feelings or types of emotion. Maslow, an early theorist, distinguished B (for being) love, which he saw as positive and implying independence, from D (for dependency) love, which he saw as negative and implying neediness. Another distinction is between passionate love and companionate love (Berscheid and Walster, 1974): passionate love is the steamy sort that Casanova and Don Juan specialized in, whilst companionate love is the kind that kin and long-term marriage partners may have. Companionate love is enhanced by an increased sense of commitment whilst passionate love derives primarily from physiological arousal and excitement.

Is love really just either madly passionate or boringly dispassionate? Is this passionate–companionate dichotomy too simple to account for all the feelings that we can have towards a lover? Another proposal suggests that there are six types of love (Lee, 1973) and that people can mix the types together in various ways. The six types are labelled with various Latin and Greek words for types of love: *eros*, *ludus*, *storge*, *pragma*, *mania* and *agape*. Each has a typical character and a brief explanation may assist us in working out the nature of love.

Eros (romantic love) focuses upon beauty and physical attractiveness; it is a sensual love that expects to be returned. People who score highly on *eros* typically believe in 'love at first sight' and are particularly sensitive to the physical blemishes of their partner, such as being overweight, having a broken nose, smelly feet or misaligned teeth. They are attracted to partners on the basis of physical attraction, like to kiss and cuddle soon after meeting a new partner, and report a definite genital response (lubrication, erection) to the first kiss.

Ludus (game-playing love) is like a game and is seen as fun, not to be taken seriously. People scoring high on *ludus* typically flirt a lot, keep partners guessing about their level of commitment to them and stop a relationship when it stops being fun. They get over love affairs easily and quickly, enjoy teasing their lovers and will often go out with someone even when they know they do not want to get involved.

Storge (friendship love) is based on caring, not passion. People scoring high on *storge* typically believe that love grows from friendship, that lovers must share similar interests and enjoy the same activities. For storgic lovers, love grows with respect and concern for the other person. They can put up with long separations without feeling that the relationship is threatened and are not looking for excitement in the relationship, as ludic lovers are.

Pragma (logical, shopping-list love) is practical and based on the belief that a relationship has to *work*. People scoring high on *pragma* ask themselves whether their lover would make a good parent and they pay thoughtful attention to such things as their partner's future career prospects. Pragmatic lovers take account of their partner's background and characteristics like attitudes, religion, politics and hobbies. Pragmatic lovers are realistic and relatively unromantic.

Mania (possessive, dependent love) is essentially an uncertain and anxious type of love; it is obsessive and possessive and half expects to be thrown aside. Manic lovers get very jealous. People scoring high on *mania* typically believe in becoming ill or doing stupid things to regain their partner's attention if ever the partner ignores them or takes them for granted. They also claim that when the relationship gets into trouble, they develop illnesses like stomach upsets.

Agape (all-giving, selfless love) is selfless and compassionate and generally loves other human beings in an unqualified way, as preached by Gandhi, Buddha and Jesus. In their close relationships, agapic lovers would claim that they use their strength to help their partner through difficult times and may say that if their partner had a baby with someone else, they would want to help to care for it as if it were their own. Lee (1973) reports that he did not encounter any persons who were perfect examples of agapic lovers, although many people reported brief agapic episodes.

Do such love styles get communicated differently in speech? What about cultural contexts also and how do they modify expressions of the feelings? If there are these types of love, then do men and women experience them to different extents? Yes. Men are erotic and ludic in their attitudes to love (Hendrick et al., 1984), whilst women are pragmatic, manic and storgic. In other words, men's love is typically passionate and uncommitted, with an element of game-playing coupled with romance. Women's love is typically practical and caring, with an element of possessiveness, a view that could be explained in terms of economic factors and the fact that in the past it has paid women to be practical and to think long term when they have had a choice. This is not to say that women do not base their love on passion or that men do not care about their lovers. The sexes mix their experience of love in different blends. However, the wide differences in love style between men and women are very broad assessments that do not do justice to the subtleties of love style, and there are now known to be several other levels of difference that moderate or complicate the general rule that men and women are different in their experiences of love. For example, there are differences apparent in different types of relationships (Hendrick and Hendrick, 1990) and differences between people in love and those who are not (Hendrick and Hendrick, 1988). Also people report their feelings of love differently in different circumstances or to different audiences (Hendrick and Hendrick, 1993). Thus the broad style of love is a springboard from which a complex, multiform compendium of emotions is expressed in talk.

Developing love?

So far we have explored love as a state of feeling that is expressed and communicated, but we should also look for expressive change as people fall in love. Aron et al. (1989) showed that falling in love is characterized by frequent expression of the fact that the other person is like the self, by comment on the other's desirable characteristics, by talk of similarity, and communication of a sense of 'mystery or magic'. By contrast, falling in friendship is reported as due simply to similarity and propinquity, with a little less emphasis on the other's desirable characteristics and practically no mention of any magic or mystery. Aron and Aron (1997) further delineate the ways in which the experience of falling in love is also an experience of self-expansion or enrichment of the sense of self by inclusion of the other. In other words, humans are geared towards the expansion of their self through exploration, development of competence, integration of incoherent experiences, or extension of awareness. The development of a relationship with someone who diversifies the expansion is deeply satisfying and enriches both persons' sense of self.

Another possibility is that falling in love is a transition between different blends of the types of love. For instance, initial attraction to a possible lover might begin as erotic love, mixed perhaps with *mania* (desire for possession) and *ludus* (game-playing). As the relationship develops, the lovers might express greater feelings of *storge* (friendship) as they develop caring on top of passion. This may lead them on to talk about the working of the relationship in the long term, that is, to discuss the partner's potential as a long-term mate, co-parent of the children, and so on – in short, to an assessment of pragmatic concerns. If the partner seems to pass that test, then they might begin to express pragma love. All of this would suggest that married couples would score more highly than other couples on pragma love, whilst new partners might score more highly on erotic love, that is, views about the 'right type' of love for different sorts of relationship will vary. As the relationship to a partner develops, so the type of love will be communicated differently also.

All of the above suggests the centrality of the way in which love is communicated. As Marston et al. (1987) found, when I feel love or think about it, I also communicate about it. When I feel it, I may even think of inventive ways to communicate it ('My love is like a red, red rose that's newly sprung in June; My love is like a melody that's sweetly sung in tune . . .'). But there is something equally important: the way in which we express love may be *coloured by the circumstances of the moment*. If we are on a date then we may be interested in openly conveying lust (if we are feeling lucky) or at least strong positive feelings (something like *eros*). By contrast, if we are discussing marriage, our minds may turn to the roles involved in long-term commitment (something like *pragma*). If we are feeling playful and having a good time, or in a group of friends who can overhear what we are saying, then we may just start teasing (something like *ludus*). These could all be different modes of expression of the same single positive attitude toward a partner rather than different types or styles of emotion. Attitudes do not have a single level of intensity or only one mode of expression. As rhetorical theorists note very regularly (Dixson and Duck, 1993), we express our attitudes and make statements in particular forms as a result of the *audience* to whom we are talking and the *situation* in which we are speaking. 'The attitude' is thus represented by many different forms of expression and is a somewhat amorphous and protean thing. I suspect that researchers of love ought to look less at the presumed single-minded and enduring aspect of the person who feels the love (as psychologists tend to do when they explore love attitudes or love styles). Instead they should pay more attention to the circumstances and rhetorical/social/interpersonal contexts or situations where love is expressed and communicated in everyday life. Although you can feel love without expressing it to anyone but yourself, the occasions that are most interesting are obviously those where it is not only felt but also expressed. There it carries social and relational consequences and yet is also constrained by social and relational forces without actually changing its nature.

The behaviour of lovers

Aside from the feelings of love which drive us into relationships, there are behavioural and communicative consequences also (Acitelli, 1993; Aron and Aron, 1997). Love is both a felt emotion and an expression of that feeling in the behaviour through which we communicate to partners – and to the outside world – that we love them. Obviously, partners who are married often choose to wear wedding rings to communicate the fact; dates hold hands; partners embrace or put their arms around one another in the street. These indications are slight but well known. They are called 'tie signs' (Goffman, 1959) in that they indicate that two people are 'tied' to one another (like other uses of symbolic spatial markers discussed in Chapter 1). Furthermore, lovers sit closer to one another than do 'likers', and they gaze at one another more than do people who are just friends (Rubin, 1973). Obviously also lovers and would-be lovers talk to one another in intimate ways that are 'readable' by outsiders and which occasionally make lovers sensitive about audiences or careful about how they behave in company (Baxter and Widenmann, 1993).

Also Sprecher and Duck (1993) investigated the ways in which first dates are converted into second dates (because at some point they obviously have to be if people continue the relationship, yet this practical aspect of relationship development had almost never been studied before). As may be expected, talk plays a critical role in the enterprise and is a central mechanism for converting initial attraction into a working form of relationship. Furthermore, as things move even further forward, the partners wind up talking about the relationship itself at some point as it becomes a topic of conversation in its own right (Duck, 1994a). Indeed Acitelli (1988, 1993) has shown that such talking is a key way in which people adjust their perceptions of one another, ratify their evaluations, and increase mutual understanding, checking out discrepancies of understanding and generally clearing the way to a better grasp of one another's inner core. The very act of talking about the relationship is a key way in which love is indicated, especially for women (indeed men sometimes assume that something must be wrong with the relationship if the partner wants to talk about it!).

One part of love then is a direct communicative display of the fact that we love our partner. However, as Acitelli's work shows, some of the cues that are contained in communication are subtle and indirect, and not only reassure the partner but tell the outside world that the relationship exists and draw subtle boundaries around the relationship. Of course, the sorts of display that we choose on a given occasion are also likely to be influenced by the rhetorical situation, the social context and the interpersonal environments as discussed above. Presenting a partner with a ring, doing a really big and inconvenient favour, and disrobing are all, in their own ways, capable of conveying a message of love and fondness through behaviour. Nevertheless, each is appropriate only to a particular set of circumstances or for a particular audience and would be inappropriate in other circumstances or with other audiences.

For this reason, *loving behaviour* itself develops and changes as love attitudes themselves develop. Developing love is not simply an increasingly powerful attitude but is also a changing constellation of behaviours. As Aron et al. (1989) show, the experience of falling in love is usually described in terms only of attitudes and feelings, based on other people's personalities or physical characteristics, similarity to oneself or propinquity. Aron and Aron (1997), however, go on to describe the importance of shared activity – and in particular exciting shared activity – in the process of developing love, especially those that involve high levels of physical activity (dancing, hiking, bicycling) or newness and exoticness (attending concerts or studying nature).

In addition to the feelings associated with falling in love there are some pleasant consequences and some side effects. There is a strongly reported change in behaviour as well, such as increased eye contact, physical closeness and self-disclosure. Beyond this there is a broader change to the structure of everyday life behaviours. For instance, we gradually pay more attention to a new lover and spend less time with old friends; we start to share more activities and adjust our lifestyles as we let our new lover into our lives; we arrange to spend more time with our partner and less with other people (Milardo and Wellman, 1992; Parks and Adelman, 1983). In short, part of falling in love is an increased binding together of the habits of daily life and a developing routine interdependence. More than this, a big part of it is extending the range of ways in which love can be expressed and communicated. However, such behaviours frequently create stress or difficulty in ways that confirm the point that daily life is about management of conflicting forces (Baxter and Montgomery, 1996; Duck and Wood, 1995).

Baxter et al. (1997) show that persons who are withdrawing from inter-action with their network of friends in order to facilitate or extend a deep romantic relationship actually experience competing loyalties. The problem is how to distribute a fixed amount of time when different relationships (friends, family, lover) regard it as part of their relational rights to have access to a person's time.

Perhaps for this reason, people who fall in love frequently report that it is highly disruptive and that they develop a high level of nervous disorders and skin problems (Kemper and Bologh, 1981), but when love is going well, people report feeling good both in mind and body (Hendrick and Hendrick, 1988). Disruption to love is more problematic, however. People who have never been in love claim that they have a high number of minor bodily disorders like colds and 'flu, and people who have recently broken up with a partner suffer such physical disorders too (Kemper and Bologh, 1981). Those whose partners had broken off with them typically report sleep problems, headaches and loss of control of emotions. Those who caused the break-up suffered less, except that females reported stomach upsets.

Jealousy in love

Love makes us feel valued by someone else, and we feel jealous when we fear that he or she does not value us or that s/he is spending too much time with someone else. (On a technical point of definition, one is jealous of what is one's own, but envious of that which is other people's. Thus one is jealous – or possessive – of one's own partner, but envious of – covetous of – someone else's.) Positive emotions are often reported in a way that suggests they make us feel competent whilst negative ones are explained in terms of inadequacy (Davitz, 1964) – that is, inadequacy relative to other people and their feelings for us. The negative emotions in relationships (like jealousy) are often unpleasant precisely because they affect our self-esteem or our sense of competence as a social performer or partner (Bringle, 1991). They are also complex blends of feelings, thoughts and behaviours (in the case of jealousy these are often treated by researchers as if they are coping behav-iours) and some researchers (Pfeiffer and Wong, 1989) have recently begun to assess jealousy as a multidimensional construct. This breaks jealousy down in to three elementary components: cognitive, emotional and behav-ioural. The authors' own multidimensional jealousy scale includes questions about these three categories. For example, how often have the following thoughts occurred to you: I suspect that X is secretly seeing someone of the opposite sex . . . I am worried that someone of the opposite sex is trying to seduce X? How would you react emotionally to the following situations: X is flirting with someone of the opposite sex . . . X hugs and kisses someone of the opposite sex? How often do you engage in the following behaviours: looking through X's drawers, handbag or pockets; questioning X about his or her telephone calls?

Box 2.3   Jealousy and envy

- Smith (1991) notes that envy is very often characterized by a sense of injustice that partly 'legitimates' the feeling.
- Hupka (1991) argues that jealousy is at least in part a human creation based on the social structures in which human activity is organized (see text here on social rules for expressing jealousy).
- Clanton and Kosins (1991) also note that jealousy is a sign that something is wrong with the relationship rather than with just one of the partners.
- Hansen (1991) points out that jealousy also has implications for family structure and family stress and is not truly an individual emotion, at least in its consequences.
- Buunk (1995) indicated that jealousy often reflected back on the jealous person, especially if the person was a woman – that is to say, a woman who discovered that her partner was having an extramarital affair often developed not simple anger but feelings of self-doubt and self-accusation or a feeling of inadequacy.
- Sharpsteen (1995) further noted that jealousy occasionally provokes strong *affirmation* of, rather than threat to, a relationship and causes partners to 'seek proximity to the partner' or to accommodate to the errant partner's desires or needs.

Communication of jealousy emerges early in life, with children as little as one or two years old being clearly able to register and communicate jealousy (Masciuch and Kienapple, 1993). By three and a half, children are experienced enough in the ways of the world that they can even distinguish different types of social situation which elicit jealousy, with maternal attention to a sibling waning in importance as a source of jealousy as the child ages. In later life the experience of jealousy is more likely to be associated with jealousy over the behaviour of sexual partners, but it can also be related to experiences of denied promotion at work (Zorn, 1995) or a general sense of competition or quarrelling with neighbours or other acquaintances (Retzinger, 1995).

Research on jealousy indicates that men feel jealous when they feel inadequate or when they experience a threat to their self-esteem, but women feel jealous when they feel dependent on a relationship (and believe that it is better than any other relationship possibilities presently open to them). Men are more likely to react to jealousy with anger and women with depression (Hansen, 1991).

Obviously, it is a powerful emotion, but what exactly is jealousy? Buunk and Bringle (1987: 124) define it broadly as 'an aversive emotional reaction evoked by a relationship involving one's current or former intimate partner and a third person. This relationship may be real, imagined, or expected, or may have occurred in the past'. In other words, it is a negative feeling that we get when our partner 'steps out' of the relationship – or when we 'think' he or she might.

This definition is broad and allows for considerable personal differences in jealous reactions. Look, for instance, at the phrase 'likely to occur'. People will differ in beliefs about the likelihood of a partner getting into an extra-dyadic relationship. Such beliefs and judgements will depend on a whole mix of possible influences (e.g. our feelings about the partner's attractiveness, knowledge of the partner's behaviour, age and availability of alternative partners, partner's trustworthiness – even our own personality, possessiveness and ability to trust others).

Buunk and Bringle's (1987) work is based on sexual affairs although most of us have felt jealous when we see partners just showing an interest in other people (or having an interest shown in them by others). In some cases, people also report feeling jealous not about a real partner but about a desired one. One sign of increased desire for involvement with someone is precisely when we start to get upset that he or she is going out with someone else.

Since we can feel jealous about different sorts of relationships and since the different relationships have varying levels of importance to us, it is possible that they are afflicted by different sorts of jealousy. What we need to understand is what exactly makes us feel one sort rather than another. Is it entirely personal, or are we influenced by social rules about how we 'should' experience jealousy? Let us look first at types of jealousy and then at the point about rules.

Perhaps there are different types of jealousy, just as there are different types of love. Mazur (1977) distinguished five types: possessive, exclusive, competitive, egotistical, and fearful:

Possessive jealousy is a response to perceived violation of 'property rights'. We feel this type of jealousy about things or status or even other people if we think that they belong to us or are our property. For instance, we sometimes feel possessive jealousy if our partner acts in an independent way.
Exclusive jealousy is a response to occasions when we are omitted from a loved one's important experiences or when we are not allowed to share a loved one's private world. For instance, if our partner wants to go camping in the mountains to commune with nature and specifically forbids us to accompany him or her, then we might feel a twinge of exclusive jealousy.
Competitive jealousy with our partner is our reaction to a feeling of inadequacy and an attempt to restore the balance. In this case, we may feel competitive jealousy if our partner is actually better than we are at something where we ourselves wish to excel.
Egotistical jealousy is the feeling that our way is the only way and an inability to expand our ego awareness or role flexibility. It consists of difficulty in altering our perspective or accepting the need to change ourselves or our routine ways of behaving. In short, it is a desire to stay as we are, under no influence to adapt to other people's wishes or needs.
Fearful jealousy is a reaction to the threat of loneliness or rejection. This type is felt when we are rejected and left alone by our partner, whether or not that partner runs off with someone else.

Is jealousy identified with any particular visible display of behaviours? No, but different instances of jealousy do all seem to have one underlying theme, namely loss of control (or believed loss of control) over our partner's feelings for us. This results in a general sense of hurt or anger (Ellis and Weinstein, 1986), but this sense is 'blended' in different ways by different persons on different occasions. As Ellis and Weinstein (1986) argue, this is partly because the expression and communication of emotion are mediated by symbols that have meaning to the person feeling the emotion. Thus there is no direct and agreed way for people to express or feel jealousy, but each person does it according to his or her own system of meaning. Also different people refer to quite markedly different blends of feelings that, for them, make up jealousy. A common core of hurt, anger and fear is frequently described, but even then the exact recipe for the pain of jealousy is variable (Ellis and Weinstein, 1986). Sharpsteen (1993) in fact proposes that jealousy is a blended emotion based on knowledge, but sharing features similar to those in other emotions like anger and fear.

We might feel hurt and angry on some occasions, whereas in other circumstances we would feel only mildly aroused. For instance, we may feel a mild type of excitement if we know that our partner is just teasing us with the prospect of entering another relationship (indeed, we may now recognize it as ludic love), but we would probably feel both hurt and angry if we found out that the partner really had another relationship (at least we would if we lived in a society that assumed all such relationships needed to be 'exclusive' in order to be really sincere).

Our blend of feelings is provided partly by the context and by particular interpretations or symbolic meanings that we give to the acts that 'cause' jealousy on a given occasion. These will probably direct a person's attention to specific parts of the whole jealousy-evoking event (e.g. to a sense of feeling helpless or to angry words). Contexts vary as a result of the degree of 'attachment' or relationship intimacy between the relevant parties (Ellis and Weinstein, 1986). They vary according to the 'valued resources' that flow through and are controlled by that attachment (i.e. whether the relationship runs through our life fabric or is marginal and peripheral to it); and to the perceived degree of 'intrusion' into that attachment by the third person (whether he or she really threatens it or just slightly unsettles it). This latter is important because no-one expects a relationship with someone else to exclude all outsiders in all respects all of the time. We recognize that our partner will need and want other friends too: we cannot have the partner all to ourselves. Rather, we feel jealous when a third party threatens an area that is seen as central to our attachment to a partner (e.g. we would feel jealous if someone else looked like becoming our best friend's best friend), or else when feelings of discontent are brought about by another's evident superiority (Smith, 1991).

In our society, we usually have labels – 'friendship', 'marriage' and 'engagement' – that help us to mark out our relationships and warn outsiders that our partner is central to our attachment in this way. The labels indicate where the limits of the attachment lie, and the community helps in various ways to enforce the relationship. Thus, to announce an engagement or a marriage is to use a tie sign to tell the community to act as an extra guardian against intrusion or trespass on the relationship by outsiders. To put this another way, interpretations of situations are made on the basis of knowledge of the systematic behaviour of the partner, and also from rules and knowledge from which to infer those interpretations of the person, such that the interpretation is based on normative or cultural expressions of meaning; these meanings can be used to invoke the aid of others in watching over the proper performance of a relationship.

Rules about jealousy

Feelings are shaped partly as a result of social context and partly as a result of general social rules about the appropriateness of expressing certain emotions about relationships (Buunk, 1995). We may feel outrage as well as jealousy if someone infringes cultural rules – for example, by committing adultery with our spouse. In Victorian times, husbands were often encouraged to go and shoot their wife's lover(s). However, if the relationship between sexual partners has not been formally agreed by society (e.g. if we are living together but are not married) then no rules govern the expression of feelings about those same sexual transgression. We may feel jealous but get no social support for feeling outraged.

Further, personal experience of our partner and the ways our lives are intertwined by routines together provide a basis for interpreting the meaning of certain behaviours that may affect our reactions. For instance, if we both agree that flirting with other people is an acceptable behaviour then we should not feel jealous when we catch a partner doing it (Bringle and Boebinger, 1990). In open marriages, for instance, partners feel jealous of their partner only when his or her behaviour violates the agreed rules about sexual conduct in the relationship and not just because the behaviour occurred (Buunk, 1980). 'Swingers' note that it is acceptable for their partner to have sex with another person so long as he or she does not 'get emotionally involved'. Such swingers would not feel jealous because the partner had extramarital sex but they would feel jealous if the partner became emotionally involved.

Such rules stabilize the relationship and act as guides for feelings about the partner's behaviour in it (Hochschild, 1979). They can even specify when a society expects a person to be jealous and in what circumstances (Davis, 1936). For example, Trobriand Islandsmen used to be expected to 'offer' their wives to a visitor and were specifically forbidden to feel jealous if the visitor accepted (Malinowski, 1929). In our own ways, we often attempt to suppress and control jealousy, partly because it may be socially disapproved, partly because we may feel that it reveals too much of a dependency on the relationship, and partly because it creates an unpleasant degree of restrictive possessiveness of the partner.

An emotion like jealousy can be experienced in everyday life, then, in a social context that defines the appropriateness even of strong emotions (Sharpsteen, 1993). With jealousy, it seems that loss of control or of social 'face' is one important element in the emotion. Jealousy is an appropriate emotion to feel when either our social status or self-esteem or control over a relationship is threatened (Buunk, 1995; Radecki-Bush et al., 1993).

To put it slightly differently (but only slightly), jealousy is a response to an imagined loss of influence over a routine part of life, namely over the feelings of another person towards ourselves (Radecki-Bush et al., 1993). When we imagine that we have lost influence over another person's feelings for us or when we are given evidence that they do not care, then we experience jealousy. Such a reaction can take the form specifically of a sensed threat to security, even when a person is *imagining* the situation (Radecki-Bush et al., 1988). The more we take loving feelings for granted and the more extensively they are threatened, the more jealousy we feel, unless, of course, we were in manic love and experienced a strong sense of threat and dependency.

Shyness and social anxiety

Shyness is rather similar to embarrassment in some ways but is an affective-behavioural syndrome consisting of social anxiety and inhibition. Shyness is caused by an anticipation of a discrepancy between a person's desired self-image and his or her way of projecting the self-image so that the actual projection is expected to fall short of the desired one. Shyness is embarrassment in advance, created by the belief that our real self will not be able to match up to the image we want to project.

Everyone feels shy from time to time, but some people are likely to feel more shy than others. Also obviously some people feel shy about certain topics (e.g. discussing sex) but not others. Some 41 per cent of people believe that they are shy and up to 24 per cent think that it is a serious enough problem for them to do something about it (Pilkonis, 1977). If you are not shy yourself, then two out of the next four people you meet will be and one of them will feel that it requires seeking professional help.

There is one key feature to shyness and it revolves around problems with interpersonal communication (Kelly, 1982). A central problem for many shy people is their unwillingness to communicate (i.e. 'reticence'), characterized by avoidance of, and ineptitude at, social interaction and performance in public or at the centre of attention in a social encounter. Is the cause deficient communication skills; or anxiety about communication (so-called 'communication apprehension'); or simple avoidance of communication? In other words, is it because the person generally dislikes communication, or becomes paralysingly anxious about it, or just cannot do it well behaviourally? In practical terms there are few differences among the results of these three possible causes (Kelly, 1982), although the first two seem to be attitudinal or cognitive causes whilst the last is a behavioural or communicative problem. Programmes that improve (behavioural) performance actually reduce anxiety also, so we cannot distinguish the behavioural and the attitudinal components easily. What is readily distinguishable is that part of shyness is the experience of dyadic communicative difficulties and that part of it is the communicative difficulties themselves. This raises the intriguing question of whether shyness is a particular sort of social interaction rather than a trait of particular people.

Whichever of these possibilities is ultimately correct, a serious problem for shy people is that reticence is evaluated by outsiders as if the shy person felt hostile and negative towards people rather than being shy or nervous about them (Burgoon and Koper, 1984). When strangers are asked to assess videotapes of reticent persons talking to other people, the strangers rate the reticents quite negatively. They see reticents as expressing too little intimacy/similarity, being detached and uninvolved in the interaction, and showing too much submissiveness and emotional negativity. They also rate reticents as not credible or somewhat 'shifty'. When the shy persons' friends see the same videotapes, however, they usually rate the behaviour as more positive. In other words, shy persons' behaviour appears negative to strangers, but their friends had already become used to it and discounted it. Once shy people gain friends they are seen positively; the problem is that their behaviour is such that strangers probably would not want to become their friends in the first place.

Leary and Dobbins (1983) show that there are quite severe relational consequences of shyness, in that surveyed persons who were highly shy had had fewer sexual experiences, less sexual intercourse and a smaller number of sexual partners than people who were not very shy. Dating, a usual preliminary to sexual encounters, is a situation that gets rated as highly anxiety-provoking by between 37 per cent and 50 per cent of men and 21 per cent to 50 per cent of women, in any case. Presumably, the very shy are at a considerable disadvantage in dating; their shyness effectively cuts them off from initiating normal social life, though ultimately the habitual daily forces and activities that bring people together (such as the workplace and its routines) can smooth the path to developing a relationship by forcing people together and exposing them to one another's behaviours and conversations without their having to make it happen otherwise.

If we can define the precise nature of the problem then help can be prescribed. There are different elements to shyness. Some stem from anxiety about communication ('communication apprehension') and some from reticence or lack of skill in performing communication adequately. In the latter category are a speech impediment or a belief that we have nothing to say that would interest people or an awkwardness and inability to converse easily (Kelly, 1982). The end result is the same – the person does not communicate – but the reasons are different.

Tragically, the anxious person may be a perfectly competent communicator if the anxiety could be overcome. Many such people are perfectly good communicators when they are relaxed in the company of friends, but the unskilled person would perform badly even when not anxious (Leary et al., 1987). The anxious, or 'privately shy' person typically focuses on the subjective discomfort and fear of negative evaluation whilst the 'publicly shy' person thinks of the behavioural inadequacies as the main problem.

It does seem as if something about shyness fundamentally affects a person's system of social communication with other people and as if that serves (unintentionally?) to keep others away. Communication problems contribute to the difficulties of the shy person and help to ensure that they stay lonely. It may work the other way around, such that social isolation contributes to communication difficulties, for instance, through lack of practice (Zakahi and Duran, 1982). One particularly important problem is that shy or communicatively incompetent persons become used to not being intimate or open with others. They thus 'learn' to give out signals in their routine social behaviour that are interpreted as meaning that they are not interested in relationships with other people (Zakahi and Duran, 1985). Clearly, a state like shyness is built into a person's routine ways of handling life, other people and new situations, and is the habitual style of behaviour in such new situations. Thus, shy persons contribute nonverbally to their own social rejection and hence to their future loneliness.

Loneliness

Loneliness is more common than we may believe, is not confined to a group of odd or abnormal people, is associated with both unhappiness and illness, and can be cured. People who are lonely do not necessarily have fewer relationships or daily interactions than other people have, but they are often less satisfied with the ones they do have. Equally it is clear that the experience of loneliness is not associated with total isolation and even those who are chronically lonely have a few friends too (Tornstam, 1992). This is particularly important because satisfactory interactions – especially cross-sex interactions – are associated with better feelings about health (Wheeler et al., 1983).

Who becomes lonely?

Who becomes lonely? We all do. Roughly 26 per cent of a large sample reported feeling 'very lonely within the past few weeks' (Bradburn, 1969), and almost everyone experiences intense loneliness at some time or another (Peplau and Perlman, 1982), although men are rejected more often than women if they admit to loneliness (Borys and Perlman, 1984). We often think of loneliness as more rampant in elderly rather than younger populations, but research casts doubt on this (Schultz and Moore, 1988) and actually shows that loneliness is higher in high school students than in the elderly. For elderly people what is important is the availability of a close confidant (Peplau et al., 1982) and whether the person has been used to being single through life (Shanas et al., 1968). In one study, contrary to popular myth, only 15 per cent of old people report that they feel lonely quite often (Tunstall, 1967). Moreover, Tornstam (1992) found a large sex difference in loneliness, with women being more lonely than men, especially married women aged between 20 and 49. Women have a tendency to higher expectations for intimacy in a relationship and also to have lower self-esteem, but Tornstam (1992) showed that this did not explain the sex difference, which was more likely due to the females' greater sensitivity to strain and stress in relationships.

There are some situations where everyone becomes lonely, and we can distinguish *trait loneliness* (a stable and persistent pattern of feeling lonely – definitely a feature of the person; he or she invariably takes the feeling into new situations) and *state loneliness* (a transient, temporary feeling of loneliness – probably resulting from the situation or a move to a new environment rather than to the specific person; everyone might feel lonely in such circumstances). When people move to college they all tend to experience loneliness but some cope better with it than do others. Interestingly, males who are lonely tend to form a more negative view of themselves than do females, since they attribute it to personal failure rather than to forces over which they have no control (Schultz and Moore, 1988).

What is loneliness?

Clearly, loneliness is not necessarily the same as being alone (DeJong-Gierveld, 1989). We can be lonely in a crowd and can be perfectly happy on our own sometimes in the 'bliss of solitude'. The crucial feature of loneliness, according to Perlman and Peplau (1981), is a discrepancy between what we're doing and what we expect or hope to do. To put it more precisely, loneliness results from 'a discrepancy between one's desired and achieved levels of social relations' (Perlman and Peplau, 1981: 32). If we desire a small number of friends (say 1 or 2) and that is what we have, then we will be happy and not lonely. If, on the other hand, we desire 15 friends and have only 14, then we shall feel lonely.

To assess loneliness, we must look at the person's desired or needed levels of social contact rather than at just the levels of social contact that he or she actually achieves. Our expectations, desires and needs can fluctuate from time to time independently of our actual levels of social contact. For example, when we are under some sort of stress we might want company, but when we are working on a difficult task we would rather be alone and would find company annoying. Also, the Perlman–Peplau model is perfectly comfortable with the finding that our experience of loneliness can vary according to internal factors like feelings or beliefs even when our number of friends or social contacts stays objectively the same. In other words, even when our contacts stay the same and our number of friends is constant, we could still feel lonely on some days and not others or in some circumstances and not others, depending on our present desire for company or solitude.

For example, people feel more lonely just after they have been beaten at racquet ball (Perlman and Serbin, 1984), whilst teenagers experience more loneliness at weekends (Larson et al., 1982), not because they have fewer contacts then but because they expect to have more active social lives at weekends.

Expectations about relationships and about loneliness will be influenced by personality, beliefs about attractiveness, and whether one tends to take credit for social successes in meeting new people or blame for failures to make friends. Duck et al. (1994) showed, for example, that lonely people feel negative about interaction with other people and also about their own performance of relational behaviours that would make them attractive to other people. When lonely people watch videotapes of their own conversations with other people, they are particularly likely to be negative about themselves. Solano and Koester (1989) showed that a strong element of the low competence of lonely people is their extreme anxiety about social performance which tends to interfere with their performance of appropriate social behaviour and so becomes a vicious cycle of self-fulfilling prophecy.

We learned in the preceding section that shy people habitually fear making new friends and may be anxious in ways that could affect their adequacy in carrying out new encounters. Those who usually assume that social failures are their own fault ('because of the person I am and the problems I always have') are likely to overlook other obvious factors that could account for loneliness – such as 'circumstances' or 'moving to a new neighbourhood'. They will probably blame their isolation in the new circumstances on their habitual and personal difficulties even when no-one else would make that inference. Accordingly, they are much more likely than everyone else to feel negative about themselves and to experience a sense of personal hopelessness. Trait lonely people (i.e. the long-term lonely) are found to have exactly the characteristics that make it more likely that they will blame themselves in this way. They have a low opinion of themselves, see themselves in negative terms, dislike talking about their feelings, and are low in intimate behaviours (Jones et al., 1981; Solano et al., 1982).

Later work (e.g. Marangoni and Ickes, 1989; Rook, 1988) has urged researchers to differentiate loneliness, emphasizing variations in the duration of loneliness, and different levels of motivation, such as social anxiety, or interpersonally deficient causes of loneliness, such as social skill problems. As Solano and Koester (1989) show, the anxiety component may be more powerful than any other component such as social skill deficits. Several other theorists (Vaux, 1988) have distinguished different sorts of loneliness also. *Social loneliness* is a deficiency in the social network (i.e. a small number of contacts) perhaps due to a change in circumstances such as moving to a new town; emotional loneliness is a deficit in close attachments, especially romantic ones. In the case of social loneliness, the numbers of relationships are low, but in the case of *emotional loneliness* the quality is low (especially of certain types of relationships). The possibility obviously exists that these forms of loneliness result from different sorts of deficits in the person involved. Mikulincer and Segal (1990) break the experience of loneliness down into psychological components: cognitive (what you think about loneliness and other people in general); emotional (what you feel about loneliness and other people); motivational (how concerned you are to do anything about loneliness when it happens); and behavioural (what you actually do about it). There are also those researchers who distinguish the situations of loneliness and differentiate it in respect of different relationships. Some people find it quite easy to be amiable to everyone but find close intimacy difficult for various reasons, like past experiences or personality structure (Duck, 1991). Others feel shy in company, except in the company of one specific person, such as their romantic partner.

Lonely people may have several deficits rather than just one. They may have poor social skills (see Chapter 1 and the next section), they may be poor at perceiving others' needs in conversation or social situations, or they may be poor at adopting the roles necessary in interaction. Wittenberg and Reis (1986) explored all three possibilities and found that they all contributed to loneliness (hardly surprising if you imagine what a person with all these deficits would be like to talk to). However, those subjects who were assertive and responsive to others were best able to avoid loneliness. Spitzberg and Canary (1985) found that although lonely subjects were less competent at communication than other subjects, they also tended to recognize this. Interestingly, they also devalued and criticized the social skills of their partners. Despite this, Vitkus and Horowitz (1987) showed that lonely people were just as good at adopting roles given them by the experimenter as were any other subjects. Perhaps if lonely people are given roles to adopt then they can fulfil them but in everyday life they do not do so because, as Spitzberg and Cupach show, they devalue the whole social performance. Thus they do not feel like getting involved in it by playing the appropriate roles well for themselves.

What do lonely people do?

Lonely people do habitually report quite consistent feelings (Rubenstein and Shaver, 1982). These are: *desperation* (being panicked and feeling helpless); *depression* (feeling sad and worthless); *impatient boredom* (restlessness and boredom simultaneously); and *self-deprecation* ('What's wrong with me?' and 'Why am I so useless?'). Chronically lonely males have characteristic sets of beliefs about themselves and other people that lead them to act in an aggressive and hostile way (Check et al., 1985). Lonely males are more punitive than nonlonely males are, particularly towards female partners who make errors on a learning task that the male is 'supervising'. Many violent males, particularly rapists, are found to score highly on loneliness scales and to have been socially isolated well before they committed their violent assaults (Howells, 1981).

Chronically lonely persons tend to be self-absorbed, nonresponsive, negativistic and ineffective in their interactions with strangers (Duck et al.,

1994). They spend more time alone, particularly at weekends, and are less involved with voluntary organizations, dating, relatives and neighbours or social activities generally (Jones et al., 1985). They sometimes show 'sad passivity', which involves overeating, oversleeping, watching television, crying, drinking alcohol, or taking tranquillizers (Rubenstein and Shaver, 1982). They also watch more TV than average, especially news broadcasts (Rubin et al., 1985), which might suggest that their loneliness is associated with a sense of lack of stimulation. Also found in this study, though, is that lonely people tend to 'interact' with a favourite local news anchor, often talking to the newscaster or commenting aloud on the reader's appearance and performance.

Other typical styles of coping with loneliness are to engage in 'busy-busy' activity, solitary hobbies, jogging alone, or taking vigorous exercise. Other people react to loneliness by self-indulgent actions, particularly buying themselves 'toys' like microcomputers and remote control miniaturized stereo systems, or just generally running riot with their credit cards. When we get lonely we often turn into 'big spenders' in an effort to make ourselves feel better about ourselves. More useful are coping strategies that involve visiting other people, writing to friends, telephoning them, or just attempting to increase social contact.

The key feature is the belief system that we hold about the causes of our loneliness and about our ability to control it. If we believe that it will go away as long as we take positive action, then we are more likely to attempt to socialize. If we believe that it is somehow 'our fault' – and a permanent feature or, at least, a stable feature of our lives at that – then we are more likely to become depressed. Several studies show that it is possible to reduce loneliness by giving the person a sense of control over it. Thus, for instance, Shulz (1976) found that old persons who were allowed to schedule visits from volunteer workers felt less lonely than those whose schedule was fixed for them by someone else – even though the total number and length of the visits was the same for both sets of people.

When you are forced to be alone

Variations in the sense of control are probably one reason why not all 'being alone' is loneliness, as the Perlman–Peplau model makes clear. If our desired level of social contact is low for some deliberately controlled reason (e.g. if we are feeling creative and want to write a novel) then low levels of social contact will be highly enjoyable and high levels of social interaction may actually be unattractive to us.

The problems arise when someone is forced to be alone willy-nilly. For instance, students typically report feeling lonely soon after they arrive in their new university at the start of their first year (Shaver et al., 1985). Friends rather than dates or lovers are the best buffer against loneliness in those circumstances (DeJong-Gierveld, 1989).

The loneliness of the new college student What happens, then, when new students go to college? Shaver et al. (1985) looked at ways of predicting which students would stay lonely and which would develop fuller networks in the new environment and so cope with loneliness. Their results show that the transition to college was particularly stressful for males, whose loneliness increased four times more than females'. Also males' dating frequency declined more than females'. The latter may have resulted from first-year male students having a smaller pool of dates available to them since there is a cultural norm that encourages females (but not males) to date older as well as same-aged members of the opposite sex and to decline requests for dates from younger males.

Old relationships back home declined both in number and perceived quality, whereas new ones did not quickly reach the satisfaction levels of pre-college ones. The transition to college caused the end of almost half (46 per cent) of the pre-college romantic relationships and also produced strain in the other 54 per cent, which were rated much less positively after the transition than before it.

On the more positive side, the students were quick to establish new groups of casual acquaintances, but experienced considerable uncertainty about them. Their feelings about family and kin became more positive, and they experienced less conflict with parents even though they did not see them as often – or perhaps because of it. Seemingly, though, this was a subjective change rather than a real or objective one, since there obviously was little interaction going on with the family that could improve; the students just felt better about their family.

Curing chronic loneliness

Loneliness causes loneliness. That is, people who are presently lonely may, like shy persons, communicate in such a way that other people do not feel inclined to relate to them or might disregard them and find them unattractive (Spitzberg and Canary, 1985). Whole programmes of research are now geared up to identifying the interpersonal skills (or rather the lack of skills) of the chronically lonely person in an attempt to understand the most effective ways of helping them (Jones et al., 1985).

The basic argument here is that lonely people, like shy people, lack certain skills in communication and social behaviour, such as assertiveness, or else they are higher in shyness and self-consciousness (Jones et al., 1981) and experience inhibited sociability (e.g. difficulty making friends). Lonely people in a laboratory setting select less effective power strategies and are generally less effective in meeting new people (Perlman et al., 1978). Lonely students are below average at sharing their opinions on personal topics (Hansson and Jones, 1981). Jones et al. (1984: 146) conclude provocatively that 'the interpersonal behaviours often associated with loneliness may actually reduce the likelihood that the lonely person will be able, without intervention, to restore mutually satisfying relationships with others'.

A number of successful programmes for treating chronic loneliness have been developed recently to help people to cope with loneliness, prevent the more serious consequences like depression and suicide, and help them to create broader and more satisfying networks – as well as preventing people from becoming lonely in the first place (Rook, 1988). In essence there are four approaches:

1 *Cognitive treatment*, aimed at changing lonely people's expectations that they will be rejected in social encounters (similar to the one used on shy people in the preceding section);
2 *Social skills training*, aimed at improving people's ability to be effective in encounters with other people;
3 *Group therapy*, aimed at increasing sensitivity to other people;
4 *Community-based approaches*, aimed at increasing people's opportunities for interaction.

The community-based approaches are not much use to people with underlying social skill deficits since 'Go out and meet more people' really just amounts to 'Go out and be rejected by more people' unless the underlying problem is solved first (Duck, 1991).

In one social skills training programme, Jones et al. (1982) trained some very lonely males to increase their attention to their partner in a conversation (e.g. by asking questions about the partner; continuing, rather than changing, the topic of conversation; showing interest in the partner's views). Training involved exposure to audiotapes of 'good' and 'bad' conversations in which the instructor pointed out places where attention to the partner would have been particularly appropriate. In a similar programme, Gallup (1980) trained lonely people in other interactional skills (e.g. paraphrasing partner's comments; summarizing their statements; giving positive evaluations). In both programmes, lonely people became more skilful in conversation and reported subsequent increases in sociability, reductions in loneliness and reduced feelings of shyness.

Cognitive treatments, on the other hand, aim to restructure the way in which the lonely people think about themselves and the interpersonal events in which they participate. Individuals who are lonely usually are high in social anxiety, just as shy people are, and they feel that they are being judged or ridiculed by other people. Treatments such as Young's (1982) cognitive therapy are intended to change these attitudes and to encourage the person to engage in activities with other people, including open disclosure of his or her feelings and emotions.

One method of effecting such change is to challenge the person to produce evidence that other people are ridiculing or judging him or her. Examples of other people making errors are then discussed and comparisons made of the subject's reactions to them. Often, it can be shown that the lonely person has a higher standard for his or her own behaviour than for other people's, a proposal confirmed by later work (Duck et al., 1994) as discussed above.

It is encouraging that such therapies are being developed. Loneliness is something that we all experience from time to time and that we all try to avoid or correct. It is thus a common human concern for which systematic study can provide some answers and correctives. It is a good instance of the fact that relational problems affect our lives fundamentally by getting incorporated into our routine ways of interacting. We should also note that since relational problems lead to pronounced loss of concentration, one of the most dangerous people in the world is a lonely air traffic controller.

Summary

The emotions that we have looked at here share a number of features:

1 They occur in relationship to other people, involve expressive and communicative behaviour, are closely connected to the notion of worth and competence in relationships and are based on standards set within particular cultures. Each in its own way is a form of expression that communicates our assumed value and worth to other people in that cultural context.
2 These emotions do not need specific external events to spark them off but can all be rekindled just by thought and by fantasy or imagination about social encounters, past, present, or future. They can be experienced in the absence of other people but are 'about' them.
3 They are sometimes experienced as just hot surges of emotion, but are more often enduring emotional states reported in dispositional *language* ('I am in love'; 'I am a shy person') or seen to have possible long-term effects on relationships. They can become ways of social life, enshrined in ways of communicating and expressing ourselves through behaviour or else can have long-term effects on the relationship.
4 They are structured into or impact upon social routines and everyday behaviours. That we feel jealous or shy or lonely or in love influences the way we *communicate with other people* in the long term, as well as in the short term. It can affect how we look at them, how we speak to them and how we deal with them, as well as how we choose to relate to them. In short, personal emotions have dyadic, communicative effects also and are based within the language system with which a person thinks and speaks.
5 The isolating feelings (shyness, loneliness) can be treated by training programmes that affect the person's communicative behaviour, as well as other people's responses and hence the lonely or shy person's feelings about their own worth.

In short, I have been making the case that *social emotions* are essentially dyadic, communicative and relational ones, and as such occur in a cultural context that adds layers of meaning to them by providing a context in which the 'meanings' of specific behaviours are interpreted and moderated.

Further reading

Cupach, W.R. and Metts, S. (1994) *Facework*. Thousand Oaks, CA: Sage.

Duck, S.W. and Wood, J.T. (eds) (1995) *Confronting Relationship Challenges*. (Vol. 5) *Understanding Relationship Processes*. Newbury Park, CA: Sage.

Miller, R.S. (1996) *Embarrassment: Poise and Peril in Everyday Life*. New York: Guilford.

Retzinger, S.M. (1995) 'Shame and anger in personal relationships', in S.W. Duck and J.T. Wood (eds), *Confronting Relationship Challenges*. (Vol. 5) *Understanding Relationship Processes*. Thousand Oaks, CA: Sage. pp. 22–42.

Salovey, P. (ed.) (1991) *The Psychology of Jealousy and Envy*. New York: Guilford.

Wood, J.T. and Duck, S.W. (eds) (1995) *Under-studied Relationships: Off the Beaten Track*. (Vol. 6) *Understanding Relationship Processes*. Thousand Oaks, CA: Sage.

3

Interaction and Daily Life in Long-term Relationships

'People are actors in giving communicative life to the contradictions that organize their social life, but these contradictions in turn affect their communicative action . . . *Praxis* focuses on the concrete practices by which social actors produce the future out of the past in their everyday lives.' (Baxter and Montgomery, 1996: 13–14)

Chapter 2 looked at some Big Emotions, and connected 'feelings' to language, culture and 'praxis' or the doing of relating and the conduct of daily life. I wrote about 'love' as an emotion, though I wrote less about how people enact it in daily life, for example. Yet we do not experience emotions on some abstract plane: they hit us in the face as a part of daily life or in response to relational experience. As Duck and Wood (1995) suggested, relational emotions are basically to do with management of behaviour or the organization of daily life and the routines and expectations that ordinarily make them up. True, we think of relationships as based in emotions and abstractions but we do them all the same. Also if we think of relationships only as being based on emotions we miss perhaps the most important point about relationships: they happen in daily life where lots of other things happen too besides emotions – things like gossip, hassles, decisions about our calendars and time organization, manipulation of impressions by others, trivial organization of leisure time, sharing of experiences, reading about other people's relationships in magazines . . .

It is true that when we are asked about what matters to us most in life and gives it its fullest purpose, the majority of people give one simple answer: relationships (Klinger, 1977), meaning most probably the positive ones. However, I doubt if people are really talking about *emotions* in relationships when they answer that way; I'd bet they are talking about the experience of relationships in all its complexity. What is more I'd bet that enemyships also matter in practical conduct of life and in some cases are more powerful forces on our thinking and behaviour than are the loves and friendships that surround us (Wiseman and Duck, 1995). Also important is the handling of little details: it is OK to like someone but where do you find the time to talk to them if you have pressing work to do, or other people competing for your attention and time or other relationships you are in? What is sacrificed if you spend time with them and what does it mean if you don't choose to make that sacrifice?

Relationships are obvious sources of joy and happiness: we like being with friends; we enjoy the company of others; being in love is wonderful when we think of it in the abstract and forget the non-idealized parts. On the other hand, good relationships can be hell when they go wrong or get into trouble and cause us pain, or when a partner calls on us to fulfil a relational obligation (like providing support and help) when we don't care to do it. Chapter 2 showed us that specific emotions about, or experiences in, relationships have very powerful effects on people yet the chapter often decontextualized relationships by stripping them out of daily life because much research work also does that. The present chapter shows the import-ant role of relationships as a whole, particularly change in relationships, not only in social life but also their effect on our 'sense of being' or sense of self-esteem. One thing you need to notice is that although we think of rela-tionships as stable places where we live, most of our daily experience is in fact varied and unstable. For example, we and our partners have moods; some days things keep going wrong; people can be a hassle when at other times they are not, and so forth. Somehow or other we manage to create a sense of unity and character from this ebb and flow of variety (Duck, 1994a). We also talk about relationships in emotional terms yet we probably spend most of our time dealing with them in practical terms.

We can make sweeping statements about the value of relationships but there is, of course, also a negative side to relationships. Poor relationship skills are associated with criminality, violence and aggression, neurosis and depression, illness, shyness, drug and alcohol problems, marital difficulties, divorce, spouse beating and child abuse (J. West, 1995; Wood, 1997). They also create demands on us to provide help, comfort and resources to others or oblige us to be available to others when they are in difficulties, especially in times of illness and stress (Stein, 1993). The phenomenon of 'care-giver burnout' has been widely researched (Miller et al., 1988) whether in respect of mental health service professionals and counsellors who experience exhaus-tion from all their caring for others (La Gaipa, 1990) or merely untrained folk who care for sick relatives (Lyons and Meade, 1995). People also give us daily hassles (Bolger and Kelleher, 1993) and present us with binds and dilemmas (Wiseman, 1986) or stretch our loyalties (Baxter et al., 1997). In living practical relational lives, these are variations with which we must be prepared to contend, and considering what we may be letting ourselves in for, there might be a case for never getting into relationships at all!

Starting relationships

Just as we tend to think of relationships in the abstract so we have a number of relatively simplistic ideas about the ways in which they start and finish. The whole notion of a clear start to a relationship is at odds with some of our other experiences of life. When did you start the relationship with the assistant at your supermarket check-out? Does the way you 'started' the relationship with your mother really matter that much? Have you ever had a relationship where you really had to think back quite hard to remember how it started because it just grew out of some relatively frequent contact? Did you and your partner ever disagree about how it started or have you always seen the start of the relationship in identical terms? Doesn't that strike you as remarkable (either way)? Of course people ask one another out on dates and can pinpoint that time as the start of the relationship, but it may be that the *planning* to ask someone out on a date is the real start, not the date itself. Or perhaps the date itself is not really the start, but the relationship grows out of the date. Let's think this one out a little more . . .

In everyday life we are enormously influenced by first impressions. Job applications, interviews, and the whole course of a relationship can be 'set' by the first few moments. In everyday life, we make many snap judgements about people and form instant likes and dislikes. Of course we don't do this alone either. We often get to hear about someone first from our acquaintances, not by direct experience ourselves (Berger and Bradac, 1982), or we may hear gossipy or 'reputational' things about someone before we ever get to meet them – hence the line 'Good to meet you at last, I have heard so much about you.' We also know that from information received or impressions we make ourselves we can create 'irrational' first impressions, sudden lusts and likings, and intense hatreds for people we really do not know. We can like the manner of a person we do not know and can form instant dislikes of someone who has not even uttered a word to us.

So it is actually paradoxical that the study of initial responses to strangers makes sense as a starting point for understanding long-term human relationships; it is an identifiable point when relationships are most often thought to start or fail to start, but very often plenty precedes that 'starting point'. Even so, things can be derailed by trivialities: we may decide (not) to date someone whose appearance does (not) appeal to us, and so we may (fail to) embark on a relationship that could have changed our lives. Rodin (1982) indicates that if we reach the early decision that 'this is a non-relationship' (with a restaurant waiter, for example) then we close down certain kinds of cognitive processing and do not bother to search for indications that might otherwise become the basis for a relationship. Indeed, there is evidence that in as short a space of time as 30 seconds partners usually decide whether a date is going to be a success or failure (Cortez et al., 1988).

Aside from appearance, what makes us initially attracted (and attractive) to other people? Common sense will answer 'You were attracted because you have similar attitudes and personalities.' That is a reasonable proposition, but how does it stand up to investigation?

Laboratory investigation of attraction

If we find that friends have similar attitudes, we may congratulate ourselves that we have found an answer to the question until we realize that we have

---

Box 3.1   Exercise on relationships

- Think for a moment about the people with whom you are particularly friendly. What do you like about them and how did the relationship get started? How does the relationship with each person differ from those that you have with other people?
- Write out two short lists (say 10 items each) giving: (a) the features of a friend that you like (seven items) and those that you dislike (three items) (b) the sort of activities that you perform or topics you talk about almost exclusively with friends (seven items) and those that you do with other people too, but that are 'better' with friends (three items).
- Think for a moment about an attractive person you have seen but not really met – one you would like to start a relationship with if you were completely free to do so. Write two short lists (10 items each) giving: (a) what you find attractive about them (seven items) and what you find unattractive about them (three items) (b) seven things you would do or talk about with them if you got to know them and three items you would definitely not talk about or do.
- Compare your various lists and try to work out the important differences among them, if any. Consider the differences involved in 'relating' to strangers and friends, and think what it is that changes when strangers gradually turn into acquaintances and friends.
- Take a look at the chapter by Rodin (1982) that outlines the bases for comparisons between such lists.

---

not shown whether similarity causes liking or liking causes similarity. (After all, we do try to discuss things with friends and persuade our friends to adopt our ideas and become more like us, don't we?) For a social scientist, the challenge is to find a way to alter similarity levels between people so that you can see what it does to their attraction for one another.

The problem was cleverly solved by Tony Smith (1957), a solution that was also independently developed by Donn Byrne (1961, 1971), though Byrne's own approach became the focus of a certain amount of criticism over the years (Byrne, 1997). The essence of the solution involves experiments on attraction to strangers where subjects filled out an attitude questionnaire and then were given another scale (allegedly) completed by a stranger. Byrne then assessed subjects' responses to the stranger (who was actually non-existent, i.e. was bogus or hypothetical, in honour of whom the method was called 'the bogus stranger method', although the experimental subjects did not *know* that the stranger was fictitious). The subjects would be presented with the information allegedly provided by this stranger, and they would then be asked what they thought of him or her. Byrne carefully arranged the information so that the stranger's attitude scale matched up with the subject's own to a precise degree (say 80 per cent or 65 per cent or 20 per cent), according to the needs of the experimental design.

Byrne's work, also known as 'the attraction paradigm' (or 'the paradigm that would not die'; Bochner, 1991), assumed that attitude similarity is an example of 'reinforcement' or reward – something attractive, desirable, and positive that we like to experience. The important point, according to Byrne, is that it is *reinforcement* that we like and it happens that attitude similarity is usually reinforcing. Note that Byrne does not say that attitude similarity is always reinforcing or attractive (sometimes it may be boring to meet someone whose attitudes are absolutely the same as ours). But usually, Byrne says, attitude similarity will be reinforcing, and so we usually find it attractive. If you are asked to write a critique of Byrne's work then please remember that point, because you will certainly read papers by other scholars who do not take account of it and are quite simply wrong in the way that they represent his work (Byrne, 1997; Duck and Barnes, 1992).

When all we know about someone is his or her sex and a sample of his or her attitudes, then we will like that person in proportion to the amount of reinforcing similarity between us; the more similar, the more we like him or her. If we know a little more about the person then the picture becomes more complicated: for instance, it matters whether we have a positive view of him or her (e.g. that we have not found out that the person is a thief or a homicidal maniac or mentally ill – unless we are, also). It also matters whether the similar attitudes are important to us, whether the reasons given for holding them are similar to ours, and whether we believe the strangers are stating their true opinions. In brief, as the picture becomes more complicated, so the plain and simple commonsense rule that 'similarity is attractive' turns out to be more and more inadequate and in need of refinement. In investigating this area Byrne and colleagues established an enormous amount of detail about this particular phenomenon, assessing the truth of the basic assumptions (Byrne, 1997).

In sum, we usually like people whose attitudes are similar to our own, so long as we like ourselves and the other people are normal, sensible people stating their true opinion. This fact is also obviously the basis of the method used by dating agencies who match partners up by selecting people with similar attitudes and beliefs – though the strangers there are real, not bogus. Byrne often tested the validity of his work outside the 'laboratory'. He found that bank managers give bigger loans to people with similar attitudes, for instance; that jurors are more likely to be lenient to defendants with attitudes like theirs; and that similarity of attitudes can overcome the prejudices of racial bigots so that prejudiced whites actually express liking for blacks who have similar attitudes (Byrne, 1992, 1997).

Laboratory-based, experimental, manipulated studies of liking may not penetrate real liking. In life we rarely gain such unambiguous access to someone else's attitudes. When was the last time a stranger came up to you and gave you a written list of his or her attitudes? Sometimes, we have to be 'detectives'; we know that people often conceal their true attitudes and we have to uncover them through communication. For instance, they may conceal their true attitudes from us in order to get something from us or to ingratiate themselves. Also, sometimes, people withhold their 'true' attitudes for other reasons, such as desire to create a positive impression or fear of

how their 'true confession' might be received by us. We all also know that
we have behaved in these concealing ways ourselves.

Social processes operate to ensure that initial encounters (and even later
ones) are not always the open, frank exchanges of unambiguous information that we sometimes think about in ideal circumstances. For example,
social conventions occasionally encourage us to be polite (which is an
interesting form of dishonesty in some sense), present images, or manage
impressions, or conceal embarrassing facts (Miller, 1996). For these reasons,
we correspondingly have to work at uncovering the true picture behind
other people's words; and some of us will be more proficient than others.
Thus my argument here (also adopted by Bochner, 1991) is that the
business of initial attraction is not just one of *matching* our attitudes or
characteristics with someone else's but of *communicating* about them and
assessing the manner in which they make sense from our point of view
(Duck, 1994a; Duck and Barnes, 1992). I'd also invite you to think whether
attitudes are communicated *only* by attitude statements uttered seriously,
probably with an expectant and dramatic roll on the drums heard in the
background to indicate significance. In everyday life, Big Time Important
Things are not what we hear: we hear much more about trivia, and we see
attitudes enacted in small behaviours (or else we deduce attitudes from the
style of someone's behaviour rather than from bald and strong direct
statements). Thus in real life the task of working out someone's attitudes is
really quite complex and indirect or inferential.

This opens up the possibility that individual differences in the detecting
skills of 'normal adults' are likely to be influential in relationship begin-
nings. It is also likely that young children will be less good at interpreting
people's attitudes, as will be some psychologically disturbed patients. These
extreme examples merely make the point that differences in detecting skills
can exist. Perhaps the shy and lonely 'normal adults' are at the poor end of
the scale when it comes to determining whether someone has similar
attitudes, and so they get off to a bad start with strangers.

When strangers are introduced – even in the laboratory – to have a
conversation, the effects of attitude similarity 'wash out' (Sunnafrank and
Miller, 1981). Similar subjects do not like one another any more than do
dissimilar ones after they have had a brief interaction. Also, dissimilar
partners who are able to interact also like their partner more than do
dissimilar ones who do not interact. Interaction has a positive effect on
liking, and it modifies the effect of dissimilarity on its own. When communication exceeds a 'one-off conversation' and is extended over time and
to explicit discussion of attitudinal issues, then again it is the dissimilar
stranger who gets a better rating (Sunnafrank, 1991).

Attitudes, attraction and relationships

Researchers of initial attraction are usually well aware that they are studying a small part of a broader set of issues (e.g. Byrne, 1997). Often, they are

both startled and hurt by critics who effectively say 'This work on strangers is silly because it tells us nothing about marriage.' Work on obstetrics tells us little about senility, but that is not a reason for not doing it. Many real-life examples make initial attraction an obvious and important area of concern. What we must bear in mind, however, is that of course not all attractions lead to relationships (Byrne, 1992).

'Attraction does not mean relationship'   There are myriad reasons why we do not set up relationships with every attractive person we meet, the most significant being a lack of a wish to do so (e.g. already married or engaged, going steady, not enough time, too many commitments); inappropriateness (e.g. differences in status, circumstances not conducive); or, perhaps more poignant, incompetence. Many people who report being lonely or shy feel unable to carry out their wishes to set up desired relationships. Occasionally, I get letters about this, saying things like 'I am a 25-year-old male and have this inability to converse, communicate, or form any sort of relationship with the opposite sex. It is a long-standing problem. Women do seem attracted to me but as soon as it gets on to speaking, conversing, etc., it goes no further' (actual letter). Obviously, we might begin by looking at the social skills of such persons (see Chapter 1), but the commonness of the problem is significant. It is the most frequent problem dealt with by the various counselling services on university campuses. If you can't deal with strangers you won't get friends without some help (perhaps from third parties, matchmakers, or the environmental forces that 'make' us get to know people willy-nilly, as the workplace environment does).

All the same, attraction to strangers is the starting point for all relationships that do eventually start. Researchers have sought to know why we select between strangers, why we prefer some to others, and what happens once we move on from our initial attraction. A problem with laboratory work on attraction is that it 'freezes' situations out of context: subjects go to a room for an experiment, meet a stranger (or don't meet a bogus one!), and then go home. This might lead us to think of all interactions as frozen and context-free – like separate snapshots rather than single still frames from a continuous movie. Life is not made up of such separate snapshots, but is continuous and much more like a movie film. In life, one meeting with a person often leads to another. When we know that fact, it probably affects what we do and how we treat those strangers whom we may see again and get to know better. So we must expect that our reasons for initial attraction are not necessarily those that influence long-term development of relationships or help us to stay in relationships. Why should they be? Perhaps as Bochner (1991: 487) argues, 'Whether individuals actually have similar or dissimilar attitudes is not as important as the assumption shared by most individuals that they should have something important in common with the other (e.g. attitudes) if they are to form a relationship.'

Acquaintance is made up of several different elements, dimensions and stages, each with its own influences as things proceed (Van Lear and

	Undeclared	Declared
Nonevaluative	Commonality of experience = events	Mutuality
Evaluative	Equivalence of evaluation	Shared meaning

Figure 3.1 *Four components of 'similarity' (Duck, S.W.* Meaningful
Relationships: Talking, Sense, and Relating, *p. 118, copyright © 1994 by
S.W. Duck. Reprinted by permission of Sage Inc.)*

Note: The *declaration* dimension distinguishes the fact that two persons may have common
events in their backgrounds (commonality) and either may or may not know it. The *evaluative*
dimension distinguishes the fact that 'similarity' as normally construed involves both the
common facts and the common evaluation of the facts.

Trujillo, 1986). Acquaintance is thus a process with long-term ramifications
(Wood, 1997). Long-term acquaintance is probably not simply caused by,
say, physical attraction even if that is what grabs our interest initially. The
development of relationships is not simply caused by initial attractions.
Relationships do not work like electric motors, which just start and run
whenever we press the right switch. That sort of mechanical metaphor,
surprisingly, is widely held ('we just clicked'), even though it is an inadequate idea. Of course we have to do something communicatively in the long
term to make relationships work: we do not just 'sit there looking pretty' in
the hope that the rest is automatic. Relationships do not develop only
because two people start out with compatible personalities. But rather than
dismissing the impact that attitudes and personality may have on relationships, we need to understand their role in our lives, and to understand
the mechanisms by which such understanding is developed (Duck, 1994a:
chapter 4). Figure 3.1 helps to guide us through the understanding of the
process. As we work through the research on initial attraction, note that the
similarity that has been talked about in research and the sorts of similarity
that come to mind when we just sit and think about it actually have four
layers when you strip things down in terms of social *actions* that take place
in the practical world of everyday life (Acitelli et al., 1993; Duck, 1994a).

Attitudes and personality as elements of relationships

Sometimes, we act as if two people *are* similar and that's that (this is
'commonality' in Figure 3.1). But in the praxis of real life, things are not so
simple: even if two people are similar, they must communicate that
similarity to one another before it can have an effect ('mutuality' in Figure
3.1). Bochner (1991: 487) claims that 'One of the main functions of communication in early, and perhaps even in later, encounters is to foster
perceptions of attitude and personality similarity and also to create the

impression of being an interesting and stimulating person.' So obviously we talk to one another and in so doing we create the mutuality noted in Figure 3.1.

In line with the argument that I am developing here, Cappella (1988) argues that relationship formation is interactional; it is predictable not from the way in which two persons happen to 'click together' but from how they *make* the pieces click together. We never see the internal states or attitudes of other persons directly so we can only infer them from the sorts of nonverbal and verbal behaviour discussed in Chapter 1. Because of this, the two people's reading of each other's nonverbal behaviour will be crucial to this inference process and highly significant in acquaintance. Also important will be the ways in which they 'mesh' that behaviour to make the interaction smooth and enjoyable (Burleson et al., 1996). The microstructure of inter-actions does change as relationships develop, so nonverbal behaviour also changes to reflect and illustrate growth of relationships (Cappella, 1988).

Revealing (and detecting) information in the acquaintance process

Precisely how and why do we go about choosing information about our-selves so that we can communicate it to other people who can use it? To answer this, let us look at the work of negotiating and creating a relation-ship out of all the information that partners work with in interactions.

We become acquainted by an extended process of uncertainty reduction that continually shifts its focus and moves on to new, unknown areas (Berger, 1993). However, the development of relationships is not simplis-tically equivalent to the revelation of information nor to the decrease of uncertainty. The process of relationship development is created by the *interpretation* of such things by the partners, not by the acts themselves (Duck, 1994a), and it involves the evaluation phase noted in Figure 3.1. When we understand a person at a superficial level, we look more deeply and broadly into other parts of his or her make-up. When we know someone's attitudes to romance, for example, we may want to know more about his or her deep personal feelings about parenthood, for instance, but this is not simply because we desire more facts – it is to give us a better framework for understanding what we already know. The process of getting to know someone is the process of framing and understanding the other at as many levels as we can. But it is also a process that continues forever – unfinished business that proceeds right through our lives and the life of the relationship (Duck, 1994a), since each new day, every new interaction, and all meetings with the partner are fresh and informative and could change our under-standing as time goes by. Therefore, we are continually exploring our partner as we see him or her in the unfolding practical circumstances of life.

Historically the focus on different matters as acquaintance progresses has been called 'filtering' (Kerckhoff and Davis, 1962). We can see why: it is as if we have a sequence or series of filters or sieves and when a person passes through one they go on to the next. Our first 'filter' may be physical appearance. If we like the other person's looks then we will want to go on and see what his or her attitudes are like and whether we can relate to them (Duck, 1976). 'Attitudes' could then be the second filter, and so on. We assess our acquaintances within a progressive series of 'tests': those who pass one test go through to a deeper level of friendship – and on to the next test. At each point we learn more about the person's thinking.

In my own adaptation of this old approach (Duck, 1994a; Duck and Condra, 1989), such tests are subtler and subtler comparisons of one's own attitudes, beliefs and personality compatibility with the partner, as partners seek to enmesh their respective meaning systems. In pursuing this process we start by latching onto the indicators that are available. For instance, we may begin with 'ball park' indications of someone's pattern of thought ('Are they extroverts – or introvert like me?'), and become more and more fine in our 'tuning' as the relationship goes on. What specific values do they hold most dear and are they the same as mine? What little things upset them when they are in a bad mood? What are their deep, deep, deep fears about themselves and what does that tell me about the way they 'tick'? We work through such filters because we wish to understand and create a thorough picture of the partner's mind and personality in as much detail as possible. The tests, or filters, help us to reduce uncertainty and draw our partner's personality in finer and finer detail as the relationship deepens and develops. Indeed, Duck and Craig (1978) found that, in the long-term development of relationships, such processes are precisely what occurs.

Filtering theories are more sophisticated than the 'switch on' models that suggest that relationships are caused by one simple feature, like attitude similarity or physical attractiveness. However, I now realize that filtering theories overemphasize thought and cognition, and they really only propose a more sophisticated sequence of motors to be switched on. Honeycutt (1993) proposed an interesting variation on this theme and suggested that when people describe their relationships as moving through stages they are in fact responding to a cultural script that depicts 'stages' as the way to think about relationship development. The apparent 'movement' in relation-ships is in fact a perceptual or memory device established by individuals and societies. In other words, rather than being something 'real' in relationships, relationship development is *perceived as if* it followed predigested patterns that are recognized by cultural beliefs or by the processes of cultural contextualization indicated in Chapter 1.

One result of such beliefs is that people feel they should reveal personal information about themselves as appropriate to the script for stages. These revelations serve as a sign of growing intimacy and trust of our partner. 'Self-disclosure' occurs usually by words but occasionally by nonverbal means, as when we let someone sit closer or touch us more than before. We self-disclose when we tell someone how we have been upset by something recently or 'what I am most ashamed of about myself' or 'what I dislike most about my parents'. We self-disclose when we tell secrets or give other people access to private attitudes that we share with very few others. We can also self-disclose nonverbally by 'giving ourselves away', for instance, bursting into tears unexpectedly or suddenly blushing.

In most social psychological work, self-disclosure refers to verbal intimacy, particularly the content of messages that are so disclosed. This work assumes two things: (1) that we can tell how intimate others are merely by examining the words they use, the topics they talk about and the subjects they introduce to a conversation; (2) that intimacy proceeds by the successive revelation of layers of information about oneself, like peeling the layers off an onion (Altman and Taylor, 1973). Such topics have occasionally been listed and rated for intimacy level. For example, Davis and Sloan (1974) put 'How I react to others' praise and criticism of me' at the bottom of their list and 'My feelings about my sexual inadequacy' at the top of their list for very intimate topics.

Remembering the discussion in Chapter 1, you may find this a bit dissatisfying. In life, there are more indicators of intimacy than just words; nonverbal cues as well as the relationship between the partners help to define and communicate intimacy. For this reason, Montgomery (1981a) talks of 'open communication' rather than just self-disclosure. She describes it as composed of five elements, some of which occur more often in some types of relationships whilst others appear more frequently in others. *Negative openness* covers openness in showing disagreement or negative feelings about a partner or situation. *Nonverbal openness* relates to a communicator's facial expressions, vocal tone, and bodily postures or movements (see Chapter 1). *Emotional openness* describes the ease with which someone's feelings or moods are expressed and his or her concealment of emotional states. *Receptive openness* is a person's indication of his or her willingness to listen to other people's personal information. *General-style openness* refers to the overall impression that someone creates.

Even if we look at just the content of speech then we can split openness into different elements, of which topic intimacy is one (Montgomery, 1981a). However, intimacy of a topic is not the same as 'intimacy of topic in a relationship'. For instance, the context for what is said about a topic can make it intimate or non-intimate and the target of the disclosure likewise. Thus, the question 'How is your sex life?' looks like a promisingly personal and intimate topic unless we reply 'pretty average' or if it is our doctor who asks us about it. In short, even intimate-sounding topics can be discussed non-intimately, or in non-intimate contexts, and there really is no such thing as an absolutely intimate or absolutely non-intimate topic (Spencer, 1994). Other factors that make for intimacy in conversation are, as we have learned before, verbal immediacy, nonverbal accompaniments and relational context. Openness, then, includes both verbal and nonverbal aspects of behaviour and deals as much with the function of a message as with its medium (Montgomery, 1984). When we look at open communication in context, it is apparent that content and topic intimacy alone do not discriminate between high and low open communicators.

However, Dindia (1994) indicates that relational self-disclosure is a more complex and contextualized occurrence than this. It involves a complicated mixing of intra-personal processes (for example, decisions about one's readiness to discuss a particular topic, beliefs about a partner's likely reaction to the topic itself rather than to one's disclosures about it – i.e. a judgement about the other person not just about the topic itself). As noted by Duck (1980), many of the processes of relating are conducted only in the mind and are influenced by expectations about another person's likely reactions. Thus work on self-disclosure that treats it as driven only by the 'pure intimacy' of a topic misses the important practical consequences of the fact that we live everyday lives where topics assume intimacy (or not) *in context* and *in relationship*, not in any unattached or pure way.

Spencer (1994) also notes that self-disclosure is not simply a device for revealing information about self but is also a mechanism for giving and receiving advice. If I self-disclose to you that I have a problem about shyness then you can implicitly advise about how to deal with it by self-disclosing one of your most embarrassing experiences and how you overcame it, for instance. You can self-disclose that you have had the same problem and then start to self-disclose some examples of situations where it happened and how you dealt with it, thus subtly presenting me with advice about how to deal with it. In that case, self-disclosure serves a relationship purpose (helping me out) and shows intimacy and loyalty (because you help me) and is not simplistically about the successive revelation of layers of yourself.

How strategic are we in making acquaintances?

Has it struck you how passive much of the work on self-disclosure has assumed that we are, if it implies that we successively and inevitably reveal information about self in layers, more or less routinely? Do we actually try to make other people like us sometimes or do we just sit back, smile, flash a few attitudes around and hope that people will react positively to our successive revelations? I believe that we actually spend quite a lot of time *trying* to get other people to like and appreciate us and also to check out how we are doing. We become upset when we fail to create positive feelings in other people; it is a great source of personal distress and dissatisfaction. We must have strategies for making others appreciate us and an awareness of 'how we are doing'. Douglas (1987) explored the strategies that people use to discover whether another person is interested in developing a relationship ('affinity testing'). These are listed in Box 3.2. In essence, people rarely ask directly whether someone is interested in a relationship or not (well, the person might say 'no' and that would be that). Because it puts us on the line if we ask directly, there is a preference for indirect strategies that get us the information without us having to ask directly. Or we may ask ambiguously so that if the other person turns us down we can deflect the negative implication of rejection: for example, instead of saying 'Will

Box 3.2   *Douglas on affinity testing*

Confronting
Actions that required a partner to provide immediate and generally public evidence of his or her liking.

1   I asked her if she liked me.
2   I asked her if I appealed to her.
3   I put my arm around her. It made her say yes or no.

Withdrawing
Actions that required a partner to sustain the interaction.

4   I just turned myself off and just sat there real sedate. I knew that if he started jabbering (which he did) then he was interested.
5   I would be silent sometimes to see if he would start the conversation again.
6   We were at a disco and I said, 'Well, I'm leaving.' I wanted him to stop me. You know, to say, 'Are you leaving already?'

Sustaining
Actions designed to maintain the interaction without affecting its apparent intimacy.

7   I kept asking questions. You know, like, 'Where was she from?' 'What music did she like?'
8   I met this girl. I liked her. I asked all these questions. 'What do you do for a living?' 'Where do you live?'
9   I tried to keep him talking. I asked him questions. I told him about me.

Hazing
Actions that required a partner to provide a commodity or service to the actor at some cost to himself or herself.

10   I told him I lived 16 miles away. Sixteen miles from the church I mean. I wanted to see if he would try and back out.
11   I told her I didn't have a ride. She said that was OK. She said she would take me. I told her where I lived; it took about an hour to get there. I told her she couldn't come into my house even if she gave me a ride. I knew that she liked me because she accepted the situation I put her in.
12   I met this guy at a party. He asked me if I wanted to go see a movie. I said OK. When we got there, I told him I didn't want to see it, I wanted to go home. I didn't really. I wanted to see how much he would take.

Diminishing self
Actions that lowered the value of self; either directly by self-deprecation or indirectly by identifying alternative reward sources for a partner.

13   I asked her if she wanted to talk to somebody else. You know, 'Was I keeping her from something?'
14   I told him I wasn't very interesting. Waiting for him to say, 'Oh, no.'
15   There were these other guys there. I kept pointing them out to her.

continued overleaf

Box 3.2   (cont.)

Approaching
Actions that implied increased intimacy to which the only disconfirming partner
response is compensatory activity.

16 I would touch his shoulder or move close to see if he would react by staying
    where he was or moving closer.
17 I moved closer. He didn't move away.
18 I moved closer to her. We were sitting in a bar. You know, at one of those
    benches, I wanted to see if she would move away.

Offering
Actions that generated conditions favourable for approach by a partner.

19 I waited for him to come out of the restroom. Everyone else had left by that
    time. If he wanted to ask me out, he could
20 I helped him carry some things out to his car. I made it to where we were by
    ourselves so that if he was going to ask me for a date, we would be in a
    position where he could do it.
21 I knew we would have to play with someone close to us in line. So I stood in
    front of him. I wanted to see if he would pick me.

Networking
Actions that included third parties, either to acquire or transmit information.

22 I went over and asked his friends about him. I knew his friends would tell him
    about it. Then, if he came over to me again, I would know he liked me.
23 I told other people there I liked him. I knew it would get back to him. I knew
    other people would tell him. If he ignored it, I would know he wasn't
    interested.
24 There was one guy at a party. We chit-chatted and he looked pretty inter-
    esting. There were some of my friends these, so I left and, later, I asked them
    what he had said about me.

Source: Douglas (1987: 7–8)

---

you go out with me to this movie?', you may say 'This movie is on at the
Cineplex, do you like that kind of movie?', which gives the person the
chance to treat the question as an invitation (and to reply 'Yes, shall we go
together?') or as a straightforward request for information but *not* as an
invitation to go and see it together ('Yes, those films are interesting and I
also like the ones by the director's son'). To choose to answer the question
alone is also in effect to reject the invitation but to do so without causing
offence.

   Have a look at Box 3.2 to find out some of the indirect strategies that we
use to test out our chances of developing a relationship. At the start of a
relationship we might need to assess the partner's interest in further
meetings, such as may be discovered by use of the strategies in Box 3.2.
Alternatively we might be in an established relationship and wish to test out

the partner's level of commitment. The ways which partners in relationships conduct 'secret tests' of the state of the relationship were studied by Baxter and Wilmot (1984). Baxter and Wilmot argued that partners are often uncertain about the strength of their relationship yet are reluctant to talk about 'the state of the relationship'; they regard it as a taboo topic (as Baxter and Wilmot, 1985, found in a different paper). Our usual solution is to apply direct and indirect tests – secret tests – as means of discovering how things stand. Such methods involve, for instance, asking third parties whether your partner has ever talked about the relationship to them. Alternatively one might use trial intimacy moves to see how a partner reacts – and so gives away some indication of intimacy. Such moves can take the form of increased physical or emotional intimacy, but might be more subtle. For example, a person might use 'public presentation': inviting the partner to visit parents or talking about your own intentions to have children some day. The real but concealed questions in each case are: how does my partner react, and does he or she accept the increased intimacy or the open commitment? Other methods described by Baxter and Wilmot (1984) are the self-put-down (when you hope the partner will respond to your self-deprecating statement with a supportive, intimate statement) and the jealousy test (when you describe a potential competitor and hope to observe a possessive, committed response by your partner).

If we are successful in initially attracting someone to us, what happens to deepen the relationship? Recall that some self-disclosure is a sign of good mental health and influences the course of relationships. A certain amount of intimate disclosure is expected in our culture, whether as an indication that we genuinely trust another person or as an indication that we are psychologically normal and healthy. We are supposed to say a few disclosing and revealing things in order to open out. Women are particularly expected to self-disclose and are often pressed into doing so if they do not do so voluntarily; closed women are asked direct questions that make them open out (Miell, 1984).

Reciprocity of self-disclosure is also expected, at least in the early stages of relationships. If I self-disclose to you, you will self-disclose back. It confirms a desire to develop a relationship since you could have chosen not to reveal the information, especially if it is quite personal. Conversely, we could hold back a relationship, if we wanted, by just not revealing something personal to our partner even if our partner did so to us (Miell and Duck, 1986). Self-disclosure is used strategically both to develop relationships (Davis, 1978) and to hold them back or to shape the relationship into one form rather than another (e.g. to keep someone from getting too intimate, too fast, or to protect the relationship from straying on to taboo topics; Baxter and Wilmot, 1985; Miell, 1984; see Box 3.3). It is also worth noting, however, that reciprocity of self-disclosure wears off as relationships mature. As Wright (1978) puts it, 'Apparently, in the more comfortable and less formal context of deeper friendship, the partners do not feel they owe it to one another, out of politeness or decency, to exchange trust for trust: the trust is already there.' Furthermore, Miell (1984) showed that some people are subtle enough to be able to use self-disclosure to interrogate other people or to find out information. It works like this: I know that there is a norm of reciprocity about self-disclosure; I therefore know that if I self-disclose about some topic in the right kind of circumstances and do it appropriately, then you will feel normative pressure to self-disclose back also; therefore I know that if I self-disclose 'well', you will tell me something personal back again. Thus if I self-disclose appropriately, I can find out things about you because my self-disclosing will tend to open you up and evoke self-disclosure back from you in reciprocation of my own self-disclosing.

This latter approach, however, points out that in everyday life self-disclosure is not used in any simple way, but is used actively to do all sorts of things: to project oneself as normal and open; to obey social norms of reciprocity and civility; to reveal oneself as a sign of intimacy in the relationship; to shape up a relationship; to construct a level of comfort with self; to find out information about other people; to develop relationships (Dindia, 1994); to establish trust or give advice (Spencer, 1994) or to manage and present impressions (West and Duck, 1996) rather than simply to reveal layers of one's personality. For example, people can reveal something personal about themselves in order to show the other person that he or she is trusted to keep things secret, or a person could tell a story about their personal experience or their feelings in a way that is intended not simply to reveal information but to help the other person ('I was very shy myself too when I was your age and I felt so ashamed of the fact that I blushed a lot and was awkward, but I soon learned that I could feel better if . . .'). In such cases the comment is serving many goals and it would be wrong to see it as *only* a disclosure of private personal feelings or information about self (Spencer, 1994). Likewise a person could say 'My friend is gay and he's really cool', which is both a disclosure of personal information (how I feel about my friend's homosexuality) and an *alignment* with the friend, indicating support and admiration. Thus a disclosure of personal feelings can also be a statement of attitude or even a political statement or the management of the impression that one is open-minded (West and Duck, 1996). As I have been suggesting here, then, any statement has to be seen in rhetorical context as something that achieves different purposes and not as an activity with a single purpose or only one possible meaning. Meanings are developed between people in interaction in context and are not absolute things that exist simplistically in the words: they happen when interaction happens, in a context, and between people.

Establishing, developing and maintaining relationships

What is the psychological relationship between initial attraction and long-term liking? What are the processes by which we convert 'gut attraction' into a working relationship? Note also, of course, that most meetings with

---

Box 3.3 Strategic self-disclosure

Partners use self-disclosure as a tool for the control of relationships. For instance, we will occasionally make a disclosure just so that we plunge our partner into a 'norm of reciprocity' requiring him or her to respond with something equally intimate and revealing (Miell, 1984; Miell and Duck, 1986).

Acquainting persons frequently use false disclosures to provoke an argument or debate (Miell, 1984). By doing this we find out what our partner really thinks (i.e. we induce our partner to self-disclose by a devious means rather than by a direct question asking for our partner's views).

Self-disclosure serves an important role in creating relationships and helps partners to construct a story of the origin of a relationship (Duck and Miell, 1984). Partners begin to construct 'relational disclosures' to make to outsiders to indicate depth of involvement.

Sprecher (1987) compared the effects of self-disclosure *given* and *received*, rather than treating self-disclosure as one global concept, as many previous researchers had done. Amounts of disclosure the person received from the partner were more predictive of the feelings that a person had about the relationship than was amount of disclosure given to the partner. Overall, however, the amount of disclosure in the relationship predicted whether the couple was still together in a four-year follow-up!

There is a reverse side to this, however. There are 'taboo topics' that we recognize and respect (Baxter and Wilmot, 1985). Some themes are 'dangerous' ones to explore (e.g. partner's past relationships; the present state of our relationship). *Lack* of self-disclosure can thus sometimes be strategic and can help to preserve the relationship because it keeps us away from topics that can be inherently threatening.

Duck et al. (1991) indicate that self-disclosure does not occur in everyday conversation to anything like the extent that is assumed by laboratory research and in everyday life there are important aspects of conversation other than self-disclosure that are influential on relationships (e.g. the mere occurrence of conversations even on trivial topics). Duck et al. (1994) also found that persons in a conversation tend to see the conversation as less significant than do outside observers. Researchers are likely to have simply both overestimated the impact of self-disclosure for a variety of reasons, and also misrepresented its social importance in relationships by focusing on its role as a revelation of one's 'self'. In fact, as the text here discusses, self-disclosure does lots of different things in relationships.

---

strangers do *not* develop into intimate relationships (Delia, 1980) and for that matter neither do lots of relationships with people we know, such as shop assistants, classmates, colleagues at work, or even some family members. Also interesting but so far unaddressed by mainstream research is the question of how we actively keep relationships at a distance and actively stop them developing.

In real life, my experience is that we plan to meet people and we share points of contact but also that predictable routines constantly force us together frequently with those we know well. If researchers study only meetings between interchangeable, anonymous strangers in contextually sanitized laboratory environments, we miss the point that our real-life encounters are only occasionally unforeseen, unexpected, and accidental but can also be predictable, anticipated, and (most often) prearranged or unavoidable (e.g. with roommates). Because meetings are like this, they come from somewhere and we have coded memories about the persons and the relationship in which they arise: stories about where the relationship came from, what it means to us, and where it is going. Miell (1987) has shown that a person's beliefs about the future of the relationship are very often influenced by the last three days of routine experience in the relationship more than by the whole history of its long-term idealized past. Duck et al. (1994) have shown that memory for past relational events is influenced very strongly by the *present* state of the relationship. This makes a lot of sense: when relationship problems occur, they occur in the present, the 'here-and-now', and all the fond memories of the distant past become degraded or idealized by the insistence of urgent present feelings. Such a view runs counter to that offered by theories that assume relationships are based on the exchange that has taken place in them in the past, however, or that commitment is an enduring thing based as much in the general past as in the immediate present.

Relationships are often buried in daily routines

Most of the time, daily life is remarkably humdrum, routine, predictable. We take our long-term relationships for granted most of the time and assume that the partner we slept next to will wake up still feeling like a partner tomorrow. We do not go through a ritual each breakfast time where we treat each other like strangers and run through a whole range of rewarding techniques to re-establish the relationship and take it to where it was the day before: we behave that mental way only with friends we have not seen for ages. The remarkable fact about daily life is that continuities exist in our minds and do not have to be worked for, once the relationship is defined and established (Duck, 1990). Friendships can feel as if they exist and continue over years and miles without any contact except the occasional 'phone call, Christmas card or letter (Rohlfing, 1995). Relationships have their permanence *in the mind*, on the basis of beliefs not just of rewards (Duck and Sants, 1983). Relationships survive distance, climate, revolt, pestilence and Act of God, as long as people *think* they do.

Relationships which have major effects on people are of this perpetual but dormant kind: parent–child relationships, marriages, friendships, collegial relationships at work. They are part of the unchallenged and comfortable predictability of lives made up of routine, regular conversation, expectation, and assumptions that most of tomorrow will be based on the mental foundations of today. However, relationships do not just pop out of strings of routines but from the way the partners *think* about those inter-actions and connect them mentally/communicatively, or reflect on them when they are not actually 'in' them (Duck, 1980) and *talk to one another* in and about them (Duck and Pond, 1989; Sprecher and Duck, 1993).

Box 3.4 Social participation and everyday talk

Wheeler and Nezlek (1977) devised a structured diary method (called the 'Rochester Interaction Record') that records, for instance, whom the subject met, where, for how long, what was talked about, and how the subject felt about the interaction. They find that 56 per cent of interactions that last more than 10 minutes are with persons of the same sex. The women subjects spend more time in interaction in the first part of their first university year than do men, but by the second part of the year this difference disappears. This may show that women adjust to the stress of their new arrival at university by seeking to involve themselves in social life.

Reis et al. (1980) show that physically attractive men have more social interaction than less attractive men. For women, there is no relationship between their physical attractiveness and their level of social participation. However, both attractive men and attractive women report greater satisfaction with their social interactions than do the less attractive persons.

Employing a new technique that adds assessment of *communication* to the other elements of social participation, Duck et al. (1991) have shown that the quality of women's communication is judged higher than men's in day-to-day interaction and that most regular day-to-day communications are low in self-disclosure and have low impact on the future of the relationship (except conversations of lovers). They also found that there is a tendency for conversation on Wednesdays to be more conflict-laden than conversation on other days of the week.

Using the above techniques (the Iowa Communication Record or ICR), Duck et al. (1994) explored the interactions of lonely people and found that they evaluated their own and other people's everyday conversations more negatively than other people did.

Making sense of relationships

Sometimes people think about their relationships and sometimes they do not. We may think about a relationship when we are face to face with our partners, but we also do it frequently when they are not there – as when we daydream, fantasize, plan, plot, experience private disappointment, expectation and hope. We can plan the relationship; we can think back over encounters and try to work out what went wrong with them or what we can learn from them. We can learn about our partners by thinking things over in this way since we can easily pick up on some crucial point that may have escaped us before. This 'out-of-interaction' fantasy, or thought work, is a very important aspect of both the building and destroying of relationships (Duck, 1980). By thinking about and recalling interaction, we actually construct a context for its future and its past.

One essential feature of relating is the need to provide a 'story' about it, and, clearly, these stories could be readily made up in the course of such out-of-interaction thinking. Try keeping a diary of how you feel about your partner, then you'll know what I mean. You will also see how much a relationship is characterized by *variation* in thinking about the other person, not by the monotonous constancy of feelings that is often assumed by research based on ratings of commitment or liking (Duck, 1994a). This kind of musing also might help us to create a sense of continuity – a sense that the relationship is a lasting venture, not a temporary phase. This is functional in that it preserves us from the need for continually re-establishing new relationships or continually re-enacting our existing ones on each new day, and is based in the structure of language (Chapter 2).

Beliefs, routines and future projects are central to everyday life, but we are not always completely sensible, thoughtful people. I see myself making mistakes and wrong assumptions, being inconsistent, losing my temper, taking unreasonable dislikes to people, unfairly teasing people, feeling uncertain, embarrassed and ashamed occasionally. Yet it is all too easy to overlook these little foibles and assume that no-one else does these things. It often looks to me as if the rest of humanity is going around soberly and seriously processing information in the manner of true scientists, in rational, statistically defensible ways, reaching conclusions, being competent, liking people who are well dressed, attitudinally similar and who order their arguments properly. Yet, I know I am often persuaded by people not for these reasons but because I cannot be bothered to argue about some issues, do not think of the effective debating point till I am halfway down the street, am in a rush to do something more important to me, or I simply do not know enough about the topic to challenge them adequately.

As in the rest of life, so in relationships I think we can easily misunderstand what really goes on if we overlook the importance of 'trivial' behaviour. It does not feel to me as if the world is full of relationships where perfect strangers grasp one another's collars in breathless attempts to shake out the other person's attitudes in a search for reinforcement. Neither do I see people in long-term relationships going round giving grades to partners for their every action and calculating whether the cost-benefit arithmetic works out well enough for them to stay in the relationship for the next 10 minutes. Not every encounter is a surprise; not every person a blank slate upon which rapid calculations have to be performed. Not every member of the family has either just fallen in love with you or is about to file for divorce, or is either a young child with a tendency to initiate violent acts or an elderly incontinent who feels lonely. Neither is precisely the same level of feeling felt towards each partner all the time irrespective of mood or circumstances, but rather our feelings about people – even people we love – can vary not only over a long time but even in the course of an interaction.

Relationships are a part of life, and everyday life is a part of all relationships. As those lives change through our aging, so do the concerns we have and the things we do (Bedford and Blieszner, 1997; Dickson, 1995). As days go by, so our feelings and concerns are subject to change or variation. Our friendship needs vary through life as do our opportunities for getting them and our bases for seeking them (Dickens and Perlman, 1981). They also vary day by day in the face of circumstances (Bolger and Kelleher, 1993). In teenage years, the main search is for a group of friends and for sexual partners (Berndt, 1996); later, most people become committed to one partner and their network of friends stabilizes for a while (Notarius, 1996). If we marry the partner and have children, then our friendship needs are affected by these circumstances and by career developments (Veroff et al., 1997). When the children leave home, parents often become involved in the community more extensively and start up new friendships in the middle years of life (Adams and Blieszner, 1996). As life develops new demands and new routines so we change friendship 'work'. Our feelings can go up and down as joys and resentments arise, recede and gain resolution. Thus the statements that we make about liking and loving are likely to be *summary statements* (see Chapter 2) that can be more or less accurate reflections of how we felt three days ago or two hours ago or last year, just as any 'average summary' is only a more or less accurate reflection of a specific case.

A consistent element of all life routines consists of such trivial variation, and we apparently waste a lot of time doing seemingly unimportant things. For example, we spend much of our time talking to other people about commonly experienced events (Duck, 1994a), gossiping, and giving views of one another (Bergmann, 1993). For that reason, regular behavioural measures of friendship (especially measures of talk in everyday relationships), are better predictors of relationship growth than are monolithic cognitive structural ones (Andersen, 1993). Acitelli (1988, 1993) shows that when people talk about relationships they are not only describing and celebrating them, as researchers have previously thought, but also formulating them and perhaps changing their attitudes towards the relationship.

Do partners always agree about their relationship?

Discrepancies of interpretation, even between close partners, are an inevitable part of everyday social life (McCarthy, 1983). When researchers find such disagreements, it should surprise them less than it does. Our own and everyone else's cognitive processes are inaccessible to us; if we do not know what other people are thinking, we can depend only on guesswork and we often guess wrongly. Yet Hewes et al. (1985) show that people have sophisticated knowledge about the likely sources of error in information that they have about other people and are able to correct for biases in 'second guessing'. By talking to others in routine ways, we can assess their cognitive processes more and more accurately, but to do so we may have to work through disagreements during conversation (Wood and Duck, 1995). Secondly, we seldom discuss our views of relationship openly and explicitly with our partners except when we think something is wrong (Acitelli, 1988, 1993). So we do not get much experience of seeing explicit agreement about our relationships (though they are nice when we get them), and the experiences we do get will emphasize the discords instead.

The *problems* with relationships are more likely to be visible, accessible and familiar than are the smooth parts. In particular, we misperceive other people's feelings in one important respect: we tend to be uncertain about partners' commitment to relationships and assume that they might change their mind – as if we are their friend for only as long as *they* think we are (Duck, 1994a). More importantly, partners probably each see different events as crucial in the relationship, so there is no good reason to expect partners to be in total agreement about the nature or course of the relationship (McCarthy, 1983). What happens when disagreements are detected is that people talk them through (or at least talk about them), so once again in everyday life, conversation is an important tool for developing and sustaining relationships.

Does it matter what 'outsiders' think?

In real life, relationships take place in a context provided by talk with other people not just by the partners' own thoughts and feelings. The presence of others (and what they know about the relationship) distinguishes between our behaviours in public and secret relationships, obviously, but can also affect the things we do in cooperative and competitive, open, trusting and closed, threatening relationships. Much research shows that we are aware of such outside influence on relationships both at the personal level and from such sources as media and social culture (Duran and Prusank, 1997; Fitch, forthcoming; Klein and Johnson, 1997; Milardo and Wellman, 1992). Outsiders can affect the course of a relationship by expressing general disapproval or encouragement (Parks and Eggert, 1991), but there are other effects, too. First, as we pull into one new relationship we correspondingly have a little less time for our old friendships (Milardo and Allan, 1997). New friendships disrupt old ones; marital relationships reduce opportunities for 'hanging out' with friends. Second, outsiders, in the shape of the 'surrounding culture', give us clues about the ways to conduct relationships. For instance, Klein and Milardo (1993) show how outsiders are often arbitrators of conflict between members of a couple or give them advice on how they 'ought' to handle it. Equally, motivated by concern over the reactions of other people, we may try to hide affairs and hope that the newspapers or our acquaintances do not find out about them, yet we are happy to publicize marriages in those self-same newspapers and to those acquaintances.

As partners become more involved in a courtship, so this adversely affects their relationships with friends (Milardo and Wellman, 1992). Respondents in the later stages of courtship interact with fewer people, relative to persons in the earlier stages of courtship, and see them less often and for shorter periods of time. However, the most noticeable changes in rates of participation occur with intermediate friends rather than close ones. Changes in frequency and duration of interactions subsequently lead to a decrease in the size of network (Milardo and Allan, 1997). In other words, as we see our date more, so we see our casual friends (but not our close friends) less until they finally drop out of our network altogether, if the courtship progresses satisfactorily (Allan, 1993; Milardo and Allan, 1997). Courting partners are thus less of a 'substitute' for close friends than for casual acquaintances. However, emotional commitment to one romantic partner sends ripples through the larger network to which we belong.

Some of the preceding suggestions show that a developing relationship between two people not only has meaning for them but begins to have meaning for *other* people, too, and that affects the way it works. It becomes an 'organization' over and above the feelings that the partners have for one another and begins to carry social obligations, cultural constraints, normative significance and the shaping hand of expectation (Allan, 1993; McCall, 1988). Whilst social psychologists explore the ways in which feelings for one another pull partners together, and communication scholars explore the ways in which those feelings are expressed and communicated, sociologists are interested in relationships as social units over and above the two members in them (McCall, 1988). In a sociological analysis of friendships, Allan (1993, 1995) points to the ways in which social life in turn structures our choices of partners and creates patterns of activity that help us to express emotions, regulate our feelings in relationships and provide opportunities for relationships to take a particular form. Sex, class position, age, domestic relationships and pre-existing friendships all pattern and constrain an individual's choices and limit freedom in everyday practical life in ways not considered by those who imagine that attraction and friendship choices are the simple result of emotion or of cognitive processes of information management. You will not be allowed to marry Madonna, even if you love her. Instead our analysis of relationships has to recognize the effects of context on such emotions and processes and hence we need to attend not only to what people *think* but to what they *do* in everyday life, not only in their development but also in their break-up (see also Chapter 4 and Box 5.1).

Handling the break-up of relationships

So far I have focused on the bright side of relationships but much talk and many routines are also directed towards the less appealing side of relationships: when they break up, need repair or have to be straightened out. By far the most common experience of negative things in relationships is the management of minor irritations and trivial hassles that arise day to day in relationships of all kinds (Duck and Wood, 1995). The rosy picture of relational progress drawn so far is thus only part of the truth (and Cupach and Spitzberg, 1994, devote a whole book to the dark side). For instance, why have researchers just focused on love and overlooked needling, bitching, boredom, complaints, harassment and enemyships (Duck, 1994b)? Why do we know more about romantic relationships than we do about troublesome relationships (Levitt et al., 1996)? Things often go wrong in relationships in all sorts of ways and cause a lot of pain when they do, some of it intentionally hurtful (Vangelisti, 1994). Sometimes it is Big Stuff and leads to break-up of the relationship, but most of the time it is relatively trivial and leads to nothing except hurt feelings and the conflicts involved in *managing* the occurrence. How does it happen?

When things go wrong

There are several parts to acquaintance, and so we should expect there to be several parts to the undoing of acquaintance during relational dissolution. This is partly because relationships exist in time and usually take time to fall apart, so that at different times different processes are taking a role in the dissolution. It is also because, like a motor car, a relationship can have accidents for many reasons, whether the 'driver's' fault, mechanical failure or the actions of other road users. Thus, in a relationship, one or both partners might be hopeless at relating; or the structure and mechanics of the relationship may be wrong, even though both partners are socially competent in other settings; or outside influences can upset it. All of these possibilities have been explored (Baxter, 1984; Duck, 1982a; Orbuch, 1992). However, I am going to focus on my own approach to these issues and refer you elsewhere for details of the other work. One reason for doing this is that my own theory of relationship dissolution is closely tied to my approach to relational repair (Duck, 1984a) as well as to my approach to the development of acquaintance (Duck, 1988) and so provides links between what has gone before here and what follows.

The essence of my approach to relational dissolution is that there are several different phases, each with a characteristic style and concern (Duck, 1982a). Thus, as shown in Figure 3.2, the first phase is a breakdown phase where partners (or one partner only) become(s) distressed at the way the relationship is conducted. This generates an *intrapsychic phase* characterized by a brooding focus on the relationship and on the partner. Nothing is said to the partner at this point: the agony is either private or shared only with a diary or with relatively anonymous other persons (bar servers, hairdressers, passengers on the bus) who will not tell the partner about the complaint. Just before exit from this phase, people move up the scale of confidants so that they start to complain to their close friends, but do not yet present their partner with the full extent of their distress or doubts about the future of the relationship.

Once we decide to do something about a relational problem we have to deal with the difficulties of facing up to the partner. Implicit – and probably wrongly implicit – in my 1982 model was the belief that partners would tell one another about their feelings and try to do something about them. Both Lee (1984) and Baxter (1984) show that people often leave relationships without telling their partner, or else by fudging their exits. For instance, they may say: 'I'll call you' and then not do it; or 'Let's keep in touch' and never contact the partner; or 'Let's not be lovers but stay as friends' and then have hardly any contact in future (Metts et al., 1989). Given that my assumption is partly wrong, it nevertheless assumes that partners in formal

BREAKDOWN: Dissatisfaction with relationship

↓

| Threshold: I can't stand this any more |

↓

INTRA-PSYCHIC PHASE
Personal focus on partner's behaviour
Assess adequacy of partner's role performance
Depict and evaluate negative aspects of being in the relationship
Consider costs of withdrawal
Assess positive aspects of alternative relationships
Face 'express/repress dilemma'

↓

| Threshold: I'd be justified in withdrawing |

↓

DYADIC PHASE
Face 'confrontation/avoidance dilemma'
Confront partner
Negotiate in 'Our Relationship' Talks
Attempt repair and reconciliation?
Assess joint costs of withdrawal or reduced intimacy

↓

| Threshold: I mean it |

↓

SOCIAL PHASE
Negotiate post-dissolution state with partner
Initiate gossip/discussion in social network
Create publicly negotiable face-saving/blame-placing stories and accounts
Consider and face up to implied social network effects, if any
Call in intervention teams?

↓

| Threshold: It's now inevitable |

↓

GRAVE DRESSING PHASE
'Getting over' activity
Retrospection; reformulative post-mortem attribution
Public distribution of own version of break-up story

Figure 3.2 *A sketch of the main phases of dissolving personal relationships (Reprinted from Duck (1982a: 16) 'A topography of relationship disengagement and dissolution', in S.W. Duck (ed.),* Personal Relationships 4: Dissolving Personal Relationships. *London: Academic Press. Reproduced by permission.)*

relationships like marriage will have to face up to their partner, whilst partners in other relationships may or may not do so. The *dyadic phase* is the phase when partners try to confront and talk through their feelings about the relationship and decide how to sort out the future. Assuming that they decide to break up (and even my 1982 model was quite clear that they may decide *not* to do that), they then move rapidly to a *social phase* when they have to tell other people about their decision and enlist some social support for their side of the debate. It is no good just leaving a relationship: we seek other people to agree with our decision or to prop us up and support what we have done. Other people can support us in ways such as being sympathetic and generally understanding. More important, they can side with our version of events and our version of the partner's and the relationship's faults ('I always thought he/she was no good', 'I could never understand how you two could get along – you never seemed right for each other'). This is the *grave-dressing* phase: once the relationship is dead we have to bury it 'good and proper' – with a tombstone saying how it was born, what it was like and why it died. We have to create an account of the relationship's history and, as it were, put that somewhere so that other people can see it and, we hope, accept it. In this phase, people may strategically reinterpret their view of their partner, for example by shifting from the view of the person as 'exciting' to being 'dangerously unpredictable' or from being 'attractively reliable' to being 'boring' – exactly the same features of the person are observed, but they are given different *labels* more suited to one's present feelings about the person (Felmlee, 1995).

In breakdown of relationships as elsewhere in life, gossip plays a key role. Here it works in the social and grave-dressing phases and in a dissolving relationship we actively seek the support of members of our social networks and do so by gossiping about our partners (La Gaipa, 1982). In some instances, we look for 'arbitrators' who will help to bring us back together with our partner. In other cases, we just want someone to back up and spread around our own version of the break-up and its causes. A crucial point made by La Gaipa (1982) is that every person who leaves a relationship has to leave with 'social credit' intact for future use: that is, we cannot just get out of a relationship but we have to leave in such a way that we are not disgraced and debarred from future relationships. We must leave with a reputation for having been let down or faced with unreasonable odds or an unreasonable partner. It is socially acceptable to say 'I left because we tried hard to make it work but it wouldn't.' It is not socially acceptable to leave a relationship with the cheery but unpalatable admission: 'Well basically I'm a jilt and I got bored dangling my partner on a string so I just broke the whole thing off when it suited me.' That statement could destroy one's future credit for new relationships.

Accounts often serve the purpose of beginning the 'getting over' activity that is essential to complete the dissolution (Weber, 1983). A large part of this involves selecting an account of dissolution that refers to a fault in the partner or relationship that pre-existed the split or was even present all along (Weber, 1983). This is the 'I always thought she/he was a bit of a risk to get involved with, but I did it anyway, more fool me' story that we have all used from time to time.

However, accounts also serve another purpose: the creation of a publicly acceptable story is essential to getting over the loss of a relationship (McCall, 1982). It is insufficient having a story that we alone accept: others must also endorse it. As McCall (1982) astutely observed, part of the success of good counsellors consists in their ability to construct such stories for persons in distress about relational loss.

Putting it right

If two people wanted to put a relationship right, then they could decide to try and make it 'redevelop'; that is, they could assume that repairing a relationship is just like acquaintance, and go through the same processes in order to regain the previous level of intimacy. This means that we have to assume that break-up of relationships is the reverse of acquaintance, and that to repair it, all we have to do is 'rewind' it. This makes some sense: developing relationships grow in intimacy whereas breaking ones decline in intimacy so perhaps we should just try to rewind the intimacy level.

However, in other ways this idea does not work. For instance, in acquaintance we get to know more about a person but in breakdown we cannot get to know less, we must just reinterpret what we already know and put it into a different framework, model, or interpretation ('Yes, he's always been kind, but then he was always after something').

I think that we need to base our ideas about repair not on our model of acquaintance but on a broader model of breakdown of relationships that takes account of principles governing formation of relationships in general. Research on relationships has begun to help us understand what precisely happens when things go wrong. By emphasizing processes of breakdown of relationships and processes of acquaintance, we have the chance now to see that there are also processes of repair. These processes do, however, address different aspects of relationships in trouble. This, I believe, also gives us the chance to be more helpful in putting things right. Bear in mind the model just covered, as you look at Figure 3.3, and you will see that it is based on proposals made earlier. There are phases to repair of relationships, and some styles work at some times and not at others (Duck, 1984a).

If the relationship is at the intrapsychic phase of dissolution, for instance, then repair should aim to re-establish liking for the partner rather than to correct behavioural faults in ourselves or our nonverbal behaviour, for instance. These latter may be more suitable if persons are in the breakdown phase instead. Liking for the partner can be re-established or aided by means such as keeping a record, mental or physical, of the positive or pleasing behaviour of our partner rather than listing the negatives and dwelling on them in isolation (Bandura, 1977). Other methods involve redirection of attributions, that is, attempting to use more varied, and perhaps more

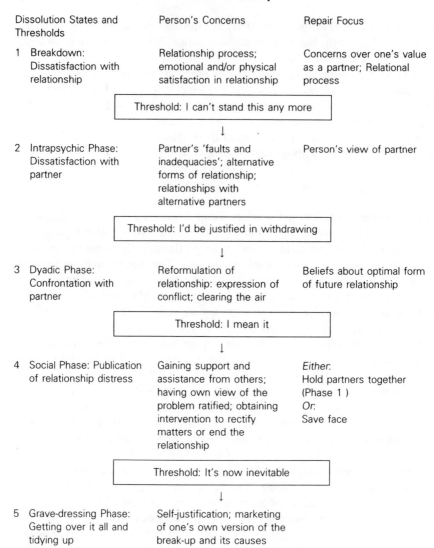

Dissolution States and Thresholds	Person's Concerns	Repair Focus
1 Breakdown: Dissatisfaction with relationship	Relationship process; emotional and/or physical satisfaction in relationship	Concerns over one's value as a partner; Relational process
Threshold: I can't stand this any more		
↓		
2 Intrapsychic Phase: Dissatisfaction with partner	Partner's 'faults and inadequacies'; alternative forms of relationship; relationships with alternative partners	Person's view of partner
Threshold: I'd be justified in withdrawing		
↓		
3 Dyadic Phase: Confrontation with partner	Reformulation of relationship: expression of conflict; clearing the air	Beliefs about optimal form of future relationship
Threshold: I mean it		
↓		
4 Social Phase: Publication of relationship distress	Gaining support and assistance from others; having own view of the problem ratified; obtaining intervention to rectify matters or end the relationship	*Either:* Hold partners together (Phase 1) *Or:* Save face
Threshold: It's now inevitable		
↓		
5 Grave-dressing Phase: Getting over it all and tidying up	Self-justification; marketing of one's own version of the break-up and its causes	

Figure 3.3   *A sketch of the main concerns at different phases of dissolution (Reprinted from Duck (1984: 169) 'A perspective on the repair of relationships: repair of what when?', in Duck, S.W. (ed.),* Personal Relationships 5: Repairing Personal Relationships. *London: Academic Press. Reproduced by permission.)*

favourable, explanations for the partner's behaviour – in brief, to make greater efforts to understand the reasons that our partner may give for what is happening in the relationship.

At other phases of dissolution, different strategies of repair are appropriate, according to this model. For instance, at the social phase, persons outside the relationship have to decide whether it is better to try to patch everything up or whether it may serve everyone's best interests to help the partners to get out of the relationship. Figure 3.3 thus indicates that the choice of strategies is between pressing the partners to stay together or helping them to save face by backing up their separate versions of the break-up. An extra possibility would be to create a story that is acceptable to both of them, such as 'It was an unworkable relationship . . . and that is nobody's fault.'

Essentially, this model proposes only three things: relationships are made up of many parts and processes, some of which 'clock in' at some points in the relationship's life and some at others; relationships can go wrong in a variety of ways; repairing of disrupted relationships will be most effective when it addresses the concerns that are most important to us at the phase of dissolution of relationships which we have reached.

The ways we change our 'stories' about a relationship provide important psychological data, and they indicate the dynamic nature of the help that outsiders have to give to relationships in trouble. Different parts of the story need to be addressed at different phases of breakdown. Is one and the same kind of intervention appropriate at all stages of a relationship's decline? Probably not. It makes more sense to look for the relative appropriateness of different intervention techniques as those dynamics unfold. There are few 'scripts' for handling break-up of relationships and many intriguing research questions surround the actual processes by which people extricate themselves (or can be helped to extricate themselves) from unwanted relationships. For example, Miller and Parks (1982) look at relationship dissolution as an influence process and show that different strategies for changing attitudes can help in dissolution. It is now a major aim in the personal relationships field to explain dissolution and repair of relationships.

Summary

This chapter has looked at personal relationships by exploring the ways in which they are *practical*, rather than emotional, matters that start between strangers. It has elaborated the processes (attitude similarity, self-disclosing, uncertainty reduction and organization of routine behaviours) that are needed to develop relationships. It has stressed that this process is not a simple one of merely comparing attitudes and personality characteristics with those of other people, but is a social, dyadic and communicative process of discovery and bonding, embedded in influential social contexts. It has emphasized the view that relationships are continually developing processes and are not static states begun and defined only by partners' initial psychological make-up or reward levels. The chapter has also stressed the ways in which outsiders influence the shape and development of partners' feelings and organization of their relationships. The chapter emphasized the creation of relationships; the effects of time and process; the interaction of beliefs with social skills and behaviour; and the role of outsiders' perspectives and influences on the relationship. Decline, dissolution and repair of relationships were considered in tandem with the role of everyday routines and everyday talk.

Now, we can look at the family and at children's relationships, perhaps the two most important kinds of relationship in life for us all.

Further reading

Bochner, A.P. (1991) 'The paradigm that would not die', in J. Anderson (ed.), *Communication Yearbook 14*. Newbury Park, CA: Sage.

Duck, S.W. (ed.) (1993) *Social Contexts of Relationships*. (Vol. 3) *Understanding Relationship Processes*. Newbury Park, CA: Sage.

Duck, S.W. and Wood, J.T. (eds) (1995) *Confronting Relationship Challenges*. (Vol. 5) *Understanding Relationship Processes*. Thousand Oaks, CA: Sage.

Orbuch, T.L. (ed.) (1991) *Relationship Loss*. New York: Springer Verlag.

Wood, J.T. and Duck, S.W. (eds) (1995) *Under-studied Relationships: Off the Beaten Track*. (Vol. 6) *Understanding Relationship Processes*. Thousand Oaks, CA: Sage.

4

Relationships with Relations: Families and Socialization

'A family is a set of relationships determined by biology, adoption, marriage, and, in some societies, social designation and existing even in the absence of contact or effective involvement and, in some cases, even after the death of certain members. This implies that the boundaries of a family cannot be described by an observer: one must ask the respondent because family, according to this definition, is subjective.' (Bedford and Blieszner, 1997: 256)

What sort of picture comes to mind when you think of the typical family? Two youngish, attractive, well-groomed, smiling parents with 2.4 happy children driving in an average-sized shiny new car to an ordinary super-market to buy their wholegrain breakfast cereals, right? The advertisers and politicians love to represent families that way, even though some estimates are that only 10 per cent of families are actually like that (Lawson, 1996). Even average people in ordinary families like to think of families as typified that way. There are many aspects to family functioning that fascinate researchers, too, and relationships in families (particularly as they form the basis for a child's beliefs about relationships with other people in general; Cooney, 1997) raise a number of particularly interesting issues for us. Not least is the recent reconceptualization of the notion of 'family' away from the above myth to include single parent families, families where both parents are the same sex, and families where parents do not marry but instead decide to cohabit (Sher, 1996). Many people also choose to stay single or create blended families that combine persons previously in other marriages (Coleman and Ganong, 1995). Thus the idea of 'a family' can be represented in different ways. Fisher (1996) differentiates between the *traditional nuclear family* (two married parents and their children); *single parent family* (an unmarried, separated, divorced or widowed parent with children); *extended family* (consisting of three generations in the same household, usually grandparents, parents, children). The extended family is a type of family style that is very common in some cultures and many groups in North America. *Kin networks* are particularly common in black communities where families are 'organized around large informal networks of blood relatives and also may be long-term friends who are considered family members' (Fisher, 1996: 314). *Blended families* are formed where a single parent joins a household with another adult who may already be a parent or may be child-free. Thus, in case it is not clear from the above, the defining characteristic of 'a family' comes down to only one thing: the presence of at least one child who is the responsibility of at least one adult. This, however, is a limiting concept because we should not forget that as time passes so children take over responsibility for care of their aging parents (Bedford and Blieszner, 1997), and this reformulation of family structure is enormously important in the middle and later years of the lives of adult children (Lewis and Lin, 1996).

Another cosy myth in our culture is that most families are enjoyable and safe environments in which to live or grow up. Our adherence to the pastime of keeping family albums and tracing family trees testifies to most people's wish to remain in a family and form part of their identity on the basis of seeing themselves as a part of it through their life. Yet, surprising as it sounds, outside the armed forces, the family is the most physically violent group or institution that a typical person is likely to encounter (Straus, 1985). We are more likely to see, commit or be a victim of violence within the family than in any other setting. We are more likely to be murdered, beaten or physically abused by our spouse, mother, father or siblings than by a random stranger (Eiskovits et al., 1991; Straus, 1990; Straus and Gelles, 1986).

Equally, families are not particularly stable. At least 50 per cent of all first marriages end in divorce (Vanzetti and Duck, 1996) and some estimates go up to 67 per cent (Martin and Bumpass, 1989). About a quarter of those who marry today will be divorced before their seventh anniversary (Notarius, 1996). There now seems to be a trend away from long-term commitment and toward serial monogamy (Vanzetti and Duck, 1996). By the time they are 18 years old, one out of every two children will experience some of their upbringing in a single parent household (Cherlin 1992; Glick, 1989). Furthermore, it is now much more common than previously for spouses to live apart in commuter relationships (Rohlfing, 1995).

Lastly, while the Victorian family was something of an emotional iceberg, modern families are mythologized as emotional refuges and strongholds. These shifting demands couple with new economic and social conditions to place new strains and demands on the family as a unit (Bass and Stein, 1997). Spouses are now asked to be satisfying lovers, caring friends, and even mutual therapists. Many are also faced with managing the stresses of family and two careers in the same household (Crouter and Helms-Erickson, 1997). At first, we might see all this as a welcome development, but the increased importance of these competing roles has the paradoxical effect of making it more likely that the members of the family will fall short of the emotional demands placed upon them (Sher, 1996). Some scholars have presented a radical critique of the family that argues that when it functions best, the family is the ultimate destroyer of people by social means (Braverman, 1991). It draws people together through a sense of their own incompleteness, it impedes the development of an individual's identity, it exerts too strong a social control over children, it indoctrinates family members with elaborate and unnecessary taboos (Fisher, 1996). But the family could still buy wholegrain breakfast cereals.

Developing an exclusive relationship

From first date to marriage

The previous chapters have made the point that emotions *per se* are not the causes of relationships and this is true of families and marriages as much as of other sorts of relationships. Despite the romantic novels, when lovers walk off hand in hand into the sunset, such a 'lovers' relationship' has only just started to need work, rather than reached its point of stability – and the early years of marriage contain significant problems for most couples (Veroff et al., 1997). Forget, for the purposes of this chapter, that marital relationships magically result from love. Recent research (e.g. Sher, 1996) shows that far more important than gooey love are the ways the relationship is built and made to work through everyday life behaviour including such things as organization of recreation time, socializing and the disposition of practical aspects of everyday life (Notarius, 1996). Thus it is – perhaps strangely – important to look at the ways in which partners structure their interaction and patterns of daily life. This structuring is important whether partners are heterosexual or homosexual. As Huston and Schwartz (1995) show, homosexual couples have particular problems in working out structures for their relationships, since their activity is in many cases rooted in a concern to protect the precise nature of the relationship from the public so as to avoid the negative reactions of family or other social groups.

In understanding the role of social context in the foundation of relationship patterns, however, it is very important to understand also that the expressed reactions of others are a force on all relationships (Klein and Milardo, 1993; Wood, 1993). We all care about the responses of other people to our relationship and are influenced by the social context in which it occurs (Milardo and Allan, 1997) and most of us also recognize that if marriages are not made in heaven, then we have to do most of the work on them ourselves. Old research on young heterosexual couples (Huston et al., 1981) focused on the different routes, pathways or trajectories through courtship, and some of them seem to bind the couple together more effectively than do others. Huston et al. (1981) found four different pathways towards marriage that were based on different ways of handling affectional activities, leisure activities, and instrumental activities such as household chores. The four courtship types were: (1) *accelerated-arrested*, which begins with a high level of confidence in the probability of marriage, but slows down in its final progression to marital commitment; (2) *accelerated*, which starts off more slowly than type 1, but proceeds smoothly and directly to certainty of eventual marriage; (3) *intermediate*, which evolves quite slowly and gradually, with the most turbulence and difficulty occurring at the last stages; and (4) *prolonged*, in which courtships develop slowly and uncertainly, with much turbulence and difficulty. Partners in the intermediate courtships are the most independent of one another, particularly as regards feelings and joint actions (i.e. the so-called affectional and instrumental domains). They show less affection and joint activity. Partners in prolonged courtships report less affectional activity and lower proportions of leisure activities done together. Accelerated courtships are characterized by close affiliations and high, strong levels of liking, but partners are not necessarily more cohesive or bonded together when it comes to activities and time shared with other people.

However, this early work overlooked the fact that such pathways are implicitly scripted by society (Honeycutt, 1993), as discussed in Chapter 3. The pathways may therefore not be truly reflective of the issues that face couples or predict success and failure (Notarius, 1996), but might only represent a good story into which a variety of real events can be idealized (Bochner et al., 1997). The very notion of a pathway itself, as we saw in Chapter 1, is a convenient (but not necessarily accurate) metaphor for the ways in which relationships are experienced to grow in intimacy (Duck, 1994a). In fact pathways, like the stages that some theorists posit for relationship growth, are not automatic nor clear cut. Milardo and Allan (1997) note that while we think of 'society at large' as providing the context for marriages in this way, such norms of society are actually directly enforced and sustained by the intricate styles of connection that individuals form with one another face to face, with family, or with networks of acquaintances. Such structural interdependence affects the flow of information (the people with whom you choose to talk about particular topics, for example) and the sanctioning of individuals' behaviour (by the neighbours or in-laws, for instance) in ways that reinforce norms of conduct for relationships (Wood, 1993), including the stories and narratives about their formation, stabilities and dissolution, as we saw in an earlier chapter.

Another metaphor that we use to describe relationships is 'bonding' (Baxter, 1992). 'Bonds' is a metaphor that implies tying, connection – chains, even. When we talk of a 'couple' we are actually using a similar metaphor. How do people couple or tie themselves to someone else through the restructuring of their daily routines and thus become part of one another's life? As I pointed out in Chapter 3, such routine connections are the basis of relationships – a basis that mere feelings do not provide alone. There is even evidence that partners have to adjust their sleeping habits (Larson et al., 1991). If people are classified according to their life preferences ('morning person' or 'night person') then couples with one night and one morning person have greater dissatisfaction with their relationship than do couples who match on sleep habits. Also all couples are not kept together by great sex or by the fact that they hold similar attitudes but, as Huston and Schwartz (1995: 95) put it, by the fact that 'they will have something mutually interesting to discuss over breakfast'.

Making a courtship work?

The simple feelings that partners have for one another are thus not necessarily a good predictor of their success at creating a sound relationship and much of a relationship is conducted in talk (Wood, 1993). Talk not only serves the instrumental purpose of being a means to organize tasks but is used in social settings to chatter away like piano keys and conduct arguments, to divide work, to plan holidays and to create an imagined future (Duck, 1994a). Couples who are deeply in love may nevertheless fail in the task of setting up an effective relationship, may become frustrated at the length of time it takes to carry out courtship successfully, or may give up and either leave the relationship or marry anyway and just hope that it will all work out. Bonding takes place through time and talk – and it affects the activities and routines with which the couple intertwine themselves (Crouter and Helms-Erickson, 1997). Those that lead to greatest satisfaction with the courtship are those in which the couple's daily lives become most fully entwined as the routines of their day get more closely interlocked (Suitor, 1991). Also increasingly clear is that couples who embed themselves firmly in strong and stable networks will experience greater consistency in their growth toward a more lasting marriage (Milardo and Allan, 1997; Parks and Eggert, 1991).

Working out such issues as 'who does what' will involve discussion, if not conflict, and there are good and bad kinds of conflict to have during courtship. Some conflict seems to help the relationship but some of it most decidedly does not (Kurdek, 1994). 'Good' conflicts that facilitate the courtship are those about negotiation of tasks or activities or roles in the relationship. Couples may expect to argue about who does what, who goes where how often, what I shall do for you if you do this for me, who decides who does what, and the like. By sorting out role and relational organizational issues, even if it causes a few arguments at first, the couple is actually binding itself together more effectively as the two separate individuals start to function as a social unit. So those kinds of conflict (and their resolution) can be helpful. Those that are not helpful are the ones that centre on incongruent goals or inconsistency of desired outcome in the relationship. If we argue about the nature of the relationship (e.g. whether it is to be a marriage or just a friendship) rather than who does what in it and how it should be organized, then we are in trouble. However, Klein and Johnson (1997: 470) also note that 'similar conflict issues may play out differently in different family types', with traditional male-breadwinner families discussing the issues of household chores differently from spouses in peer marriages or lesbian partnerships.

If partners handle these aspects of their courtship successfully, they lay the foundations for handling them successfully in the later marriage where tasks and duties shift and new problems occur (e.g. during the transition to parenthood, Clements and Markman, 1996). The effects of conflicts or unresolved negotiations at this stage do not always show up until later into the relationship (Notarius, 1996). Even serious conflicts in a courtship do not necessarily prevent couples from carrying on and getting married, but these conflicts do predict dissatisfaction with the marriage five years later (Markman et al., 1993). The important lessons for us readers, then, are to do with the manner of constructing properly interwoven daily lives, communicating about the issues and routines there, and interactively conducting the relationship. These interpersonal communicative ventures are fundamentally more important than any simple, and essentially abstract, 'psychological structures'.

Managing sexual activity in courtship

One difficult aspect of courtship is the question of sexual behaviour. In relation to heterosexual dating, Christopher and Cate (1985) identify four typical pathways towards sexual intimacy, as indicated in Box 4.1. In homosexual dating, the partners appear to be influenced by the cultural norm that men, more than women, are taught that sexual intercourse is justifiable for its own sake (Huston and Schwartz, 1995: 92) and so gay men are likely to adopt a view of romance that sees 'sex early' in courtship as normative. Lesbians, however, have fewer institutional and socializing influences that foster a positive attitude to casual sexual relationships. This can lead to an impasse where neither woman is completely comfortable making the first move (Huston and Schwartz, 1995), but obviously does not prevent sexual relationships occurring any more than shyness does for heterosexual men.

Thus in both heterosexual and homosexual couples, sexual behaviour can be a source of difficulty and awkwardness or of pleasure and mutual satisfaction in a couple, but it has to be 'managed' and raises issues of 'who makes the first move', 'who has power', and so on. Questions arise as to frequency, initiation, context and type of sexual activity agreed or permitted in the relationship. How often should it occur? Should it grow only from mutual desire or may either partner initiate it? How early should it happen? What styles and variations are acceptable? Who is allowed to say 'No' and what does that mean? Such matters are negotiable, and lots of conflict in the creation of a couple centres on these negotiations and behaviours (Christopher, 1996).

Couples often find that they are arguing about (or, at least, discussing) sexual matters as both the relationship and expectations develop. Satisfaction with the level of sexual activity is usually closely matched with overall satisfaction in the relationship (Blumstein and Schwartz, 1983). Conversely, sexual dissatisfaction is a major source of unhappiness in relationships, leading to arguments, affairs, and non-monogamy (Buunk and Bringle, 1987; Silverstein, 1981). However, nothing is ever simple and marital therapists sometimes see couples who have a great sex life but who have little else in common. The important element in these cases, as in the sexually dissatisfied couples, is that the routine 'organization' of the couple or relationship is out of tune in some important dimension, possibly because the partners do not talk to one another often enough about their relationship (Acitelli, 1988).

Box 4.1   Pathways to sexual intimacy

There are four different pathways to sexual intimacy through the stages of (a) first date, (b) casual dating, (c) considering becoming an exclusive couple, to (d) partners seeing themselves as an established couple:

- *Rapid involvement.* Such couples begin their sexual interaction at a high level during the early stages of dating, often having intercourse on the first date.
- *Gradual involvement.* These couples are characterized by a slow incrementation of sexual activity from first date to the 'couple' stage with orgasmically oriented sexual interaction starting typically at the stage when the couple begins contemplating becoming 'a couple'.
- *Delayed involvement.* Such couples are characterized by a gradual incrementation that nonetheless starts from a level lower than that of gradually involved couples. Sexual intercourse is typically delayed until after the couple see themselves as 'a couple', at which time there is a dramatic rise in the average level of sexual involvement and in varieties of sexual activity.
- *Low involvement.* Such couples start at a minimal level of sexual involvement on first date, and, by the time they become 'a couple', they are still at a preorgasmic level of sexual intimacy.

Rapidly involved couples report high conflict but also high levels of love at the early stages, and, for the other types, increases in sexual involvement are associated with increases in both conflict and love.

Source: Christopher and Cate, 1985

Christopher and Frandsen (1990) examined the different sexual influence strategies used by premarital partners and found four general strategies: *antisocial acts* (ridicule, insult, guilt manipulation, threat, for instance); *emotional and physical closeness* (expressing love, claiming that relationship with the partner is special, flattery, hints, for instance); *logic and reason* (claiming to be knowledgeable about appropriate levels of sexual involvement; compromise on level, persuasive arguments, for instance); *pressure and manipulation* (using drugs or alcohol, manipulating mood, talking fast and telling white lies, for example). The authors suggested that the different strategies have different impacts on the development of relationships.

Getting the relationship organized

Thus far, we have learned more about the relatively obvious points that: families, marriages and courtship have a history; the different parts of the history have to be established and organized through talk, agreement and negotiation; and these communications are quite likely to influence one another. The family, the marriage and the courtship involve at least two of the same persons. The different labels that are applied to that pair of people ('courtship' then 'marriage') mean that only some aspects of the relationship are new or different. The partners are the same and live life in many of the same old ways throughout. For this reason, many of the same sorts of issues and problems recur for the couple throughout that interconnected history from courtship to marriage (and, maybe, to divorce) – thus many

external factor

attribution

Box 4.2   Marital satisfaction and communication

Many couples these days are dual-career couples and this fact has significant impact on the relationship in several ways discussed in the text. It also affects especially the stresses that are felt in transition to parenthood (Crouter and Helms-Erickson, 1997).

One important effect of dual-career relationships is that workplace friends become important in the life of the couple and may become a more significant sounding board for discussion of couple relational issues than other sources of support (Crouter and Helms-Erickson, 1997).

Veroff et al. (1997) report that men are more 'love-dependent on marriage' than are women and especially African–American men have a special sensitivity to being accepted as men by their wives. This sense of affirmation as a man is especially important in the early years of marriage.

Veroff et al. (1997) report that in the early years of marriage successful couples idealize and protect the image of their partner by attributing negative behaviour to the situation and positive behaviour to personal characteristics, or by recasting flaws as virtues or highlighting some positive effects of the flaw. Such affirmation can make this partner feel more positive about him/herself.

Acitelli et al. (1997) examined the first three years of marriage and showed that constructive acts of behaviour are more important than destructive acts to third-year marital well-being, whereas destructive acts were more predictive of first-year marital well-being than were constructive acts. In other words marital interactions in the first year may be so predominantly positive that it is the destructive acts that are noticed immediately and make the difference in levels of reported satisfaction early in marriage.

Acitelli et al. (1997) also found that wives' understanding of husbands' constructive behaviours in the first year was positively related to third-year marital happiness for black couples and negatively related for white couples whereas the association had been positive for both groups in the first year. Both of these results indicate that positive interactions are pretty much ambiguous and uninformative relative to negative acts, but that spouses' interpretations of these positive acts have a more enduring effect than do negative acts themselves.

---

researchers now look at early relational organization as the best predictor of divorce five years later (Gottman, 1994; Notarius, 1996). We will do the same but will also look at the ways in which relationships are organized in the context of other aspects of life (for example, how work affects relationships – see Box 4.2).

As we saw in Chapters 2 and 3, relationships become organized in several ways – for example, distribution of responsibility, power structure, time organization, development of idiomatic forms of language, even establishment of routines of daily life. In this respect they take on many of the properties and qualities of other organizations, such as shared history, private jokes and languages, and a sense of belonging (McCall, 1988). These are additional to the feelings that the partners have for one another, but they are just as important since they provide predictability and stability (Allan, 1995). Relationships can succeed or fail as much because they become disorganized as because the partners stop liking one another as people (Suitor, 1991). In perhaps unwitting ways, that we have not connected together yet, we have all heard people complain about relational organization, and it is not all about chores or division of labour. The relationship has to have a satisfactory emotional organization also; and people complain when 'The relationship was too intense' or 'The relationship wasn't going anywhere' or 'We liked one another, but the relationship just didn't work out.' These organizational predictabilities help to explain why breakdown, development and repair of relationships are disruptive. Distress at disruption and loss of relationships is often precisely because they are so humdrum and routine and 'comfortable' that they become built into the other routines of our lives (Hagestad and Smyer, 1982). These taken-for-granted routines build in ways that we do not always realize until they are removed. Their loss takes away unspoken and unrealized parts of ourselves.

One required element of relational organization is making it consistent with available social forms that others recognize. The couple's attempt to 'become a socially recognized unit' is not an automatic consequence of their liking one another, and the couple has to do work in the network in order to be recognized and accepted by other people. For instance, as a courtship becomes more intense, so the couple will withdraw from contact with friends to some extent as we saw above (Milardo et al., 1983). If the friends know about the courtship then the withdrawal is unlikely to cause offence, though sometimes such withdrawals are secretive at first (Baxter and Widenmann, 1993). Even the honeymoon has this kind of role in helping the couple to withdraw from society in order to carry out a transition (Hagestad and Smyer, 1982): the honeymoon helps the couple make the important transition from one role or couple type (engaged) to another (married) by having them pull away from their normal range of associates for a while and go somewhere special. We might think of this ritual as having the function of allowing the couple to enjoy one another for a while, but sociologists have interpreted it as serving a social reorganizational function also. Immediately after being formally joined by the wedding, the couple go away from all the friends and relatives who knew them as 'unjoined' individuals. When they return, they return as a socially recognized couple and the absence created by the honeymoon period gives everyone the chance to adjust to the transformation. Of course, for gay and lesbian couples such transitions are often not socially approved and so they present the couple with an extra emotional issue to resolve (Huston and Schwartz, 1995). For instance, Weston (1991) indicates that homosexual couples may be estranged from their 'blood family', who reject the couple's orientation, and for this reason homosexual unions are often celebrated with family-of-choice present but the 'blood family' absent.

Other factors that influence a couple's satisfaction also depend on socially recognized organization of the relationship. Such factors could be, for instance, knowledge of the average statistics for frequency of sexual intercourse, which may affect the partners' views of whether they are behaving 'normally'. More important examples come from societal definitions of the 'proper' distribution of labour in marriage, good relationship conduct as contained, for example, in magazine agony columns or articles about relationships whether in men's magazines or women's magazines (Duran and Prusank, 1997).

If a society generally believes that the 'good husband' carries out certain duties whereas the 'good wife' performs other quite distinct duties, then the couple who arrange things in that differentiated way will feel that their marriage is ideal in that respect (Crouter and Helms-Erickson, 1997). But, if the society generally expects both partners to share all duties equally, then the same couple (or one member of it) will feel aggrieved and dissatisfied. The difference in the two cases is not the actual work or duties carried out but the context of attitudes in which they are carried out (Allan, 1993). Furthermore, what counts as a perfectly acceptable distribution of labour in the 1990s bears no resemblance to that in the ideal marriage in the 1890s. Couples from the two times who felt perfectly contented would probably look on each other's marriages with disbelief and even shock. Also in recent times, the issues of dual earning couples have become very significant (Crouter and Helms-Erickson, 1997) and marital satisfaction must be understood in terms of its connection to the experience of work 'outside' the relationship as well as in terms of the experiences 'inside' the marriage on its own. Clearly daily experience of work spills over into the home life twice as often when both spouses bring home their concerns from work.

Part of the feeling that a marriage is working well depends on what the partners expect, and expectations can come partly from the beliefs that society has about marriages (Sabatelli and Pearce, 1986). Zimmer (1986), for example, indicates that the very prospect of marriage causes strong anxieties about the stability and success of the marriage, with partners getting cold feet and going through a turbulent phase just at, or after, the point where they have decided to get married. Often couples doubt the possibility of being able to have both security and excitement in the same relationship. Yet partners can see how their marriage matches up to society's ideals for the relationship. If they see themselves carrying out their roles well, then they will be satisfied. Dissatisfaction can be created by partners' feelings that their relationship does not live up to the societal ideal (Storm, 1991). Most of us are guided in our feelings and behaviour by some such influences, but some people actually take the lead almost entirely from social norms. Norms show people where they stand and increase their satisfaction with the relationship since norms make it easier for people to know what is required of them.

Such exogenous (or external) factors as social norms matter as much as the factors we usually assume to be significant (i.e. the endogenous or emotional factors) in marital satisfaction. The partners' feelings for one another, their communication style, and their relative power are examples of endogenous factors. The three (feeling, communication and power) really represent one and the same thing: expression of affection is done through communication, and power is a communicative concept, too. When we talk of power in a relationship, we are describing partly the way in which one person's communications affect the other person and partly the way in which that other person responds. As Kelvin (1977) points out, power does not 'reside in' a person: you do not have power unless someone else treats you as if you do. Power is thus a *relational* concept and depends on the acceptance of a person's power ploys by the person to whom they are directed or by others with some institutional authority. In the case of violent abuse, for example, the abused partner may be quietly constrained to accept whatever the abuser does because institutions like the Church encourage the view that one must accept both better and worse aspects of a marriage (J. West, 1995). Thus a lack of social support translates into a force that deprives a woman of real choice and becomes ultimately one extra source of the abuser's power (Mayseless, 1991).

Communication and satisfaction

How does this all have impact on a couple? When one person acts and the other responds in a couple, they have accommodated, or adapted, to one another (Giles et al., 1973). Dyads, or pairs of people, communicating to one another do accommodate in various ways (outlined in Chapters 1 and 2 here). Couples communicate in terms of their ability to resolve conflicts, express affection for one another, be open in self-disclosure of thoughts and feelings and the like. Satisfaction is related to these communicational variables, and the primary predictor of marital satisfaction and dissatisfaction is the communication that occurs between partners. Most forms of communication between partners are reciprocal or couple-based, which, we have seen, is true of power. Acitelli (1993), as noted above, found that relationship talk influences couples' perceptions of, and feelings about, the relationship. In general, the more a couple talks about the relationship, the more satisfaction they feel about the relationship, although I have already noted that some men assume that one needs to talk about a relationship only when it is in trouble (Acitelli, 1988).

Therefore, the dynamics of communication style of the couple should be far more important for their satisfaction and success than, say, originating demographic background and pre-existing psychological characteristics are. In any case, the social meaning of any personality characteristic comes from the way that 'personality' is operated by the communicative behaviour of the persons (Duck, 1994a; see also Figure 3.1). Abstract personality variables do not predict marital happiness: happiness is predicted by the communication in which personality variables come to life in practice.

Relational behaviours predict satisfaction and create the interconnectedness of different parts of the courtship/marital history of a couple. A couple's communication influences their level of satisfaction and affects the atmosphere in the rest of the family also. If courting partners mesh their daily personal routines together, they improve the chance of working out ways to deal with new relational routines that become necessary as the relationship changes (e.g. to cope with the birth of children). Kelly et al. (1985) studied couples before marriage and then followed them up after their marriage to see whether features detected during courtship were predictive of marital stability, and if so, which ones. (Make your own predictions and then check them out below.)

What is a good premarital predictor of marital stability? It is the ability to deal with conflict in the time before marriage (Sher, 1996) – a communicative factor rather than an individual or compatibility factor. On the other hand, ineffective nonverbal communication and poor communication skills are also associated with marital dissatisfaction (Pike and Sillars, 1985), and nonverbal cues provide a context for verbal communications. Nonverbal affective patterns (i.e. showing affection by smiling, touching, etc.) are more important than verbal disclosure and explicit verbal attempts to avoid conflict. Gottman (1994) has concluded that couples' interaction patterns early in the relationship predict problems later and this is evident even in videotapes where the sound has been turned off and when all you can observe is nonverbal communication! Box 4.3 indicates other work that clarifies the role of communication in satisfaction.

Obviously such work as the above helps marriage (and premarital) counsellors trying to prevent marital problems. Their effort is to try and create in courtship a stable basis for the subsequent marriage over and above the intention to increase the couple's satisfaction with their courtship. Some couples, for instance, volunteer for 'enrichment programmes' without feeling that their relationship is in serious difficulties, but they merely want to get more out of it in the present or future (Notarius, 1996). Nonetheless, Notarius and Markman (1993) show that the more positively couples rated each other's communication during negotiation exercises, the more satisfied they were with their relationship later on (both two-and-a-half years and five years later on). This was so even when the degree of positivity/negativity of communications was not related to partners' satisfaction at the time when the assessments were initially made. In other words, partners' future satisfaction is predictable from how they feel about present communication patterns, even though they do not notice this predictive relationship at the time and it even attaches to NVC (Notarius and Markman, 1993).

Co-dependence and relationships

I noted earlier that relationships are not all good for people all the time and that families can cause people problems. When we observe such problems as alcoholism or drug abuse then our first assumption is that this is a problem of an individual and we are likely to see the family as the unfortunate people who have to deal with this person. However, some therapists see such problems as alcoholism and drug abuse as *family* problems, or individual psychoses as generated by bad relationships with parents or see

---

~~coM~~   *Box 4.3 Communication and relational satisfaction*

Happy couples give more positive nonverbal cues than do unhappy couples (Rubin, 1977) whereas unhappy couples have more disagreements, have fewer agreements, and exchange more criticisms than do happy couples (Notarius, 1996).

Distressed couples, relative to non-distressed ones, attribute their partner's behaviour to enduring, stable traits (Fincham and Bradbury, 1989), whereas happy couples express more agreement and approval for the other person's ideas and suggestions (Birchler, 1972).

Satisfied couples confirm and support one another whilst dissatisfied ones reject and disconfirm one another – not only in respect of verbal statements but even in their very existence, often making statements that seem to imply 'You are nothing to me'; 'You do not exist for me'; 'Your comments and opinions do not matter to me'; 'I don't care' (Watzlawick et al., 1967).

Happier couples talk more about their relationship, and couples with high satisfaction are ones where husbands tend to talk more about the relationship (Acitelli, 1988), are more willing to reach compromises on difficult decisions (Birchler, 1972), and express agreement more often than they express disagreement with the spouse during problem solving or conflict (Gottman, 1979; Riskin and Faunce, 1972).

Alberts (1988) showed that adjusted couples were more likely than maladjusted ones to voice their complaints about the other person's behaviour, and to express positive affect when doing so. Maladjusted couples tended to voice personal character complaints, to display negative affect and to counter-complain when the partner voiced dissatisfaction.

Distressed couples are more likely to reciprocate negative communications than are happy couples (Gottman et al., 1977), and happy couples are more likely to reciprocate positive communications than are unhappy couples (Gottman, 1989).

Zietlow and Sillars (1988) compared the characteristics of communication in younger, middle-aged and older couples and found that retired couples tended to be the least analytic and least conflictive in their communications. Middle-aged couples were also non-conflictive on the whole but when they detected 'issues' they tended to analyse them hard. Young couples were much more analytic and confrontative but also used humour during conflict.

Pike and Sillars (1985) found that less satisfied couples had more negative reciprocity in their communication than did more satisfied couples, and that satisfied couples tended to avoid conflict rather than confront it. They also found that nonverbal behaviour seems to have a fairly generally accepted meaning but that the verbal communications of couples are more personalized in their meaning and interpretation.

---

problem individuals as representing and acting out symptoms of the family's distress (Wright and Wright, 1995).

How can an individual's alcoholism or drug abuse possibly have anything to do with the family? The heavy (problem) drinker may not merely be an individual who happens to have impact on a family (i.e. it is not adequate simply to see the drinkers as 'the problem'). Although obviously there are such one-way impacts (e.g. on children of parents who drink excessively; Wright and Wright, 1995), there are some problems with this kind of interpretation. For one, a large proportion of families are quite resistant to improvements in the family member with the problem (Orford, 1980). Spouses themselves sometimes break down when their partner's drinking problem is cured (Orford and O'Reilly, 1981). Also partners sometimes describe 'the other person when drunk' in terms more favourable than they describe 'the other person when sober' (Orford, 1976). In particular, wives often describe their 'drunk husbands' as more masculine and dominant (which they happen to regard as attractive characteristics) than they describe their 'sober husbands'. Orford et al. (1976) even found that unfavourable 'when sober' perceptions of a spouse were predictive of poor outcome for the drinking problem over the subsequent 12 months. If we prefer the behaviour of our partners when they are drunk (e.g. they may be extremely funny when drunk but very depressed and withdrawn when sober), it is unlikely we shall substantially support their attempts to stay sober. The feelings of one family member towards another who has a problem can help to sustain the problem and interfere with attempts to solve it. This kind of 'co-dependency' essentially comes down to a *relational* process that 'influences individuals' self-definitions and conduct in interpersonal contexts' (Wright and Wright, 1995: 128). One feature of the situation where a parent is alcoholic is that the spouse often employs a variety of tactics for denying or minimizing the problem or concealing it from others. This typically involves the discouragement of children from acknowledging or responding to the problem, whether by parents passively modelling denial, or actively instructing the children to adjust to the alcoholic parent. When one parent is incapable and the other is pretending nothing is wrong, the children are soon discouraged from talking about the problem and can become convinced that nothing really is wrong, or if it is, that the problem is something to do with them or is somehow 'their fault'. Such children lose their trust of other people, do not talk openly to others and often lose the ability to express emotion clearly. In short the children are pulled into a complex family game and become altered themselves as a result of the roles that they adopt to keep the family functioning.

Another example of a general co-dependency in relational processes is observable in people who have problems with drugs (Lewis and McAvoy, 1984). Partners and children of opiate abusers, such as heroin addicts, are frequently called on to structure their lives in a way that, as it were, depends on the addiction of a family member. For example, the partner and children may spend the day routinely stealing money to pay for the drug. Such routines of life are important to us as frameworks in which to conduct ourselves. Suppose the addiction is treated. How does that alter the way in which the addict's partner and children need to spend their routine day, and does that change their attitudes to themselves? In a sense, they are no longer needed: their functions have become redundant. As we might predict, these people frequently resist the therapeutic exercise and lead the addict back to the addiction, thus re-establishing their own routine usefulness to the addicted family member (Lewis and McAvoy, 1984). In such cases, treatment for opiate abuse often includes treatment for the abuser's family. Treatments strive to provide some alternative structure and routine for the abuser's family so that the addict's return to normality does not simply empty their lives together (Lewis and McAvoy, 1984). Wright and Wright (1995) conclude their review of the evidence by seeing such co-dependency as a relational activity that does not necessarily imply any underlying individual pathology – it is, instead, an adaptive means of making sense of what is going on and keeping life stable for those in the unhappy situation. In brief the participants adapt and play out 'situated identities' based on the context provided by their human relationships in the family. Thus Wright and Wright (1995: 128) conclude: 'relationship processes influence individuals' self-definition and conduct in interpersonal contexts'.

The transition from couple to family

Another influence on marital satisfaction is the presence or absence of children. Many married couples eventually have children and more and more same sex partnerships choose to adopt or have children too. Whereas we think of children as 'bundles of joy', the transition to parenthood is one of the greatest stressors of a relationship (Clements and Markman, 1996). Satisfaction with marriage declines sharply after this transition and conflict increases. In part this may be due to the disruption of sleep that occurs as a result of infant care but is also partly because of the extra relational organizational problems associated with the project of becoming a family.

There has been enough thinking about the impact of parental upbringing on 'life chances' for truisms to have reached the popular media as far back as the 1960s (e.g. 'Hey! I'm depraved on account I'm deprived' in the 1961 classic film *West Side Story*). Such truisms stem in part from the important pioneering work of Bowlby (1951), who claimed that an infant's relationship with the main caretaker, traditionally the mother, is predictive of later adolescent relational success. In brief, Bowlby's claim is that an infant separated from the mother developed psychological complexes that impaired subsequent relationships and could lead to delinquency in adolescence and adulthood. It is accepted as commonsense nowadays that the infant needs a steady relationship with loving significant adults, even though Bowlby's work was revolutionary in its time. How often have we heard people say that their relationship with their parents is responsible for later life events? But do they mean to blame a relationship that happened before they could even speak? Do we really believe that people turn into delinquents just because their relationship with their mother was inadequate for the first four to six months of life?

This work has been seriously questioned (Rutter, 1972). One problem is that the 'maternal deprivation hypothesis' seems to assume that the most important events are those in the first 12 months of life and that everything that happens between the ages of one year and, say, 17 years does not have much influence. Instead, more recent work urges us to look at the activities that occur during the rest of childhood and the impact on the child's social life of the child's view of itself as a social being (French and Underwood, 1996). Self-esteem influences our views of our attractiveness and so has a major effect on our relationships. So, let us take a look at the experiences in the family which affect self-esteem and give us the basis for our relationships with other human beings.

The specific variable of parental style of control in a family not only can affect the child directly but can provide a model for the child's subsequent social relationships (Hinde, 1989). Ladd et al. (1993) show that parents often structure their children's play or social experiences in ways that expose the children selectively to different sorts of experiences of control over their own relationships: for example some parents forbid a child to play with particular other children, or parents may 'hang around' a lot when a child plays and make specific suggestions about play, games, or roles to take in playing with others. Pettit and Mize (1993) look closely at the less direct ways in which parents influence children's styles of relational behaviour. For instance, parents 'teach' children tacitly through their own interaction style as well as explicitly by verbal comments about social relationships and how to 'do' them. I would think it obvious also that children learn tacitly from stories in books and TV as well as at school (Duck, 1991).

You should note that this new style of approach to parental teaching of relationships is in direct distinction to the old work (Baumrind, 1972) that identified three styles of parental treatment of children and then presumed that such styles 'produced' children with different social characteristics. The *authoritarian parents* try to control and evaluate the behaviour of a child using some absolute standards of behaviour. They stress obedience and punishment – often physical punishment but also withdrawal of love or psychological blackmail. Secondly, *permissive parents* relate to the child's behaviour in non-punitive and accepting ways, often consulting the child about its behaviour, offering rationales for the standards that are used, and relying on reason rather than punishment in child-rearing. Finally, an *authoritative style* is one based on direction of the child through reason but not on the basis of equality nor, necessarily, of acceptance of what the child is doing. Such a parent exercises firm control, but does so by verbal interchange and communication rather than physical force. This style of parenting is more successful in 'producing' children who are independent, cooperative, friendly and achievement-oriented, and is generally the style recommended by family therapists. Of course one also needs to take into account the style not only of the parent but also of other persons in the family and also of the composition of the family itself. In particular, children learn a lot from siblings (Dunn, 1996), not only from interacting with them but also from seeing others interact with them. For instance, a child could acquire a negative view of itself from seeing parents consistently treat a sibling in a more favourable manner.

All the same, the idea that there is such a direct one-way effect has been challenged (Lollis and Kuczynski, 1997). Psychologists and family scholars do not normally believe that single causes lead to general effects in any simple way – for example that a parent's own experiences as a child in a family simply affect the ways in which he or she organizes his or her own child's life in a family (Pettit, 1997). However, it has been a relatively recent turn for attention to be paid to such experiences as a frame for the creation of experiences for others. Thus Kramer and Baron (1995) considered the intergenerational linkages created by parents' experiences with their own brothers and sisters as frames for the ways in which they evaluate relationships between their own children. Of course, if my own experience of 'being an older brother' is that 'younger brothers are favourites' then I may attend more carefully to my elder son in order to ensure that he does not suffer the disadvantages that I perceived to go with the role when I was in it myself. Kramer and Baron (1995) reported that mothers who claimed negative sibling histories were most likely to have children who interacted positively with one another as a result of the mother's selective child-rearing practices, such as less differentiated treatment of siblings, decreased use of authoritarian techniques and greater reliance on redirective discipline (i.e. turning the child's attention away from the problem rather than focusing on it and emphasizing punishment). Likewise, Putallaz et al. (1993) noted that mothers' recollections of the joys and miseries of their own childhood affected the matters to which they attended in shaping their own children's experiences.

What is going on here in a broad sense and how does it relate to the principles outlined in Chapters 1 and 3? It should not surprise us that parents use their own past experience in order to generalize to the future of their children or in order to structure their approach to the new experiences of parenthood. We are basically spending our whole lives doing that sort of extrapolation from one experience to another (as in Chapter 3). Humans typically use their past interpretation or thoughts about events as guides for the future (Duck, 1994a), but this does not mean that they do so without adding their own spin, fantasies, hopes or good ideas when they can. We should note however that the above instances of 'intergenerational transmission' of values and practices are based on the assumption of freedom of choice and not all parents are fortunate to be in circumstances where they have such freedoms. Furthermore, it should not surprise us to find that the two persons in a relationship influence each other, even if one of them (the child) seems on the face of it to have less formal power than the other (the parent). All relationships have bi-directional influences where each person influences the other one even if they are unequal in power (Duck, 1994a). The new part of the recent research is the emergence of a solid set of studies that have shown how it works for parents and children specifically and that a child can 'control' a parent (e.g. by throwing tantrums that then have to be handled by the parent).

As part of this change of view in research, away from the simple idea that parents just imprint their children and the children respond, more recent research has emphasized the constructive/interpretive role of the child in the rearing process and begun to see that the child has never been a simple passive receptacle for parents to put ideas into during child-rearing (Pettit and Clawson, 1996). Children are now known to have several different paths to the achievement of peer competence, whether they adapt to parental style (Baumrind, 1972), observe siblings and peers (Dunn, 1996), follow explicit parental advice (Pettit and Mize, 1993), or experience the benefits (or costs) of parental memories of childhood (Putallaz et al., 1993), or parental management of the social environment (Pettit and Clawson, 1996). In any case, in recent research a solid set of studies had emerged that has shown how it works for parents and children specifically and that a child can 'control' a parent by its behaviour as much as a parent can control a child by giving out instructions (Manke and Plomin, 1997). As such this is an instance of a more general trend to credit all relational partners with their own interpretive abilities and constructive frameworks that mean that relating is never just the activity of one person upon another, but instead is two constructive persons working together reciprocally and responsively (Duck, 1994a).

From all the above, we should recognize that a 'family' is made up of many interacting and reacting systems and subsystems that do not interact in equivalent ways. For example, one parent may prefer Child A and treat Child B less well; that difference in itself may influence the behaviour of each child as a growing individual and of each child towards the other. It may have impact upon the development of each child's self-esteem as well as its interactions with each parent. As another example, if one child in a family has a disability (Lyons and Meade, 1995), then this may cause the parents to behave differently towards the several children in the family, and if the disability is severe then the other children may get very little attention at all. Finally, parents are obviously not the only models for children; children are exposed also to the behaviours of grandparents, aunts and uncles, teachers and neighbours, to say nothing of friends' parents and their friends themselves (Parke and O'Neil, 1997). Thus a family is more than a pair of parents, and as a child develops, so the social world is increasingly made up of more than just the immediate family anyway. Nonetheless, the family remains a major source of the child's learning about human relationships, both through the child's experiences in the family and its observation of the family.

Children's friendships

Outside influences

After it was realized that a mother's relationship to her infant in the first six months did not necessarily predetermine the rest of the child's social life, researchers looked first into two main sources of later influence: to adolescent gangs and to family life. For instance, work began to attend to fathers and show that a child could be securely attached to its mother but anxiously attached to its father (Park and Waters, 1988). Two other major areas also opened up: the impact of peer or sibling interactions (Dunn, 1996), and the relevance of style of fathering (Teti and Teti, 1996). Researchers began to realize that brothers, sisters, fathers, and friends – and childhood – had somehow been omitted from the earliest thoughts on this issue (von Salisch, 1997). Lastly, they also began to pay much more attention to the bi-directional nature of the relationship noted above – to see how children influence parents, not just vice versa (Manke and Plomin, 1997). In short, researchers began to ask many important questions about the relationships among relationships (Dunn, 1988, 1996) and the influence that children can have upon parents as well as vice versa (Mills, 1997).

Are children essentially passive and receptive to various significant forces that stamp themselves on that developing person, or are children active persons who exert their own individual influences? Perhaps they are interactive. Perhaps the child is an active participant exerting influence and effects on others as much as being influenced and affected by them. Clearly the child perceives, and to some extent interprets, the parents' behaviour just as the parent interprets and supports the child's (Parke and O'Neil, 1997). Thus the dominant view in developmental psychology now is that the parent–child relationship is an interactive and mutually influential one (Lollis and Kuczynski, 1997). Seeing the idea that only parents influence children as the 'sound of one hand clapping', Lollis and Kuczynski (1997) list many ways in which *both* partners in the parent–child relationship influence the other. There is obviously bi-directionality of influence between each partner's behaviour and the other's thoughts in any immediate interaction as each person responds to the partner's conversation, actions and ideas (Duck, 1994a); influences of each partner's expectations about the other; influences of beliefs about the other person based on past behaviour; and influences of expectations of continuity and transformation across time (parents often do things in light of beliefs about children's *future* development rather than only on the basis of their present behaviour – for example, some disciplinary activities are based on the belief that the child needs to develop a social conscience, even if the actual behaviour itself is not really that important when taken out of that context).

None of this is to deny that our first interactions with our parents are a basic framework for understanding and evaluating our own personal worth (Parke and O'Neill, 1997) and indeed an important research issue concerns the amount of the social base that is laid down in infancy and how much by later experience (Teti and Teti, 1996). From this base, children work out their own value as a social object for other people; an understanding of the nature and structure of relationships between people; and the kinds of relationship that they are best at establishing with others (Barrett, 1997). Such thoughts can be formed by influences as subtle as the mother's speech style. Garrard and Kyriacou (1985) found that mothers who use a language code based on awareness of others' feelings increase the child's social sensitivity, the ability to comprehend others' feelings in friendship, and the awareness of others' needs and goals in social settings. Putallaz et al. (1991) also note that mothers with predominantly anxious or lonely recollections of their own childhood took the most active part in their children's social development and actually had the most socially competent children.

Many influences on a child's willingness to relate to others are equally subtle – even, for instance, the age of the parents. As adults mature through their own life cycle, so their pattern of friendship alters in various ways (Adams and Blieszner, 1996). Homel et al. (1987), for instance, found that parents with stable and dependable friendships were more likely to have children whose self-rated happiness was high and who had better school adjustment as compared to parents without such networks. Also parents' networks expand and contract as a result of the pressures on them from careers, family, and age itself (Pettit and Mize, 1993). At some ages (usually mid-twenties to mid-thirties), parents' own friends have young children and these, therefore, make natural playmates for one another. If, however, a pair of parents are of unusual ages for parenthood (say they are much older than usual) then their friends may not have young children any more. There, a natural shortage of playmates exists for their own children, who may thus be exposed to fewer social experiences with other children. Pettit and Mize (1993) also indicate the ways in which parents structure environments for children and have influence on the sorts of playmates who are encountered, how often they play together, and what sorts of toys and play are allowed.

Perhaps it is a small point then, but as a child develops, so do the parents and other members of the family system, who have their own life-tasks and concerns. Anderson (1985) shows that both mothers and fathers show sharp increases in role stress when their eldest child first enters school. For the average pair of parents, however, a child's entry to kindergarten or infant school presents them with a new range of friends themselves. Children's parents are sometimes enabled to become friends with one another just because the children meet at school and become friends. The parents' paths cross more frequently, and they begin to share common interests and concerns. Once again, we see that these 'events' have impact and direct effect on the communication patterns of the parents and the children (Crittenden, 1997).

This is an important change because very young children play with other children only if they are pointed at them (Pettit and Clawson, 1996). Obviously, they do not have the resources or mobility to go round choosing or visiting friends. They play with those who are 'put in front of them'. Yet, even at young ages the child probably needs experience with other children. The smiling encouragement of caring parents is not enough; even when it paves the way, the way has to go somewhere, and eventually it points to the school playground.

Peer and family influences on children's relationships at school

Who says that children's friendships with each other do not matter? If you were unpopular at school you are more likely to become an alcoholic, a depressive, a schizophrenic, a delinquent, a dishonorable discharge from the army or a psychotic (Duck, 1991). Recognizing the importance of relationships at school, researchers have begun to explore the bases of children's friendships, the ways in which they change with age, the ways in which they go wrong, and the most effective means for putting them right. Researchers have also begun attending to problems of bullying and victimization at school (Boulton and Smith, 1996; Smith et al., 1993). Researchers have looked at the psychological structure of the individuals in relationships and at the dynamics of children's relational communication and behaviour (Yingling, 1994). Also quite recently a great deal more emphasis is being placed on the whole context of the child's interactional experience, including the experience created in the family (von Salisch, 1997). Furthermore, Bhavnagri and Parke (1991) have explored the role of parents as direct facilitators of the child's social experience, in structuring their play and other interactions. Thus in the discussion that follows, we should remember that the child does not lead an insulated life but rather is subject to many social influences upon interactive experience, over and above those that he or she creates personally, and that there is a bi-directionality of influence: children influence their social environment as well as vice versa (Pettit and Lollis, 1997).

Cognitive bases of children's friendships

It seems to make sense to ask whether children's friendships are based on their general mental development or on their knowledge of social rules (Bigelow et al., 1996). In other words, is social development related to cognitive development? Children acquire moral reasoning and intellectually manipulated skills in a predominantly systematic and progressive fashion. Are their friendships based on similar principles? Is there a predictable sequence in children's approaches to friendship?

In a single sentence, children become less egocentric and less instrumental in their friendships between the ages of zero and six, develop relationships based on cooperation during the ages of five and 10, and begin to appreciate more fully the value of a friend's deep psychological qualities, such as character, from about the age of nine (Bigelow et al., 1996). These developments and sophistications continue in adolescence (Duck, 1975b). To put it even more briefly, the focus shifts from 'Me and what You can do for me' to 'You and Me and what we can do together' to 'Us and how we can help one another to grow as people'. Figure 4.1 gives a comparison of two major approaches and shows the various labels that have been given to the stages behind my preceding short summaries.

Children early (i.e. aged three to seven) define friends in terms of proximity and availability. Somewhere between the ages of four and nine

Selman and Jaquette[a]			Bigelow and La Gaipa[b]		
Stage	Friendship awareness	Perspective-taking	Stage	Dimension	Grade at onset
0 (3–7)[c]	Momentary physical playmate	Undifferentiated: egocentric	I	*Situational* 1 Common activities 2 Evaluation 3 Propinquity	2 3 3
1 (4–9)	One-way assistance	Subjective; differentiated	II	*Contractual* 4 Admiration	4
2 (6–12)	Fair weather cooperation	Reciprocal; self-reflective	III	*Internal-psychological* 5 Acceptance 6 Loyalty and commitment 7 Genuineness 8 Common interests 9 Intimacy potential	4 5 6 7 7
4 (12+)	Autonomous independence	In depth; societal			

[a] Adapted from Selman and Jacquette (1977) and Selman and Selman (1979)
[b] Adapted from Bigelow and La Gaipa (1975) and Bigelow (1977)
[c] The numbers in parentheses are rough guidelines of the age range in each stage

Figure 4.1 *Two major theories of children's friendships (W. Dickens and D. Perlman (1981: 96), in S.W. Duck and R. Gilmour (eds) (1981), Personal Relationships 2: Developing Personal Relationships. London: Academic Press. Reproduced by permission.)*

children acquire an ability to differentiate another child's viewpoint from their own, but a friend is still valued for 'what he or she can do for *me*' rather than on any reciprocal basis. Between six and 12 ('fair weather' cooperation), children come to appreciate reciprocity in friendship and realize that the other person has rights, needs and wishes also. However, these are still seen as self-interested rather than mutual, and a child will satisfy a friend's needs only if it suits. From around nine the child realizes that friendship is collaborative: mutual and common goals are important. Only around the age of 12 does complex appreciation of friendship appear and begin to take a more adult form, namely, recognizing that autonomy and independence can go together with friendship (e.g. the other person will have/need other friends but that fact does not threaten our friendship).

Also during this set of growths and transitions, children are learning not only to perceive others' perceptions but also to understand social rules and roles (Bigelow et al., 1996). Much that is learned then is not simply about *understanding* others but about *cooperating with* others (which is partly facilitated by understanding others and partly facilitated by knowing what to do, of course).

Children's behaviour and friendship

Friendship is no more 'all cognitive' in children than it is in adults: behaviour and communication have major parts to play, and both of these change as the child grows up. It is through behaviour, particularly through reciprocity and cooperation, that children learn the social and cultural rules for social behaviour (Bigelow et al., 1996). In particular, they come to know about other people through social collaboration within the existing cultural framework (Schneider et al., 1997). Our knowledge of ourselves and of other people comes from an increasing understanding of social relationships built up from social interaction (Miller, 1993), a greater understanding of the organization of social life and hence a greater ability to carry out social commitments or take responsibility for what is happening (Bigelow et al., 1996).

The interaction of thought and behaviour is only one side of the coin: even if children do develop through stages at a reasonably steady rate, we need not assume that children all start with the same levels of abilities: some are tuned in to friendship and some are not (von Salisch, 1997). Children scoring high in friendship motivation are different from other children in their detailed understanding of friendship (Barrett, 1997). They also show very sociable behaviour (which is independently classified by teachers as 'friendly', 'affectionate', 'cooperative', 'sincere', 'happy' and 'mature'). Those with higher scores on motivation also have deeper friendships and they are very stable in best-friend choice (von Salisch, 1997; see Box 4.4).

On the opposite side of the popularity chart we can distinguish between actively rejected children and those who are merely neglected; these are different sorts of unpopularity (Asher and Parker, 1989). Neglected children

---

Box 4.4   Children's competence in relationships

Parents' own social networks influence the play partners of children but also provide models of sociability for the children (Parke and O'Neil, 1997).

LaGreca and Santogrossi (1980) identified children who were accepted by their peers and gave a group of them training in social skills whilst two other groups served as controls. Relative to these controls, the training group showed improvements in skill, knowledge, and performance in structured settings or initiations of play. However, on its own, the training did not increase popularity.

Gresham and Nagle (1980) extended such ideas to test out a training/coaching programme, a modelling programme (where unaccepted children watch skilled ones and are taught to identify key aspects of their performance), and a mixed coaching/modelling programme. All three methods improved the 'play with' sociometric/popularity ratings of the children.

Unaccepted children can be taught specific conversational skills, and they improve in ability to perform the skills until the follow-up four weeks later (Ladd, 1981). Popularity also increases for these children at that time.

Attili (1989) reports that children who are 'difficult' cause a depressed reaction from the mother that itself feeds into the children's increased difficulty. Apparently the mother's attitude towards the children reflects upon the children's own feelings of emotional security and adversely affects the child's adaptation to school.

Siperstein and Gale (1983) specifically selected rejected children, rather than those who were ignored or unaccepted, as in the preceding examples. After coaching, such children increased in popularity and also showed a decrease in the amount of self-isolation or bystander–onlooker 'hovering' behaviour outside groups of other children (when the child becomes an onlooker of a group he or she obviously wants to join but dares not do so).

Smith et al. (1993) showed that bullies and victims at school are different from other children in the ways they conduct relationships with peers but that they also have different experiences of relationships in the family. For example, bullies develop an interpersonal style that lacks warmth and is concerned with power, and their families are usually lacking cohesion. Bullies may nevertheless be popular with some peers even though they are often manipulative.

Pettit and Clawson (1996) have suggested that the style of parent–child interaction and parental coaching skills contribute to children's experience of their peers whether directly by creating a warmth of interpersonal style, or indirectly by parental practices that help the child to understand social relationships with others.

---

are ignored whilst rejected children are actively disliked and tend to get rejected in new groups too if they are placed in them without training. In particular, they are much more likely to complain of feeling lonely than are neglected children or those with low social status, and they are more 'at risk' of having feelings of inadequacy and low self-esteem (Asher and Wheeler, 1985). What, then, differentiates them from other children or, to put it another way, what do they do wrong?

Actively rejected children have unusual ways of explaining the causes of social events (Sobol and Earn, 1985), poorer social skills (Pettit and Clawson, 1996), and a more disturbed and disturbing way of interacting with other children at play (Smith et al., 1993). These differ from the explanations given by children who are merely isolated by neglect (i.e. non-participants who are not actively rejected) or controversial (i.e. frequently accepted by some peers but equally strongly rejected by other peers). Unpopular, rejected children see the world in more stable terms and, therefore, they see their rejection as quite likely to persist, more or less irrespective of whatever they do (Barrett, 1997). Self-esteem, first acquired in interactions with parents and siblings, sets the scene for later feelings about friendship as represented in friendship motivation. This affects behaviour in social settings which interacts with beliefs about our popularity and acceptability to others. Together this affects our approach to explaining our social successes and failures.

Curing childhood unpopularity

The first question really is 'what are we trying to achieve when we try to "cure" childhood unpopularity?' Is it adequate to assume that all we need to do is treat the unpopular child and implant some magical, 'spray-on' attractant, or should we take the whole children's group and deal with the complexities of their interconnections as a system? Is the child's problem possibly one of lack of general communicative competence? No, I believe (Duck, 1989) we should differentiate social skill, general interpersonal competence in social or play settings, communicative competence in talking to other children, and relational competence (i.e. the specific competence of sustaining personal relationships).

There are many different kinds of skill involved in successful relating in childhood, and hence there are many levels at which difficulties can arise (Adler and Furman, 1988; Pettit and Clawson, 1996; Box 4.4). For instance, the child's behaviours may be inappropriate – in which case some form of social skills training may help – or the child's motivation for relationships may be low. Alternatively, the child may lack the relevant social knowledge about behavioural routine or the nature of relationships. The child may be deficient in internal feedback and poor at evaluating his or her own behaviour or general capabilities. The appropriate way to tackle the problem will depend first on correct identification of the underlying problem causing the behavioural inadequacies (Furman, 1984). By implication, no general style of approach will be universally effective.

Let us start by looking at the separate ideas suggested. One approach we could use is based on 'targeting' the child who has social difficulties, then training the child in various skills that may otherwise be lacking. For instance, some children do not talk enough to their peers or do not engage in cooperative play or never take the initiative in entering games. Direct coaching of such children can be beneficial (French and Underwood, 1996). In the Oden–Asher (1977) programme, children are trained for 10 sessions in: participation in other children's play; cooperation and methods of collaborating rather than competing with others; communication skills of listening and talking; validation, support and nonverbal reinforcement by means such as looking, smiling and offering encouragement. We know from Chapter 1 what a stupendous impact such skills have on the flow of social behaviour and on our acceptability to other people. We also know that these skills are usually acquired at random, because efforts to train and guide children in them have typically been haphazard (Berndt, 1996; Pettit and Clawson, 1996). Paradoxically, governments spend vast amounts of money on teaching children academic skills, but ignore those relating skills which are just as important to adult happiness and success (Duck, 1991).

Such programmes of social skill training are obviously beneficial, but they may not be enough on their own. Even if the unpopular child is trained, the child's peers may not notice. The child's reputation for unpopularity might still exist in the minds of the child's classmates, who may not notice the child's improved style of behaviour (Ladd, 1989). In that case, merely training the unpopular child may be ineffective in the long term if the classmates' behaviour is not affected, too. What is then required is a method that involves the classmates and peers also (Walker and Hops, 1973) or brings in parents and others (Pettit and Clawson, 1996). This method centres on reinforcing peers for interacting with isolated children: the peers are encouraged to approach and play with the previously rejected or ignored child, thus giving the child the experience of acceptance and joint play. In another instance, non-handicapped children were encouraged to play with handicapped children by the direct means of teaching them how to do so (Guralnick, 1976). 'Normal' children can be taught to persist in engaging withdrawn children in play even if they had initially met with a cool and withdrawn reception (Strain et al., 1976). As Furman (1984: 115) concludes, 'peers can be effective therapeutic agents'.

Another strategy is to encourage mixed-age social interaction. An immature child given experience of play with younger kids can learn to take control, to have responsibility, and to direct the activities of others. Furman et al. (1979) successfully used such a technique to improve the interaction rates of withdrawn children. For later ages, however, the reverse strategy is proposed (Duck et al., 1980), namely, giving socially immature children the chance to observe older children's friendships so that they can use these as models. With aggressive children, this may have the additional effect of showing them the dangers of using aggression against 'stronger opponents', so that they are encouraged to develop non-aggressive strategies for interaction. In other cases, it is more suitable to train the child in techniques of entry to groups of other children. A particular characteristic of neglected and rejected children is that they 'hover' on the outside of groups as bystanders or onlookers and do not show effective means of getting themselves admitted to join in (Putallaz and Gottman, 1981).

For a child with problems that persist across situations, and who is obviously the major source of the difficulties, various techniques have been tried. Bierman and Furman (1982) attempted to coach such children in conversational skills by making videotapes about peer interaction and giving the children 'practice' in how to do it. Children are taught social skills based on reinforcements for increasing interaction, for talking to other children and the like. But these forms of training are combined with group experiences where the skills are practised (under expert observation) in the environment where they will ultimately be used by the child alone. Such subject-oriented and peer-oriented combination programmes seem likely to prove effective in the long run (Furman, 1984; Pettit and Clawson, 1996; Schneider et al., 1989). However, the most advanced approaches now are those that involve the whole mix of people in a child's social environment, including the family and teachers (Pettit and Clawson, 1996).

Happy families?

A general point that is clear enough from the above is well recognized by family experts: that a family – however it is made up – is not a simple unit but a complex of relationships between individuals (Fisher, 1996) and that these individuals have many types of relational experiences beyond the family. In seeking to understand the family we need to see 'it' as both a context for personal relationships (e.g. family atmosphere provides a context for a child's growth of self-esteem) and *as* a set of relationships that all impinge on the individual and as something that functions in a variety of social networks and cultural contexts. Naturally as with other relationships involving people who are growing, learning, developing, changing or aging – which is all of us – the relationships in a family change over time. Babies become children, children become adolescents, adolescents become adults, parents become grandparents, and adult children may take over the role of caring for those who once took the role of caring for them (Cooney, 1997). In particular it is short-sighted to view the parent–child from a point that sees the parent and child as independent and different when in fact they are mutually interdependent and increasingly similar as time goes by (Cooney, 1997). Only in a trivial sense is the relationship between these relatives the same across time; in the non-trivial sense the relationship is mightily different as a result of the changes in age, and concurrent responsibility and style (Lewis and Lin, 1996; Pearson, 1996). Thus families are essentially entities that are dynamically *changing all the time*. Families should not be seen naively as defined and fixed entities. If families could never change then there would not be any family therapists, but as we have already seen, families can not only be dysfunctional, they can even create problems for their individual members.

Family break-up

All through this I have written about distressed families that stay together nevertheless. Many couples, however, get divorced (although an increasing trend is for couples to avoid marriage in the first place; Bedford and

Blieszner, 1997). What 'causes' divorce? Answers range from demographic factors, like race and religion, to personality factors like achievement motivation and extroversion, to interactional factors, to relational processes (see Orbuch, 1992). However, we must avoid treating divorce as an event for which a simple cause should be sought. Rather, divorce is a transitional process not an event (Duck, 1982a, 1991), and researchers are now looking for those causal factors which combine to fuel the relentless, unforgiving development of that process. Divorcing takes so long because there is more to it than just 'falling out of love'.

There are at least three parts to marriage that have to be unpicked in divorcing (Hagestad and Smyer, 1982). As we saw in discussing courtship, partners have not only to love one another (one part) but to be successful in meshing their activities and daily routines together (second part). As their relationship becomes well bonded and the routines, work or division of labour in the relationship are sorted out, so the partners develop attachment to the role of spouse – the 'being a husband or a wife' (third part). These three things (love for partner, attachment to established routines, attachment to the marital role) are all built up in courtship and marriage. All have to be disassembled during divorcing where a fourth element (legal commitment) is dissolved. There are many types of divorce that have been identified (Hagestad and Smyer, 1982). The first distinction is between orderly and disorderly divorce.

In *orderly divorces* the partners detach themselves successfully not only from their feelings for one another but from their attachment to the role of 'husband' or 'wife', from their involvement in an established set of daily routines, and from the legal role. They have to decide that they do not love their partner, do not want to be 'a spouse', do not miss the routines of their daily life together, but do want to be legally divorced.

Disorderly divorces are those where at least one aspect of these disengagements is not successfully completed. For instance, one partner may stay in love with the 'ex', or may find it impossible to adjust to 'not being married'. Hagestad and Smyer (1982) list seven types of disorderly divorce. Given that in an orderly divorce the partners detach from all four of the elements noted above (attachment to partner, attachment to role, shared routine and legal commitment), the disorderly divorces are made up from the seven remaining possible combinations of scores on the four elements. For example in the first type ('divorced in name only') the partners are legally divorced, but still emotionally involved, still invested in the spousal role and still sharing routines, possibly even living together. Type 2 ('I wish it hadn't happened') is in evidence when partners' daily activities are disconnected from one another and they are legally divorced but one partner still feels love for the other and still connects with the spousal role. The partners in Type 3 ('I've got you under my skin') share no daily routines, no desire for the spousal role as such and no legal connection, but all the same they are still emotionally attached to their spouse. As one subject put it: 'If we ran into one another it used to just kill me. I used to take the long way home just so I wouldn't see him.' In Type 4 ('the common law arrangement') the partners do not want to be married, as such, and are legally divorced but do feel love for one another and desire to be connected in routine. These couples are essentially cohabiting after divorce instead of before marriage! Type 5 ('why not be roommates?') encompasses those who share their lives and like the marital status, even though they do not have a legal marital role and do not have any other emotional attachment to the partner. Type 6 ('marriage has its advantages') includes people who think that the state of marriage is better than singlehood, even though they are not attached to their partner and do not share routines. Type 7 ('business as usual') comprises couples who want to be legally divorced and do not love one another but continue, essentially for convenience, to stay in the same house and do the same sorts of things in daily life as they have always done.

Three points about divorce   First, divorce is a stressful process with both physical and psychological side-effects (see Chapter 7). It affects and disrupts the partners' daily lives, routines and sense of identity as well as making them unhappy. Second, the divorce of two persons has consequences for many more people than just the two persons who are separating. It obviously affects the children of the marriage. Since we are looking at the family as a system, and the parents of the divorcing pair as well as their siblings, we should think about those effects. Third, and less obvious, to become divorced, couples have to separate – that is, to unmake, 'brick by brick', the relationship they have previously painstakingly put together. To do this they have to undo all the things just listed in the previous section, but to do so against a background of family and societal pressures and forces that may want them to stay together. Just as society creates exogenous influences on couple's courtships and marriages, so it creates barriers to the dissolution of marital relationships. Two obvious ones are:

1   'Divorced' is a negatively valued state that people do not like to have to apply to themselves. One adjustment that divorcees have to make is to the sense of shame and failure that is often felt by the person or imposed by outsiders. In our society, it is believed that a divorce is a *failed* relationship (rather than, say, a courageous and honest response to an unworkable partnership).
2   Society is organized in a way that 'expects' people to belong to couples, so that it is actually regarded as embarrassing, say, to invite a single person to a dinner party without inviting another 'single' of the opposite sex to balance things out. What may seem right to the hosts, however, can sometimes be embarrassing to the 'single' guests who probably take mild offence at being crudely paired off like that.

However, many divorced people remarry or enter new roles and so reconfigure their family and thus their experience of what 'a family' is (Coleman and Ganong, 1995). While the restructuring is not the only thing that happens, it is the element of the whole process that most researchers focus on. One thing to bear in mind also is that about 25 per cent of previously married men and women move into gay or lesbian relationships after divorce, although the most common reconfiguration is a remarriage or a new cohabiting heterosexual relationship (Coleman and Ganong, 1995). Families reconfigure in a variety of ways, do so quickly after a divorce (which in some cases was presumably precipitated by an affair which then becomes the new, replacement relationship anyway), and reconfigure several times.

Children and divorce or reconfiguration

Divorce is an extended transition that inevitably 'affects the entire family system and the functioning and interactions of the members within that system' (Hetherington et al., 1982: 233). It does not stop once the marriage is ended but flows on into the people's lives in innumerable ways for years afterwards (e.g. in terms of a legal requirement to pay certain costs of the ex-partner; strains in required discussions about the children's future; loss of trust in relational partners; poor relationships with one's own children). The outcome and experience of the divorce affect different members of the family differently, and the problems faced by the divorced parents are likely to be different – and to require different skills – from those faced by the children (Kitson and Morgan, 1990). There is no such thing as a victimless divorce – that is, one where no member of the family reported any distress or exhibited disrupted behaviour. Even reconfigured families are 'incomplete institutions' (Coleman and Ganong, 1995): as all too many people discover sadly, there is never a place on an official form (e.g. at school) for a step-parent to sign and take responsibility for a child. Coleman and Ganong also note that society has an ideology that permits officials and policy makers to intrude into family life at the point of a legal divorce (e.g. deciding who pays for which of a child's needs) in a way that they rarely feel able to do when a marriage is still intact, even though the relationship involves the same people.

Children in distressed families, particularly those which experience separation and divorce, develop certain personality styles or views of themselves and also manifest social–behaviour problems when interacting with other children (Amato, 1991). Children experiencing parental divorce tend to suffer from depression and psychological disturbance, such as excessive feelings of their own guilt – they particularly tend to assume that their parents' divorce is somehow their fault (Kitson and Morgan, 1990). Hetherington also found that boys manage better with their fathers and girls manage better with their mothers, although if living with their mother the boys adjust better than girls to a stepfather (Hetherington, 1979).

In the first year, particularly, of the divorce, children from divorced families are more oppositional and obstructive, more aggressive, lacking in self-control, distractible and demanding than are children from families that are still together. This is true even if the comparison (i.e. intact and undivorced) families are showing high rates of marital distress and discord. The divorce itself is a significant factor, but the children are also adjusting to new custodial and emotional arrangements that are often puzzling and difficult to accept (e.g. 'Why do I spend one weekend at this house and the next weekend at another house?').

Being labelled 'the child of divorced parents' is something that children find difficult to cope with (Amato, 1991). For example, they may get a 'hard time' at school for 'having no mother or no father'. In an attempt to explore this issue, Gottlieb (1983) reports a programme in Canada designed to deal with the aftermath of parental divorce. By introducing children of divorced parents to one another, Gottlieb was able to establish support groups for them. The support group shows them they are not alone in their experience and helps them to share and develop ways of coping with their problems. This technique makes use of what researchers now have learned about children's friendships outside the family.

Children's relationships with their parents also change somewhat predictably after divorce. For one thing, only 33 per cent of children have monthly contact with the non-residential father (Furstenberg et al., 1983), and 44 per cent of 12 to 16 year olds had not seen their father in the previous 12 months. Part of this may be due to the fact that only 16 per cent of children are involved in joint custody of any type (Donnelly and Finkelhor, 1993), but in part it is supported by the fact that absent fathers stay in contact with daughters more than with sons after a divorce.

Coleman and Ganong (1995) apply the above Hagestad and Smyer (1982) model to the issues of family reconfiguration and look at the processes by which parents become disattached from their roles as parents, whereas Hagestad and Smyer originally looked at the ways in which people became disattached from their roles of married persons. The process of relationship loss is made up in this model by a complex of different features and most are experienced as loss of control and hence are enormously stressful. In reconfiguring families, the emotional attachment to children, attachment to the role of parent, and attachment to the routines of daily family life are all affected. If a father has no custodial rights then an uncontrollable loss of the role of 'father' (as normally understood) will be experienced. Accompanying this sense of loss, according to many divorced fathers, is a sense of reduced masculinity and loss of rights as either a head or a participant in a household (Arendell, 1993). Many fathers respond to such senses of loss by becoming as absent from the other roles as possible also, whereas those who retain some custodial rights do not (Umberson and Williams, 1993). Coleman and Ganong (1995: 90) suggest that 'the ambiguity of the non-residential father role may be too uncomfortable for some men, so they withdraw from their children, essentially abandoning the role rather than continually face situations in which they feel awkward and unsure of how to continue fathering'. If you have time to discuss this idea in class, you might find it interesting to do so.

Summary

Complex interrelationships affect our social behaviour. Relationships, like people, have a history and have come from somewhere, often taking a long time to emerge and develop. A marriage can be affected by the style of the preceding courtship adopted by the partners; a family, as a whole, can be influenced by the kind of marital interaction between the two spouses in particular; the child at school can be affected by the quality of previous interaction in the family home. The learning that the child gathers about relationships from the family environment can carry over and influence the child's approach or avoidance with other children in the neighbourhood or at school. This chapter took the view that the parent–child relationships, like other relationship pairs in the family and the relationship of the family itself to outsiders, are also bidirectional. That is to say that it is too simple to say that parents influence or direct children or that families are not affected by networks and vice versa; instead there is a two-way street of influence where each element acts with and responds to the other. Even very young children have their own ability to interpret and understand – and hence to react to or even resist – what another person does or says to them. Hence relationships are created by reciprocity with the persons involved, and with outsiders, and with contexts surrounding the relationship.

Further reading

Duck, S.W., Dindia, K., Ickes, W., Milardo, R.M., Mills, R.S.L. and Sarason, R.B. (eds) (1997) *Handbook of Personal Relationships* (2nd edn). Chichester: Wiley.

Pettit, G.S. and Clawson, M.A. (1996) 'Pathways to interpersonal competence: parenting and children's peer relations', in N. Vanzetti and S.W. Duck (eds), *A Lifetime of Relationships*. Pacific Grove, CA: Brooks/Cole.

Pettit, G. and Lollis, S. (eds) (1997) 'Bidirectional influences in child-parent relationships' (special issue), *Journal of Social and Personal Relationships*, 14(4) August.

5

Influencing Strangers, Acquaintances and Friends

'One cannot do justice to the individuality and dynamics of social relationships if one follows the, in itself, correct observation that social relationships arise only when the participants know something about one another.' (Bergmann, 1993: 53)

As I have noted in the opening chapter of the book and in other places later, *all* communication involves persuasion, brings in various cultural and social baggage to our interactions, and carries relational outcomes. Even at times when we are just chatting with friends we may do so in ways that happen to reveal a new way of facing a problem, or that happen to reinforce their view of self, or their feeling of being supported in a general kind of way (Leatham and Duck, 1990). Even everyday chat about apparently trivial matters can therefore serve to persuade in such unintended ways and the everyday talk becomes important because it provides a continuous background for much else that we do that *is* deliberately persuasive: it lays the ground and creates a long-term context for those bigger moves, such as support in a time of crisis. So although many situations are ones that we recognize as obviously 'persuasive', they are actually just special instances of the general truth that communication is *always* subtly rhetorical and indirectly persuasive. Talk always represents the speaker's view of the situation, the audience, one's own identity, and one's preferred way of understanding things, to which we invite our partner's or our audience's acceptance (Duck, 1994a). However, situations labelled as 'attitude change' are not the only places where persuasion occurs and the present chapter continues to develop the theme by showing the deep structural connections between 'persuasion' and 'relationships', even in the relatively familiar everyday experiences where we deal with others who face us with predicaments or difficulties.

As Cupach and Metts (1994) note, daily experience occasionally involves preventing, coping with, or digging ourselves out of predicaments, and Miller (1996) further discusses the sorts of public embarrassment that are horribly familiar, when our public performance fails to present a cool or competent image in the face of other people's attention to that performance. When we go about our daily business, we are occasionally confronted with unexpected situations that force us to deal with awkward strangers, usually to persuade them to stop some behaviour that is offensive to us – strangers who light a cigarette in a no-smoking area, who jump ahead of us in a queue, who irritate us in launderettes, or who may even sexually harass us. On other occasions, the problem is to deal with people whom we know a little but not very well, and ask them to do something for us that they may be inclined to resist. Our regular bus driver may have to be persuaded to accept and change a large banknote; we may have to ask our class instructor to extend the deadline for an assignment; or a person in the adjoining apartment may need to be asked to turn down the stereo. Sometimes we may even want to persuade a friend to do us a troublesome favour or to bring a close partner or family member round to our way of thinking. At other times there may be relational matters that we do not typically even see as 'persuasion' at all. For instance, we don't see it as persuasion when we ask a classmate to come out on a date with us, but it *is* a form of persuasion. So it is when we (persuade someone to) end a relationship, or (persuade someone to) have sex or accept a marriage proposal, or (persuade someone to) heed our advice on something or accept an offer of help. In ways we may not always immediately recognize such situations involve us in the business of changing someone's mind, persuading or influencing them, their behaviour, their beliefs, or their impressions of us, or getting people to do things for us. Of course, daily life brings us into contact with many different sorts of people, some of whom we know and some of whom we do not. Some may even be enemies (Wiseman and Duck, 1995) with whom we are forced, by circumstances, to interact. At other times we may be faced with an importunate friend or acquaintance or someone who expects us to do them a favour, fulfil an obligation, or carry out a duty of friendship that imposes a burden on us. Sometimes we may do things for people easily because we like them. Sometimes we may resist an easy request because we *don't* like the person.

Because of this, there are two goals in this chapter: first, to show that the processes of persuasion are intricately tied up with processes of *relationships* so that daily relational activity involves persuasion more widely and deeply than may appear at first; a second goal is to show how the relationship between two people deeply affects the type of persuasion that is appropriate and how it 'changes the standard rules of engagement' in ways that turn such rules from being generally applicable to being relationally specific. Relationships are an implicit basis for much persuasion and indeed this is one reason why car salespeople and advertisers try to mimic such relational activity and act over-friendly and caring or appear to establish friendly relationships with customers as part of the whole process. They don't play just to our logic but to our feelings of acceptance or belonging. Also our relationship duties and obligations or our willingness to do things for people 'because it's you' represent another instance of 'persuasion by relationship'. How often have you heard someone say 'I don't do this for everyone but I will do it for you because you are a friend'?

In this chapter, therefore, I want to start out with a relatively traditional discussion of persuasion (which I have always – I'll be honest – found dry and boring) and show how much more interesting and informative it gets once we get down to the relational underpinnings and look at persuasion *as* relating. It is true that in each of the cases of strangers, of acquaintances and of friends, the issues are somewhat different, despite the underlying similarities of the persuasive processes, but we should look at both similarities and differences.

When dealing with strangers we can only assume that they are average, sensible members of society about whom we know only what we can see; we have to assume that they will be influenced by the usual average things, such as power and logic, and have average, normal attitudes. Since we have no relationship with them except as one anonymous human being to another, they are contextless for us and there is no special knowledge of their personal characteristics on which to draw. By contrast, with acquaintances we attempt persuasion and compliance in a different relational context: we probably do want to emphasize that they know us a little and that they should consequently treat us as persons with individual characteristics. That they do know us means that we can claim special treatment: we are not 'just another person who wants something done in a hurry' but someone to whom they have a minor obligation to grant special treatment.

With friends, we use whatever special knowledge we have about them, but are probably also concerned to preserve the relationship between us. However, friendship is a source of obligations, and part of the role of 'friend' is willing acceptance of chores, duties and obligations to do favours that help the other persons (Stein, 1993). We do unwelcome or inconvenient things for them precisely because we are their good friend. Wiseman (1986) has pointed out that a part of the 'voluntary contract' of friendship involves us tacitly agreeing to support our friends in times of need, to offer them help even if it is personally inconvenient, to take time away from our own business in order to attend to *their* business, and to engage with their demands upon our psychological and physical resources. Thus, the context for influence is rather different in a friendship as compared to an acquaintanceship, but on my own limited reading of work on persuasion and attitude change it seems that these relational differences are elided as scholars search for *absolutely* effective ways of persuading or inducing compliance. Such literature typically pays little attention to everyday tasks like persuading someone to come on a date, have sex, pick up the catastrophe that is their bedroom, turn down their stereo, curb their dog or leave us alone. It also pays little heed to the broader context for persuasion that is provided by a relationship, or by membership of a network, and by that relationship knowledge or the fear of relational consequences.

In looking at persuasion and compliance, then, I shall make two big moves: after reviewing some standard literature on persuasion I shall focus on its relevance once everyday relationships are seen as a context for persuasion. I shall not focus exclusively on grand issues like political persuasion, voting behaviour, advertising effectiveness, the campaign for/against nuclear arms, or the general attempt to persuade people to give up smoking. When it comes down to the nitty-gritty in everyday social life, we most often want to get someone to change what they are doing (i.e. to comply with our desires) rather than to change their attitudes for ever on a key topic (Leatham and Duck, 1990). If you need a regular review of attitude change research that deals with Big Issue Persuasion between people who do not know one another, that can be read in any other introductory text. In keeping with my own emphasis on daily life in this book, I happen to believe that large-scale decisions and attitudes occupy much less of people's time than the amount of work on Big Issue Persuasion might lead us to imagine. I believe that partners spend longer arguing about the best way to decorate the living room, the most desirable car to purchase, or where to go for a meal or a holiday than they do confronting each other about political issues or prejudice toward racial groups. I do not mean that the latter issues are not important; they are. However, to study them to the degree to which they are often studied in attitude-change texts is seriously to misrepresent the contours of social life and to fail to create a proper representation of human experience.

From the point of view of classical rhetorical theory a person persuades by three basic means: logic (*logos*); emotions (*pathos*); character (*ethos*). Traditional approaches to attitude change in social psychology and communication have focused on all three and I will try to sketch each of them before showing that in everyday life *ethos* – the identity, personality, and character of a speaker — is the most influential with friends and family and acquaintances. It is 'who you are' more than 'what you say' that matters in persuading friends. On the other hand, in dealing with strangers there is more of a mix of logic and emotion involved.

Influencing strangers

In dealing with strangers we usually lack knowledge about their particular characteristics as *people*. What we see on the surface is all we have to deal with. Accordingly, we are likely to draw upon different aspects of the persuasive context from those we use when we deal with acquaintances or with friends. Yet we may also be attentive to our own *ethos* – others' perceptions of our character – in the setting. For instance, we may be concerned about other outside observers' views about the episode. If our behaviour towards a stranger 'causes a scene', we may be concerned about our appearance to any other people that are present; when dealing with friends, we probably also have their feelings and interests in mind as much as our own. Consider the following example.

Strangers on the train

At the time when I was beginning work on the first edition of the book, I had to go to London for two days to record a television programme on 'social skills' with a man who specializes in assertiveness training. The journey back involved a three-hour train ride, which, on this occasion, took more than four hours because of poor weather. I always choose a non-smoking section, which is clearly marked with a red circular notice on every window, showing a cigarette crossed out, the words No Smoking, and a statement of the penalty for violating the rule. The carriage filled with another 31 passengers, and we departed more or less on time. I looked around at the strangers who were my fellow passengers. Directly opposite was a young woman who looked as if she were a student and a young man who was stapling together leaflets about solvent abuse, warning teenagers about the social, health and legal disadvantages of glue sniffing. He soon started chatting to the student and it turned out that he was a vegetarian who jogged every day and helped to run a youth sports centre. I began to see why he had chosen a non-smoking section: he cared about health. Across the central corridor of the open-plan compartment was a table occupied by two large and hungry people who began tucking vigorously and, to my mind, unwisely into a selection of 'junk food' bags. I sat reading a paper about loneliness in college students whilst I listened to *The Lark Ascending* by Vaughan Williams on my personal stereo. I could keep an eye on things by 'looking out of the window' since it was a dark winter's evening and the carriage lights reflected the carriage events clearly. These cameos continued amiably enough along their own paths for some hour and a half, as the train lurched on from London towards Lancaster interspersed with announcements from the guard/conductor and bar steward.

Then one of the big eaters lit a cigarette.

I drew his attention to the fact that it was a non-smoking section and asked him to go to a different section of the train. He replied that someone further down the train was smoking but, as a computer manager from Manchester pointed out to him, that did not actually contradict my point that *he* was sitting in a non-smoking section. Out of the other 30 passengers just that one man joined in the argument and supported my request whilst the others looked on with a mixture of amusement, embarrassment and British reserve.

When the smoker would neither put out his cigarette nor move there flashed across my mind one of the points from the television programme I had just finished recording: stick to your guns. However, it was with something of a sense of failure that I went looking for the guard/conductor who asked the man to move, which he then did, flashing in my direction one of those looks that would kill a toad.

What we had here was a 'social confrontation episode'. As Newell and Stutman (1988) point out, the key feature of such an episode is that one actor in the situation points out to another actor 'that his or her behaviour has violated a rule or expectation for appropriate conduct within the relationship or situation'. Key elements are the legitimacy of the invoked rule; the legitimacy of any other rule that might supersede the first rule; whether or not the person actually performed the illegitimate behaviour; whether the behaviour actually amounts to a violation of the rule; and whether or not the accused accepts responsibility. If we analyse the present problem and the ways in which it unfolded we can see that all of these elements were invisible and silent cultural normative societal fellow travellers in that railway carriage on that dark and stormy night!

What about these other passengers? The solvent/health man later left the section for a while and as he returned to his seat, placed a pack of cigarettes and a lighter in front of him. He had said nothing, I assume, because he felt divided loyalties. On the one hand, he smoked, but on the other hand he recognized the need to consider other people's rights while doing so and had himself left the non-smoking carriage when he wanted to smoke. Or perhaps he didn't want to be involved in another scene where he would be asked not to smoke. His behaviour did raise an interesting issue, though, since his other actions and statements pointed to a concern over health and a care for others: so why did he smoke? The student was a non-smoker who had said that she always chose non-smoking compartments, so why did she say nothing?

Some scholars would point to the first smoker's attitude structure: his beliefs about smoking, his beliefs about the legitimacy of his action, and, given that he could see others smoking, his consequent belief that he was being unfairly singled out for criticism. Some would argue that he felt his freedom was being constrained and so he reacted against the constraint. Others would look at the internal, logical structure of my request and its evident ineffectiveness. Some would point to other relevant circumstances, such as the passivity of the others in the compartment that provided a context for the support of rule-breaking and no support for me. Some of these ideas have been applied generally to all persuasive contexts, but I think that some are more likely to be important in this setting and others elsewhere. Some matter in dealing with strangers and some do not; some are more important in dealing with friends – for instance, whether a challenged behaviour threatens the relationship itself.

Being noticed

When dealing with strangers, a first requirement is to be noticed and have them pay attention to our request. To do this we have to present ourselves in a way that makes it clear that we have the right to have our request dealt with. By contrast, when dealing with friends, our right to be heard and noticed is built into our relationship: friends heed us because they know us. With strangers, however, we might need to use some guile and devices.

Attention to a persuasive message is well established as a critical factor for persuasion to occur (Hovland et al., 1953). People attend more closely to a credible source, that is, one that appears to justify our attention, one that has authority and can be trusted or believed. In the 1950s, when Hovland's studies were conducted, it was found, for instance, that Robert Oppenheimer, who headed the team that created the atom bomb, was more readily believed and accepted by a US audience than was *Pravda*, the Russian newspaper, whether or not the topic was nuclear bombs.

Source credibility is freely manipulated in advertisements. Advertisers like to say 'Doctors recommend' or 'As used in hospitals' as a way of tying their product to credible sources. Other indirect means are also used to appeal to symbols recognized in our culture as respectable and authoritative symbols of credibility. For instance, when persons are shown recommending drugs or pharmaceutical products, they are frequently figures in white coats ('scientists') or smart business clothes ('executives') – with greying hair if they are male ('authority'). They usually wear glasses ('intelligent'), carry clipboards ('data'), are seen giving other people directions ('power') against a background of test tubes ('science'), and they use fountain pens ('class'). The same person saying the same thing about pharmaceutical products on a football field in sports gear would probably appear less credible even if the message, the facts, the words, the argument, the claims, were all precisely the same. What we respond to are the cues in the context; all are cues carefully prepared to suggest credibility within our culture. Here credibility is produced by cultural symbols of expertise (or, in the case of advertisements, assumed expertise; after all, most viewers would realize that the 'expert' is not really an expert but is just an actor playing that part – yet we still might believe what is said).

In dealings with strangers source credibility is one of the most important factors. In the smoky warmth of my dark social predicament on the train, I could have tried to claim such credibility in a number of doubtful ways ('Hey, I'm a professor/brain surgeon/fighter pilot . . . please stop smoking') or in one of two other more effective ways that make use of physical attractiveness and similarity. If we are attractive and are like the stranger in ways that are relevant to the message (e.g. if we wear sports gear when trying to persuade a sporting audience) then we are more likely to be persuasive, according to well-established studies by McGinnis (1970) and by Berscheid (1966) respectively. We are not all physically attractive (although people who appear in advertisements usually are – presumably because they are selected for the job because they get more attention and hence are more credible), but we can improve on nature if it is important and we have the time and the forewarning to make those adjustments. If we are able or willing to do so, then we can also take some steps to become – or to seem – similar to the targets of our persuasion attempts. For instance, we dress up smartly for interviews with important people and take care over our appearance to impress people. We may also go to considerable lengths to agree with them and support their ideas (i.e. we ingratiate by appearing to be similar to them).

The findings on source credibility are helpful with strangers when we have time to prepare, but as researchers soon began to find, source credibility alone is not enough to explain persuasion nor is it always a helpful guide. We are quite often thrown into persuasive contexts quite unexpectedly by the unpredictable actions of other people, and we need to influence them then and there. 'Please serve me next, I was here before this person'; 'Please move your car, you're blocking my exit'; 'Please stop smoking, you're in a

---

Box 5.1   Source credibility

- Credibility of a source affects a listener's likelihood of changing his or her attitudes (Hovland et al., 1953).
- Expertise, trustworthiness, attractiveness and similarity to the target are important elements of source credibility (Petty and Cacioppo, 1981).
- A person is more credible when he or she argues against his or her best interests, perhaps because it is taken to indicate trustworthiness (Walster et al., 1966).
- The racial origin of a communicator can influence the speaker's credibility for prejudiced audiences (Aronson and Golden, 1962).
- A communicator who takes a predictable line (e.g. a fervent Catholic who speaks against pornography) is less persuasive than one who speaks in contrast to the direction one would expect to be taken (e.g. a fervent Catholic who speaks for the cathartic value of pornography; Eagly et al., 1978).

---

no-smoking section'; . . . 'Why don't you turn down your stereo, I'm trying to work.' Everyday life is not always conveniently arranged, and yet we have to deal with the actual context in which we find ourselves. If we happen to be nicely turned out, and wearing spectacles, then we may have influence, but we may happen to be in running gear or a bathrobe or to have just (been) woken up. In any case, appearance alone does not guarantee persuasive success.

When we are dealing with familiar people whom we know, however, what about source credibility then? When friends and family want to influence us in those circumstances, credibility comes not from the usual cues of clothing and the rest, but from what we know about the person, his or her relevant competencies, and how we feel about him or her. Since I know my brother is a professor of economics, I am more likely to credit his statements on economics. Also I am more likely to credit the arguments of someone I love or have come to respect, even if he or she does not dress well and is not outwardly similar to me. Those I have come to know as irritatingly incompetent probably will not persuade me, however they dress up. People I regard as enemies will hardly ever be able to persuade me to do things, even if they sweeten the deal with gifts and promises (as Virgil, the Roman poet, put it in the *Aeneid*, 'I fear/distrust the Greeks even when they are bearing gifts'). Relative power positions are also well known in our everyday encounters and are significant in this context. Over a period of time, we get to know who has authority or credibility and who has not; we learn which friend is the group leader or gives reliable advice; we know which student in class is bright and a good 'consultant' about class-work; we have ideas about which colleague carries authority or has a strong political base in the department.

I believe that those real-life cues based on personal knowledge and relationships affect our perceptions of credibility in everyday life much more than the business clothes or the glasses. A friend is credible to me because I know and trust him or her, not because of the clothes. In everyday life, power, credibility and trust are based on vibrant, familiar relationships, on everyday talk, and on built-up trust (Boon, 1994), not on the fripperies of the advertising image. When familiarity is lacking and we are with a stranger, a shopkeeper, a bus driver who will not change a large note, or a sexist waiter who presents the bill to the man in the party when the woman booked the table, then we probably cannot rely on source credibility alone and we need other strategies, like appearing friendly ('Hey pal, turn down the stereo') or choosing words carefully and taking great thought over the structure of our persuasive message, or appealing to bystanders for their help and intervention.

The apathetic context

Our predicaments in social life – even among strangers – often involve us in taking a stand on some matter when other people are there to see, like other people standing in the queue that someone tries to 'jump'. Awareness of the reactions of strangers or friends, whether physically or only psychologically present, often guides our action and helps us to feel good or bad about the situation. We may well be guided in our actions and words by thoughts of 'What would the neighbours think?' or 'What do these other people think of all this?' These powerful relational and social contexts are extremely influential.

In the non-smoking compartment I found myself in that embarrassing public situation: my request to the smoker was uttered before an audience of other people who were also affected by the smoker's behaviour. No one else did anything and no one else (bar one) took my side. That means that there were 28 people sitting around saying and doing nothing whilst the two-act melodrama went on in their midst. In particular, it meant that the smoker was not being made to defend himself or being publicly 'boxed into a tight corner' by social pressure. This provided an important psychological context for my persuasive attempt. In terms of the Newell and Stutman (1988) analysis above, this apathetic context tacitly suggests the unimportance or illegitimacy of the rule that I invoked and explains why my efforts to enforce it were doomed.

It is an important fact, not just a coincidence, that we live our lives as members of social and psychological communities that provide such contexts against which to evaluate our actions, thoughts and beliefs. We are strongly affected by the views and actions of relevant other people, and we habitually compare our behaviour, dress, attitudes and beliefs to other people's (Festinger, 1954). The essential argument of Festinger's 'social comparison theory' is that we are all inclined to assess ourselves against a relevant group of other persons to see if we compare equally, if not favourably, and we prefer to be liked and accepted rather than disliked and rejected. Have you had the experience of turning up to a party dressed in the 'wrong' kind of clothes? Then you have experienced the consequences of social comparison theory. Festinger indicates that we compare our attitudes, opinions and emotions also: when we want to know if we are acting or thinking in an acceptable manner or making a sensible emotional response we compare ourselves with other people to see how they react. If they do as we do, then we are 'OK'.

Festinger's point is vital because it is such a common part of human life: we are *always* comparing ourselves to other people and we want to be accepted or acceptable. For instance, as students, we often want to know what sorts of exam/test/essay grades everyone else earned, so that we can evaluate our own performance more thoroughly. Just knowing our own score may not be sufficiently reassuring. Whenever we feel the urge to compare our own jogging times, test grades, body weight or salary against average figures, we are experiencing the phenomenon of social comparison. It guides us as we attempt to find out if we are normal or right, and can even be used as an argument in persuasion, as in the statement any parent of an adolescent has heard: 'Can I stay at the party till 12.00? Everyone else will.'

If we look at what happened – or, rather, what did not happen – in the non-smoking section of the train, we can see social comparison at work, silently telling me I am in the wrong. For one thing, the smoker's first response was to indicate a comparison group elsewhere to 'make his behaviour right' (he pointed out that others were smoking in the train). Second, a more subtle comparison was that only one person was concerned about the smoking and no one else reacted. The smoker may look round and think, 'This smoke doesn't bother anyone else or they'd be reacting. I'm doing OK. The guy here is overreacting.' I look round and think, 'I am upset by the smoking but no one else is saying anything. Perhaps my reaction is inappropriate.' Since people tend to assume that others are similar to them (Stotland et al., 1960), a nonreaction is equivalent to support for the status quo rather than for a new proposal. Through apathy, the others are supporting the 'smokus quo' rather than the proposal that it should stop. The message from the comparison group to me, then, is 'You care and we do not, so you are wrong.' In terms of the Newell and Stutman (1988) analysis, they essentially, but passively, deny that the smoker is violating a rule, or perhaps implicitly suggest that the rule written on the window (i.e. No Smoking) can be superseded by another rule (i.e. No Smoking Unless Other People Are Not Very Bothered By It In Which Case You Can Do It Anyway).

How could I have reinterpreted their indifference so that it becomes supportive of me and provides me with a comparison group? A careful piece of oratory or a well-structured message directed at the apathetic bystanders might have energized a bit of support that could have changed the balance of opinion for comparison. The stratagem would be to make the other people feel good about themselves, and so to interpret their apathy as something positive and supportive of me. For instance, I could have tried suggesting that they were all too nice to speak up as I had done. ('These other people are too polite to say so but they are offended too.') If they are *really* apathetic, then they will not contradict and say 'No, I am not just being polite; I am really not offended', but they *might* and then my position would look a bit limp. In dealing with friends we have two different sorts of behaviour available to help us: (1) friends are very likely to be similar to ourselves in elaborate ways (Byrne, 1997; Duck, 1994a) and to provide useful social comparisons and support for our behaviour (Duck, 1991); (2) we have known friends a long time and have a basis for understanding what sorts of behaviours they will tolerate and what not, so the social comparisons and judgemental standards are built into the situation and relational context and we know them to be generally supportive.

The dog owner's dilemma

Another fascinating incident showed me the power of comparison with other people's behaviour and also how fate can intervene to correct bystander apathy. I took Christina (then aged nine) and Jamie (then aged four) to the children's playground where a special section for the under-fives was fenced off and had a sign: 'Dogs are not allowed in this area.' There were about 20 parents there, each with at least one child, when one turned up with two small children and a dog, which he brought in and allowed to run strenuously around. Apathetically, the rest of the parents looked from one to another, raised eyebrows, muttered to one another in general terms about 'dogs' and made social comparisons – no one else did anything directly, so why should I be the first? We all said nothing, all expecting someone else to take the initiative, and all unwilling to risk the dog owner's reactions, since he had a generally uninviting look about him. We were all rapidly transformed into nonapathetic good citizens, however, when the dog started to chase one of the children, then several of us heroically united to draw the dog owner's attention to the sign. His response was one of those staggering real-life retorts (it is given below) that no one ever expects. The dog's sudden refocusing of energy made an extra contribution to the incident that forced us from feeling good about ourselves in one way (we are tolerant, open-minded, unofficious) to feeling good in another way (we are good citizens protecting children from danger). That was the crucial change that led to our intervention.

   What did the dog owner say when we pointed his good eye at the notice? With marvellous aplomb, he said 'It's only a small dog; they don't count.' This points to something that is missing from the accounts of predicaments given so far: any reference to the fact that the target of our persuasion has a mind – in this case quite an inventive one. He probably felt about himself, as most people do, that he was a normal, rational human being, who is basically all right, acts in a reasonable way, and has an above-average sense of humour. How might this have affected his actions and accounted for his beliefs about the dog?

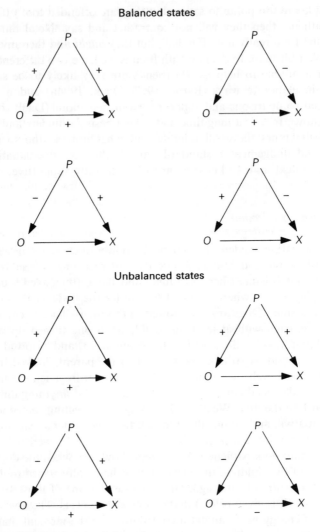

Figure 5.1 *Balanced and unbalanced states*

Balance and consistency

People seem to feel better about themselves when they act in a way which they feel is consistent (Heider, 1944, 1958). Note my careful wording of that statement: it does not state that we *are* consistent, but that we like to *think* we are. Consistency theorists suggest that we prefer consistency or 'balance' among our different attitudes. When we become aware of imbalance or inconsistency among them, we are then motivated to change something.

In Heider's model there are usually two persons (P, O) and one object about which they have an attitude (X). P and O can feel + or – about each other and about X. Balance is the result if the signs all come out positive when multiplied algebraically (i.e. $+ + +$ or $- - +$), and imbalance is the result of negative product (i.e. $+ + -$). So in our case, we have me (P), the dog owner (O) and the presence of the dog (X). Things would be imbalanced for me if I liked the dog owner (+); I disliked the dog's presence (−); and the dog owner liked the dog (+), that is, if the algebraic product of the $+ / -$ signs comes out as negative overall. $(+) \times (-) \times (+)$ comes out negative, according to rules of algebra. However, I did not like the dog owner (−) or his little pooch (−), but he liked it (+), so I am in a balanced state: the overall algebraic product of $(-) \times (-) \times (+)$ is positive. So I shall not change my attitudes and I shall continue to believe that the dog should go. The dog owner is balanced too: he does not know or like me (−); he knows that I dislike the dog (−); but he thinks that the dog is nice and too small to count as a dog (+). Once again, then, $(-) \times (-) \times (+)$ comes out positive, so he is balanced, and he will not move the dog from the area.

On this model, if I want to persuade the dog owner, I have to create imbalance, so that he will be motivated to restore balance. I want to change his attitude to the dog's presence by this method, so I must create imbalance in him by affecting one of the other two items of the three. If he knows I dislike the dog but does not care, then he will not change, so I must make him care about my opinion. If I make him like me then he will care about my opinion and feel imbalanced. I need to create the following thought system: I like P (Steve) (+); P does not like the dog being here (−); I want the dog to stay (+); this comes out negative overall $(+) \times (-) \times (+)$, so the dog owner would be imbalanced and would want to change something – for instance, his attitude towards the dog's presence. I should make him like me first, then tell him to take his terrorist terrier elsewhere.

Critics of consistency theories have noted that it's not so simple in real life – especially in interactions with strangers. How do I ensure that the attitude that such a stranger changes is the one towards the dog's presence and not the positive attitude to me that I have suddenly induced him into having? Heider's theory, unfortunately, cannot predict which one of the two will be altered to restore balance (Newcomb, 1971). Since his new-found liking for me would have been a recent attitude whereas dog-loving is an old-established one, it's much more likely the dog owner would restore balance by changing from liking me to disliking me and would hang on to his belief that the dog can stay. One difficulty with Heider's approach here, then, is that the relationship between the two strangers is as likely to be affected by the persuasion attempt as is the attitude I want to change. In friendships, the consideration of the effects of a persuasion-attempt upon the relationship is, however, very likely to figure strongly as an influence on choice of persuasion strategy. In face-to-face attempts at influence, either the two parties do not know one another (so they will not care a great deal about their attitudes about one another and are very likely to change those feelings quite capriciously) or the two parties know one another well and will not want to bicker over a petty attitudinal disagreement, so they might agree to differ or not to fight. In either case, balance theory loses its predictive value when placed in relational context.

Dissonance

Another model, Festinger's (1957) dissonance theory, focuses on the attitudes of one person (P) only (not those of P *and* those of O) and also admits P's *behaviour* into the equation. (Note: Festinger's dissonance theory is different from Festinger's social comparison theory.) In brief, it argues that a person will be motivated to restore balance (or, in Festinger's terms, to restore 'consonance') when the person holds two attitudes which lead to psychologically inconsistent conclusions or when the person's behaviour and attitude about it do not accord. Thus, if we disapprove of smoking but find that we have just lit a cigarette, we ought to experience dissonance.

Dissonance theory appears in all the psychology textbooks, although its original findings have hardly ever been unambiguously replicated (Stroebe, 1980). It is a striking theory and many of the results from studies into it are striking, too. People have lied for small amounts of money but not for large amounts (dissonance: I lied; the money did not justify it; therefore, it was not a lie). They have bamboozled themselves (dissonance: I find this group very boring; I went to a lot of trouble to join it; therefore, it is not a boring group).

Dissonance was probably felt by the solvent/health man in the non-smoking section. It takes two forms: (1) I am a health enthusiast, but I smoke; (2) I am a smoker, but I am sitting in a non-smoking section. We know how he resolved the second simple instance: he moved elsewhere when he wanted to smoke and thereby removed that particular bit of dissonance. As to the first case, it is much more interesting. It would have created or *increased* dissonance for the health enthusiast both to support me (he would be thinking 'I am a smoker telling someone else to stop') and also to support the smoker ('I am a smoker advocating smoking in a non-smoking section when I care about other people's rights'). Hence his silence.

How would dissonance work with the dog owner, though? To get him to change his behaviour we have to create dissonance in him somehow. Our blatant attempt to do that ('You have a dog here'; 'You're in an area where dogs are prohibited') failed because he found a way to deny the applicability of the rule ('Small dogs do not count'). We could have tried to affect other attitudes of his, for example, the positive attitude that he probably holds about himself. We could have tried to make his positive view of himself inconsistent with his actions. (I once heard this used effectively on a plane: 'If you put your bag in that overhead rack it might fall on me and I know you'd feel bad about that. I'd prefer you not to feel bad so why don't you put it somewhere else?' It worked in that case.) We could have pointed out what dissonance he would feel about himself, what a jerk he would think he was, if a nice person such as he did something to upset a lot of other people, for instance, by letting his wild dog loose in a children's play area. But, because he is a stranger to us, we do not really know just by looking at him how much dissonance he can tolerate. Maybe he has a high threshold and can easily withstand it. Relevant to his tolerance here is the fact that, if he takes his dog away, he would have to move himself and his children and all his bags of shopping and the baby-buggy. If it comes to dissonance versus inconvenience, he may choose to tolerate the dissonance. As it turned out, in another brilliant stroke of human ingenuity, he picked up the dog and put it inside his coat, thus stopping it running around (that kept us happy), but not moving it from the play area (that kept him happy).

The dog owner's behaviour (bringing in the dog, and letting it loose) is what creates the difficulty and permits us to apply the principles of dissonance theory. What if he had not brought the dog in before we spoke to him – that is, what if we said our piece after he got his children out of the baby-buggy but before he let the dog through the gate?

Behavioural intentions

A key element of a person's attitudes to anything is provided by behavioural intentions (Fishbein and Ajzen, 1972). That is, the best predictor of someone's eventual performance of an action is not that person's expressed attitude to the act but his or her *intention* to perform it. So the best place to exert persuasive pressure is on the intention to perform the act rather than on the act itself. Once he had let the dog in he was committed, and a whole range of new psychological processes was triggered. Before he admits the dog, his intention to do so has not been put into effect, and we could influence his behaviour by influencing his intention.

Undoubtedly, our mistake was to wait until he had committed himself to bring the dog in with him. By attempting to get him to stop – rather than attempting to prevent him from starting – we affected his sense of freedom, and we initiated *reactance* (Brehm, 1966; Brehm and Brehm, 1981). Reactance is a state brought about by the feeling that our freedom has been constrained. When reactance is aroused, so the theory goes, we attempt to restore our lost freedom, to restate our right to enjoy it, or to regain our control over things. Research shows that reactance can lead people to do exactly the opposite of what they were requested to do – just to show that the persuader does not have control over them. 'This person told me to do X. Right, then! X is the last thing I'll do!' We have all seen other people do this, and, probably, we have all acted that way too. The dog owner was only being human: we should have acted sooner to prevent his reactance.

Problems with these ideas

In sum, then, even though I give these approaches sketchy coverage here because you can read them more fully in any text, you can see that there are problems that have led to them being reconsidered. To use their principles, we must know in advance just what would be 'consistent' for the target, and, therefore, how to inject enough uncomfortable inconsistency into a personal situation for the person to be sufficiently disturbed to want to remove it. When dealing with strangers, this is precisely the kind of knowledge about them that we never have. On the other hand, if we know the other person well, we can take account of individual personal styles and we need to talk to them differently based on that personal knowledge (Planalp and Garvin-Doxas, 1994).

A second reason why consistency theories are problematic is because they misrepresent human lives. We are not actually consistent, but often wish we were or try to represent ourselves as if we were. People have all sorts of double standards and can happily do things that (to an outside observer) appear to be inconsistent or illogical. From the inside, however, the blinding logicality and consistency of our own actions is only too apparent ('Small dogs don't count, so I'm being consistent'). Consistency theories will, in my opinion, never be accurate predictors of all behaviour, but they will often predict the ways in which we will report behaving or would like to behave, or would like to see ourselves – rather than what we actually do. They are of little use when we meet strangers, except in extremely vague and general ways. We have to know people better before we know how to create specific feelings of inconsistency without having them simply decide to dislike and ignore us. Thus we are likely to rely on well-known, generally effective means of organizing speech to persuade (the *logos* that I mentioned earlier).

Logos: messages and persuasion

In any situation, the pattern of the messages that we choose is fundamental but the extent to which the pattern is based on personal knowledge of target is quite varied. Some message structures are more persuasive than others (Dillard, 1989) as has been recognized since the time of Aristotle, who provided the term *logos* to apply to this aspect of persuasion. There is the 'foot-in-the-door' technique (i.e. asking for a small favour before asking for the big one), or the 'door-in-the-face' technique (i.e. asking for a big, unreasonable request, being refused, and then settling for a small request, which was actually the one you wanted all along). Thirdly, there is the 'low-ball' method, a technique that gets another person committed to something on the basis of false information (e.g. by quoting the costs as lower than they are). Once a person feels committed, he or she is likely to carry on with the behaviour even when hidden extras or increased costs are subsequently revealed.

'Foot in the door'   Door-to-door sales people use a method of trying to put a foot in the door – literally or figuratively – and getting the prospective client to make a very small and harmless-looking commitment initially (e.g. a commitment to approving the format of a series of books). Once that is made, the commitment is increased gradually (e.g. to taking the first volume of the series on approval, then to agreeing to have a few volumes in the home to see how the set looks, and so on up to the seller's original aim:

getting you to pay for 26 volumes). The technique is based on small increments of commitment at each stage so that the client really feels that each step is a logical and hardly noticeable progression from the previous step, until lo and behold, the client owns a fine, extremely expensive encyclopedia.

Would you erect a large and unsightly billboard in your back yard, even if it was for a good cause and encouraged careful driving? Not likely. In fact, only 16 per cent of residents in Palo Alto, California, agreed when asked directly (Freedman and Fraser, 1976). Of those who were first asked to put a small sticker on road safety in a window of their home, however, 55 per cent subsequently agreed to put up the large sign, too. Comparable results are found by several other researchers and DeJong's (1979) review of them concludes that the technique is effective as long as the initial request is small and when no compelling reasons, such as financial inducements, are offered for doing it.

One explanation is that the foot in the door works because the initial compliance allows the persons to feel good about themselves. Kraut (1973) finds that if people are 'labelled' positively when they give to one charity they give more to a second one also. The method of labelling is simple: 'You are really a generous person. I wish more people were as charitable as you.' For such an effect to work, however, the labelled action must be seen by the actor as resulting from 'internal' factors – those under the actor's own control – otherwise there is no credit for having acted that way. External causal factors – those not under the person's own control – often cause people to do things, so the positive label would probably not work if the actor felt that the actions were brought about by other than their personal free choice (Dillard et al., 1984).

Intelligent, generous, and discerning readers like you who have made a thoughtful choice in buying this book will obviously find many ways of using this method in predicaments with strangers and friends. The technique is useful only if we have control over the circumstances or can choose the precise timing of the requests. Also, a useful relationship can be established even by some very small expression of commitment to help – and that can then be exploited. For instance, Cook (1977) notes that some seducers first attempt to get a partner to do a small favour for them before they make any explicit sexual 'move', and they take willingness as an encouraging sign. Then they increase the scale of the requests and begin to steer to sexual themes.

'Door in the face'   Will persons who refuse a big demand be more likely to agree to a small one (the so-called door-in-the-face method)? In the original study of this possibility (Cialdini et al., 1975), subjects were first asked to serve as voluntary counsellors at a county juvenile detention centre for two years. Almost everyone turned this 'opportunity' down. When they were subsequently asked to agree to a much smaller request – that is, to chaperone some juveniles on a trip to the zoo – many did so.

The method seems to work if the initial request is almost ridiculously large, so that the person does not even entertain it as reasonable, and so does not feel negative about himself or herself when turning it down. It also works when the second request is made by the same person who makes the first one – possibly because we would feel bad about ourselves if we turn the same person down twice in a row. It would make us feel mean or unhelpful if we do this. The method is also more successful if the second, smaller request is related to the first, such as filling out a small insurance company survey after declining to fill out a much longer one (Mowen and Cialdini, 1980).

'Low ball'   The low-ball technique (Cialdini et al., 1978) consists of raising the cost of doing something, once the target (client) agrees to do it in ignorance of the true full costs. For instance, if you consent to show up for an experiment you will be more likely to agree to come before dawn if I hold off on information about the time it starts until after you agreed in principle to participate. This technique differs from the foot in the door only insofar as it involves initial commitment to the *same* behaviour that is ultimately requested, whilst foot in the door involves initial commitment to a *different* smaller request. It is useful in some circumstances (e.g. selling a car) and even more useful for prospective customers to be aware of. It really depends on there being little or no personal relationship between the people. It loses its effectiveness once we come to realize that someone might use it quite constantly. It is also an extremely offensive and exploitative approach, and will lose more friends than it will persuade, so it is typically a technique that does not work for (and is not normally chosen by) friends to use on one another.

Reflections

There is one odd implication in the material reviewed so far. It mostly assumes that persuasiveness 'resides' in the external characteristics of the persuader (e.g. we are persuasive because we dress well or look good); in the internal psychological structure of the target (e.g. people generally change their attitudes in the direction of consistency); or in the broad relationship of parts of the message to other messages that have recently been sent and received (e.g. persuasion follows recent rejection of other persuasion attempts). The effects are largely assumed to be absolute. The strategies are presumed to work irrespective of personal circumstances or of the situation or of the relationship between participants.

Also, the previous work assumes that our only goal is to persuade the other person, but in most predicaments we actually have multiple goals (Clark and Delia, 1979). For instance, we want to ensure no smoking in non-smoking areas, but we do not want to feel bad about ourselves; we want to stop someone letting their small dog into a children's playground, but we do not want to look to other people as if we are overreacting or officious; we want to get friends to do us a favour, but we certainly do not want to leave them feeling exploited or feel that we are abusing them or that we are 'bad people'. What is needed, then, is to recognize these multiple goals and explain the ways in which *relational* goals might affect the shape of requests that we make on top of other purely persuasive goals.

Was it something I said?

Let us assume that we all have a range of persuasive strategies to choose from in any set of circumstances (Miller and Boster, 1988; Miller and Parks, 1982); we choose different methods in different encounters, with different people, or on different occasions with the same person, or from circumstances that grow from our relationship to the listener or to the interaction. For instance, one thing to which we may give particular attention when trying to persuade friends or acquaintances is their social face and their sense of identity as good people. We want them to feel good as well as to do what we ask; we want them to continue to understand that we respect them even if we request their help with something personally inconvenient to them; we want them to appreciate the obligations of friendship but not to feel *too* obligated; we want to feel we are good people who are not too dependent or needy even when we have difficulties with which we need help.

Forms of a request   What are the factors that particularly influence the form of a request and represent our concern about how the other person feels? Two influences are variously called 'dominance and intimacy' (Cody et al., 1983), or 'status and familiarity' (Tracy et al., 1984). These focus on the amount of liking that exists between the two actors (or the degree to which they know one another) and on their relative status (cf. Chapter 1 on the form of language as a result of the status and solidarity variables). When we know, like, or have power over someone, then we choose strategies not used with strangers. The third factor that influences choice of message type is, rather naturally and predictably, the size of the request or the amount of inconvenience or imposition that will result for the target of the request. The larger the request or favour is, the more the requester takes account of 'felicity conditions' and 'face wants' (Tracy et al., 1984). 'Felicity conditions' refer to two elements of messages: (1) the speaker makes clear why the request is being made and hence establishes that there are legitimate needs for making it: (2) the speaker inquires about the hearer's willingness to perform the requested act (in other words, the person establishes that he or she is making a request rather than giving an order or asking for fulfilment of an obligation; Fitch, forthcoming). 'Face wants' refer to the concern that the speaker has for presenting a positive image of self and partner (Tracy et al., 1984). There are three elements to this:

1   Messages differ in the degree to which they acknowledge the hearer's desire to be liked and appreciated ('I really appreciate your help on this; you're very kind').
2   Messages differ in relation to the negative face wants of the hearer (i.e. the person's desires for autonomy, freedom of action and freedom from imposition). Speakers acknowledge this need by showing reluctance to impose on the hearer or by showing uncertainty in their request ('I hate to ask you this, but . . . would it be at all possible for you to . . . ?').
3   Messages differ in the attention they give to the speaker's own positive face (e.g. when we ask to borrow money we might make it clear that we have saved some already, but not enough). Note that attention to face wants directly relates to something that we have found here to be vital – making the other person feel good about himself or herself – and that felicity conditions do so less directly but still could help to do so.

Strategy selection   What strategies do we see ourselves having available to us and why do we make particular selections? Certain 'types' of person may habitually choose certain types of strategy or certain types of situation may lead to certain types of strategy-selections by more or less everyone. For instance, powerful people may regularly choose punitive strategies, explicitly or implicitly, and people who want to be seen as powerful may think that those strategies are the ones to use. Men and women may also choose typically different strategies; women are found to prefer to start with reward-based strategies, but their reaction to reluctance or noncompliance depends on the type and strength of the relationship between the two parties and the consequences for that (de Turck, 1985). When persuading acquaintances (as distinct from friends), we do choose persuasive strategies that do not 'give us a bad time' if things go wrong (Miller, 1982). Our first thought is 'What are the consequences for me if I do not succeed here or things go wrong?' On the other hand, when attempting to persuade friends, we avoid strategies that the target cannot resist without feeling obliged by friendship to do something for us that he or she would really much prefer not to (Miller, 1982). We ask 'What are the consequences for the friend and for our relationship if things go wrong?' Roloff et al. (1988) also show that the more intimate a person is with the target of the request, the less likely is any elaborate explanation of the request or any form of inducement. However, if the request is turned down, then intimates are more likely to come back with a less polite message than are people who are less intimate. The relationship between us and the target influences both the strategies and the messages that we choose.

Everyday talk as persuasive

Let us now explore some of the preceding issues from two new relational vantage points: first, from the assumption that, in everyday relational contexts, the two related parties are concerned about the preservation of their long-term relationship at least as much as they are concerned about persuading one another; second, from the point of view of the fact that all relationships and all persuasion occur in a network of other relations to which the partners are also attentive. Just as a person may not be willing to risk losing a good relationship with a partner in order to get a request fulfilled, so the person may be concerned about the good opinion of *other* close friends or family also and that concern can provide a powerful context for behaviour in persuasion.

One prominent influence on our behaviour is the way that we feel about ourselves and our way of handling a situation. Equally, we all like to feel satisfied not only with the outcome of an attempt at persuasion but with the manner in which we dealt with the situation. If we are deciding about ways to tackle a predicament or to get another person to do as we want, then our relationship with him or her may affect this assessment of our satisfaction following one or other of a choice of alternative strategies. Just think, if our neighbours turn their stereo up too loud, we *can* call the police, but it is not necessarily the best action from a long-term social or personal point of view. Even if the other person is a stranger to us, our satisfaction with the outcome may depend not only on getting what we want but on doing it in a way that reflects well on our self-image and social presentation. In negotiations, for instance, it often helps to enter with a claim for slightly more than we actually want so that we have something to give away as a concession that creates a favourable image of our reasonableness as negotiators. Likewise in everyday persuasion of acquaintances, we are likely to want to appear reasonable, fair, open-minded and as the sort of person who considers the partner and the relationship as well as the specific result of persuasion itself.

The relational context

An important everyday fact, then, is the significance of the persuasion attempt in the here-and-now of the person's social life: persuasion has consequences for me now here, yet other people might ultimately comment on the specific interaction between myself and the specific target. We often have to make persuasive attempts knowing that we must continue in the same social or relational situation afterwards or that other people will get to hear about it or that a particular outcome today could carry long-term relational consequences. If we try to get a neighbour to turn down the stereo, we may be making our future life less comfortable since the neighbour may become ill-disposed towards other requests and may become 'difficult', or other people may see us as interfering and troublesome and may start to gossip about how we behaved. Little persuasive attempts in the present can, therefore, have large personal and social consequences in the future. We would be making a big mistake if we regarded everyday compliance-gaining and persuasion as neatly packaged within the interaction itself, done at a distance from insistently helpful friends and friendly advisers, or out of the influence of gossip and group membership; or, if we saw 'compliance-doing' as a pure act of 'information processing' that is relatively rapid and based only on sensible logical, non-social principles, and is not mentally connected to the relational consequences that would fall out on the participants.

A second point is that compliance-gaining in everyday life might take up a lot of time if it violates friendship norms – we'd get into a long discussion about friendship and what it means. Persuasion can be a drawn-out process for other reasons in long-term relationships. It is not usually a simple, once-for-all event. The target is likely to resist us or challenge us, which will require us to take another shot. Furthermore, some compliance takes time to plan. Attempts to seduce a partner or have an essay grade changed by a familiar professor can be thought about or planned in advance, can be modified, and can be thought about later, too, if they fail the first time. Also, as Christopher and Frandsen (1990) showed (see Chapter 4 here), individuals often use clusters of sequential strategies in order to achieve such goals as premarital sexual intercourse and may persist over a longer timespan – say, several encounters. Thus selection of persuasive strategies within a friendship or romance is, I think, a developmental incremental activity rather than an isolated, one-off action. In close personal relation-ships the structure of messages is modified by the long-term context provided by the relationship and is not a 'pure' act of attitude change or persuasion deprived of that context.

Furthermore, when we look at the routine side of real life we see that our knowledge of one another helps us to plan and gives us some awareness of likely consequences since we know the target quite well. When we have to get a parent to lend us the car, persuade a friend to lend us a valuable book, or obtain an extension of a deadline for an assignment, there are inbuilt relational forces that affect not only the target of the persuasion but also the person attempting to achieve the outcome. For one thing, both parties have a view of themselves and the nature of their relationship – and probably wish to preserve it. Sometimes, we would rather give up on an argument than risk losing a friendship. For this reason, we shall most probably be unwilling to act in a way that threatens the relationship, and we may make this fact a key element in our persuasion attempt. If we make a request that we recognize is too demanding, we might choose to accompany it by some relational preservative like an appeal to the person's good nature, an offer to restore the balance one day, a reminder of a past occasion when the positions were reversed, or a reference to our overwhelming need and the role requirements of friendship. In other circumstances when the relation-ship is more formal, such as between teacher and pupil, such relational references will refer to the demands of the *role* and the participants are unlikely to persuade by trying to imply that there is a close personal friendship.

Once we recognize that most persuasions occur in such a context of living relationships – not only in partnerships but in networks – and in real social lives and within our long-term goals or projects, not just our short-term persuasive objectives, we see that we need to look carefully into the impact of such contexts on our attempts to gain compliance, including the moral context provided by our close associates (Klein and Johnson, 1997; Klein and Milardo, 1993). A very important fact that I have repeatedly alluded to in the course of this chapter has been the fact that relationships quite simply legitimate certain sorts of persuasion by their very existence: I may ask you to do something difficult for me simply by virtue of the fact that we are friends. Your friendship obliges you to perform certain kinds of supportive actions and the persuasion to perform them is inherent in the acceptance of the role of friendship. I may structure my request in a way that reminds you that you are a friend and that friends have to help one another: basically we both accept that friendship means that each of us should do things for the other's good and that's that. It would be quite ridiculous for us to spend a long time structuring persuasive arguments, getting our feet in the door or our doors in the faces of friends and parents and relatives in quite the way that some of the old research might lead us to expect to be necessary.

The moral context

One of the complaints I made earlier about classical research on attitude change is that it strips persuasion out of these everyday relational contexts that direct the way influence actually proceeds. We have now spent some time looking at the ways in which relationships themselves provide a context for persuasive attempts but I have not yet returned to a point I made at the start concerning the importance of the network and social context in which any individual persuasive attempt occurs. When we persuade a single individual our behaviour is open to the scrutiny of others either directly or as a result of the reports of either party to third parties. If someone tries to bully me, I may tell friends or family and the word could soon reach many other ears when each person tells their own friends and allies that 'X is a bully'. On top of that, the moral context provided by membership of a community also exposes our behaviour to the persuasive influence of social accountability: what I mean by that is that our own behaviour can be shaped and moulded not only by the influence of media or magazine ideals or cultural norms and prescriptives (as discussed in Chapter 1) but by the fact that our own behaviour is subject to the moral scrutiny of our specific community of acquaintances and our network of friends and relatives. When we deviate from agreed and desired goals, we may become the subject of gossip.

Gossip has long intrigued psychologists (Goodman and Ben Ze'ev, 1994; Suls, 1977), but it is only recently that scholars have begun to look at gossip not simply as a phenomenon of message transmission or social comparison (see above) but as a mechanism for social sanctioning, moral persuasion and relational structuring (Bergmann, 1993). When a person becomes the subject of gossip, the person is essentially being subjected to the moral judgement of the gossipers and the people's behaviour is made the subject matter of these people's social persuasions. Recognizing this, people very

---

Box 5.2   *Gossip and social order*

We often learn about other people from gossip and – let's be honest – a lot of daily communication is gossipy. The important thing to recognize is that this utterly trivial activity is highly significant in social life in general and relationships in particular. Not only is discussion of others with third parties a normal – if unreliable – source of information about other people, it also has other features discussed below.

Gossip serves to (mis)inform but also to entertain and amuse, yet it also serves to give a speaker status in a group since he or she knows something the others don't.

Gossip is usually about other people's private behaviour about which we can really actually know very little except though inference or speculation, which therefore involves a complicated mix of moral judgements and narratives that spin the story for us.

Gossip is often represented by the gossips as 'only trivial' or 'only a bit of fun' or something they are really 'not doing' ('I don't want to be a gossip but . . .', 'Don't think I'm prying but . . .'), since gossip *per se* is typically seen as a negative thing to be caught doing. However it is important in an obvious and non-obvious way. First it is obviously an important way of interpreting someone's behaviour and affecting their reputation. Second and less obvious, it is an important way of enforcing moral codes informally, by subjecting people to (the fear of) third party ridicule or censure (Bergmann, 1993).

---

often hold back from doing something just because they fear the consequence that the neighbours or the family might find out and disapprove; thus there is a hidden persuader in society that prevents activities that, if discovered, are likely to attract censure from others. Even relational behaviour itself is subject to the direct evaluation of third parties who may intervene and persuade the partners to behave differently, using the moral persuasive force of their position as representatives of the wider society in which the behaviour takes place (Klein and Milardo, 1993) or the right to comment on relationships that is conferred by their social position (in-laws do this a lot!). The tools for handling relational conflict itself also include the censure of outsiders' comments on the behaviour as a means of persuading people to cease and desist from the conflict (Klein and Johnson, 1997). As Bergmann (1993) notes, gossip is therefore a form of persuasion both active and passive: fear of becoming the subject of gossip passively persuades people not to engage in some forms of behaviour and the comments of other people can actively dissuade a person from some courses of action. Thus when we place persuasion in the everyday context of lived experience in relationships within a culture and its attendant expectations, we can see yet another side of it which is not reached by classic analyses of attitude change and persuasion: the moral and interactive relational context in which the persuasion is carried out.

The moral context is also easily recognized in cases where one person gives advice to another, since advice is often directly about choices of actions and so is morally loaded. Equally advice is often the same thing as social support as when it helps a person to solve a problem, supports their way of acting, or validates an alternative that they have proposed (Sarason et al., 1997). Furthermore, in long-term relationships the advice given to one person on a small matter may provide a basis for the two people to set up expectations of support and assistance in other contexts. For example, by finding frequently that Person X helps me with little tasks or talks constructively and encouragingly about daily trivia, I can form the impression that the person is a supportive and helpful friend. Thus, when there comes a need for some big help with something hugely disastrous or significant, it is this person rather than another person in my network to whom I would turn for support (Leatham and Duck, 1990). Daily conversations thus provide a subtle building of context for the provision of social support that merits more research attention. Such conversations also serve to structure networks for us mentally in the sense that from the experiences obtained in these trivial conversations we can build up some sense of the organization of our network (Milardo, 1992) into those who are best helpers, those who help under protest, and those who never help at all. Thus we build up a sense of the relative difficulty of persuading such persons to come in and make an effort for us when we need it (Leatham and Duck, 1990).

Persuading in relationships

Another example of relational persuasion is provided by the case of asking someone out on a first date and that typically involves either obvious or indirect persuasion. (Less well-studied is the way in which first dates are turned into second and subsequent dates (Sprecher and Duck, 1993), but that too can be seen as a persuasive activity at some level, and so can other relationship moves such as the invitation to have sex.) The traditional form here is for a man to ask out a woman (Mongeau et al., 1994), though I will look at other forms below, and show (as has been my theme in this chapter) that relational work like this involves a lot more than simple persuasion of one person by another even though it does include that. It is normal for a dating request to be made explicitly, and for the other person to respond to it with acceptance or rejection one way or another. You can probably reflect back through some of the other topics in the chapter here and see that persuading someone to go on a date involves issues of the legitimacy of the behaviour (is it an appropriate request to be making to this person in this situation?), some elements of making a person feel good about themselves (it is flattering to be asked in most cases, and bad to be rejected), and it could involve the careful structuring of the message in a way that plays into the target's face wants (see above). Some women report playing hard to get and making the man work harder by rejecting the first request in a way that implies that a second request would work and others report that there is sometimes an image problem involved if one accepts too quickly or too enthusiastically. Thus the request for a date involves many of the processes that I have talked about above.

Of course, the usual assumption is that the request for and acceptance of a date reflect the mutual attraction and desire for future interaction (Mongeau et al., 1994), though there can be multiple reasons for initiating a date (Lindsley, 1993). Men and women may initiate dates differently, given present social norms that typically presume that the man will be the one to ask. In the case where it is a woman who asks a man out on a first date, Mongeau and his colleagues (Mongeau et al., 1994) have found that men evaluate female behaviour on the subsequent date as reflecting *less* intimacy than the females reported feeling in the men's behaviour. Intriguingly, about 100 years ago the roles were reversed and the male was invited by the female to 'call' at the home (and hence to observe her domestic skills all the while under the vigilant supervision of her parents). For the last 50 years or so, the male typically invited the female to go on a 'date', but recently roles have equalized and either sex may invite the other out on a date. Some surviving expectations still persist, however, and a female who invites out a male may attract impressions of forwardness and sexual availability that her passive sisters do not (Mongeau et al., 1995). The broad truth seems to be that such stereotypes are moderating (Mongeau et al., 1994), though as a female's behaviour becomes more direct so it is regarded as increasingly unexpected (Mongeau et al., 1995). Curiously, although female-initiated dates are reported as actually being less intimate, as noted above, the males enter them with increased sexual expectations. Can you think of any reasons to explain this curious fact?

Although the first date is not the only experience that determines the form and future of a romantic relationship, it may set a tone that takes time to overcome and modify. For the reasons that a female initiation of a date may lead the male to greater expectations of sexual intimacy, the subsequent 'normal' level of interaction on the date may violate the male's expectations (Mongeau and Carey, 1996) and so set a pattern of decreased interest for later dates. However, since there are very few studies of the ways in which first dates are made to carry over or turn into second dates and thence into romantic relationships (Sprecher and Duck, 1993), we cannot do more than speculate about the sorts of persuasive communication, rhetorical strategy and expectancy creation that are involved here, though we can draw something from research on gay and lesbian relationships.

In the case of gay and lesbian relationships, Huston and Schwartz (1995) report that lesbians often do not feel comfortable making the first move to request a date, given that their primary socialization as women has been that they 'should' take a passive role in relationship initiation. Obviously this is overcome somehow and although the mechanisms are not well understood, it appears that some lesbians simply adopt a less passive and more initiative role that defeats their primary socialization. This does raise the interesting question of how people in general 'accomplish tasks for which they had little or no training as children or adolescents' (Huston and

Schwartz, 1995: 93), as well as the issue of whether any form of relationship training is something that any of us receives adequately in childhood and adolescence (Duck, 1991).

Research on gay men suggests that dating initiation is accomplished to a greater extent by situational manipulation, such as by seeking out establishments and contexts where people go to establish first contacts, such as gay bars. This puts the men in a context where dating moves are expected but the situation is complicated by the fact that this context also represents a setting where casual sex is often accepted more than some gay males seek (Huston and Schwartz, 1995), so that these men find themselves in a setting where 'sex is expected' to result from date initiation and they may not feel right about that. However, the situation is interesting because the context itself provides some of the justification for the activity that occurs there and hence the persuasive force of context is once more indicated. In considering relational persuasion in everyday life relationships, it is clearly inadequate to focus only on message structure or on balance or on dissonance and to ignore the power of context and situation or social expectations and history as important contextual elements in persuasion that ratify and warrant certain types of compliance or persuasion-attempts. As I have tried to show through the chapter, such contexts are provided by cultural norms, places, situations, relationships, times and other contexts that were discussed earlier in the book. In short, persuasive dealing with strangers and friends is a contextual activity and relationships are contexts: it's not all about psychological manipulations.

Summary

We have looked at some real-life examples where one person chose to try to stop another person from doing something he wanted to do and I have tried to draw out the ways in which the relationship between speaker and target modifies what happens there. I described, and tried to apply, a number of techniques that have been studied by social psychologists and communication scientists for many years, but I have emphasized the ways in which these overlook the importance of the context provided by the relationships between speaker and target also, and should shift the focus of persuasion towards real-life relational experience and away from idealized sorts of persuasive contexts only. By contrast I have shown that in everyday real life, the relationship between the persuader and the target is vital, and there are a number of ways in which the social and relational context for real-life decision making could affect the ways in which we decide to attempt to persuade someone else. However small many of our persuasions are in real life, many of them can be drawn-out and anxiety-provoking in ways not true of persuasion about 'big' attitudes (for example, about nuclear power or the environment or politics). Our decision making and persuasion in the context of our everyday life concerns involve us in thinking about the consequences for our relationships with our partners, friends and work colleagues, as well as in simply assessing the merits or demerits of two sides of an argument or of two alternatives that lie open to us. I discussed the role of gossip in indirectly but firmly persuading people to do moral things, and I looked at a number of interpersonal and relational activities that are at their roots persuasive, such as asking people out on dates or sharing advice and requesting social support. My main points were that such activities are ones that we slither into during everyday life without special signposts; they happen as a routine part of everyday life and emerge seamlessly from it. They are played out within cultural norms about 'who does what', and various personal and relational concerns about one's self-image, the cultural practices of friendship, and the roles of men and women. It makes no sense – at least it makes no sense to me – to try to explain persuasion merely in terms of the psychological features of individuals that take no account of such important hidden persuaders as context and network and experience of the society.

Further reading

Bergmann, J.R. (1993) *Discreet Indiscretions: The Social Organization of Gossip*. New York: Aldine deGruyter.
Billig, M. (1991) *Ideology and Opinions: Studies in Rhetorical Psychology*. London: Sage.
Duck, S.W. (ed.) (1993) *Social Contexts of Relationships*. (Vol. 3) *Understanding Relationship Processes*. Newbury Park, CA: Sage.

6

Human Relationships Take the Witness Stand

'Psychologists and other researchers are becoming more sophisticated about the legal system.' (Bartol and Bartol, 1994: 193)

The previous chapter looked at the role of relationships in persuasion in general. The present chapter follows on directly from that by looking at relational influences on persuasion in the particular context of the court-room. At first sight, the workings of the law and the workings of relation-ships have little in common, except that jurors form impressions of witnesses and defendants much as strangers form impressions of one another in potential relationships. Yet jurors – especially in long and important trials – also form relationships with one another, and other processes of relational persuasion are silently present in many other ways we shall explore. Furthermore, the law is connected to relationships in other ways that are not immediately obvious. Relationships are personal and particular whereas the law is public and general, yet there are laws about personal relationships (against domestic violence; for marriage; custody rights; granting or restricting access to sexual favours, and so forth). Relationships also demand our exclusive loyalty to specific others to whom we are committed through thick and thin ('. . . in sickness and in health'), and to whom we grant special privileges, information, services and favours. For example, we are supposed to protect our children even when they are ill-behaved or insubordinate and parents may be held legally liable for the actions of their children. We are also expected to look after our parents when they become old and frail, to defend our friends when they are in trouble or need our help, and not to abuse our spouses. These are special responsibilities and requirements of the social norms of relationships. By contrast, the law often expects us to treat all others equally without fear or favour. For these sorts of reasons, although the processes of relating are important they occasionally conflict with expectations of the law and are also surprisingly overlooked as forces in the actual operation of the law and the legal system.

Relationships and the law

Even given the belief in equality and indifference, the law does recognize relationships in various ways – for instance, in giving parents certain rights to control the future of their own children but not the future of the children of other people at random; allowing tax breaks to couples who are legally married but not to couples who are not; limiting the extent to which spouses can be forced to testify against one another; or permitting extension of legal liability from one person to another (e.g. making a parent legally liable for the actions committed by the parent's child; Rubin, 1987).

Also the law has recently begun to get interested in whether cohabitors are, to all intents and purposes, rather like spouses as far as the rights to property are concerned after a relationship breakup. In 'palimony' trials, there are sometimes questions about the measurement of love and the extent to which there are different types of love (e.g. whether live-in lovers are in love in the same way as spouses are, see Chapter 2 here), how love should be valued, what it entails, how much an intertwining of daily life routines is an indicator of the existence of a 'relationship' and so forth. The law also defines certain sorts of relationships as acceptable and others as not acceptable. For example, it does not accept marriages between children of five years of age, prohibits incestuous marriages, revolts against sexual relationships between adults and children, widely approves of single serial marriages between adults of different sexes but disapproves of bigamy and adultery and in many places marriages between people of the same sex, and recognizes the rights of spouses to inherit one's property under certain circumstances where a will does not exist.

The law even extends its interest to NVC (nonverbal communication; cf. Chapter 1) where in a recent case of Pennzoil versus Texaco, the jury apparently placed great weight on the fact that an 'agreement in principle' was sealed nonverbally by a handshake between the parties (Rubin, 1990a). Also there is increasing evidence that trial judges' NVC can have unwanted effects on the outcome of a trial, such that 'appellate courts have cautioned repeatedly that juries in criminal trials accord even the most subtle behaviours of judges great weight and deference. One judge concluded that juries "can easily be influenced by the slightest suggestion coming from the court, whether it be a nod of the head, a smile, a frown, or a spoken word"' (Blanck et al., 1990: 653).

Clearly also the law is the only way to establish or end the very existence of certain types of relationship whether these be contractual partnerships or the more routine pairings of life. Marriage, after all, results *only* after a legally recognized ceremony and so does divorce, if you call that a ceremony. Further, by refusing to recognize same-sex marriages in certain places, the law runs directly into conflict with relationship practices of certain groups and so intrudes into the personal sphere (Huston and Schwartz, 1995). Lastly, the legal system is able to break up (by a legal divorce) those families that it formerly recognized as legitimate, to set limits on the kinds of frequency of meetings between children and non-custodial parents, and to regulate the sorts of behaviour that married couples can perform with one another (for example certain kinds of sexual practices, such as sodomy, are illegal in some states in the USA whether or not the partners are married).

Consider other connections also between law and relationship processes. Now that the previous chapter has looked at interpersonal persuasion in everyday life, what about special persuasive circumstances, like trials, where the whole point is to persuade a jury of 12 people who have just entered a new relationship with one another? We know the importance of the topics covered so far (NVC, language, space-usage, liking/disliking, interpersonal persuasion, etc.), so we can expect that they are also relevant to the court- room and that they help us to increase our understanding of what goes on there. My purpose here is not to give an exhaustive review of work on law and social behaviour, but rather to apply specifically the earlier material on human relationships to supplement the understanding of courtroom behaviour by showing its *relational* underpinnings. I also seek to raise some issues about the role of *relationship* processes in such occurrences as courtroom cross-examination or jury decision making which have previously not been fully researched.

There are many questions about the legal process that interest social scientists and several have a relational substructure that is presently just implicit. For example, although Rubin (1990b) points out his excitement as a social scientist learning to practise law, he does not mention its obvious relational underpinnings. He says he recalls 'being struck by the central importance of psychological assumptions, not only with regard to such psycho-legal staples as insanity and criminal intent, but also with regard to such commonplace questions as what constitutes "acceptance" of an offer (in contract law), what makes a payment to a former employee a "gift" (in tax law), and what sort of behaviour is "negligent" (in the law of torts)'. I want you to notice how much relationship research has to add to such things as gifts between friends, understanding of acceptance of a sexual proposition or a request for a date, or negligence in caring for a friend. I also believe that lawyers will begin to appreciate the ways in which rela- tionship research can feed into their work, through the elaboration of the ways in which relationships are defined in practical daily life and the ways in which acquaintances treat each other (Duck, 1994), the expectations that relationship partners form toward each other or the schemata by which they judge the existence of relationships (Andersen, 1993). In cases where the breakdown of relationships is at issue, then the assessment of relationship quality against prototypical expectations for love could be relevant (Fehr, 1993), or the role of parental styles of education about relationships (Pettit and Clawson, 1996) could be an important factor in a decision about suitability for custody.

How can we apply relationship research to legal issues? For one instance, we have already seen how language and relationships influence one another, convey relational information about liking and trust, or indicate power differences, such as we considered in Chapters 1, 3 and 4, so we could look at *relational* implications of language in the courtroom. We are ready, then, to explore the ways in which lawyers use such things as relational linguistic 'tricks'. We can also think about the relationally based persuasion that goes on in court, and will revisit some of what was learned in Chapter 1 on relational language forms and styles as well as relational persuasion from Chapter 5. Another area of research concerns the influence of the personally attractive or unattractive characteristics of the defendant upon the outcomes of trials and whether good looks lead to good verdicts – or to put it another way, whether the fair-looking get greater fair-ness. We will thus revive some of the issues about attraction to others (dealt with in Chapters 2 and 3). Does physical attractiveness improve your chances of getting a verdict of not guilty? We are ready to look at that one in terms of the influence of liking on social judgements. A final set of issues concerns the ways in which jurors, as a group, reach their decisions. Given the mission of this book, we could ask a relatively new question about the relational underpinnings of jury decisions: how do relationships form between jury members and do these relationships influence trial verdicts? Are powerful members of smaller juries more likely to establish the kinds of influence that come from liking than they are in larger groups? We could also look at the ways in which personal contact between jurors influences the manner in which decisions are reached and whether the jurors are likely to consider the detail of evidence in an *interpersonal and relational* context. For example, are the personal dynamics between jurors any more or less influential than the facts of the case? Are jurors likely to be swayed by the evidence or also by the personalities of the other jurors *discussing* that evidence? I will propose that relational principles and a knowledge of relationship processes help us here to deal with such questions.

These are some new ways in which I shall add relational research into an examination of the court and its activities (relational language; physical attractiveness of defendant; relationship issues in juries). They are all closely related to the issues that we have been dealing with so far and help to show that research on relationships can illuminate questions explored by other social scientists and by practising legal professionals. We can begin to look at these matters by going to the very roots of legality and looking at the ways in which the law makes assumptions about law-abidingness.

Assumptions of the law versus results of empirical studies

Do lawyers' assumptions about human nature – or lawyers' models of human beings – match up with research on daily relational interactions? For example, take the law's abstract concepts like the 'reasonable person'. Juries are often instructed that the conduct of a 'reasonable person' is not the same as jurors would do in the circumstances, nor even what the average person would do in similar circumstances, but what this 'reasonable person' would do, having account of all the facts. You, or the average person, for example, might react angrily to an insult and lash out, but a reasonable person might not. This makes the concept essentially non-empirical: in other words, it asks juries to think hypothetically and to detach themselves from their daily experience. This would be like asking you to imagine what the perfect student might be like on Mars: you'd have a few ideas culled from your experiences here on Earth, but you might find it hard to imagine what difference it might make being green and having your eyes on stalks. As I have been noting throughout the book, real-life relationships are experienced as cumulative, sequential and patterned even if variable. The cumulative weight of repeated humiliations is more important in explaining someone's sense of shame and anger in a relationship (Retzinger, 1995), or one person's oppression of another in a relationship (West, 1995) than is the occurrence of a single act of humiliation. Thus, whereas a reasonable person faced with a single insult may shrug their shoulders and let it pass, someone who has experienced many insults and much humiliation may regard the latest insult as another escalation in a patterned sequence (Scheff and Retzinger, 1991) and hence as something patterned all together into their system of meaning (Duck, 1994a). For this reason, the *relational context* of specific actions is relevant to the interpretation of the response (Duck et al., 1997).

The law, however, represents a relatively hypothetical environment. For example, the law assumes that 'reasonable people' do not take account of their social and personal relationships in deciding whether to report a crime, even if that report will adversely affect their friendships, marriages or social relationships. Yet stop for a minute: do you think you would find it harder to report on a crime committed by your enemy than by your father, for example? As Rubin (1987) indicates, the law expects that children, in most circumstances, will testify against their fathers if called upon to do so and can be punished for not doing so. This is one clear case where the law assumes that something – a higher duty – should be the case even though it cuts right across relational norms and experiences of everyday people.

Crime and crime reporting

If we can assume some effect of '*who* you know', can we expect an effect of '*what* you know' from daily life and from your interactions with people to whom you feel close? Do everyday folk take the same view of the nature of criminality as the law does? Obviously, people's attitudes to crime, to criminals, or to criminal acts will depend on what they think criminal acts are and the relational environment or social network in which one lives. If someone you love does something criminal would you feel a stronger urge to protect and be loyal to the person or to be a good citizen and turn them in to the police? Is it a crime not to prevent a crime (without actually assisting), for example? If people don't think something is a crime or if they happen to believe that a given law is unwise (as, say, many people believed that the laws prohibiting alcohol in the USA in the 1920s were) then they are less likely to report those whom they see breaking it. If you think that what has happened doesn't amount to a criminal offence, or you are not aware that there is a crime involved, then you won't report it. If you are ignorant of what the law says in a particular case, then you wouldn't go and report to anybody that someone has broken it. If the general attitude in your network is that the law is unfair or biased against your group then perhaps it is 'reasonable' in such a relational setting to be suspicious of law officers or to experience a lot of social pressure from friends to ignore or disrespect the law and its agents. In totalitarian states, fear of being exposed or betrayed by others for failing to report crime can lead to people exposing or betraying others so that they can be seen as good citizens (Mamali, 1996). Also in such contexts, citizens develop warning codes (like 'personal idioms' in Chapter 1) in order to alert one another that a third person present is not to be trusted (Mamali, 1996). In our own real living world, too, where daily contact with friends and networks is the experience of life (Milardo and Wellman, 1992), it is reasonable to assume that daily interaction reinforces the attitudes or beliefs of both the individual and the group in which the person relates to others (Duck et al., 1997), and that people develop relational systems so that they can balance civil duty against personal relational responsibility (Mamali, 1996).

Clearly, then, a network's beliefs about criminal offences will influence our behaviour in dealing with them. What the law actually says, however, is that every citizen has to be presumed to know what the law is and, by and large, is presumed to accept it. You may not escape punishment by claiming to be unaware that your action was against the law; you are supposed to know what is against the law and you are supposed not to do it. Of course, this assumption is partly expedient. If anyone could claim ignorance of the law then we'd all be able to get off the charges for each first offence against a particular law. As John Seldon put it in 1689, 'Ignorance of the law excuses no man [*sic*]: not that all men know the law, but because 'tis an excuse every man will plead and no-one can tell how to confute him.'

The law also assumes that you should be concerned to uphold the law. This is a different point since a lot of people know what the law is and don't try to uphold it. You are subject to prosecution for your own violations, of course, and should not aid and abet others, nor conspire with them when they commit crimes, even if they are your best friends. The law also assumes that you must act in a socially responsible manner even if it is not in your best interests personally. For instance, even if it puts you physically at risk you may still be required to help the police to pursue or restrain a fugitive. There are some crimes which are completely defined by the fact that you have failed to carry out this duty. For instance, har-bouring criminals is an offence which simply means you are not living up to the duty of reporting on people you know are criminals, even if they are your relatives or friends. Secondly, being an accessory after the fact (in other words, you weren't involved in the crime itself, but you helped somebody after they had done it) is another crime because it defies this duty to assist. The final example, an obvious one (receiving stolen goods), means that you weren't actually involved in the theft but you accepted goods knowing or believing that they were stolen and didn't report the fact or give them back.

Box 6.1   When is a crime not a crime?

Are other people's relationships just their own business? A particularly startling study of the belief that they are our own business also indicates the subtle role of relationships in the legal arena. Shotland and Straw (1976) staged an assault in an elevator – using a man and a woman confederate. Whenever the elevator stopped where there were people outside, the woman would scream and the man would appear to be assaulting her. What would you do if you saw this happen? What the subjects did, by and large, was nothing. Most people outside the elevator wouldn't do anything at all if the woman just shouted for the man to leave her alone. A more effective strategy for the woman was to shout 'I don't know you.' People intervened if the woman made it clear that the assaulter was a stranger – otherwise they apparently assumed that the combatants *did* know one another: for example a common assumption was that it was a marital tiff or an argument between boyfriend and girlfriend, that it was none of the bystanders' business to intervene. Apparently people think it is 'OK' for men to batter their wives or girlfriends, but it is not all right for them to batter women that they don't know! So not only does a presumed human relationship between two persons influence observers' likelihoods of stopping an assault, the relationship creates evident dangers also.

People generally fail to report shoplifting, particularly when there is a readily identifiable victim, like a large corporation which, they felt, could absorb the costs of minor thefts (Gelfand et al., 1973).

Persons from small towns or rural areas are more likely to report shoplifters than are persons from large cities (Gelfand et al., 1973).

The more valuable the item stolen, the more likely it is that the shoplifter will be reported (Hindelang, 1974).

There is no clear sex difference. Whilst Dertke et al. (1974) found that more females than males reported a shoplifter, Gelfand et al. (1973) found the opposite, while several studies find no effects (e.g. Bickman and Green, 1977).

If a person is made responsible for the items stolen (e.g. 'Please watch my bags while I go to the ticket counter'), then that person is more likely to pursue and stop the thief (Moriarty, 1975).

All of the above examples imply a duty not only not to commit a crime but also to report one if you observe it being committed by anyone else or come to know that it has been committed (see Box 6.1). Interestingly, all of these crimes arise from *relationships* with the 'real' criminal, or else from your decision to do something that, in other circumstances, would be regarded as a prototypically friendly action (such as helping somebody, giving aid and comfort, taking care of their property for them . . .). Nevertheless, the law assumes that legal duty can be expected to overpower feelings of relationship: in a very poignant way in some cases, then, the law pits the prohibitions of citizens' duty against the social norms for relating.

In everyday life you obviously have human relationships with the people you live or associate with, and there are social and relational consequences that will make you want to treat those people in special ways (see Box 6.1). The law, however, assumes that you will not – for example, it assumes that you will rat on a friend who commits a crime. But I'd bet you would consider the social and relational consequences first, and assess whether you'd be subjected to rejection by friends, social disapproval, unpopularity in the neighbourhood, or exclusion (West, 1995) or whether the civil consequences would outweigh the relational ones (Mamali, 1996). For most of us, close relationships may matter more than the carriage of justice about a petty crime. Thus the decision whether or not to report a crime is at least complicated by human relationships. The same thing holds what we found in the previous chapter: namely, that the claim 'I don't do this for everyone, but because it's you I will . . .' will deflect the processes that would otherwise be expected to operate. Likewise, as J. West (1995) shows, many social institutions such as the Church take on a special responsibility for putting relationships first and holding marriages together at all costs, even if it is sometimes best for a wife to get out to escape abuse. In short, the general human willingness to act as good citizens is affected by the nature of human relationships in that culture. All the same, our relationships are sometimes regarded as more important than our personal suffering precisely because we all live in personal communities where specific loyalty to friends or spouses may be counted higher than some generalized duty as a citizen or personal pain.

Trial by jury: interpersonal influence in the legal process

Having shown how the existence of human relationships between people complicates their decisions and operation on legal/criminal issues, let us now go into the courtroom and see how human relationships research illuminates that august institution. First I want to make a short – but relevant – digression about the legal system. Although we tend to take the English and American legal systems as 'normal' and right, there are in fact many different systems which are used to try people, some of which are to establish guilt or innocence and some of which serve other social functions (Cooke, 1990). In France, for example, the evidence is sifted in advance of the trial by an examining magistrate. He or she has powers to call witnesses to give evidence, to recall them to give evidence again, to cross-examine them, to examine them in private if desired, or in places other than a courtroom, and has various other powers, too. By the time the French 'trial proper' occurs, the assumption that the person is *guilty unless proved innocent* is actually more sensible than it sounds to those of us familiar with the opposite assumption in the USA and UK.

By contrast, a major purpose of the Chinese legal system is intended to be to provide educative functions *after* the establishment of the defendant's guilt (Berman, 1977). A large part of the trial process is thus devoted first to developing correct thinking in the criminal who is on trial, and second to reinforcing good citizenship in the non-criminal observer of the trial by showing everyone what was wrong with the criminal's thinking when he or she committed the crime. In such trials the establishment of guilt or innocence is not the only point: their point is also to illustrate what was wrong with the logic or state of mind of the criminal at the time of the offence, and to encourage public repentance – over and above the imposition of punishment for the offence (Berman, 1977). In Chinese law the function is thus also persuasive: to change attitudes and reinforce, amongst non-offenders, their beliefs in the basic wisdom and goals of Chinese society. For this reason the Chinese law and the legal professionals have a 'nurturing role' intended to guide, train and improve the logic of the criminal and the public. Therefore the criminal's extensive recounting of shame and repentance is a major feature of a Chinese trial.

By contrast with these systems, the English and American legal systems are most concerned first with the establishment, *during the trial*, of guilt or innocence and second with punishment of the guilty. Although some decisions about guilt or innocence take place before the trial (e.g. the decision by a client and the lawyers over the plea to be entered – guilty or not guilty) and may even involve the lawyers from both sides (e.g. plea bargaining), guilt or innocence is primarily established solely and exclusively in the court during a trial – and the trial is held in a courtroom, not at the scene of the crime. Although this system may strike us as perfectly natural because we are familiar with it, it has a strange and unusual feature: what happens in court is the only thing that counts. In essence, one side presents a persuasive argument and the other side tries to cut it down, based on the credibility of witnesses, on the plausibility of evidence, on the likelihood that X or Y 'fact' was true at the time of the crime – in short, on the *persuasiveness* of one side against the other.

Such trials have their origin way back in English history where guilt or innocence was established on the basis of a test or trial. The assumption was that a decision could be made by God, who would indicate what the truth was. Accordingly the ordeals were 'attended with elaborate religious ceremony, which accounts for the credence placed in their efficacy' (Walker and Walker, 1972: 15). The test or trial was put into one of several forms such as a trial of strength or trial by ordeal. One method ('trial by ordeal') involved making the accused person hold a red hot bar of metal or put a hand in boiling water for a given length of time. The hand was then bandaged up and left for some days. If after that time it had come out in a blister or the hand had not healed, that was taken to mean that God was indicating that the person was guilty, and if the hand didn't come out in the blister that meant that he or she was innocent (or dead from the wound). A similar idea worked for witches: trial by ordeal for alleged witches involved binding them hand and foot and putting them in a sack to be thrown in a river. If they floated, it meant that the water rejected them because of their guilt and if they sank it meant that the water accepted them and they were innocent – but again, probably dead by the time anybody pulled them out. In any case, the guiding idea in such trials was to refer the issue of guilt or innocence to God, who would indicate the verdict by means of a sign ('verdict' incidentally originally meant 'statement of truth' rather than the present-day meaning of 'result', because in those days the public belief was that God somehow pointed to the truth of the matter at issue by means of a sign).

Other kinds of trial were 'trial of strength' or 'trial by combat' and in both cases this was originally reserved for the knightly class – people whose rank or nobility allowed them to carry weapons. The idea was that two opposing parties fought it out between themselves and the one who was left alive or still willing to continue at the end was presumed to have God and right on his (in those days) side and hence to be the innocent one. Not unnaturally several alternative forms of trial were developed, one of which relied originally on human relationships quite explicitly. This one (the 'wager at law') involved the defendant producing a number of friends or acquaintances (generally 12 of them, so the size of your network was important then too) who, amidst appropriate religious ceremony, would wager their immortal souls on an oath that the accused was innocent (and, for those interested, the word 'jury' is actually derived from the ancient French word – juree/jurer, from the Latin *jurare* – meaning 'to swear on oath'). In an age where such oaths about eternal life would be taken quite as seriously as we would regard open heart surgery without anaesthetic, it was doubtless difficult to obtain the necessary social support in cases where guilt was even possible let alone where it was probable or certain (Walker and Walker, 1972).

The original basis of trial by jury thus introduces one important relational aspect of legal process: the accused's relationship to the jury. Trial by jury originally introduces the notion of convincing 12 *acquaintances* that you are innocent and thus friendship is an ancient forerunner of the jury system. It was also supposed to be done by 12 people (men, of course, in those days) who were of equal rank to the accused, who were from the same community, and who therefore were familiar with the life circumstances and daily routines of the situation in which the accused may have been before the alleged crime. In these ancient times, *relationships* and everyday routines thus became the basis for our present-day legal system's trial by jury. Nowadays the jury is not on one side or the other, and indeed, it is strongly intended to be impartial and *not* to have any social or personal relationship with any party in the trial.

At first an accused could not be compelled to submit to trial by jury without first consenting, but a refusal to plead was often taken as an admission of guilt and, in the case of a crime, the accused could be subjected to 'inducements' to plead, such as being crushed by lumps of iron (*'peine forte et dure'*) until either consent or death resulted. Nice people, our ancestors! Actually this procedure was not formally abolished in the UK until 1772, when the courts decided simply to accept a refusal to plead as an admission of guilt.

If you had power in a society like that, what would *you* do? . . . Of course you would and so did they: they allowed themselves 'understudies' to undergo the trial for them. In the case of trial by combat, many people in

---

Box 6.2   Images of the trial

Miller and Boster (1977) present three different images of the trial:

1   The trial as a rational, rule-governed event. This is perhaps the most widely held view of the trial, much supported by TV melodramas in which clever attorneys argue rationally and skilfully against one another, the victor being the hero (who brings brilliant argument, new testimony or perspicacious deductions to bear). Unfortunately, as Miller and Boster indicate, lawyers often break the rules (e.g. by deliberately introducing inadmissible evidence that will affect the jury, knowing that, even if the judge directs them to ignore it, the jury probably can't).
2   The trial as a test of credibility. There is more on this in the text of the chapter, but essentially the model relies on the idea that the opposing sides are in a search for credibility rather than, necessarily, for the truth. See text.
3   The trial as a conflict-resolving ritual. In this model, trials are essentially social rituals that take the place of other ways of resolving conflict, like fighting or arm-wrestling. See the text of the chapter for an account of the evolution of trials that supports this notion to some extent.

---

the knightly class preferred to delegate their possible death to someone else and employed champions to fight the trials of strength on their behalf, so that even if they lost the fight, they did not also die in the process. In the course of time these champions eventually evolved into lawyers who spoke, rather than fought, on your behalf! Originally a counsel was allowed to speak on your behalf only on matters of law, not on issues of fact, and a person could not necessarily call witnesses nor give evidence on his or her own behalf. In those days also (i.e. fifteenth-century England until 1670 and Bushell's case) a jury could be fined for reaching a verdict that the judge didn't agree with or considered perverse (in fact in recent times, judges agree with juries in 79 per cent of cases anyway; Saks, personal communication). In a trial by combat you would obviously try to pick the physically strongest understudy; in the case of trial by our system you are inclined to pick somebody who is a good advocate or a strong and inventive speaker (if you can afford it) and has the best record of persuasive skills.

The idea that remains from the original system is that you are represented by some kind of 'champion' and that the two sides of the case are put by these two adversaries (defence and prosecuting lawyers) – which leads to it being called the 'adversarial system' (see Box 6.2). Some countries do not follow or adopt the adversarial system and in these cases the court or the judge does the examining of witnesses instead (Cooke, 1990). In the latter society, the judge or examiner asks the questions and interprets the answers, can ask whomever he or she wants whenever he or she wants and can call them back again. This differs from the adversarial system where one side presents its case and is followed by the other side presenting its case, which is a notable feature of the Anglo-Saxon system. Here the judge's role is one of ensuring fair play and acting as a general guide to the jury rather than interrogating witnesses. In this system, the pursuit of the 'whole truth' is not really the goal: rather (at least in criminal cases) it is a test of the prosecution evidence and an attempt to assess whether a case can be proven beyond a reasonable doubt by persuading the impartial jurors by convincing argument (Mortimer, 1983).

The system also has rules for excluding evidence that might be unsafe or unfair (such as hearsay, or confessions obtained by force), but human stereotypes and the effects of human relationships can probably never be completely excluded from any system that runs on human fuel.

Deciding the facts

There is one key reason why this background, whilst brief and a little superficial, is significant when we try to apply relational principles to the courtroom. In the system which has evolved in our particular society, (legal) truth is established on the basis of plausibility and credibility. The issue in such a trial is whether the witnesses are *believed* at the time – not whether their statements are 'objectively' accurate. Also, because of the emphasis on establishing guilt or innocence during the course of the trial in the courtroom, there are rarely attempts to assess whether the claims of the witnesses are true by other means except than just asking them more questions. If I say that something is true then I could be challenged only by showing that I look like a liar or by someone assessing whether my claims seem to make coherent sense, by reference to their own internal logic, their agreement or conflict with common sense, how they match up with the statements of other witnesses or experts and their ability to withstand attempts to make them look wrong-footed or appear implausible. It is very rare for the court (for instance the judge) to examine a scene of crime and return to court saying 'Look, you've told us this is a six-inch line, and it's an eight-inch line, therefore, you are a liar' and for the jury then to decide whether to believe the witness or not. Instead a lawyer will say 'You said it was a six-inch line, other witnesses have said that it was larger, and I put it to you that it is an eight-inch line.' The important psychological point in such trials is therefore whether witnesses can be made to look as if they know what they are talking about. Thus the whole issue of the factors that make people seem credible to others (see Chapter 5) becomes relevant. As we have seen, relationship factors influence judgements of credibility and authority much more than has previously been realized.

One important point in criminal trials, then, is that juries – people – have to decide the facts of the case as presented in court, because the law assumes that the people on the jury go in with neutral and unfettered minds that they will use reasonably and rationally and independently of personal, relational or 'irrelevant' influences in the court or the jury room. Lawyers, on the other hand, assume that jurors are cauldrons of biases; lawyers therefore have instigated considerable research into juror biases (Saks, 1986). What lawyers forget is that relationships, rather more than abstract attitudes, account for the lion's share of our special preferences and treatment in real life and these are to a large extent excluded by the provision that requires the jury to have no relationships with the parties to the case or with the lawyers. This is particularly important because the whole issue in a court is whether or not somebody is found guilty – yet guilt is determined in law, not just by what the accused persons actually did, but by what the jury *thinks* they did.

The jury may have to decide whether the defendant had the required intent at the time the crime was committed, or, if the person admits the intent, to decide whether it was criminal, and so the jury's biases and presuppositions could have life or death importance. Here the law uses the concept of *mens rea* (which is to say, a guilty mind). There is 'specific intent' (related to specific purposes) or 'general intent' (which may be relevant in cases of negligence or recklessness). Your act will be defined as criminal only if you had bad intentions or criminal motives (*mens rea*) when you did what you did. If you had no *mens rea*, your act could have been accidental – and the consequences for you are different. If you happen to be cleaning a shotgun and you shoot somebody with it by accident (i.e. without *mens rea*) that is probably an accident but not murder. If, on the other hand, you take a shotgun, deliberately aim it at somebody knowing that it is loaded, and deliberately pull the trigger intending to kill them, then you have *mens rea* – you have a guilty mind or criminal intent. You are therefore guilty of murder, not of causing an accident, even if the effect for the victim is the same in both cases (i.e. death).

What is important as far as the law is concerned is your state of mind at the time when the trigger was pulled and this, of course, is one thing that juries often have to make complicated attributions and inferences about (Sarat and Felstiner, 1988). One of their jobs is to assess the defendant's likely state of mind at the time of the offence. In earlier chapters we looked at the ways in which the formation of a relationship with someone is a process of building up a map of their meaning system (Duck, 1994a). In long-term face-to-face relationships these maps can be modified, tested, and generally improved by actual conversation with the partner, by observing the partner in different settings, and by gaining some sense of the varieties of their behaviour (Duck, 1994a). In a trial, a juror's exposure to the defendant is brief, relatively uniform, and either black (prosecution) or white (defence), a situation that subverts the normal processes of getting to know someone and is likely to increase the chances of the effects of bias. In looking at trials, then, it is important that we think about the biases, prejudices and unfounded theories of personality that may add to the other problems that afflict a jury. The point is quite simply that the jury is made up of human beings, not legal ideals, and human beings have various kinds of social psychological processes built into them which don't function in ideal kinds of ways. They are also open to persuasion by other members of the jury group, and as we have seen in Chapter 5, human relationships and self-image can matter as much as pure evidence or logic.

We can find a lot in the courtroom to fascinate us, given all this. For instance, thinking back over the reasons why we disregard or dislike others or suspect deception (see Chapters 2 and 3), if credibility is the issue, what do lawyers do to make witnesses look stupid or unlikeable, or to create an atmosphere of disbelief or to try to imply that witnesses are deceivers or to attack witnesses' motives in giving evidence? What about the NVC that indicates lying, and what about the fact that, as we saw in Chapter 1, most of us cannot identify when someone is really lying nearly half so well as we think we can?

Bearing in mind what we have covered so far, there are several different aspects of trials that we can now analyse from a strictly relational point of view, beginning with the physical environment of the courtroom, the way that it is set up, and how that affects relationships and interactions there (cf. Chapter 1 on use of space). Then I will look at the nature of the trial and 'consensual truth explanations', that is to say, where truth is defined by what people say it is or what the majority of people agree it is. As students of human relationships we should expect many 'irrelevant' factors to influence what jurors think – things like likeability and attractiveness of defendants, discrediting of key witnesses, similarity of jurors to defendants, and relational persuasion. Finally I will offer some thoughts about relationships, antagonisms and alliances amongst jurors, using some of the relational research that we have been looking at earlier.

Order in the court

In Chapter 1 we saw how the organization of space in social settings will affect the ways in which people get treated, since it indicates something about the nature of the social and personal relationships between them. This is true of the ways we stand and the places we stand in, the amount of space which we use, the horizontal distance between actors in social space and the vertical arrangement of space also, that is, who is placed in a powerful, high position and who is low down.

What does a student who has read Chapter 1 immediately notice about a courtroom? The courtroom is an intriguing example of the arrangement of such social space and implicitly accords greater respect and importance to the statements made by certain actors in the scene. Judges always sit in the highest position; defendants usually sit in an exposed but fixed position in the courtroom; jurors sit together on one particular side of the judge, also in a special place – though of course jurors could probably hear equally well from any other position. The lawyers are placed centrally but are usually allowed to move around.

Furthermore, what can we make of the nature of the interactions that take place and the effects this has on the presentation of testimony? The interactions in a courtroom are extremely formal and very much outside the range of most people's experience. Ordinary people are inclined to act in a dignified courtroom with some anxiety, and hence in a stilted and self-conscious way. It appears different in the TV courtroom dramas – but then, they're actors! Witnesses all feel very much 'on stage' in these kinds of formal interactions. This will be particularly true in court since judges really do have power. There are various special sanctions and rules which apply in court (e.g. the court has the power to deprive you of property, money, liberty and relationships, as in divorce or child custody cases).

The normal spatial arrangement of a court, then, conveys messages about the relationships between the actors and show who has authority and who does not. Witnesses are likely to be affected by their unfamiliarity with the experience of being in court and with what goes on there. They might be overawed by the structure of the courtroom and the fact that there are rituals, unusual forms of speech and the fact that some of the people are wearing robes (and, in Britain, wigs). These solemn aspects are outside the routines of ordinary people's common experience, so we might find that a courtroom affects the behaviour and demeanour of witnesses. We might expect them to feel intimidated, awkward, put on the spot, embarrassed. We could predict that some witnesses will cope with the pressures more effectively than others (for example, people whose job involves them in talking to large groups might be at an advantage as against those who are not used to doing so). It will not surprise us, then, to find that these predictions are, by and large, readily confirmed by experimental work (O'Barr, 1982).

One reason why the law regards trial by jury as a mainstay of the criminal legal system of Anglo-Saxon courts is precisely because it is felt that ordinary men and women are the best judges of other ordinary men and women in such difficult surroundings. Lord Denning, formerly Master of the Rolls (the senior civil judge in the British legal system) noted, 'Trial by jury has been the bulwark of our liberties too long for any of us to seek to alter it. Whenever a person is on trial for a serious crime or when, in a civil case, a person's honour or integrity is at stake, or when one or other party must be deliberately lying, then trial by jury has no equal.' He thinks that juries are reasonably good at deciding whether witnesses are telling the truth or not, whether they are distressed or intimidated, and whether they are showing themselves in a fair light. We have already seen in Chapter 1 that this assessment may be somewhat optimistic, because we are often bad at detecting deception (Stiff and Miller, 1984), and are more likely to be influenced by credibility than by real truth, and so on. But in practice juries get extended exposure to witnesses (who may often be examined for several hours) and their impressions are not the simple one-off impressions that we sometimes find in experimental studies of juries and witnesses.

Bearing false witness?

What types of evidence affect juries? We already have seen (Chapter 3) that a person's physical appearance affects our liking for him or her in predictable ways and that liking makes us less careful about fairness – we tend to favour people whom we like. Does this happen in court, where we are supposed to be fair rather than favourable?

How we think criminals look   Most of us hold stereotypes about 'the criminal'. We share a clear, but wrong, idea of what criminals are like and this tends to be a physical stereotype based on whether the person *looks* aggressive or wicked. If all criminals looked like criminals, of course, then every law officer's job would be a lot easier (which may be one of the many reasons why criminals used to be branded, in a prominent place, with a letter denoting the type of crime they had committed).

So far as the law is concerned a criminal is somebody who commits a crime. On the other hand, people in general assume that criminals are ugly or have scarred faces, and that people with scars are criminals. We can test this stereotype by finding out how people react to photographs of people with and without scars (Bull, 1977). In such an experiment a photograph of a man's face had the negative 'doctored up' so that it looked as if he had a scar down his cheek or some kind of stigma such as a strawberry birthmark. Some subjects are shown the clean original and some the doctored version. Do people respond differently to each photo? Bull (1977) asked, 'Is this person a lifeboatman who goes out helping people, or is this person a criminal?' When the face has no scar on it subjects assert that the person is a lifeboatman and when the face has a scar on it, that he is a criminal. Evidently, we expect that criminals look like criminals and that people who look like criminals *are* criminals. Esses and Webster (1988) also showed that sex offenders in Canada who are average looking or unattractive physically are more likely to be assessed as dangerous and so deserving of the unlimited sentences allotted to dangerous offenders under the Canadian Criminal Code.

One explanation for this is quite simply that circulated police descriptions tend to dwell on identifying or distinguishing marks. They invariably note that the person has a scar down his or her left cheek, for instance, so people get used to hearing these kind of physical deformities associated with criminals. It is then an understandable, if illogical, leap to assume that *all* criminals are like that.

Perhaps criminality does have a physical basis. For years psychologists, sociologists and criminologists have asked whether there is, in fact, a criminal physical type. One of the first to do so was Lombroso (1918) who worked with Italian prison populations. He found that prisoners typically had sloping foreheads with narrow hair lines, big ears, eyes close together, large noses and big jaws. Try to conjure up a picture of such a person and quite frankly you can understand why they would turn to crime!

Even if there is not a criminal face or physique, maybe there is a genetic factor in criminality. For instance, there is some evidence (Prins, 1983) that more criminals have chromosomal disorders than do non-criminals. Another possibility is that people end up looking like criminals because they lead criminal lives or take to crime because of some physical capacity that suits them to it. For instance, someone who is a burglar and has to get through small windows is likely to be advantaged by being short and thin. To that extent their physique is likely to be related to the crimes they commit because their physical stature suits them to their crime. People who habitually engage in violence would probably be muscular because they use their muscles a lot, but they might have been on the receiving end of physical violence, too, so their face might indeed have been moved around a bit.

There is at least some relationship between physical appearance and crime, but to go as far as Lombroso did and claim that there is a criminal type just by looking at the structure of the face and head is risky. What is certainly true is that most of us act in a way that shows that we secretly share Lombroso's theory and we identify ugly or misshapen as bad people, villains in films and so forth. While the law assumes that people are reasonable and unbiased, evidence from research suggests the opposite: people are biased. People make unfounded assumptions about criminals' appearance; we will unjustifiably be prejudiced against people who have physical deformities (Lyons et al., 1996), and possibly will favour those who look attractive, just as in Chapter 3 we found that people do in forming the attractions that are the basis for long-term human relationships.

Attractiveness and justice   We have already seen in previous chapters how human beings tend to favour people that we like. Do juries do this and if so what makes them favour a likeable defendant? Chapter 3 taught us that two relational cues are particularly strong in fostering attraction: attitude and physical attractiveness. Are these also influential in the courtroom?

Attitude similarity often leads to attraction, so does that affect a jury's reactions to a defendant? Although jurors have very little opportunity to learn a defendant's attitudes (since defendants often do not testify and where they do, they are limited to what is 'relevant' to the law governing the crime), jurors tend to take the side of a person who seems to have attitudes similar to their own (Byrne, 1997). If the jurors think the person on trial is similar to them, thinks the same way as them, has the same sorts of attitudes about life, the same sorts of values – well, that person can't be all bad, so must not be guilty! Normally the defendant does not know how to adopt the attitudes of the jurors, although by dressing smartly and trying to present a good image most defendants try to aspire to the ideals that our culture holds dear and so to look 'good' and law-abiding. It is one of the strengths of the jury system that defendants have no prior relationship with jurors, no knowledge of their attitudes and little influence over the selection of jurors. Obviously when defence lawyers challenge jurors and try to have them barred from sitting on a particular jury, it is often because they assume that the juror holds attitudes different from the defendant's and so may be unfavourable to the defendant (Saks, 1986).

Do physically attractive people get a better deal in court than other people? We have some evidence from studies using fake jurors in simulated or 'pretend' trials. Physically attractive people were given lighter sentences in these simulated trials (Landy and Aronson, 1969). This was a general finding except when defendants had used their physical attractiveness in the commission of the crime, for instance if they were confidence tricksters. Where confidence tricksters had done this to 'con' people, then subjects gave them harder sentences. It had always been assumed from the Landy and Aronson study that they would get acquitted more often, but evidently this is not so. Physically attractive subjects were given lighter sentences by experimental subjects but they did not get acquitted more often (Stewart, 1980). So the findings about attractiveness are a bit uncertain – and we cannot necessarily assume that they would 'work' on real-life juries to the same degree. In any case, physical attractiveness is 'unlikely to be a major determinant of case outcomes' (Bartol and Bartol, 1994: 201).

How we think criminals behave in court   Just as we hold to a few assumptions about the ways in which criminals' faces look, so we are probably going to be influenced by their nonverbal behaviour in court – just as we are in everyday life anyway. It is odd that, given the amount of social psychological work devoted to the study of nonverbal behaviour in everyday life settings (see Chapter 1 here), only recently has any time been devoted to understanding the effects that it has in court (Blanck et al., 1990). A lawyer's facial expressions or eye contact with the witnesses and jurors, a witness's manner and nonverbal style, spatial behaviour, movement and vocal characteristics such as speech rate, pitch and inflection, can all affect his or her credibility with a jury (Stiff and Miller, 1984). Presumably a witness's nonverbal behaviour therefore can affect the ways in which a jury assesses him or her and evaluates the testimony that he or she gives in the courtroom (Pryor and Buchanan, 1984). Accordingly, the US courts take specific note of this and guidance to jurors often explicitly states (as in the following quotation from the Florida Supreme Court) that 'In determining the believability of any witness and the weight to be given to his or her testimony, you may properly consider the demeanor of the witness . . .'

Remembering from Chapter 1 that Stiff and Miller (1984) found that observers were actually very bad at detecting deception in real-life contexts, what would you expect to find happening in a court? Looking at some specific behaviours that normally indicate nervousness, Pryor and Buchanan (1984) compared nervous and relaxed defendants. They used self-manipulation (nervous fidgeting), eye contact or lack of it, and speech errors or fluency as indices of nervousness in a defendant and then looked to see the effects on a jury's ratings of that person. In this study, the jurors were given a summary of the case and then saw a videotape of the defendant before receiving a judge's (standard) guidance on determination of the case. Some of the jurors saw a videotape where the defendant was very nervous, some saw another videotape where the same defendant was not looking nervous at all. This study was particularly interesting because it found that moderately nervous defendants were judged to be the most guilty. The calm and confident ones were thought to be most credible and least guilty. Interestingly, female jurors reported being more influenced by the nonverbal signals than males did, as we might predict from Chapter 1; however, when Pryor and Buchanan looked at their actual scores, they found that the females had not in fact been influenced by it any more than the males had. This is quite surprising in view of the findings by Keeley and Hart (1994) that females invariably are found to be superior in decoding NVC.

The sequence of events in the courtroom   In forming impressions of strangers or acquaintances, we know that certain information (e.g. about attitudes) carries especial weight and that it can be very important whether we hear a piece of information at an early point in an interaction or later. Indeed, in Chapter 3 we spent some time considering 'filter theories' of relationship development and pointing out that information is more relevant to relationships at some particular points than at others.

In the area of formation of impressions about people, researchers have thoroughly explored the issue of primacy versus recency or, in other words, what matters most – the case that comes first (primacy) or the case that is most recently heard (recency)? Kassin et al. (1990) found that the issue is not a simple one. Some subjects, specifically those with a high need for cognition (i.e. a strong desire to understand things), are influenced more by arguments preceding the evidence (which therefore give the evidence a structure that the subjects can follow) than by the evidence itself. Subjects with a low need for cognition, on the other hand, were influenced by arguments *following* the evidence (i.e. those arguments coming after they had made their own judgements of what was significant and what was not, and needed to hear how to put it in context).

In a study on a related but different point, Pyszcynski and Wrightsman (1981) examined the way in which the prosecution made its opening statement and the subsequent effect that this had on a jury's thoughts. They showed, rather surprisingly, that lengthy prosecution opening statements are really the best bet for a prosecution. The longer the opening statement the better the cards are stacked their way.

The reasons for this are quite simple (assuming that there is no 'time out' between the statements). If the defence also makes a lengthy statement in reply then the jury will probably begin to nod off; if, alternatively, the defence subsequently makes a brief reply because they want to avoid boring the jury, then the jury assumes it is because they have not really got a good defence. So it pays the prosecution to make as long an opening statement as possible – at least in an experimental setting. Conversely, if the prosecution makes a brief opening statement, then the jury tends to think that the prisoner is not guilty, whatever the defence does. The study thus suggests that it is in the best interests of the prosecution to make a lengthy opening statement.

The same primacy–recency effects influence reactions to individual pieces of testimony. What matters is the structure of the messages – as we found in Chapter 5, too. Paying attention to the strength with which people make their points at the beginning and ends of their statement, Pennington (1982) showed that if the strongest points come first then observers (jurors) are more likely to believe what is said. Therefore, if the prosecution puts its best evidence first rather than keeping it in the bag and bringing it out with a flourish at the end, they are more likely to get verdicts of guilty.

We have to be careful in interpreting such studies though, since many of the effects are actually created in very brief manipulations in the laboratory. By contrast, in a full court hearing much time is spent on those same details. Chapter 3 showed us that there can be important brief effects on initial attraction but that relationships themselves are not necessarily formed by them alone. In a full trial – which could last weeks – the jury sees much longer samples of each participant's behaviour and initial impressions can easily be overturned by later evidence (Sunnafrank, 1991).

As I have been arguing throughout this book, these differences depend on the one crucial factor in human relationships that psychology minimizes and communication studies allows to prevail, namely, whenever a witness gives evidence – not just at the start of their testimony – they *talk*! What have scientists learned about the effects of the kind of language in which testimony is delivered?

Mind your language in the courtroom

It is not enough to speak the truth in court: one has to *seem* to be the sort of person who can be believed and therefore evidence must be presented in a convincing way. One way is to speak in a manner that helps one's credibility (Cooke, 1990). Sarat and Felstiner (1988) note that the language of motives in the law is different from that in normal social relationships. Clients going through divorce tend to reconstruct the past and *explain* their own behaviour as well as the actions of others rather than just describe it (Hopper, 1993). However, lawyers tend to focus on the way the divorce process works and to explain the actions of spouses in terms not of the motive but of the process. So lawyers (and judges) come at issues of human relationships from a different angle from the one that their clients use and this is embodied, as is much else, in the linguistic differences and code uses that they manifest.

Legal language is different from ordinary language and confuses ordinary mortals pretty easily. We ordinary people say things in low code, as we saw in Chapter 1. Lawyers use forbiddingly technical high codes. Consider this example given by O'Barr (1982): where the normal person in the street would say, 'Have an orange', as they give it to somebody, a lawyer might say, 'I hereby give and convey to you my estate and interest, right and title, claim and advantages of, and in, said orange, together with its rind, skin, juice, pulp, pips, all rights and advantages therein, together with full power to bite, suck, squeeze, crush or otherwise eat or consume the same or to give away the same, whether with or without its rind, skin, juice, pulp, pips, anything heretofore or hereafter to the contrary notwithstanding.'

The problem for ordinary folks in court is therefore, 'What do I do? Should I speak normally or am I expected to use high code?' The answer seems to be that many folks fall into the trap of attempting to use high code, and doing it badly – which as we saw in Chapter 1 usually leads to judgements of the speaker's ineptness. What effects might this have?

Think of the contrast between the ordinary folks and the lawyers in court. We normally expect lawyers to use high code and would be surprised if they didn't. So we would expect lawyers to cry, 'Objection!', when they disapprove of a style of question or answer. Clearly this is not the normal everyday way of indicating disagreement. We expect judges to say, 'Sustained', or, 'Overruled' in response, which nobody says anywhere else but in court. We also expect lawyers to use formal forms of language like 'if it please the court' and 'your honour' and 'with your honour's permission'. But just imagine what would happen if ordinary witnesses from the public started doing things like that to one another, too. They'd be regarded as pompous, arrogant, weird, peculiar and discreditable.

In attempting to use 'proper' speech styles, witnesses invariably adopt a 'hypercorrectness' that is far more formal than would be used in everyday discourse. This means that they misapply imperfectly learned rules of grammar, use vocabulary incorrectly and produce overly precise pronunciation (Labov, 1972). Such speakers consequently make errors and speak in an unnatural manner that may give to the jury the false impression that the witnesses do not know what they are talking about. As examples of hypercorrect style, compare 'I lapsed into a comatose state, was not cognisant of the environment and although in a somewhat less than dire condition, was not at that precise moment ambulatory' with 'I was dazed and fuzzy about what was happening. I was not badly hurt but could not walk for a while' (based on O'Barr, 1982: 84). A witness speaking in hypercorrect style is usually dismissed as being of low social skills (Hurwitz, 1953) or as attempting to ingratiate (Jones, 1964). Witnesses using the hypercorrect style are regarded as less convincing, less competent, less well qualified and less intelligent than other witnesses (O'Barr, 1982). Mock jurors (i.e. student subjects acting as jurors) award lower amounts of compensation to defendants speaking in hypercorrect style.

By contrast, expert witnesses and probably also police witnesses are not only permitted to use the high code forms in giving formal reports, they are expected to do so. These expectations thus provide a context for interpreting the sense of their statements. Furthermore, they are practised at doing it, make fewer errors and appear to be in fuller command of their evidence.

People who break grammatical and linguistic rules are interpreted negatively and their actions are given a diminished meaning. It is important to note that the consequences of breaking the rules will be more severe for witnesses and defendants than for experts or lawyers since experts and persons with power are always permitted to deviate from rules that the rest of us must follow (Wiseman and Duck, 1995). People who speak in a way that makes them poor witnesses are believed less often, even when they are right. So what is it about a witness's relational or speech style which makes him or her a naturally poor witness? The most immediate way to be disregarded is to claim, honestly, that you are uncertain about your testimony. If a witness says, 'Well, I couldn't tell if the car was travelling at 30 mph or 35 mph, but it was somewhere around that, certainly not 40 mph but it may have been 33 mph' he or she may be telling the exact truth, but will be disregarded by the jury (O'Barr, 1982). Sadly, anyone who admits to being uncertain risks being seen as unreliable, even though, in fact, they are telling perhaps the absolute truth, namely that they really can't tell. People are also regarded as poor witnesses if they repeat themselves a lot. Such honesty or repetitiveness somehow robs them of *source credibility* (discussed in Chapter 5).

Jurors also think of a witness as a discreditable poor witness if the person overuses qualifiers and hedges (that is to say, 'sort of', 'you know', 'kind of' rather than just using the proper word on its own). Such speech has been called 'powerless', as we saw in Chapter 1, and uses repetition too, as well as imprecision in use of words. O'Barr (1982) reports a case where the outcome hinged on the fact that a woman was unable to make a judgement about how far her car had travelled after it had been involved in an accident, and instead of saying that she was unsure of the distance she said, 'I am poor with feet.' The jury presumably either didn't know what she was talking about, or thought that it was such a funny way of putting it that she must be an idiot and an unreliable one at that. The appeal court, however, took the honest view that she was a reliable witness who was simply good at making herself look stupid. By contrast, witnesses who claim to be able to remember minor details in their testimony, such as the colour and pattern of a man's tie, are seen to be more reliable even if that specific detail has no real bearing on the case (Bell and Loftus, 1989). It seems that reporting of details creates the impression of attentiveness and accuracy.

Poor witnesses also use fragmented styles of speech; that is to say, they break off in the middle of sentences, use ungrammatical forms and do not get to the end of the sentence. This sends a message that says 'I am uncertain about my testimony.' These examples of powerless speech styles not only convey lack of power, authority and influence, as was shown in Chapter 1, but in the particular case of a law court, they affect a jury's assessment of a witness's reliability.

Lawyers' linguistic liberties   Some discredit of witnesses stems from their own natural (mis)use of language, but occasionally lawyers can lead them into traps. The breaking of the social or linguistic rules can be accidental or it can be brought about by a careful lawyer trying to discredit a witness, for instance. Lawyers ask questions and witnesses answer them: therefore the lawyers have a considerable amount of control over the *style* of answers that the witnesses will produce (Cooke, 1990), even if they can't always necessarily affect the *content* of the answers (though sometimes they can).

Lawyers can affect the impression that witnesses give – and can do this by affecting the linguistic style of the evidence, for example, by making the witnesses break rules and so discredit themselves. For instance, a lawyer might want to upset the manner in which a person gives evidence or at least to control the manner of its presentation and indeed are so urged in legal training texts (Evans, 1983). Consider this instance: one of the things that makes people sound as if they know what they are talking about is if they talk in complete sentences or paragraphs, that is, a narrative form of report. Narrative testimony, where a witness gives continuous prose answers without being interrupted, gives a strong message: it says 'I know what I am talking about' (O'Barr, 1982). Such a witness does not need to be prompted to give the answers, appears to be able to talk without having to think about it too much, and so seems well informed and knowledgeable about the topic. Knowing this, a lawyer who wants to make an important witness look knowledgeable, well informed and unrehearsed can ask a question in a form that allows a narrative sort of answer, such as 'Can you tell us what happened in your own words; just spend as long as you like telling us what actually occurred.' By contrast, witnesses who seem to need controlling can look too talkative or foolish (for instance, the lawyer may say impatiently 'Just answer the question' – and that instantly makes the witness look evasive or too wordy). Equally, if it can be made to look as if witnesses must have information dragged out of them they can then appear as if they have something to hide. If the lawyer's questions are carefully phrased to obtain pat answers witnesses can then appear to be making rehearsed or prepared answers on the one hand, or, on the other hand, to seem uninformed or unsure of what they are saying.

The style of question gives the lawyers more control in other ways, too. The lawyer can cut down what a witness says so that there is less chance to introduce anything the lawyer would prefer them not to tell the court. TV courtroom dramas often show lawyers doing this. They stop witnesses when they are beginning to expand their testimony in undesirable directions: 'Just answer the question'; 'Please stick to the question asked.' All of these give the impression, if done in the right tone of voice, that the witness is being exasperating and could be unreliable. On the other hand, 'May it please the court to direct the witness to answer the question' offers the lawyer the chance to imply that the witness is concealing something. By such means (in other words by structuring and manipulating the *form* of discourse), a lawyer can exert some control over the manner in which the witness produces the testimony and thus can affect the credibility the witness enjoys afterwards. Saks (1991) observes that lawyers invariably ask narrative questions on direct examination (of their own side's witnesses) and adopt the choppier question-and-answer style for cross-examination (of the other side's witnesses).

Another technique which is often used to discredit experts is to try to lead them to look pedantic and petty (Brodsky, 1977; see Box 6.3 for some delightful examples). This is done by asking questions in a loose way that causes witnesses to object to the form of the question or to say, 'Well I couldn't possibly answer a general question like that', or to answer it in such a way that they appear to be undecided or else pedantic (e.g. 'Well, it

---

Box 6.3   Lawyers' linguistic liberties

Brodsky (1977) points out a member of techniques used by lawyers to discredit expert witnesses. Examples from his longer list are:

- Infallibility tests ('Do you know the scientific work of X and Y on this topic?' X and Y are, of course, especially chosen because they are incredibly obscure, but if the expert has to admit to ignorance of the work then he or she is made to look foolish and fallible.)
- God only knows ('What is the cause of divorce?' The idea here is to trivialize the issue or to expose how little the profession truly knows about particular areas.)
- Historic hysteric gambit ('Wasn't Pasteur ridiculed by his contemporaries?' The point here is to suggest that scientific consensus can often be wrong despite the consensus, and the lawyer's clients could therefore be right even if the evidence of prevailing scientific fashion is against them.)
- Challenging ('Have other studies replicated your work and upheld its reliability and validity?' Again, the point is to challenge the authority of the work. Scientific work is very rarely replicated in all its details.)

Cooke (1990) also notes that lawyers very often attempt to upset witnesses by jumping around from discussion of one piece of evidence to another until they are confused. Other attempts to discredit witnesses can involve the making of a prefatory statement before the question, such as 'We all know that women are worse drivers than men. In your opinion was the accused any worse than normal?' Such prejudicial comments must be objected to immediately before the question is answered. (Cooke also notes the importance of expert witnesses attending court in clothes that are 'evidence' of expertise, such as dark, subdued clothing without distracting accessories, which is consistent with what we read in Chapters 1 and 5.)

---

depends what you mean by "crossing the road"'). It is possible to phrase the questions so that somebody with expert knowledge could not possibly answer it without having to clarify what the question means (e.g. such questions might be things like 'What actually causes schizophrenia?', 'What exactly is mental illness'?). But of course as soon as the experts start clarifying the question, they make themselves look trivial, pedantic, nit-picking, hostile and antagonistic or hopelessly academic and out of touch with everyday life. They then are much less persuasive than people who appear to be friendly, knowledgeable and on your side. Obviously a lawyer wants to discredit the other side's expert witnesses and can use such tactics as asking detailed esoteric questions to which the expert will be unlikely to have ready replies (for example asking an expert psychologist 'What is the coefficient alpha reliability of the comprehension subtest of the Wechsler Adult Intelligence Scale-Revised?'). If the expert has to admit ignorance or uncertainty, then the status as expert is obviously diminished immediately for the jury.

As discussed in Chapter 1, the *form* of a message is a way of communicating: the content is informative, but so also is the way in which it is put across. Because of that, variation in form conveys messages as well, as we saw in Chapter 1 in discussing 'switching' from one style to another. If lawyers make a witness switch from non-narrative reporting into narrative then it begins to look as if the witness didn't know what he or she was talking about to start with but has now moved onto more familiar ground. Switching from one form to another is thus another way of conveying a message about knowledge, about certainty and about truth.

Language is used in court in a way that permits power and knowledge to be inferred. I noted earlier in this chapter that language style in our courts is an important topic because our courts decide cases on the basis of credibility and plausibility and consensual truth; 'truth' is essentially what the jury decides it is. The jury may have heard half a dozen different versions of the same story and have to decide who is reliable and expert, which versions are true, what is consistent and what is not. The big questions of plausibility are thus based partly on the nature of evidence and partly on the credibility of the witnesses which in turn derives in large part from the speech styles discussed in Chapter 1.

What is quite clear from all of this is that the material discussed in Chapters 1, 3 and 5 has direct bearing on a jury's beliefs about a particular witness as seen in the court during the trial. Presumably the members of the jury take these impressions with them into the jury room where they decide the fate of the accused.

How do juries make decisions?

After members of the jury have heard the evidence in court without discussing it amongst themselves – i.e. after each of them has formed an independent judgement – they all retire together to the jury room and expose their views, their thinking, their judgements, their attitudes and their personalities to the other members of the jury. Such circumstances are natural breeding grounds for relational activity and in long trials or complex jury discussions it is likely that relationships between jurors have some bearing on the outcome. What goes on in the jury room? What sort of impact will the shy and lonely jurors make, for instance? Whose views will be given the most credence? What are the effects of having to present your thinking to a group of strangers and argue with them about your own personal judgements? How do interpersonal relationships affect the decisions in a jury? Can likeability of jurors affect the weight given to their opinions by others? These questions are all, in one way or another, relational questions based on relational principles and processes. The emphasis of most previous research, however, has been on the decision-making processes and the decisions that are reached, and not on the ways in which relational issues between jurors may predispose jurors to agree or disagree with one another. Thus relational research can add something to the understanding of factors that are prior to the making of group decisions in a jury.

Actually, at the moment we can't know for sure how to answer these interesting questions since countries that have a jury system usually have strong laws to protect juries from direct interference or study, but we can work out how some of the relational principles that were discussed earlier could be applied to the situation. We have to recognize that researchers are not allowed to ask real juries about their decisions nor their decision making even though some countries (e.g. the USA) allow the press to talk to jurors after the verdict. The best that may be done is to have a substitute, or simulated, jury sitting in the same court pretending to be a real jury, and then take them off to a laboratory where they are asked to make a decision just as the true jury does. Sometimes it even happens that the mock jury and the real one reach the same decision – but often it does not.

Another method involves rerunning the trial using transcripts and actors who pretend to be the real lawyers, judge, defendant and witnesses. However, it still is not quite the same and still does not take account of relational research. Though actors are very good at acting, they are not judges and the mock jurors probably realize it. We cannot be certain whether mock jurors respond to something because they know that the experimenter is interested in it or because it really affects them. We must bear this in mind when we look at the research.

Are juries like other decision-making groups? Do they recall testimony accurately, stick to the correct issues and reach verdicts felt by others (e.g. judges or trial lawyers) to have been the right one on the facts? Because research cannot be conducted directly on real juries, simulated ones have to be used for studies on these issues. In some instances subjects are drawn from normal jury rosters and asked to listen to recordings of real trials. This work shows that higher status members of (simulated) juries exerted more influence than other jurors on decisions (Strodtbeck et al., 1957). It also suggests that, as shown in Chapters 3 and 4, women are more willing to take on responsibility for relationships between people; in juries, just as elsewhere, women are more thoughtful about their reactions to the other jury members and spend longer making positive comments about other people and being more receptive and encouraging of their ideas than do the male members of the jury.

As we saw in Chapter 1, those who speak most often are usually held to be more expert. The research on human relationships shows that we are affected by those persons whom we like and we tend to be influenced by status. Thus it seems natural that, at least from some points of view, such persons will be most influential in a jury – even though the law assumes that all jurors are equal. What should matter, therefore, is what they say.

When we look at the specific content of speech in simulated jury discussions it is found that about 50 per cent is devoted to expression of irrelevant material such as personal opinions about general matters (James, 1959). Only some 15 per cent of talk is actually devoted to the testimony, whilst 25 per cent is devoted to procedural issues in the jury itself (who should speak next, and so on). This could be used as evidence that juries are pretty ineffective and inattentive to the true needs of the court. On the other hand, it could be taken to make a much more interesting point, namely, that people in such a situation need to establish some relational familiarities with each other and to find out what sorts of people they all are before they get down to the business of making a complex decision about someone else's life. I have already pointed out in the rest of this book many times that humans spend a good deal of their time talking to other human beings and we have learned how these trivial conversational discussions help to establish and bind relationships together as a basis for getting other life-activities co-ordinated. Establishing a 'trivial' but working relationship first is a good basis for discussing the later material, as we saw in the previous chapter – and these 'trivia' can help to establish the relationship first. As we saw in Chapters 1 and 3, the routines of communication are often seemingly trivial, yet have important relational effects (Duck et al., 1991).

There are, in fact, four phases to group operation, of which the first (*Orientation*) is precisely this phase of getting to know one another (Fisher, 1970). However, two of the other three phases also have implicit relational purposes (the exception is *conflict* where each person states opinions unambiguously and strongly. This is the second phase, after orientation). In the *emergence* phase the general consensus begins to show through and so those in disagreement with it begin to make their points less strongly and more ambiguously so that they can be accepted as reasonable people and 'join the group again' (Fisher, 1970). Finally, the *reinforcement* phase consists of an orgy of mutual backslapping, where everyone comments on the excellence and effectiveness of the group and generally fosters the view that a good decision was reached by a lot of nice people in a very nice and sensible way. This again serves relational goals and makes everyone feel good about the group – and about themselves, too, of course.

So some research that seems to show that juries are ineffective may on second thoughts suggest instead – or also – that jurors are merely ordinary human beings who want to establish good working relationships with one another, just like they do everywhere else. The research reviewed in earlier chapters would suggest that such relational needs are predictable from physical characteristics, NVC, similarities, psychological styles and meaning systems, conversational strategies, and communication competencies.

An unnoticed point so far is that in giving opinions about other people (witnesses and defendants) the strangers on the jury are actually being encouraged to behave towards one another as friends do: they are self-disclosing about their personal opinions, their judgements and their value system (Chapter 3). They are giving away personal information about the ways in which they think and the attitudes that they hold. Remember that juries originated as groups of 12 members who were supposed to be friends or acquaintances of the accused and who were prepared to swear that he or she was innocent in the 'wager at law' described earlier. Times have changed but the relational underpinnings of jury work have not. In fact it is rather unusual – and therefore is likely to be an interpersonally powerful experience – to be in a roomful of strangers and tell them what personal opinions you have formed about another person and to display your meaning system (Chapter 3) so thoroughly and so personally.

It may have struck you in reading the above, as it struck me in writing it, that a lot of legal research that I have covered exhibits precisely the points that I dwelt on in the opening chapters of this book. It focuses on the individual characteristics of jurors rather than on how they get on with one another; it looks at how individual jurors form impressions of witnesses and defendants rather than on how whole groups of jurors reach 'joint impressions' that represent a negotiated group view; it also regards jurors' *relational* needs and personal aims or projects as somehow irrelevant and irritating. I would propose, instead, that relational needs and personal aims are a central feature of the operation when a group of strangers get together under the pressure of making difficult and responsible decisions – sometimes literally life or death decisions – about other human beings. Perhaps we should study more carefully the likelihood that jurors establish personal relationships with one another under pressure; and the likelihood that these influence their decisions, too.

Relationships and juries

Jurors are human beings in rather unusual contexts and we can expect them to show both some human characteristics and some of the human reactions to strangeness. We learned in Chapter 1 that people respond to the non-verbal and verbal subtleties that were detailed there and we have applied some of those analyses to the courtroom already; we also learned above that some witnesses can be put off by the context and fall into odd speech patterns. Chapter 2 showed the sorts of emotions that are operative in relationships, and in discussing the six types of love, for example, we learned some of the ways in which emotions can be honed to the situation in which they are experienced. In the case of the courtroom we can expect that jurors will form impressions of and reactions to the defendant, and we saw above that this has been widely explored, using both static physical characteristics of defendants and dynamics of their speech and deceptive communications. We can also assume that the jurors form impressions of, and liking or disliking, for the counsel in a case and also the judge. Whereas it has been shown that judges' nonverbal behaviour can influence jurors' judgements, so too it makes sense to assume that the jurors' liking for the judge can influence the likelihood of the jurors' accepting the judge's objectivity and other comments. Since no-one can check whether the judges' rulings are discussed and ignored in jury decision making, nor can we tell whether the jury discusses the attractiveness or credibility of the counsel, we can never know for sure what influences these have. However, it would be extremely improbable that the humans on the jury cease to act as humans making judgements of other humans just because the objects of judgement are judges or lawyers. Furthermore, we saw above that juries very often discuss procedure and matters irrelevant to the trial during discussions that have been observed and this is fully in accordance with the discussion of gossip and everyday communication that was laid out in Chapters 1 and 3. Thus it is a remarkably fair bet on the evidence that juries behave in most respects like normal human beings when they are deliberating about their verdict even though the situation is a peculiar one in many respects.

It is quite striking when looking at prominent books on psychology and the law (e.g. Bartol and Bartol, 1994) that jury decision making is explored in those texts in terms of the juror characteristics (e.g. the effects of race on jury decision making, the effect of juror authoritarianism on decisions, personality characteristics of jurors and decisions) or that decision making is placed in the framework of group decision making. In the latter case the decisions of juries are expected to follow the available principles established for 'zero history' groups, i.e. groups with no past relational history of the kind that decision-making groups of people at work in fact have, for instance. Thus the research focuses on issues such as the tendency for groups to reach decisions that are polarized versions of the decisions of the individual members, the likelihood that groups reach relatively poor decisions, the tendency of groups to reach lenient decisions on disciplinary cases, and so forth. Such work assumes that there will be 'group process loss', namely that groups will lose something in the process and reach decisions that are less efficient than those that would be made by the individuals in the groups (Stroebe, 1980).

This is all very well, but the one missing element is the fact that groups of people simply do not sit in a room for several days and then reach tough decisions without some of the relational processes discussed in previous chapters setting themselves into place. People can form relationships in a remarkably short space of time (30 seconds is about the record, but even on dates people can rapidly decide that the date will be a success or failure; Duck and Cortez, 1988). While they typically do not do so, normal people typically do set some of the relationship processes in train in that short time. In a jury, however, a group of people sits around in a relational pressure cooker, discussing relatively intimate things, such as their attitudes and opinions about something they have all seen, exposing and disclosing their judgements of other people's truthfulness, their beliefs about how other people 'tick', attributions about other people's motives, their abilities at understanding and thinking about evidence and so forth. Some of the OJ Simpson jurors were dismissed because other jurors complained that they were offensive people or had been harassing other jurors, and so on. As a lawyer might say, I rest my case. Jurors, especially in important trials, are likely to form personal relationships at least at the level of liking or disliking one another, establishing some order of personal hierarchy and power structure, perhaps even establishing 'characters' like the 'funny guy' or the 'picky one'. What remains to be seen is the effect of such relationships on jury decision making. It would be quite remarkable if juries were the only groups in the world where alliances and antagonisms did not develop and influence the eventual decision of the group, following some of the principles in the foregoing chapters.

Summary

Various aspects of the legal procedures are centrally dependent on language and relationship processes between participants – even down to the level of whether the jury likes the defendant. You are now, therefore, in a position to judge which of the three models of the trial (see Box 6.2 above) you think best fits in with the models of social behaviour offered in this book. I have argued that an important element in jury trials in the West is that they depend on plausibility and interpersonal persuasion – which, as we have seen, themselves depend quite importantly on the impressions that various people make on the jury and how much the jury likes them. A lot of the processes involved in jury decision making also have a relational basis: some of the jurors' apparently irrelevant actions do establish relationships and some of their discussions make them act towards one another just as friends normally do. Jurors are groups of people who are likely to form relationships with one another in the ways described in this book and to be influenced in reaching verdicts by their liking for defendants, witnesses, lawyers, judges and, most important, one another.

Further reading

Bartol, C.R. and Bartol, A.M. (1994) *Psychology and Law*. Pacific Grove. CA: Brooks/Cole.
Ellison K.W. and Buckhout, R. (1981) *Psychology and Criminal Justice*. New York: Harper and Row.
Kassin, S.M. and Wrightsman, L. (1985) *The Psychology of Evidence and Trial Procedure*. Beverly Hills, CA: Sage.
O'Barr, W.M. (1982) *Linguistic Evidence: Language, Power and Strategy in the Courtroom*. New York: Academic Press.
Sales, B.D. (1976) *Psychology in the Legal Process*. New York: Halsted.
Wrightsman, L. (1991) *Psychology and the Legal Process* (2nd edn). New York: Halsted.

7

Staying Healthy . . . with a Little Help from Our Friends?

'We are just beginning to scratch the surface of relationship functioning in illness and realizing that chronic health problems are, in essence, a relationship issue.' (Lyons and Meade, 1995: 210)

One aspect to everyday life seems, on the face of it, to have little to do with relationships, namely health. This first appearance is in fact deceptive and relationships have a lot to do with health in all sorts of interesting ways. When one looks more closely, then, health is significantly affected by personal and social relationships and by one's social networks. A 'social network' is the group of persons with whom a person is involved (usually friends); 'social support' refers to the help that they provide or are felt to provide. Not only do relationships influence beliefs about what it is healthy to do and what not, but the numbers of friends that we have and even our relationship with our doctor influence our health status. If we have more friends and we like our doctor, then the chances are that we shall be healthier. If we have a greater number of relationships with women, then we are also likely to have better health (Reis, 1986), and we already learned in Chapter 2 that falling in love, loneliness and marital conflict each have direct consequences on health, not all positive.

Relational issues in sickness and in health

Take a look at the advertising around you, and you will see how much human effort is devoted to prolonging life, trying to stay young and keeping healthy. Where fifteenth-century alchemists wasted their lives looking for chemical potions and elixirs to prolong life, we do the same thing in different social, cultural and relational contexts: we eat fibre, jog, take up yoga, use dye to cover grey hair and skin creams to 'banish' wrinkles. The results are similar, only the attitudes and beliefs are different. Nowadays, we believe that many diseases are curable by 'science' rather than by 'witchcraft', although in some cases the essential healing factors are actually not that different.

Most of us will die because of unhealthy lifestyles despite the fact that these are correctable through education (Rogers, 1983). The main causes of death and disease nowadays are not the old unhygienic infestations like cholera and typhoid but heart disease, cancer, sexually transmitted diseases (such as AIDS), and liver disease (Vanzetti and Duck, 1996). Each of these is related to our own personal choices about diet, smoking, sexual behaviours and alcohol. Other health risks in our society are also results of the way we choose to live: dangerous driving, crime, obesity, lack of proper exercise, stress, dangerous sports and loneliness. We feel better when we are in love or surrounded by friends; we may become discouraged when we feel lonely, but there could be more to it than mere feelings. Do human relationships actually affect our physical well-being and medical status? Some researchers claim that loneliness kills, that the process of divorce creates physical illness, and that some interpersonal styles of behaviour (e.g. personality, coping style and self-esteem) can make us more or less prone to heart disease (Lynch, 1987). Also as indicated by Trickett and Buchanan (1997), there are many forms of relational transitions in life that are extremely distressing to both psychological and physical health, such as changing schools, moving to a new neighbourhood, losing a job and its associated community of acquaintances, being widowed, or losing a child. Even falling in love can make you sick in specific ways as we saw in Chapter 2. On top of this, the experience of a sudden disaster, such as a car accident, flooding of one's home, or other natural disasters like hurricanes, produce far greater physical and psychological stresses on isolated individuals than they do on people who have strong relationships with other people (Kaniasty and Norris, 1997). It is also quite well established that the risk of developing clinical depression is quite markedly higher in people who are single, separated, divorced, or who lack a good confiding relationship with their spouse (Sarason et al., 1997; Weissman, 1987). There are thus many grounds for looking at health issues through the sort of relational lens that I will apply here to a general range of issues that appear at first sight unconnected with relationships at all. I hope to show that it is superficial to believe that individuals get sick alone. In fact human relationships and social contexts do matter a lot in health and sickness.

The sick role and the social side of illness

We may think that people go to the doctor because they are ill, but the true picture is somewhat more complex. Reporting of illness is not based on absolutes: for example, we are not just either sick or well. We are often somewhere in between. The health–illness continuum is a continuum, not a dichotomy of absolute health versus absolute illness (Shuval, 1981). What do human relationships have to do with the health–illness continuum, and why, when and how do we decide we are ill enough to need help? In fact it depends on whether a person feels supported, valued and esteemed by other people (Heller and Rook, 1997).

We do not report that we are sick every time we have germs, viruses and physical trauma; instead our likelihood of reporting sick depends also on how we feel about the experience. Recovery from illness is more than just a physical matter, since medical intervention focusing only on germs does not always cure people as fast as it should. Also relevant are the 'will to live' and whether we are embedded in a social network that encourages us to look after ourselves and cares about us. Also, reporting sick is at least partly influenced by a whole host of seemingly impertinent matters such as personality, way of life, or personal beliefs. These in their turn are influenced by the beliefs that exist in the surrounding culture, social relations, and the quality of relationships with people to whom we want to be close.

The decision that one is sick will depend on psychological factors based on the perception of symptoms and what they mean. Some symptoms are not reported and seem not to occur in some cultures; for instance, Mead (1950) reports that women in the Arapesh tribe show no signs of morning sickness during pregnancy, because the culture does not regard it as a normal consequence of pregnancy. Finally, wounded soldiers' reports of pain are often unrelated to the extent of their wounds. In the heat of battle perception of pain apparently can be depressed (Beecher, 1959).

Clearly, there are individual, cultural and relational influences on the perception of pain and the reporting of symptoms. These raise the possibility that illness can have personal or social functions as well as medical ones, such as making someone out to be a martyr or getting someone out of a difficult assignment (for instance I have noticed that I get migraines most often when I am driving somewhere to perform a task I'd prefer not to be doing). This is not saying that it has *only* social functions or *always* has social functions, but we should at least explore such functions when they can be legitimately suspected. Equally, illness can result from social events or experiences, which, again, is not saying that it always does. We need to look, then, at the relational context for becoming ill or defining oneself as sick.

Deciding what the symptoms mean   Some symptoms in themselves mean little (indeed, doctors tend to look for clusters of symptoms rather than single ones anyway). Accordingly we have to decide whether symptoms indicate illness – and if so, whether it is appropriate to consult a doctor. Loss of appetite, for instance, can mean nothing significant at all or it may be a sign of illness. It is, in any case, a *general* symptom of many different kinds of ailment, so we might decide that it tells us something important or that it does not, depending on our psychological attitudes to life at the time. A hypochondriac may decide that loss of appetite portends a serious illness and ought to be checked out; other people may not notice or be influenced by their loss of appetite (they may even be glad if they are trying to lose weight).

Since many pains are ambiguous, transitory, or due to any one of many possible root causes, they have to be interpreted. Jones (1982) points out that pain initiates a search for causes, and people will pin the explanation on any cause that seems both plausible and salient, even if it is actually incorrect. If a recent event seems likely to have caused the symptoms (e.g. if a sudden severe headache follows a blow to the head), then we are likely to attribute the effect to that cause even if, for example, the real cause is actually a spontaneous brain tumour.

By contrast, an individual's psychological state can contribute to the occurrence of certain symptoms (Mechanic, 1980). For instance, an extremely anxious person might develop ulcers or headaches and someone whose colleagues at work are 'difficult' may develop such symptoms more than someone whose work relationships are rewarding (Zorn, 1995). Indirectly, also, anxiety may cause us to change our habits: negative attitudes may make us careless or prepared to act in a self-destructive manner, for instance, by drinking excessively, eating irregularly and driving dangerously. Of course, anxiety and stress are often caused by relational experiences themselves such as conflicts or arguments (Kelley and Rolker-Dolinsky, 1987). Furthermore, a person can develop symptoms as a result of changes in daily routines or habits, and these can in turn come from psychological changes going on inside. For instance, if we become extremely anxious about relationships or are going through a divorce or a relationship break-up, we may start drinking or smoking and so develop liver or lung ailments, and it is well established that men who are recently divorced start frequenting dangerous places like red-light districts and are more likely to be the victims of assault or homicides (Bloom et al., 1978).

'Being ill' can itself become closely tied up with our view of ourselves, since it excuses us from poor performance: 'What can you expect? I'm sick.' Also, it may become structured into our daily relational routines rather like the routines of heroin addicts' families (Lewis and McAvoy, 1984), who come to structure their lives around the addict, the addiction and the behaviour that is necessary to sustain it (such as theft and prostitution), as we saw in Chapter 4. Also someone may be easier to deal with when they are 'ill', so the family is happy for them to stay defined that way, or encourages them to see themselves as 'ill' (just as I discussed alcoholics in Chapter 4). At least, if they are in bed they are doing no harm to any of their relatives. For many of the above reasons, Reiss et al. (1991: 290) affirm the general belief that '. . . a balanced image of the future contains a growing and equal partnership of the social sciences and molecular biology'.

This all goes to show that illness is not simply a physically created state, but one where relational experiences intertwine with physical factors. For example, Hooley and Hiller (1997) point out that it is now widely recognized that psychosocial and relational factors play a role in schizophrenia and depression. Even illnesses which are reported fairly commonly could nevertheless indicate that the person doing the reporting is actually having a relational problem.

Deciding to report sick   There is more to becoming ill than merely feeling a twinge of pain in the stomach: we decide we are sick when we feel that our physical state deserves attention; we receive some sort of relational confirmation that the physical state deserves attention (Heller and Rook, 1997); we are not satisfied with other possible explanations; we are willing to accept the consequences of being confirmed sick, and believe that some treatment would be more useful and effective than no treatment. These are psychological factors that link up with our views of ourselves, with our attitudes to pain, doctors and sickness, and with our personal or cultural beliefs about illness. If our culture assumes that illness is a punishment for sin then we may be less likely to admit to illness than if we are told it is a reward for doing good or if we assume it is caused by an invasion of viruses over which we have no legitimate, voluntary, personal control.

Equally relevant is our trust in the doctor and the treatment. This trust will depend on our beliefs about doctors in general, the way we are handled in the consultation, whether the doctor's breath smells of alcohol, and our own personal model of illness. People nowadays accept antibiotics whereas in previous times they may have believed in the efficacy of boiled newts' tongues, crocodile dung and the sweat of pregnant women – treatments which were more often effective than we would suppose (DiMatteo and Friedman, 1982).

Neither the decision to report sick nor the confidence in the effectiveness of treatment is based on absolute factors. An individual's personal beliefs and those of friends or cultures at large will also give meaning to pain and illness. Each society takes its own view of why and how people get sick and what they should do to put it right. Which of the following explains why we get sick? God is punishing us for some sinfulness; our body contains too much blood and needs leeching; a demon has crept into our body; we caught a virus; we failed to make a sacrifice to the health god; we ate the wrong diet; we have bad attitudes towards our comrades; we did not get a regular health checkup; we do not exercise enough; we smoke; a witch stuck a pin into a model of our body; we are lonely; we have just moved house, lost our job, become divorced and run into debt; an enemy gave us the Evil Eye; it was something we ate last night; we should have washed our hands. Not only have all of these views been held by some culture or another at some point in the past, but most of them are still believed by some group or another today. Our choice between them can be seen as partly influenced by culture and our connections to a supportive network (Sarason et al., 1997).

The sick role and the social consequences of illness

Being ill is therefore a social as well as a purely physical condition and allows the individual to enter the 'sick role'. To do this, a person must be legitimated by an accepted authority, such as a doctor, a caring friend, a concerned colleague, or, in the case of a child, by a parent (Parsons, 1951). Secondly, the illness must normally be beyond the person's responsibility to control (e.g. someone who is staggering and disoriented by reason of intoxication is not regarded in our culture as 'sick' whereas someone showing similar symptoms as a result of a blow to the head is accepted in our culture as truly 'sick'). Thirdly, whilst the sick role legitimately excuses us from certain regular obligations like work, it brings others. A person is obliged to 'get well soon' or to act out the role in a socially acceptable way by, for example, 'bearing pain with cheerfulness and fortitude', being uncomplaining about discomfort, and appearing to be brave in the face of impending death. People who do this in ways that our culture approves of have that fact mentioned in their obituaries, whereas those who fail to do so do not have their reactions described at all. You will never see an obituary that says 'When he was told that he was dying he just broke down and cried like a real wimp' (despite the fact that it might be an understandable reaction in the circumstances).

Illness has three further aspects to it (DiMatteo and Friedman, 1982), all with relational overtones: destructive, liberating and occupational.

First, illness is usually destructive: it causes physical deterioration, pains, disability and discomfort. This can cause anguish to loved ones, who see a father, mother, partner, child, or friend deteriorating before their eyes (Lyons and Meade, 1995). Insofar as the patient is aware of these feelings or reactions, then psychological pain, including feelings of guilt, can also afflict the patient. Equally, the patient has feelings about the destructive side of illness and feels pressure to cope not only with the pain itself but with its social management (e.g. not 'letting it show' to visitors or not letting it interfere with relationships; Lyons et al., 1996). Also of course people experience illness as especially troublesome when it does affect their ability to conduct relationships satisfactorily and a large part of the reported distress of diseases such as multiple sclerosis is that it destroys relationships themselves or the opportunity for conducting them (Lyons and Meade, 1995).

A further social consequence of the destructive side of illness is the direct effect on status and general 'social credit'. Many illnesses cause disfigurement or socially unacceptable sights, sounds and smells. These social stigmata must be endured by the patient along with the pain and they affect others' willingness to be involved socially with the patient (Lyons et al., 1996). Some illnesses disrupt social behaviour and cause inept actions like involuntary trembling, unexpected extensions of limbs, lolling of the head and tongue, dribbling, or disturbed eye movements. These, too, are stigmata that make it difficult for outsiders to interact with the patient in normal social ways and thus add to the burdens that the patient must endure (Lyons et al., 1996).

Some medication treats the illness but causes side effects with nasty social consequences like drowsiness or inability to concentrate (e.g. some antipsychotic drugs cause stiffness in the limbs and occasional uncontrollable drooling). Alternatively, some treatments restrict patients' social calendars or require them to withdraw from social contact to carry out medical procedures (e.g. going to lie down for dialysis on a kidney machine or going to a private room for regular insulin injections for *diabetes mellitus*; Lyons and Meade, 1995).

These aspects of illness make extra relational demands on the patient, over and above the need to cope with physical discomfort. As such they afflict the person's ability to carry out and enjoy normal human relationships.

Second, illness can also serve a liberating social function: illness frees people from dull routine, legitimates their non-completion of assignments, and releases them from exams, duties, tasks and obligations (Parsons, 1951). Social, intellectual and task-related failures can be excused by reference to sickness ('I wasn't concentrating: I have a headache'). These excuses are not damaging to the individual's social *persona* (or 'image'): the persons are 'off the hook', it is not their fault, they should not blame themselves, they do not lose their 'social credit'. They can blame the illness – the person is out of sorts and not fully responsible. In this case the illness feeds an excuse into poor relational performance but the link between illness and relationships is still important.

Third, illness can become an occupation that takes over a person's life like a full-time job. The person may need to restructure daily routines like feeding and toilet needs in significantly restrictive ways or go to bed much earlier than usual, cut down on social time, and make much less effort to go out and see people. Although such things are caused by the illness, they nevertheless afflict the person's social life and relationships and are experienced as additionally unpleasant for that reason (Lyons and Meade, 1995).

The sick role and failure   In the light of such points, some scholars have argued that illness is sometimes a mechanism for coping with failure (Shuval et al., 1973). Since illness gives us an appropriate, legitimate and accepted excuse to tell our friends why we are unable to perform roles, fulfil tasks, or take on responsibility, some people might become ill or report or play up an illness whenever they come up against evaluation, or when they are afraid of it. In brief, illness helps people to avoid evaluative situations, particularly ones which are important to them. Snyder and Smith (1982) suggest that illness operates as a 'self-handicapping strategy', as they call it, and so people exaggerate reports of illness (and may actually feel more ill) when they are faced with an esteem-threatening event. This is also known more dramatically as 'academic wooden leg' ('what can you expect from someone with a wooden leg?'; it's borrowed from Berne, 1964, *Games People Play*). Such people might feel they have developed some serious illness just before class tests, for instance, if it really matters to them to get a high grade, and they are worried that they are not going to make it. One way out of the problem is to claim an illness which is absolutely debilitating and gives the perfect excuse not to sit the exam or be tested. How could we possibly do well in that exam if we have mononucleosis, glandular fever or laryngitis? None of this is to say that people never get ill in the physical sense or that symptoms are nothing but self-protective strategies, but there are some cases where self-protection could be one of the major social roles of illness.

Patient and doctor

Visiting the doctor: why and when?

Even if we decide that we are sick, there is another step to be taken also – the step of getting help. What influences whether and when we go to the doctor? We go to the doctor not just because we feel sick, but only when we feel that our physical state is serious enough to interfere with our life and so deserves special attention (Zola, 1972). We thus have a considerable amount of personal leeway surrounding the decision whether our physical state does interfere enough to deserve attention. It also depends on what is going on in our life at the time that could become disrupted. If we were going to be married tomorrow, then we may well decide to postpone a visit to the doctor in order to get on with the relational task of getting married. If on the other hand we have nothing much planned, then we may react to less of 'an illness' to make us feel that we should see a doctor.

A second factor that influences the decision is a person's friendship status (Sarason et al., 1997). Persons with chronic asthma need fewer trips to the emergency room if they see their relational networks as strong and available for support (Janson et al., 1993). People with supportive, closely knit networks of friends go to the doctor at an earlier point in the illness, presumably because they have been told by their friends that they do not look too well, and it's about time they did something and took professional advice (Hays and DiMatteo, 1984). On the other hand, people with no groups of friends or with only small social networks go to the doctor more often when there is nothing wrong with them – either because they have no access to preliminary lay advice that would tell them there is no real problem or because doctors have a caring role and they are seeking out someone to care. They may even hope to meet other people to talk to in the doctor's waiting room – an occurrence that is not as rare as you might think (Duck, 1991).

Does it hurt enough to be worth a consultation?   What determines a person's timing of the decision that the pain is significant enough for help to be sought? DiMatteo and Friedman (1982) note that more deaths from myocardial infarctions (heart attacks) occur at times when it is socially inconvenient to interpret one's chest pains as a sign of heart problems rather than as indigestion or strained muscles. That is, at weekends, when doctors are off duty, patients do not wish to call them on a possible fool's errand – but by the time the patient acknowledges the true seriousness of his or her condition, it may be too late.

Other relational influences affect the decision to seek help at a particular time (Zola, 1972):

1   Some interpersonal crisis calls attention to the symptoms and makes the person dwell on them. For instance, a person may suddenly become aware of feeling faint during an argument or may experience difficulty breathing during a quarrel.
2   Some interference occurs to valued (social) activity. For instance, the person may not be able to join in a walking jaunt with friends because of breathlessness.

3   Symptoms are sanctioned by friends who, for example, may remark that the person looks ill. If friends say that the person looks ill when the person feels ill also then that proves that the problem must show. It is not all just a figment of the imagination.

4   Symptoms are perceived as threatening. For instance, when the pain becomes so severe that the person cannot move around properly.

5   Symptoms are perceived as similar to those suffered by other people in the patient's network. 'My friend had just that sort of minor pain in the morning but by six o'clock that night he was dead.'

Doctor–patient relationships   Do we get better just because of our relationship with our doctor? Willingness to report sick is affected by confidence in and liking for the doctor and so, more surprisingly, is recovery (Hays and DiMatteo, 1984). The doctor–patient relationship is one of the factors which affects psychological state, which in turn affects interpretation of symptoms and whether we maintain the prescribed medication.

Faith in the doctor has *some* curative effect. In the past, doctors frequently bled, purged, sweated or fumigated patients, attached leeches to them, and gave them all manner of strange concoctions, poultices and elixirs. It is less a miracle that anyone survived than it is that doctors were allowed to continue to practise medicine (which seems to have been what they were doing in more than one sense). Yet people had faith in these cures and frequently recovered, though one is tempted to conclude that the threat of further treatment was what brought about recovery.

Types of doctor–patient relationships   Researchers have begun to understand a little more clearly the means by which doctor–patient relationships can contribute to healing. Patients respond not only to their medical treatment but to their social treatment – the ways in which they are treated as human beings (Mallinckrodt, 1997). Nowadays, trainee doctors receive instruction on ways of relating to patients (Pendleton and Hasler, 1983) and how to conduct medical interviews (Putnam et al., 1988). Bedside manner can influence the outcome of treatment: the more the patient feels like an individual and is treated as a person, rather than just as a collection of symptoms, the sooner he or she recovers (for example, doctors' elicitation of patients' descriptions of their symptoms and doctors' explanations for the symptoms in clinical interviews can be conducted in such a way as to reduce blood pressure in hypertensive patients; Orth et al., 1987). Obviously, when treated personally we feel less humiliated by the degrading aspects of treatment (e.g. being stripped and prodded, having to cough, spit and excrete or produce personal specimens while the nurse smiles encouragingly from the corner).

Being respected as a person can make us feel more important and want to recover, because we are being attended by someone who cares about us personally. It also, incidentally, makes the doctor feel better personally (because he or she feels more skilful, more personable, more important), feel more positive about the job and more satisfied with doing it (Hays and DiMatteo, 1984). So, one hidden consequence of this relational factor is that it makes doctors do a better job because they begin to feel better about what they are doing. However, the other hidden consequence is that patients who feel understood tend to communicate more effectively about their symptoms and so receive better treatment (Pettegrew and Turkat, 1986). As the authors conclude, patient–doctor communication is not only instrumental but also relational, and style is as relevant as content.

A patient's perception of the doctor's social and medical skills affects confidence also. For instance, Parker (1960) shows that authoritarian medical *students* are disliked and disparaged, whilst authoritarian *consultants*, who are supposed to be expert, are indulged when they act masterfully, and are both liked and trusted. Unfortunately, where respect for a consultant's skills degenerates into fear there are some serious effects on health. Jarvinaan (1955), working with people in coronary intensive care units, found that the most likely time for patients to have spontaneous relapses or a fatal heart attack was 10 minutes before the doctors were due on their rounds to come and visit their patients. Evidently, stress was a cause of this, and the patients felt so belittled (in 1955 and the pre-bedside manner days) by the way they were treated by these eminent surgeons with all their students looking on, and poking them around, that they decided they would shuffle off this mortal coil (Hamlet, 1597).

What can be done to improve the doctor–patient relationship? If you cast your mind back to the materials on nonverbal and verbal interaction in Chapter 1, you should get some ideas. For instance, we could devote special care to the doctor's nonverbal style in the initial consultation when patients' expectations are set and when initial diagnosis is made. We could also look at the patients' nonmedical needs and the ways in which the doctor could be helped to anticipate and deal with them.

Communication in the doctor–patient relationship   The central problem in doctor–patient relationships is communication. To make a diagnosis, the doctor needs to obtain all the relevant information, but has a much clearer idea of what would be relevant than the patient does. The skill is to obtain the details, bearing in mind that the patient may be medically unsophisticated and unaware of whether some piece of information is relevant to a diagnosis. If you are breathless, does it matter that you also have swollen ankles, for instance? A doctor would know that these together indicate heart disease and circulatory problems, but the patient may not.

Traditionally, then, the doctor takes control of the interactions and asks questions that will lead to the most helpful information. We have seen (Chapter 1) that the full relational system of communication has both verbal and nonverbal components. Both, therefore, are involved in doctor–patient communication. We have also seen that encoding (conveying what you feel) and decoding (working out what the other person feels) are important. Let us now look at these relationally loaded activities in the particular medical context that concerns us here.

Encoding   One special difficulty for doctors is that they are bright people selected and trained for several years in a highly specialized and technical system of description about a common and familiar object: the human body, in its various appealing or grotesque manifestations. The patient, on the other hand, is concerned about a personal complaint and its cure, but is not necessarily intellectually curious about the why, the how and the wherefore. The patient comes to a consultation wanting, and perhaps needing, reassurance and 'information' (indeed a major part of the doctor's role is to explain the meaning of illness and to encourage appropriate preventive and curative measures which the patient must follow properly to do any good). Most of us know little or nothing about what our liver does, have no idea why we have a spleen, and could not say where our pancreas is, let alone our ischial tuberosity or gluteus maximus, but we all have one (and, in some cases, two) of these. Sometimes we know we do not know; sometimes we think we do but are wrong; sometimes we have an idea that is partly right.

Most often patients are anxious enough to want reassurance but cannot understand what is said to them to provide it. Patients persistently request detailed explanations of what is happening to them, yet they do so unsystematically, tending to be passive and general (Boreham and Gibson, 1978). They ask for 'information' but are unclear about the areas of concern: what do they really want to know? In any case, patients mostly fail to comprehend what is said to them even when the 'information' is provided. Part of the problem is that medicine is so complex whereas most ordinary people have very simple models of illness. We just are not aware of the mechanisms through which we could catch typhoid or do not have the faintest idea how gastroenteritis develops.

A further problem is that patients need to receive descriptions in common language whereas doctors tend to use 'medspeak' (Christy, 1979) and talk in jargon even when talking to patients who are relatively unsophisticated in medical knowledge. A doctor who knows the details of biochemistry must find it difficult to talk in terms of everyday examples that the rest of us can understand: doctors are taught to doctor, not to teach. Words taken for granted by doctors will go over the heads of most people: we may know what 'a diagnosis' is, but fewer know what 'a prognosis' means and can only ask 'How long have I got?'

Since medspeak is technical jargon, it is a high form of code (see Chapter 1) with many specialized terms, a complex structure and formality. It instantly freezes out informality and leaves little room for the friendly banter that may relax the patient enough to talk in detail about the symptoms. Patients are aware of very few central rules in the doctor–patient relationship, but two which stand out are: make sure that you are clean, and speak the truth (Argyle and Henderson, 1984). Since both rules emphasize the extreme power difference in the relationship they, too, are likely to stand in the way of a friendly encounter – if that is what the patient truly desires.

The risks are that such rules and complex talk will alienate the patient and that they will increase the risk of misunderstanding. In tragic confirmation of this Boyd et al. (1974) found that more than 60 per cent of patients misunderstood their doctor's instructions about the method of taking their medication, even when they were interviewed soon after leaving the consultation. (I have always wanted to know if Boyd et al. ever did a follow-up, and if so, how many subjects survived to take part in it.)

The best way that the doctor can improve things is to provide the low code social form of discourse that the patient would like: the informal chatty style of language that we normally use to friends. Patients would rather have reassuring communication than emotionally neutral communications or humorous ones (Linn and DiMatteo, 1983). The second component is that the patient expects more general issues to be covered than simply those that relate directly to the illness. For instance, patients are more satisfied when relational consequences of the ailment are specifically mentioned and addressed (Lau et al., 1982), in particular, how it will affect relationships with the family or the ability to socialize with friends, or sexual performance, or attractiveness (Lyons et al., 1996). It also seems likely to me that a preferred style would be one that emphasizes personal recollection of the patient's human individuality rather than simply the patient's medical history. Whether he had secretly written it onto my medical notes I do not know, but the doctor I best remember from my teenage years always ended each consultation with a question about my progress in the classical Greek class at school. Whilst I forget why I went to see him, I remembered this personal treatment and felt more confident about his medical skills than I did with another local doctor who not only forgot my name (a name like Duck?) but thought I was someone else. I'm just glad I corrected him and he didn't give me that person's medication instead of my own.

Decoding   Patients have a story to tell and often want to tell it in their own words – a well-known element of relating through narratives (Bochner et al., 1997). Therefore, the other side to the verbal interaction in a doctor–patient interaction is decoding. Whilst a doctor may need to ask some prompting 'closed questions' which produce 'yes/no' answers, 'Hearing the patient's true message is the . . . [essential feature] of a great physician' (Pickering, 1978: 554). (Interestingly, the original quotation has the Latin words *sine qua non*, where I put 'essential feature', and this tells us something about doctors' language codes – even when they are thinking about patients.) Attentive listening to a person's real meaning rather than to the words themselves is an essential part of decoding messages (see Chapter 1), so it is not a surprise to find that patients prefer doctors who have an attentive listening style (Stone, 1979). Such attention can help the doctor to learn more about the patient's psychological state (e.g. whether the person seems anxious, upset, depressed, obsessive, tense). Also, it may uncover something of the patient's relational characteristics (e.g. value system, beliefs, norms, behavioural preferences and lifestyle) without needing to ask

---

Box 7.1   Nonverbal cues in doctor–patient relationships

- Doctors who adopt a closed-arm position (i.e. with arms folded across the chest) are interpreted as cold, rejecting and inaccessible, whilst moderately open positions convey acceptance (Smith-Hanen, 1977).
- Doctors and counsellors who establish eye contact during a pleasant, accepting interaction make patients feel more positive about the encounter (LaCrosse, 1975).
- Affiliative nonverbal behaviours, such as smiles, nods, and a 20-degree forward lean, increase the patient's perceptions of a doctor's warmth, interest, concern – and attractiveness (LaCrosse, 1975).
- Touch can have reassuring effects on patients, making them feel more relaxed, more comforted, more supported, and more cared-for (Montagu, 1978).
- Touch can exert a general enhancing effect on the perceived competence and effectiveness of health professionals (Blondis and Jackson, 1977).
- Contact (e.g. in taking a patient's pulse) can influence patients' heart rate and cardiac rhythm, as well as reduce the frequency of ectopic beats – those that occur irregularly or out-of-place (Lynch et al., 1974).
- Street and Buller (1988) showed that doctors use less touch with less anxious patients, however, and also use a less dominant style with patients over 30 years of age than they do with younger ones.

---

intrusive questions about it. Such information may help the doctor to work out whether the patient will take the tablets or whether the other family members will help. The doctor may get family members to help the patient keep to a difficult drug prescription or dietary regimen.

Whereas the verbal part of interaction is significant, we know from Chapter 1 that the nonverbal component is more so (Walker and Trimboli, 1989). Predictably (from Chapter 1), both nonverbal encoding and nonverbal decoding will exert strenuous influence on the patient and doctor. The whole range of nonverbal cues has effects on the doctor's perception of the patient and vice versa, as Box 7.1 shows.

Naturally, patients are particularly sensitive to the effect that their condition has on other people too. It is therefore crucial that the doctor does not 'leak', through nonverbal channels, any sense of disgust, pity, revulsion, anxiety, or lack of optimism (Friedman, 1982). Interestingly, Milmoe et al. (1967) show that a doctor's effectiveness in referring alcoholics for further treatment is negatively correlated with the amount of anger present in the voice whilst talking about alcoholism. Doctors who 'leaked' their distaste for alcoholism by seeming angry with the patient had the effect of discouraging patients from actually taking the further treatment that was advised.

On the other hand, patients frequently leak their true state of anxiety about an ailment through body posture, voice tone, or (ir)regularity of speech and can also indicate fear or (dis)trust of doctors by the manner in which they regulate distance in the interaction (Hays and DiMatteo, 1984). A doctor who attends carefully to the nonverbal cues which accompany the verbal messages will gain extra information about the patient's state of health and also about the patient's beliefs about that state, all of which may be useful in diagnosis.

The relational art of medicine Doctor–patient communication is an extremely powerful influence on patients' satisfaction, so it is unsurprising that a number of programmes have been started with the intention of training medical students in the 'art' of medicine, which has the art of relating as one large component. Usually, these programmes consist of training in nonverbal or verbal communication skills (Engler et al., 1981). Typically, they show that the student's interviewing, empathy and general handling of patients improve. Results are not all positive (Farsad et al., 1978) and may not have long-lasting effects even when they are positive. We also do not really know whether such training leads to better doctors or to more satisfied patients (which may or may not be effectively the same thing). Nevertheless, it would be unusual for a social scientist to conclude that the outlook for such work is not promising, and I will not so conclude. If improvements in communi-cation continue, then it seems likely that such training benefits both the patients (who feel happier with their treatment) and the doctors (who feel happier with patients' responses and with their own performance as experts). The main questions are whether there is long-term maintenance of the skills and whether we can increase the proportion of doctors who can sustain them.

Social networks and health

By now you should have some inkling that research shows many ways in which our relationships and social networks help keep us alive. Recall that a 'social network' is the group of people with whom a person is involved (usually friends); 'social support' refers to the help that they provide or are felt to provide. There are major questions here of whether and how the existence of a large social support network can 'buffer' people against stress, affect our vulnerability to illness, and increase our chances of recovery (Duck, with Cohen Silver, 1990; Leatham and Duck, 1990; Sarason, et al., 1997). What matters most – the number or quality of supports? What happens when the network is disrupted? Is loss of relationships stressful and/ or life-threatening and if so, how? If I expect support from someone and he or she lets me down, will that make me ill?

To suggest that our health might be influenced by our membership of a network and by the practices that are common in that group is not a new idea. One early example of research on epidemiology is based precisely on this idea. The British researcher Snow (1854) showed that cholera was developed by villagers sharing one particular well more frequently than by others using a different source of water. He also showed that Scots who put water in their whisky were more likely to contract some diseases than was a group of people who drank whisky neat or who boiled their water to make tea instead.

The identification of such demographic or lifestyle features as correlates of disease remains one of the primary steps that researchers take. By such means, for instance, it is established that disadvantaged children tend to be born to young mothers who have not used antenatal services and who are more likely to be smokers (Department of Health and Social Security, 1976). Also the first step in understanding AIDS in the early 1980s was to discover the characteristics, lifestyles and relational histories of those individuals who contracted it (Vanzetti and Duck, 1996).

In a fundamental and exciting extension of this logic, some researchers have tried to identify specific features of an individual's particular groups of friends and family or lifestyle that may relate to the diseases that he or she contracts (Hooley and Hiller, 1997; Sarason, et al., 1997). Other researchers have looked at the relationship styles of the individual. For instance, Morgan (1990) was interested in such questions as how deeply a person is involved in a network of friends, how that feels, and what expectations are held in respect of friends and kin. Such research issues are generally described as concerned with 'social support'. There are clearly major over-laps between the work on the resources that friends provide on the one hand, and the work on the dynamics of personal relationships on the other. Surprisingly, it is only recently that there have been any explicit and wholehearted attempts to tie the two literatures together (Duck, with Silver, 1990), and Sarason et al. (1997) now note the importance of the *qualities* of relationship between supporter and recipient.

In their classic study, Brown and Harris (1978) show that the presence of a close, confiding relationship with a husband or partner significantly reduced the risk of women developing depression after a major loss or disappointment. Brown and Harris argue that long-term feelings of self-worth or self-esteem are especially significant, that these are provided by important close relationships, and that, to a major extent, these feelings could stave off psychiatric disorder in a crisis. One problem here is that the existence of strong close relationships with very small numbers of friends might be concealed in studies that check just on the numbers of friends that we claim to have (Hobfoll, 1984). If I do a study that seems to show that people are better off with large numbers of friends, I may miss the point that large numbers are made up of several sets of small numbers and the level of intimacy in these small groups – rather than the total number of bodies in our network – may be the key issue. There is certainly evidence that intimate relationships with a small number of persons are what really counts (Heller and Rook, 1997). What may be important is that a minimum level of close relationships is maintained. In other words, within a large group of friends there is at least one subset of one or two very close relationships with one or two special friends. Alternatively, regular conver-sations with specific friends provide the *sense* of support that is important (Leatham and Duck, 1990). Certainly there are features of the transactions

---

Box 7.2   Health consequences of relational disruption

- Widowed men have a higher mortality rate, occurrence of mental disorder and tendency to suicide than have widowed women or married persons (Berardo, 1970).
- Widows have a higher rate of health complaints during the year following bereavement than do a group of matched control subjects (Maddison and Viola, 1968).
- Lonely people are more likely to suffer from depression, to have general medical complaints and to attempt suicide (Lynch, 1987).
- Men who are in the process of separation or divorce are much more likely to suffer from stress-related illness (Bloom et al., 1978).
- Dissatisfied marital partners are more likely to suffer depression (Weiss and Aved, 1978).
- Taken generally, several sets of results indicate that persons in disturbed relationships have higher incidences of low self-esteem, depression, headaches, tonsillitis, tuberculosis, coronaries, sleep disorders, alcoholism, drug dependence, cancer, and admissions to mental hospitals (Duck, 1991).
- There is a markedly increased risk of separated men being the victim of a homicidal assault (Bloom et al., 1978).
- Several sorts of physical symptoms follow closely on a sense of failure in relationships (Schmale, 1958).
- Disruption of relationships late in life is particularly troublesome (Hansson et al., 1990), and instances of interpersonal betrayal in the social networks of older adults are surprisingly high, with some 19 per cent of all elderly adults having been betrayed or seriously let down during a time of vulnerability (including being psychologically or physically abused).

---

of pairs of friends that are significant (Cutrona et al., 1990), such as comforting one another (Burleson, 1990), or cheering one another up (Barbee, 1990). Also people tend to suffer stress and illness when their relationships become disturbed (Box 7.2), and the presence of strong, close relationships preserves people from the worst effects of stress (Box 7.3, below), whether the presence is just felt to be available or is actually provided (Sarason et al., 1997).

Obviously, there are two separate ideas here – both widely accepted. One suggests that absence or disruption to relationships leads to ill-health, the other that presence of good relationships leads to well-being. We have to be careful to distinguish between these two thoughts though, since they are not making quite the same point. If a researcher carried out a study showing that disrupted relationships 'cause' illness, that does not prove that good relations 'cause' health; it may be that good relations do nothing, they are just taken for granted. On the other hand, good ones could promote good health whilst bad ones could cause stress – because they bring rejection and also the need to restructure our lives to find alternative partners and establish new routines. Disruption to a relationship exposes one hidden benefit of being in a stable partnership, namely that it provides a division of labour in coping with life's problems. The dissolution of a relationship (Chapters 3 and 4) requires the person to take on extra and undivided responsibility for the labours of life and the routine chores of daily existence (see the discussion of Hagestad and Smyer, 1982 in Chapter 3). An important stressful consequence of relational loss, then, is loss of help with physical chores, as well as loss of emotional support, regular interaction, common understanding or view of the world, and all the daily conversations that make up relationships (all the things that Chapter 3 indicated to be significant).

The social network and social support

When we talk of social support provided by friends and kin, do we mean physical support (e.g. help with car maintenance or childcare) or emotional support (e.g. advice about a particularly troublesome problem) or just plain old regular human contact? Heller and Rook (1997) indicate that there are many different ways in which 'support' has been assessed, from esteem-building (making you feel good), through physical help (e.g. muscle power in shifting a piano), to fostering a sense of belonging or inclusion (making you feel you are a 'member of the club'). Which is it that matters most, help with routine, help in times of crisis, reassurance of worth, or some gener-alized support, based on a feeling of common understanding of the world and how to deal with it? Obviously these are not the same things and the everyday sense of inclusion that people get from routine daily conversation (Leatham and Duck, 1990) is different from the sense of support that people get from real physical help after a natural disaster like a hurricane (Kaniasty and Norris, 1997). Hobfoll (1988) has argued that stress (the flipside of support in some ways) is occasioned by the loss or threatened loss of resources, whether personal, physical or psychological. People feel stress when the resources are expended or seem in their own judgement to be likely to be expended. Naturally, people try to preserve their resources or exchange them for others and so keep the general resource level high. Thus both stress and support are strongly related to personal and environmental factors as well as to the social network and what it can provide.

There are three important sorts of social support that are significant but are not related to physical provision of support. These are:

1 *Emotional support* – provision of information that one is loved and cared for. This could be achieved by direct statements of love and affection or could be indicated indirectly by, e.g. buying flowers, arranging to spend time together, remembering birthdays, taking an interest in the other's welfare, and promoting that person's best interests.
2 *Esteem support* – provision of information that one is valued and esteemed. This could be achieved by direct statements to that effect or could be indicated indirectly, e.g. by requests for advice, by treating the person's opinion as important, by allowing oneself to be guided by that person.

3 *Network support* – provision of information that one belongs to a
network of mutual obligations.

   Support can be measured by looking at three elements (Cobb and Jones,
1984): the supportive behaviour that people actually provide; the properties
of the network (i.e. whether it is close and cohesive or spread out); or the
way that a person feels about it (the subjective sense of social support).
What would be helpful to know is how people actually get their friends to
give them support (Gottlieb, 1985) and how support varies in quality and
type as the relationship develops. Some scholars (Barbee, 1990; Burleson,
1990; Cutrona et al., 1990; Leatham and Duck, 1990) indicate the importance of interpersonal transactions, particularly those involving talk and
everyday conversation in this context. It is through the transactions of daily
life, grounded as they are on conversational interaction, that individuals
gain the sense of others 'being there' for them, and can also see the degree to
which others can offer them assistance or can develop their ability to cope.
As Leatham and Duck (1990) point out, such senses do not arise only when
stress occurs, but are part of the ever-present results of dealing with friends
in everyday life and they are *built upon* during actual stress (see Box 7.3).
   However, there are two other points that need to be acknowledged.
Hobfoll (1988) points out that we must see support in context – or, in
Hobfoll's terminology, we must look at the 'ecological congruence' of
support and how it matches up to what is needed. A given resource or piece
of support is not necessarily appropriate merely because researchers label it
as a resource. What may be supportive for a woman in labour may not work
in bereavement or unemployment, and if you fall in a river the kind of help
you need is a rope, not comforting words of advice. The resources then are
only truly supportive relative to the needs of the person in question (Vaux,
1988) – they must be ecologically congruent with his or her needs and
requirements. Vaux (1990) further emphasizes the processes of actively
developing the support network, though it is important not to see this as a
sudden activity that people carry out in emergencies only. As Leatham and
Duck (1990) observed, we are building networks and creating or denying a
possible basis for future support in almost every daily conversation.
   Equally, Sarason et al. (1997) emphasize the impact of the nature of the
relationship in which the social support occurs and such a point has also
been doggedly made by Gottlieb (1985, 1990). Gottlieb indicates the
significance of rephrasing the question about social support. He suggests
that we need to ask 'Is social support a property of a person or a property
of personal relationships?' In other words, is the important aspect of social
support the way I feel about it or what I actually get from my network,
through transactions and interaction with the people who are my sources of
support? Gottlieb makes it very plain that these interactions are what counts
and that the actual marshalling of support is a major part of the whole
business of social support. Of course, the matter of determining exactly
what someone *actually* gets from a network is extremely complex and

---

Box 7.3   Social support and (the moderation of) stress or illness

- Persons who are not socially isolated had much reduced incidence (i.e. about half the risk) of mortality, a nine-year follow-up study in Alameda County revealed (Berkman and Syme, 1979).
- Positive self-concept and good social support have a combined effect in preventing a state of depression and of anxiety during an acute crisis (Hobfoll and Walfisch, 1984).
- Social support is negatively related to the incidence of psychiatric symptoms, and absence of social support is a better predictor of disorders than is incidence of stressful events (Lin et al., 1979; Silberfeld, 1978).
- Support from co-workers tends to buffer the stress of the job (La Rocco et al., 1980).
- Women who have a close relationship with their husband are less likely to suffer postpartum depression (Paykel et al., 1980).
- Those persons who have a high quality of family relationships tend to report fewer general psychiatric symptoms (Dean et al., 1981) and also fewer neurotic symptoms, such as depression and anxiety (Barrera, 1981).
- By contrast, Hobfoll and London (1985) show that close networks can increase stress for Israeli women in time of severe pressure such as the mobilization of their husbands for war, since the networks served to transmit rumours and news of disasters.
- Rook and Pietromonaco (1987) point out that although friendship has its good side and provides help with life stresses and tasks, companionship and intimacy and various other resources that prompt healthy behaviour, there is also a negative side. Help is sometimes offered in ineffective ways; it can be offered when it is not wanted or can be intrusive or excessive, and it can lead to unwanted interactions.
- Ruehlman and Wolchik (1988) showed that interference with an individual's personal projects was found to be extremely stressful and that support with such projects was significantly related to well-being.
- Rook (1990) argues that our understanding of social support and the effects of human relationships on health will be gained from greater attention to the problematic exchanges that occur within informal social networks.
- Barrera and Baca (1990) explored the reasons that make people satisfied with the support that they receive and found that network orientation, or the tendency to be open about receiving aid and to value interpersonal support, predicted distress.
- Lehman and Hemphill (1990) found that patients with multiple sclerosis valued the expression of love and concern rather than specific advice about the best ways to cope, or even attempts to minimize the seriousness of the disease. They also attributed the cause of the unhelpful attempts at support to kindly motives even though these were not a lot of use.

---

researchers' attempts to do this objectively are probably fated to fail. The important issue is what a person *thinks* the network provides and how this relates to others' views of the matter. Where any of this coincides with the amount that a researcher thinks is achieved is a bonus for the researcher. In real life there is every reason to believe that there will be as frequent discrepancies of perception by 'receivers' and 'givers' and 'researchers' as there are about almost anything else that involves two or more people. Part of the lack of success of research in this area described by Hobfoll (1988) and by Sarason et al. (1997) amounts to researchers' misguided attempts to quantify objectively and absolutely what can only be subjective and relative.

As people get to know one another so they feel more supported, although they may also be feeling more obligations that can be a bind (Rook and Pietromonaco, 1987). As a relationship develops, so the partners feel they get more from the relationship, and the course of the relationship's development is going to be affected by the amount of support (both felt support and actual support) obtained at various stressful times. For Gottlieb (1985), the key issue is the way in which particular episodes of socially supportive action create in the person the sense of being socially supported. What are the dynamics, what happens, what do people do when they support one another, and how is it recognized and acknowledged by the recipient? Clearly, argues Gottlieb (1985), the wresting of supportive behaviour from the environment is more important than just the sense of support (or to put it another way, there has to be *some* relationship between what a person believes that he or she gets and what is apparent to outsiders as 'got'). Coping depends on both the manifestation of support and on the belief that others would provide it if asked, and the ability to obtain it when it is needed, not just on one aspect alone. As far as the perspective taken in this book goes, these beliefs and supports are *generated* by daily transactions in the routine social life of human relationships and then are *activated* by a person's needs or stressors in the context of what is going on in that relationship at the time (Leatham and Duck, 1990).

Stress, daily life and relationships

Stress affects everyone in life and is often caused by worry about everyday life occurrences. However, some specific events, particularly, go with stress and disease. The most impactful of these clearly all refer to human relationships (such as death of a spouse or a child, getting married or divorced, moving to a new work environment or birth of a child; Holmes and Rahe, 1967), and there are now 'life events scales' which assess and assign scores to these and other events. The scores are determined by allotted points. You get a certain number of points for the death of a relative (63), for moving house (20), for going to college (20), for changing jobs (36) and so on. (You even score 12 if it is Christmas, but since quarrels and even murders increase in the family at that time, maybe it's not surprising; Duck, 1991.) As your score increases – particularly if it does so sharply – there is a much greater risk of your suffering stress and/or severe illness. Usually, these are stress-related illnesses or problems, but all sorts of illness (e.g. hypertension and diabetes) start happening when life-event scores build up (Wyler et al., 1971).

What is the explanatory link between life events and stress? Two aspects of life events are quite significant to the individual, so which of them matters most? Many life events are *undesirable* (e.g. being fired, death of a relative), but they also have a second element, which is *change* – just the fact that something has altered, for example moving to a different home, or adopting a new job (and so a new work routine), or entering a new relationship.

What matters most, then, the undesirability of the event or the fact of the change? Rather surprisingly, Dohrenwend (1973) finds that change *per se* is the stressor and not undesirability. It is not just the negative aspect of the change that is important, it is the fact that it is a change at all, particularly if the change requires major psychological readjustment or major reformulation of identity – such as is involved in becoming a widow(er). Obviously, these occurrences affect self-image as well as the routines of life and require a person to reopen the business of making big sense of things. If we move to a new place, meet many new people and have to begin 'getting acquainted' again, or if we lose a relative who was very close to us or was part of our identity structure, we now have to rethink ourselves, as it were (Duck et al., 1997). Such changes to self-image require major psychological readjustment towards social restructuring and that is what is most difficult to cope with.

Two psychological reactions are relevant here. First, a person's belief in self-efficacy (Bandura, 1977) – that is, a learned capacity and belief in our own control over the environment and our ability to deal and cope with events. If we believe we can handle the problem, we will not be overwhelmed by it. An individual's beliefs in this regard could be area-specific: I may have great confidence in my self-efficacy at giving lectures but less in my ability to cope with insurance sellers for instance. Whilst a lecture class of 2500 students may hold no terrors for me, the prospect of a brief one-to-one meeting to discuss life assurance could frighten me to death.

Second, a general psychological reaction to stress is observed by Selye (1956) in the 'general adaptation syndrome'. According to this model, there are three stages to reactions to stress (which Selye regarded as a physical reaction to a noxious or unpleasant stimulus):

1 *Alarm reaction*: a generalized call to arms of the defensive forces in the organism.
2 *Resistance (sustained)*: a kind of emergency reaction in which the body sustains alertness to danger and preparedness to deal with it.
3 *Exhaustion*: the defences become depleted through being 'stretched' for too long.

Other work (Innes, 1981) indicates that these patterns are dangerous over a prolonged period since they simultaneously aggravate the body's inflammatory reaction to nasty stimuli whilst reducing resistance to them. In other words, risk is increased at exactly the same time as ability to cope is reduced.

Despite these findings, there is little agreement about the nature of stress. DiMatteo and Friedman (1982) define it as 'the state of an organism when reacting to new circumstances' (key words are: 'state', 'reacting', 'new', 'circumstances'), whilst Selye (1956) defines it as the 'physical reaction to noxious stimuli' (key words are: 'physical', 'noxious', 'stimuli'). From the foregoing, it may be clear that the definition of DiMatteo and Friedman takes account of the Dohrenwend findings that change *per se* rather than noxiousness can be stressful. The essential point seems to be that any unexpected and massive need to readjust fundamentally life patterns of meaning causes stress at a psychological level, although noxious stimuli have an effect also, particularly at a physiological level. The real question for research has concerned the means by which life events cause enough stress to cause illness, and there are three models proposed (DiMatteo and Friedman, 1982):

1 Life events call upon a person's coping style which is found deficient. This leads to unhealthy or odd behaviour that causes a negative social reaction from others ('What's the matter with her? She's behaving strangely') that leads to a definition of illness ('She must be sick') and acceptance of the sick role. There is no organic disease here. What happens is that disturbed behaviour (drowsiness, hostility, weeping) leads people to assume that the person must be unwell.

2 Life events call upon a person's coping style which leads them to unhealthy styles of behaviour (alcohol abuse, nervous smoking, self-mutilation, fast driving) and these can lead to organic disease (cirrhosis, lung cancer, heart disease, physical injury) which in turn can lead to illness and the sick role. In this case, there is an organic disease that results but it results indirectly rather than directly from the need to cope. Those who 'cope' by drinking or smoking lead themselves to the illnesses caused by those particular actions rather than to simple illnesses resulting directly from stress.

3 Life events overpower a person's coping style and cause physiological stress (high blood pressure) that leads to organic trauma (stroke, heart attack). In this case, there is a direct link between the life events and the illness, mediated by physiological reactions, such as shock.

These interesting proposals make it clear that there can be several kinds of stress, of reactions to stress and of mediating agents, the most important individual one of which is coping style or personality, but that this is embedded within relational supports available to the individual. Physiological, social and environmental stress can all be distinguished, and we should recognize that a person's social behaviour, social status and human relationships can expose them to these risks to different degrees.

We can conclude that perceived support relies on an individual having a view of themselves as 'someone with competencies and characteristics that imply their deserving of the support of others' (Sarason et al., 1997) and that this support represents a complex set of transactions that connect to the person's daily experience of self with others (Leatham and Duck, 1990) and particularly support from routine conversations that support the person's system of meaning (Duck, 1994a). The conversations with friends and relatives – whatever they are 'about' – are really a perpetual basis for support since they create or reaffirm a sense of comprehension of the world, a sense of comprehension that is violently overturned by certain sorts of events that force us to re-evaluate the meanings in our life.

Relationships and death

In the last four centuries not only have the most frequent causes of death changed in relative proportions but so have there been alterations in our attitudes to death. While death is always at some level a solitary thing, any death affects other people. The death of a spouse or child is a highly charged emotional experience, as is the death of a parent or close friend. Death thus has an impact on relationships but also there are some rather more surprising connections between human relationships and death.

Cultural beliefs about death

Death occurs within a cultural and relational context in which its meaning is interpreted. One of the earliest markers of social evolution of humankind is the change in attitudes to the dead. When a culture begins to bury the dead in ritualistic ways (e.g. with food and weapons), it marks the beginning of a change in beliefs about the nature of death and assumes that there is something beyond death. If we believe that people should be buried with weapons, food and slaves, that they should be ceremonially dressed, embalmed and lying outstretched, as the Ancient Egyptians did, then it is because we believe that the weapons, food and slaves will be needed after death, that the dead person will need to be ceremonially identifiable and, therefore, need badges of rank on the body, that the person will 'need' his or her body in an undeteriorated state after death, and that death is only like sleeping, or is a transition to a further form of 'life'.

Any treatment of the dead in such careful ways also presumes a set of beliefs about what happens after death, and also some thoughts about the nature of death itself (e.g. that it is similar to a journey from here to somewhere else, whose nature can be described, such as a Happy Hunting Ground or Paradise or Hades which involves crossing several rivers, such as the rivers of hate and forgetting). Early concepts of death usually regarded it as a journey to another place rather similar to the life experienced before death. The dead person, therefore, needed to have food and weapons (and even servants) buried with him or her so that the journey could be made safely.

It was quite a bit later that people began to believe that obtaining the full benefits of the afterlife depended on what we had done on earth during life itself. The Egyptians were early believers in the idea that our heart and soul would be weighed to judge our earthly life and we would get eternal afterlife only if we had been good in the bodily life. It was not actually until relatively late (i.e. Christian times) that there entered into the system of beliefs the notion of complete change of life-form – transfiguration – rather than simple continuance of previous bodily forms, ranks and activities.

In the fourteenth century, the dead were represented, if at all, in two forms – one as in life and one as in death. Elaborate tombs consisted of a representation of them lying at full length, in living dress, on the top tier of the tomb, and on a second tier – like bunk beds – beneath this was a representation of their naked, rotting body. Until the eighteenth century, a dead person was typically buried not in a coffin but in a winding sheet, and they were referred to as still being a member of the living community (e.g. the burial service said 'we commit *your* body to the ground'). After the Reformation, the dead were represented at a transitory stage, kneeling in prayer in full dress halfway between life and death. For the rich, coffins were introduced about the middle of the seventeenth century and for everyone else coffins were the norm by the early part of the nineteenth century. By then, the person was regarded as gone from the earthly community (therefore, 'we commit *his/her* body to the ground' was introduced to the burial service). By the eighteenth century, the rich and famous dead were represented only in the living form and statues now showed them standing or sitting, in full dress, doing something that typified them when alive (e.g. delivering a speech, riding a horse).

In the early days, sudden death was greatly feared, since it deprived the person of time to prepare for it by prayer and religious sacraments. It was also true that most people saw death fairly often not only because of diseases, war and famine but because public executions and public torture were well-tried methods of social control and entertainment. Naturally, all these fears and experiences, as well as the beliefs in the surrounding culture, affected people's perceptions about their own death and those that they witnessed around them.

What now characterizes our attitudes to death? One general difference is perhaps that natural death is expected by most people, although we also hope for it to be swift. A fear nowadays is that rampant technology could keep us alive as a vegetable somewhere between death and semi-consciousness (Kastenbaum, 1982). Edgar Allen Poe's and the Victorians' writings about being buried alive reflected prevalent fears within their readers; common anxieties nowadays emerge from the same problem modernized by concern over technical definitions of brain death and the use of life-support machines to sustain those who are incapable of independent life.

Along with such changes in central concerns come reduced tolerance for minor pains (the 'headache pill' society), a considerable amount of medical game-playing (since patients fear that doctors no longer tell the truth), and such pronouncements as 'the patient's bill of rights'. Death has become a relational, social, psychological, attitudinal experience as well as a physical event.

How do people cope, in a social psychological sense, with impending death? There are essentially three foci for their concern: (1) the pain, discomfort, disability and social stigma of a terminal illness (Lyons et al., 1996); (2) the reactions and emotions of others, particularly of close others or life partners (Lyons and Meade, 1995); (3) the person's own reactions.

Kübler-Ross (1969) proposed five stages of psychological adjustment to death:

1 *Denial* (it's a mistaken diagnosis).
2 *Anger* (why me?). This can lead to envy of those still fit, resentment against them, and even to surprising verbal attacks on helpers, nurses and friends.
3 *Bargaining* (dealing with fate for more time). Terminal patients often leave their body to medical science as part of an implicit bargain with death for more time, and with medical staff for better care that may help them stay alive longer.
4 *Depression*, sadness and crying.
5 *Acceptance*. This is often characterized by silence, withdrawal and a marked detachment from other people.

Some criticize this neat system on the grounds that the terminally ill more probably oscillate between the stages, rather than move steadily to each next one. Others note that some patients show all the stages at once or that the stages occur and reoccur. Whether or not these criticisms are valid, it makes sense to attend to the psychological dimension to dying and to concern ourselves with the psychological treatment of such patients as well as with their medical treatment.

Relationships and the timing of death

There is some evidence that the timing of dying is influenced by relational factors, such as whether spousal anniversaries or significant dates are approaching. For instance, Jewish populations show a marked 'death dip' (a significant decrease in death rate) during the time before their solemn holy day Yom Kippur – the Day of Atonement (Phillips, 1970, 1972). Other research shows that birthdays and anniversaries exert effects on death of widowed spouses (Bornstein and Clayton, 1972), who tend to die on days close to dates that had significance in the marriage.

Reactions to the death of a close partner have begun to interest social scientists working on relationships recently. 'Death of a spouse' carries the highest risk on the life events scales, and bereavement brings with it a considerable need for large-scale readjustments to the routines of life. Adults responding to bereavement typically show stress and health problems over an extended period of time (Greenblatt, 1978). They also show a sequence of reactions comparable to, but not identical with, the responses of patients to their terminal diagnosis: first, exhaustion and hollowness, characterized by a sense of emptiness, stress and overwhelming responsibility;

second, a preoccupation with the image of the deceased, even extending to hallucinations or imagining that the person is still alive, has been seen in the street and the like; third, guilt or a sense of things unsaid, feelings gone unexpressed, time not spent together; fourth, hostility to others or the 'leave me alone' reaction; fifth, changes to daily activity. The fifth reaction can be healthy or unhealthy depending on the nature and extent of the change, of course. Greenblatt's (1978) point, however, is that the psychological reaction to grief is a process that extends over time and is essential to the bereaved person, who naturally enough needs to reconstruct his or her life and identity. In many ways, the reactions of the grieving spouse mark out readjustments and changes to identity as the person comes to grips with the new demands upon them that stem from loss of partner and makes decisions about the parts, mannerisms, styles or traits of the lost person they wish to retain in their active life, perhaps by imitation.

Obviously also the death of a loved one and the subsequent sense of loss force a realignment of a person's relationships and so lead on to grieving and individual reactions to the bereavement (Harvey et al., 1995). That person's loss also may lead to losses for others (loss of that person's relationship time for others, willingness to engage in social contact, with-drawal from the network). Lastly, loss causes a person to relive the rela-tionship only in memory – occasionally feeling haunted or chained by such memories.

This last point – that memories become the experience of the relationship – actually leads to an interesting thought upon which to end a book on human relationships. It raises the possibility that *all* relationships are forged largely in memory (since we often reflect about our relationships and think of relationship partners and what to do with them even when they are not present). It also raises the possibility that relationships with someone can *change* even after the person is dead. As I have noted in passing in a couple of places earlier, if we change our feelings towards a person who is not able to be present, to make a reply, or to be engaged to present their point of view, whether they are dead or simply absent from the scene, we can change a relationship at that point simply by thinking about it and changing our feelings. So are relationships created and maintained largely in thought and the language that we use to describe them? Such an issue is a good one to discuss in class now that you have reached the end of this book.

Summary

This chapter has shown mounting evidence that social relationships influ-ence or are relevant in many aspects of health, illness, recovery and death. Some factors are quite obvious, some are not, but they run the whole range from attitudinal influences derived from the surrounding community to personal beliefs derived from interpersonal experiences and even influences coming from the network of other people to which we belong and the friendships that we have. Further, social scientists contribute positively to preventive medicine and attempts to persuade us all to lead more healthy lives (Rogers, 1983). Whilst it is clearly not yet time for us to cry 'This person is sick. Send for the relationships expert', a number of major features of health and illness are indisputably relational in nature.

Further reading

Cutrona, C.E. (1996) *Social Support in Couples.* Thousand Oaks, CA: Sage.

Duck, S.W., with R. Cohen Silver (ed.) (1990) *Personal Relationships and Social Support.* London: Sage.

Sarason, B.R., Sarason, I.G. and Pierce, G.R. (1990) *Social Support: A Transactional View.* New York: Wiley.

Afterword: Some Topics for Future Attention . . . and Some Hints on Using the Library

This book grew out of my conviction that relationships are a major concern in human lives but, more than that, they are major organizers of our social experience. It is therefore primarily a book showing how relationships intertwine with daily lives, our social behaviour, and personal experiences with other people. Personal relationships, I contend, can modify general rules of social behaviour in ways that present social scientific research does not acknowledge. Consider: however I may pressure people to buy soap powder, that is not how I influence a friend to take up my astrology classes. Whatever my general attitude to smoking, the way I handle a friend's lighting up in my house will differ from the methods that are appropriate for a stranger or for my boss or for the friend of one of my guests. There is a great power and social significance to the phrase, 'Oh well, seeing as it's you I will make an exception . . .' *Relationships are modifiers* and researchers need to gain a better grasp of the ways in which generalized social behaviour – which is essentially what such researchers study – is tailored to relational circumstance.

These were my main reasons for showing the need to interweave work on relationships into the materials already available in social scientific texts. Another was to generate some thoughts for future research. In writing the book, I have become aware of several promising issues that remain to be explored. How do everyday concerns, hopes, anxieties and plans about relationships affect other daily social behaviour? Why is there so relatively little work on the dark side of relationships (Cupach and Spitzberg, 1994)? For example, where are the studies of effects of disliking or disappointment or remorse or regret on behaviour in interactions? Why so few studies of boring communication or intentional social humiliation or bitchiness? There is much research on development of relationships but virtually none on the underdevelopment of relationships or the failure of relationships to develop. Why do our models of behaviour so often assume that we always know what we are doing, where we are going in relationships, and how our lives will develop when all around and within us we see instances of confusion and indecision? Despite their frequency in social life, there is no deep understanding of flirtation, forgiveness, regret, remorse, disappointment, polite refusals, impolite requests, or 'needling' and bullying. There has only recently been some investigation of the ways in which enemies are handled (Wiseman and Duck, 1995). Journal articles traditionally report that data from suspicious subjects are discarded, but, except on unexplored intuitive grounds, researchers do not actually know whether suspicion affects social behaviour, and, if so, how exactly. How exactly do two people behave when they distrust one another, when they are enemies, or when they are 'falling out'? What precise differences are there in their interaction as compared to the interactions of friends? What variables differentiate the interactions of strangers from those of friends? Why is there so much small talk to be found in daily life and so little accounting for it in theory? How do we recognize tactlessness, naiveté, offensiveness, complaints, rivalry and seduction? What are the *relational* underpinnings of compliance, authority, flattery and insults?

I hope that in presenting relationships as the organizing theme for this book I have stimulated present readers to become the future researchers in this field who may ultimately come to undertake to fill these gaps.

To help you and your instructor: library and research skills

It can be frustrating to find that someone else has taken the only library copy of the book or article that was the basis of a class assignment, but with a little extra knowledge about some library techniques – and a bit of practice – you can get around the problem. The same techniques can help you to follow up on any topics in this book that you particularly want to pursue, and you can use these methods to expand your abilities to read around a favourite topic. It is to your advantage to have these skills available to you.

Many volumes in your library are there to help you to do your own research if you are particularly interested in a topic. The most useful are: *Current Contents, Psychological Abstracts*, and *Social Science Citation Index* (SSCI).

Current Contents

Current Contents is published in sections and simply prints the contents pages of journals recently published. There are seven sections, and the one you need is for the social and behavioural sciences. By turning to the psychology or communication sections, you can see the titles of papers that you may be interested in for research. It also lists authors' addresses so that you can contact them and ask for a reprint of their article.

Useful for: showing you what has happened most recently.

Disadvantage: gives you only the title and titles can often be misleading.

Psychological Abstracts

Psychological Abstracts deals with specific years or half-years and prints and catalogues the abstracts/summaries which appear at the start of most journal articles. It also lists the source (i.e. the journal that published it), the title and authors' affiliations. It comes in two parts: index and catalogue. The index lists subjects and authors, and gives a code number for the relevant abstract; the catalogue lists the abstracts by code number. You start with the index to find the abstracts you need, then go to the appropriate catalogue section to find the abstracts. If they are of interest to you, you can find the original article in the journal where it was published.

Useful for: the list of keywords which enables you to track down, say, all the articles on 'friendship in children' or 'prejudice' or 'self-esteem'. It is excellent for broadly encompassing a particular topic, and because it prints the abstracts in full, it enables you quickly to find pertinent details of papers and so make a list of those that you should read in full.

Disadvantages: it is produced semiannually in volumes relating to a particular (half) year and so is not as up to date as *Current Contents*. It lists only those items published in a given year, without cross reference.

Social Science Citation Index (SSCI)

SSCI is published in annual volumes and is now available on CD-ROM. It gives a list of keywords (permuterm subject index), a list of papers and authors consulted that year (source index), and a list of citations made to particular authors (citation index). (Always ensure that you are using the correct section.) The citation index is extremely useful. Suppose I want to find all the papers in 1996 that referred to S.E. Asch's classic study on conformity: I would look up Asch, S.E. in the citation index and there would be the list. This is useful because you can, for instance, trace the way in which a piece of classic work has been used in more recent work or criticized by subsequent researchers. Another advantage is that if someone has taken the very article that you wanted to read out of the library, then you can find others on the same topic that cite the article on loan. This is useful for essays and seminar classes because the more recent article may give you some good ideas about how to evaluate or criticize the set article.

Useful for: coming up to date on classic work; doing a broad review of related research; finding out the different lines that have been developed from one particular starting point; finding alternative reading sources; or finding something that contains a good critique of an earlier paper that you might have been asked to evaluate.

Disadvantages: somewhat difficult to learn to use, but the effort really is worth it.

References

Acitelli, L.K. (1988) 'When spouses talk to each other about their relationship', *Journal of Social and Personal Relationships*, 5: 185–99.

Acitelli, L.K. (1993) 'You, me, and us: perspectives on relationship awareness', in S.W. Duck (ed.), *Individuals in Relationships*. (Vol. 1) *Understanding Relationship Processes*. Newbury Park, CA: Sage. pp. 144–74.

Acitelli, L.K. (1997) 'Sampling couples to understand them: mixing the theoretical with the practical', *Journal of Social and Personal Relationships*, 14: 243–61.

Acitelli, L.K., Douvan, E. and Veroff, J. (1993) 'Perceptions of conflict in the first year of marriage: how important are similarity and understanding?', *Journal of Social and Personal Relationships*, 10: 5–19.

Acitelli, L.K., Douvan, E. and Veroff, J. (1997) 'The changing influence of interpersonal perceptions on marital well-being among black and white couples', *Journal of Social and Personal Relationships*, 14: 291–304.

Adams, R. and Blieszner, R. (1996) 'Midlife friendship patterns', in N. Vanzetti and S.W. Duck (eds), *A Lifetime of Relationships*. Pacific Grove, CA: Brooks/Cole. pp. 336–63.

Adler, T.F. and Furman, W. (1988) 'A model for children's relationships and relationship dysfunction', in S.W. Duck (ed.), with D.F. Hay, S.E. Hobfoll, W.J. Ickes and B.M. Montgomery, *Handbook of Personal Relationships*. Chichester: Wiley.

Alberts, J.K. (1988) 'Analysis of couples' conversational complaints', *Communication Monographs*, 55: 184–97.

Allan, G.A. (1993) 'Social structure and relationships', in S.W. Duck (ed.), *Social Contexts of Relationships*. (Vol. 3) *Understanding Relationship Processes*. Newbury Park, CA: Sage. pp. 1–25.

Allan, G.A. (1995) 'Friendship, class, status and identity.' Paper to Annual Convention of the International Network on Personal Relationships, Williamsburg, VA, June.

Altman, I. and Ginat, J. (1996) *Polygamous Families in Contemporary Society*. Cambridge: Cambridge University Press.

Altman, I. and Taylor, D. (1973) *Social Penetration: The Development of Interpersonal Relationships*. New York: Holt, Rinehart and Winston.

Amato, P.R. (1991) 'The "child of divorce" as a person prototype: bias in the recall of information about children in divorced families', *Journal of Marriage and the Family*, 53: 59–70.

Andersen, P.A. (1993) 'Cognitive schemata in personal relationships', in S.W. Duck (ed.), *Individuals in Relationships*. (Vol. 1) *Understanding Relationship Processes*. Newbury Park, CA: Sage. pp. 1–29.

Anderson, S.A. (1985) 'Parental and marital role stress during the school entry transition', *Journal of Social and Personal Relationships*, 2: 59–80.

Arendell, T. (1993) 'After divorce: investigations into father absence', *Gender and Society*, 6: 562–86.

Argyle, M. (1967) *The Psychology of Interpersonal Behaviour*. Harmondsworth: Penguin.

Argyle, M. (1987) *The Psychology of Happiness*. Harmondsworth: Penguin.

Argyle, M. and Dean, J. (1965) 'Eye contact, distance and affiliation', *Sociometry*, 28: 289–304.

Argyle, M. and Henderson, M. (1984) 'The rules of friendship', *Journal of Social and Personal Relationships*, 1: 211–37.

Argyle, M., Salter, V., Nicholson, H., Williams, M. and Burgess, P. (1970) 'The communication of inferior and superior attitudes by verbal and non-verbal signals', *British Journal of Social and Clinical Psychology*, 9: 222–31.

Aron, A. and Aron, E. (1997) 'Self-expansion motivation and including other in the self', in S.W. Duck, K. Dindia, W. Ickes, R.M. Milardo, R.S.L. Mills and B.R. Sarason (eds), *Handbook of Personal Relationships* (2nd edn). Chichester: Wiley. pp. 251–70.

Aron, A., Dutton, D.G., Aron, E. and Iverson, A. (1989) 'Experiences of falling in love', *Journal of Social and Personal Relationships*, 6: 243–57.

Aronson, E. and Golden, B.W. (1962) 'The effect of relevant and irrelevant aspects of communicator credibility on attitude change', *Journal of Personality*, 30: 135–46.

Asher, S.R. and Parker, J.G. (1989) 'Significance of peer relationship problems in childhood', in B.H. Schneider, G. Attili, J. Nadel and R. Weissberg (eds), *Social Competence in Developmental Perspective*. Amsterdam: Kluwer.

Asher, S.R. and Wheeler, V.A. (1985) 'Children's loneliness: a comparison of rejected and neglected peer status', *Journal of Consulting and Clinical Psychology*, 53: 500–5.

Attili, G. (1989) 'Social competence versus emotional security: the link between home relationships and behavior problems in preschool', in B.H. Schneider, G. Attili, J. Nadel and R.P. Weissberg (eds.), *Social Competence in Developmental Perspective* (NATO ASI Series). Amsterdam: Kluwer.

Ayres, J. (1989) 'The impact of communication apprehension and interaction structure on initial interactions', *Communication Monographs*, 56: 75–88.

Bandura, A. (1977) *Social Learning Theory*. Englewood Cliffs, NJ: Prentice Hall.

Barbee, A.P. (1990) 'Interactive coping: the cheering up process in close relationships', in S.W. Duck (ed.), with R. Cohen Silver, *Personal Relationships and Social Support*. London: Sage.

Barrera, J. Jr. (1981) 'Social support in the adjustment of pregnant adolescents: assessment issues', in B.H. Gottlieb (ed.), *Social Networks and Social Support*. Beverly Hills, CA: Sage.

Barrera, M. Jr. and Baca, L. (1990) 'Recipient reactions to social support: contributions of enacted support, conflicted support and network orientation', *Journal of Social and Personal Relationships*, 7: 541–52.

Barrett, K.C. (1997) 'The self and relationship development', in S.W. Duck, K. Dindia, W. Ickes, R.M. Milardo, R.S.L. Mills and B.R. Sarason (eds), *Handbook of Personal Relationships* (2nd edn). Chichester: Wiley. pp. 99–120.

Bartholomew, K. (1990) 'Avoidance of intimacy: an attachment perspective', *Journal of Social and Personal Relationships*, 7: 147–78.

Bartholomew, K. (1993) 'From childhood to adult relationships: attachment theory and research', in S.W. Duck (ed.), *Learning about Relationships*. (Vol. 2) *Understanding Relationship Processes*. Newbury Park, CA: Sage. pp. 30–62.

Bartol, C.R. and Bartol, A.M. (1994) *Psychology and Law*. Pacific Grove, CA: Brooks/Cole.

Bass, L.A. and Stein, C.H. (1997) 'Comparing the structure and stability of network ties using the social support questionnaire and the social network list', *Journal of Social and Personal Relationships*, 14: 123–32.

Baumrind, D. (1972) 'Socialization and instrumental competence in young children', in W.W. Hartup (ed.), *The Young Child: Reviews of Research* (Vol. 2). Washington, DC: National Association for the Education of Young Children.

Baxter, L.A. (1984) 'Trajectories of relationship disengagement', *Journal of Social and Personal Relationships*, 1: 29–48.

Baxter, L.A. (1992) 'Root metaphors in accounts of developing romantic relationships', *Journal of Social and Personal Relationships*, 9: 253–75.

Baxter, L.A. and Montgomery, B.M. (1996) *Relational Dialectics: A Dialogic Approach to Communication in Personal Relationships*. New York: Guilford.

Baxter, L.A. and Widenmann, S. (1993) 'Revealing and not revealing the status of romantic relationships to social networks', *Journal of Social and Personal Relationships*, 10: 321–38.

Baxter, L.A. and Wilmot, W.W. (1984) 'Secret tests: social strategies for acquiring information about the state of the relationship', *Human Communication Research*, 11: 171–202.

Baxter, L.A. and Wilmot, W.W. (1985) 'Taboo topics in close relationships', *Journal of Social and Personal Relationships*, 2: 253–69.

Baxter, L.A., Mazanec, M., Nicholson, L., Pittman, G., Smith, K. and West, L. (1997) 'Everyday loyalties and betrayals in personal relationships: a dialectical perspective', *Journal of Social and Personal Relationships* 14.

Beall, A. and Sternberg, R. (1995) 'The social construction of love', *Journal of Social and Personal Relationships*, 12: 417–38.

Beattie, G.W. (1981) 'A further investigation of the cognitive interference hypothesis of gaze patterns in interaction', *British Journal of Social Psychology*, 20: 243–8.

Bedford, V.H. and Blieszner, R. (1997) 'Personal relationships in later life families', in S.W. Duck, K. Dindia, W. Ickes, R.M. Milardo, R.S.L. Mills and B.R. Sarason (eds), *Handbook of Personal Relationships* (2nd edn). Chichester: Wiley.

Beecher, H.K. (1959) *Measurement of Subjective Responses: Quantitative Effects of Drugs*. New York: Oxford University Press.

Beinstein Miller, J. (1993) 'Learning from early relationship experiences', in S.W. Duck (ed.), *Learning about Relationships*. (Vol. 2) *Understanding Relationship Processes*. Newbury Park, CA: Sage. pp. 1–29.

Bell, B.E. and Loftus, E.F. (1988) 'Degree of detail of eyewitness testimony and mock juror judgements', *Journal of Applied Social Psychology*, 18: 1171–92.

Berardo, F.M. (1970) 'Survivorship and social isolation: the case of the aged widower', *Family Coordinator*, 19: 11–25.

Berger, C.R. (1993) 'Goals, plans and mutual understanding in personal relationships', in S.W. Duck (ed.), *Individuals in Relationships*. (Vol. 1) *Understanding Relationship Processes*. Newbury Park, CA: Sage. pp. 30–59.

Berger, C.R. and Bradac, J. (1982) *Language and Social Knowledge*. London: Arnold.

Bergmann, J.R. (1993) *Discreet Indiscretions: The Social Organization of Gossip*. New York: Aldine deGruyter.

Berkman, L.F. and Syme, S.L. (1979) 'Social networks, host resistance and mortality: a nine-year follow-up of Alameda County residents', *American Journal of Epidemiology*, 109: 186–204.

Berman, H.J. (1977) 'The uses of the law to guide people to virtue: a comparison of Soviet and US perspectives', in Tapp, L.L. and Levine, F.J. (eds), *Law, Justice and the Individual in Society*. New York: Holt.

Berndt, T. (1996) 'Friendship in adolescence', in N. Vanzetti and S.W. Duck (eds), *A Lifetime of Relationships*. Pacific Grove, CA: Brooks/Cole.

Berscheid, E. (1966) 'Opinion-change and communicator–communicatee similarity and dissimilarity', *Journal of Personality and Social Psychology*, 4: 67–80.

Berscheid, E. (1995) 'Help wanted: a grand theorist of interpersonal relationships, sociologist or anthropologist preferred', *Journal of Social and Personal Relationships*, 12: 529–33.

Berscheid, E. and Hatfield [Walster] E.H. (1974) 'A little bit about love', in T.L. Huston (ed.), *Foundations of Interpersonal Attraction*. New York: Academic Press.

Bhavnagri, N. and Parke, R. (1991) 'Parents as direct facilitators of children's peer relationships: effects of age of child and sex of parent', *Journal of Social and Personal Relationships*, 8: 423–40.

Bickman, L. and Green, S.K. (1977) 'Situational cues and crime reporting: do signs make a difference?', *Journal of Applied Social Psychology*, 7: 1–18.

Bierce, A. (1985) *The Devil's Dictionary*. New Cranton, PA: Fosdyke.

Bigelow, B., Tesson, G. and Lewko, J. (1996) *Children's Rules of Friendship*. New York: Guilford.

Billig, M. (1991) *Ideology and Opinions: Studies in Rhetorical Psychology*. London: Sage.

Billig, M., Condor, S., Edwards, D., Gane, M., Middleton, D. and Radley, A. (1988) *Ideological Dilemmas: A Social Psychology of Everyday Thinking*. London: Sage.

Birchler, G.R. (1972) 'Differential patterns of instrumental affiliative behavior as a function of degree of marital distress and level of intimacy.' PhD dissertation, University of Oregon.

Blanck, P.D., Rosenthal, R., Hart, A.J. and Bernieri, F. (1990) 'The measure of the judge: an empirically-based framework for exploring trial judges' behavior', *Iowa Law Review*, 75: 653–84.

Blondis, M.N. and Jackson, B.E. (1977) *Nonverbal Communication with Patients.* New York: Wiley.

Bloom, B., Asher, S.J. and White, S.W. (1978) 'Marital disruption as a stressor: a review and analysis', *Psychological Bulletin,* 85: 867–94.

Blumstein, P. and Schwartz, P. (1983) *American Couples: Money, Work, Sex.* New York: William Morrow.

Bochner, A.P. (1991) 'The paradigm that would not die', in J. Anderson (ed.), *Communication Yearbook 14.* Newbury Park, CA: Sage.

Bochner, A. P., Ellis, C. and Tillman-Healy, L.P. (1997) 'Relationships as stories', in S.W. Duck, K. Dindia, W. Ickes, R.M. Milardo, R.S.L. Mills and B.R. Sarason (eds), *Handbook of Personal Relationships* (2nd edn). Chichester: Wiley. pp. 307–24.

Bolger, N. and Kelleher, S. (1993) 'Daily life in relationships', in S.W. Duck (ed.), *Social Contexts of Relationships* (Vol. 4) *Understanding Relationship Processes.* Newbury Park: Sage. pp. 100–9.

Boon, S.D. (1994) 'Dispelling doubt and uncertainty: Trust in personal relationships', in Duck, S.W. (ed.), *Dynamics of Relationships.* (Vol. 4) *Understanding Relationships.* Thousand Oaks, CA: Sage. pp. 86–111

Boreham, P. and Gibson, D. (1978) 'The informative process in private medical consultations: a preliminary investigation', *Social Science and Medicine,* 12: 409–16.

Bornstein, P.E. and Clayton, P.J. (1972) 'The anniversary reaction', *Diseases of the Nervous System,* 33: 470–2.

Borys, S. and Perlman, D. (1984) 'Gender differences in loneliness', *Personality and Social Psychology Bulletin,* 11: 63–74.   `

Boulton, M. and Smith, P.K. (1996) 'Liking and peer perceptions among Asian and White British children', *Journal of Social and Personal Relationships,* 13: 163–77.

Bourhis, R.Y. and Giles, H. (1977) 'The language of intergroup distinctiveness', in H. Giles (ed.), *Language, Ethnicity and Intergroup Relations.* London: Academic Press.

Bowlby, J. (1951) *Maternal Care and Mental Health.* Geneva: WHO.

Boyd, J.R., Covington, T.R., Stanaszek, W.F. and Coussons, R.T. (1974) 'Drug-defaulting II: analysis of noncompliance patterns', *American Journal of Hospital Pharmacy,* 31: 485–91.

Bradburn, N. (1969) *The Structure of Psychological Well-being.* Chicago: Aldine.

Braverman, L. (1991) 'The dilemma of housework', *Journal of Marriage and Family Therapy,* 17: 25–8.

Brehm, J.W. (1966) *A Theory of Psychological Reactance.* New York: Academic Press.

Brehm, S. and Brehm, J.W. (1981) *Psychological Reactance: A Theory of Freedom and Control.* New York: Academic Press.

Bringle, R.G. (1991) 'Psychosocial aspects of jealousy: a transactional model', in P. Salovey (ed.), *The Psychology of Jealousy and Envy.* New York: Guilford.

Bringle, R.G. and Boebinger, K.L.G. (1990) 'Jealousy and the third person in the love triangle', *Journal of Social and Personal Relationships,* 7: 119–34.

Brodsky, S.L. (1977) 'The mental health professional on the witness stand: a survival guide', in B.D. Sales (ed.), *Psychology in the Legal Process.* New York: Halsted.

Brown, G.W. and Harris, T. (1978) *The Social Origins of Depression.* London: Tavistock.

Brown, R. (1965) *Social Psychology.* New York: Free Press.

Bruess, C.J.S. and Pearson, J.C. (1993). '"Sweet pea" and "pussy cat": An examination of idiom use and marital satisfaction over the life cycle', *Journal of Social and Personal Relationships,* 10: 609–15.

Bull, R. (1977) 'The psychological significance of facial disfigurement.' Paper presented to International Conference on Love and Attraction, Swansea, Wales, September.

Burgoon, J.K. and Koper, R.J. (1984) 'Nonverbal and relational communication associated with reticence', *Human Communication Research,* 10: 601–26.

Burgoon, J.K., Coker, D.A. and Coker, R.A. (1986) 'Communicative effects of gaze behavior: a test of two contrasting explanations', *Human Communication Research,* 12: 495–524.

Burgoon, J.K., Buller, D.B. and Woodall, W.G. (1989) *Nonverbal Communication: The Unspoken Dialogues.* New York: Harper and Row.

Burleson, B.R. (1990) 'Comforting as social support: relational consequences of supportive behaviors', in S.W. Duck (ed.), with R. Cohen Silver, *Personal Relationships and Social Support*. London: Sage.

Burleson, B.R., Kunkel, A.W., Samter, W. and Werking, K.J. (1996) 'Men's and women's evaluations of communication skills in personal relationships: when sex differences make a difference – and when they don't', *Journal of Social and Personal Relationships*, 13: 143–52.

Buunk, A. (1980) 'Sexually open marriages: ground rules for countering potential threats to marriage', *Alternative Life Styles*, 3: 312–28.

Buunk, A. (1995) 'Sex, self-esteem, dependency and extra-dyadic sexual experience as related to jealousy responses', *Journal of Social and Personal Relationships*, 12: 147–53.

Buunk, A. and Bringle, R.G. (1987) 'Jealousy in love relationships', in D. Perlman and S.W. Duck (eds), *Intimate Relationships*. Newbury Park, CA: Sage.

Byrne, D. (1961) 'Interpersonal attraction and attitude similarity', *Journal of Abnormal and Social Psychology*, 62: 713–15.

Byrne, D. (1971) *The Attraction Paradigm*. New York: Academic Press.

Byrne, D. (1992) 'The transition from controlled laboratory experimentation to less controlled settings: surprise! Additional variables are operative', *Communication Monographs*, 59: 190–8.

Byrne, D. (1997) 'An overview (and underview) of research and theory within the attraction paradigm', *Journal of Social and Personal Relationships*, 14: 417–31.

Cappella, J.N. (1988) 'Personal relationships, social relationships and patterns of interaction', in S.W. Duck (ed.), with D.F. Hay, S.E. Hobfall, W.J. Ickes and B.M. Montgomery, *Handbook of Personal Relationships*. Chichester: Wiley. pp. 325–42.

Cappella, J.N. (1991) 'Mutual adaptation and relativity of measurement', in B.M. Montgomery and S.W. Duck (eds), *Studying Interpersonal Interaction*. New York: Guilford.

Carr, S.E. and Dabbs, J.M., Jr. (1974) 'The effects of lighting, distance and intimacy of topic on verbal and visual behaviour', *Sociometry*, 37: 592–600.

Check, J.V.P., Perlman, D. and Malamuth, N.M. (1985) 'Loneliness and aggressive behaviour', *Journal of Social and Personal Relationships*, 2: 243–52.

Cherlin, A. (1992) *Marriage, Divorce, and Remarriage*. Cambridge, MA: Harvard University Press.

Christopher, F.S. (1996) 'Adolescent sexuality: trying to explain the magic and the mystery', in N. Vanzetti and S.W. Duck (eds), *A Lifetime of Relationships*. Pacific Grove, CA: Brooks/Cole. pp. 213–42.

Christopher, F.S. and Cate, R.M. (1985) 'Premarital sexual pathways and relationship development', *Journal of Social and Personal Relationships*, 2: 271–88.

Christopher, F.S. and Frandsen, M.M. (1990) 'Strategies of influence in sex and dating', *Journal of Social and Personal Relationships*, 7: 89–105.

Christy, N.P. (1979) 'English is our second language', *New England Journal of Medicine*, 300: 979–81.

Cialdini, R.B., Cacioppo, J.T., Bassett, R. and Miller, J.A. (1978) 'Lowball procedure for producing compliance: commitment then cost', *Journal of Personality and Social Psychology*, 36: 463–76.

Cialdini, R.B., Vincent, J.E., Lewis, S.K., Catalan, J., Wheeler, D. and Darby, B.L. (1975) 'A reciprocal concessions procedure for inducing compliance: the door-in-the-face technique', *Journal of Personality and Social Psychology*, 21: 206–15.

Clanton, G. and Kosins, D.J. (1991) 'Developmental correlates of jealousy', in P. Salovey (ed.), *The Psychology of Jealousy and Envy*. New York: Guilford.

Clark, R.A. and Delia, J.G. (1979) 'Topoi and rhetorical competence', *Quarterly Journal of Speech*, 65: 187–206.

Clements, M. and Markman, H.J. (1996) 'The transition to parenthood: is having children hazardous to marriage', in N. Vanzetti and S.W. Duck (eds), *A Lifetime of Relationships*. Pacific Grove, CA: Brooks/Cole. pp. 290–310.

Clore, G.L. (1977) 'Reinforcement and affect in attraction', in S.W. Duck (ed.), *Theory and Practice in Interpersonal Attraction*. London: Academic Press.

Cobb, S. and Jones, J.M. (1984) 'Social support, support groups and marital relationships', in S.W. Duck (ed.), *Personal Relationships 5: Repairing Personal Relationships*. London: Academic Press.

Cody, M.J., Woelfel, M.L. and Jordan, W.J. (1983) 'Dimensions of compliance-gaining situations', *Human Communication Research*, 9: 99–113.

Coker, D.A. and Burgoon, J.K. (1987) 'The nature of conversational involvement and nonverbal encoding patterns', *Human Communication Research*, 13: 463–94.

Coleman. M. and Ganong, L.H. (1995) 'Family reconfiguration following divorce', in S.W. Duck and J.T. Wood (eds), *Confronting Relationship Challenges*. (Vol. 5) *Understanding Relationship Processes*. Thousand Oaks, CA: Sage. pp. 73–108.

Contarello, A. and Volpato, C. (1991) 'Images of friendship: literary depictions through the ages', *Journal of Social and Personal Relationships*, 8: 49–75.

Cook, M. (1977) 'Social skills and attraction', in S.W. Duck (ed.), *Theory and Practice in Interpersonal Attraction*. London and New York: Academic Press.

Cooke, D. (1990) 'Being an "expert" in court', *The Psychologist*, May: 217–21.

Cooney, T.M. (1997) 'Parent–child relations across adulthood', in S.W. Duck, K. Dindia, W. Ickes, R.M. Milardo, R.S.L. Mills and B.R. Sarason (eds), *Handbook of Personal Relationships* (2nd edn). Chichester: Wiley. pp. 451–68.

Cortez, C.A., Duck, S.W. and Strejc, H. (1988) 'The heart is a lonely communicator: loneliness and dating patterns.' Paper to the Speech Communication Association, New Orleans, November.

Crittenden, P.M. (1997) 'The effects of early relationship experiences on relationships in adulthood', in S.W. Duck, K. Dindia, W. Ickes, R.M. Milardo, R.S.L. Mills and B.R. Sarason (eds), *Handbook of Personal Relationships* (2nd edn). Chichester: Wiley. pp. 99–120.

Crouter, A.C. and Helms-Erickson, H. (1997) 'Work and family from a dyadic perspective: variations in inequality', in S.W. Duck, K. Dindia, W. Ickes, R.M. Milardo, R.S.L. Mills and B.R. Sarason (eds), *Handbook of Personal Relationships* (2nd edn). Chichester: Wiley. pp. 487–504.

Cupach, W.R. and Metts, S. (1994) *Facework*. Thousand Oaks, CA: Sage.

Cupach, W.R. and Spitzberg, B.H. (1994) *The Dark Side of Interpersonal Communication*. Hillsdale, NJ: Erlbaum.

Curran, J.P. (1977) 'Skills training as an approach to the treatment of heterosexual–social anxiety: a review', *Psychological Bulletin*, 84: 140–57.

Cutrona, C.E., Suhr, J. and McFarlane, R. (1990) 'Interpersonal transactions and the psychological sense of support', in S.W. Duck (ed.), *Personal Relationships and Social Support*. London: Sage.

Daly, J.A., Vangelisti, A. and Daughton, S. (1987) 'The nature and correlates of conversational sensitivity', *Human Communication Research*, 14: 167–202.

Davis, J.D. (1978) 'When boy meets girl: sex roles and the negotiation of intimacy in an acquaintance exercise', *Journal of Personality and Social Psychology*, 36: 684–92.

Davis, J.D. and Sloan, M. (1974) 'The basis of interviewee matching of interviewer self disclosure', *British Journal of Social and Clinical Psychology*, 13: 359–67.

Davis, K. (1936) 'Jealousy and sexual property', *Social Forces*, 14: 395–405.

Davis, K.E. and Todd, M.J. (1985) 'Assessing friendship: prototypes, paradigm cases and relationship description', in S.W. Duck and D. Perlman (eds), *Understanding Personal Relationships*. London: Sage. pp. 17–38.

Davis, M.S. (1983) *SMUT: Erotic Reality/Obscene Ideology*. Chicago: University of Chicago Press.

Davitz, J.R. (1964) *The Communication of Emotional Meaning*. New York: McGraw-Hill.

Dean, A., Lin, N. and Ensel, W.M. (1981) 'The epidemiological significance of social support in depression', in R. Simmons (ed.), *Research in Community and Mental Health*. New York: JAI Press.

DeJong, W. (1979) 'An examination of the self-perception mediation of the foot-in-the-door effect', *Journal of Personality and Social Psychology*, 37: 221–39.

DeJong-Gierveld, J. (1989) 'Personal relationships, social support and loneliness', *Journal of Social and Personal Relationships*, 6: 197–221.

Delia, J.G. (1980) 'Some tentative thoughts concerning the study of interpersonal relationships and their development', *Western Journal of Speech Communication*, 44: 97–103.

Department of Health and Social Security (1976) *Smoking and Pregnancy*. London: HMSO.

Dertke, M.C., Penner, L.A. and Ulrich, H. (1974) 'Observers' reporting of shoplifting as a function of thief race and sex', *Journal of Social Psychology*, 94: 213–21.

de Turck, M.A. (1985) 'A transactional analysis of compliance-gaining behavior: the effects of noncompliance, relational contexts and actors' gender', *Human Communication Research*, 12: 54–78.

Dickson, F.C. (1995) 'The best is yet to be: research on long-lasting marriages', in J. Wood and S.W. Duck (eds), *Under-studied relationships: Off the Beaten Track*. (Vol. 6) *Understanding Relational Processes*. Thousand Oaks, CA: Sage. pp. 22–50.

Dillard, J.P. (1989) 'Types of influence goals in personal relationships', *Journal of Social and Personal Relationships*, 6: 293–308.

Dillard, J.P., Hunter, J.E. and Burgoon, M. (1984) 'Sequential-request persuasive strategies: meta-analysis of foot-in-the-door and door-in-the face', *Human Communication Research*, 10: 461–88.

DiMatteo, M.R. and Friedman, H.S. (1982) *Social Psychology and Medicine*. Cambridge, MA: Oelgeschlager.

Dindia, K. (1987) 'The effects of sex of subject and sex of partner on interruptions', *Human Communication Research*, 13: 345–71.

Dindia, K. (1994) 'The intrapersonal–interpersonal dialectical process of self-disclosure', in S.W. Duck (ed.), *Dynamics of Relationships*. (Vol. 4) *Understanding Relationship Processes*. Newbury Park, CA: Sage. pp. 27–57.

Dixson, M. and Duck, S.W. (1993) Understanding relationship processes: uncovering the human search for meaning', in S.W. Duck (ed.), *Individuals in Relationships*. (Vol. 1) *Understanding Relationship Processes*. Newbury Park, CA: Sage. pp. 175–206.

Dohrenwend, B.S. (1973) 'Life events as stressors: a methodological inquiry', *Journal of Health and Social Behavior*, 14: 167–75.

Donnelly, D. and Finkelhor, D. (1993) 'Parental relations, socioeconomic status, and father–child contact following divorce.' Paper to NCFR Conference, Baltimore, MD, November.

Douglas, W. (1987) 'Affinity testing in initial interaction', *Journal of Social and Personal Relationships*, 4: 3–16.

Dovidio, J.F., Ellyson, S.L., Keating, C.F., Heltman, K. and Brown, C.E. (1988) 'The relationship of social power to visual displays of dominance between men and women', *Journal of Personality and Social Psychology*, 54: 232–42.

Dresner, R. and Grolnick, W.S. (1996) 'Constructions of early parenting, intimacy and autonomy in young women', *Journal of Social and Personal Relationships*, 13: 25–39.

Duck, S.W. (1975) 'Personality similarity and friendship choices by adolescents', *European Journal of Social Psychology*, 5: 351–65.

Duck, S.W. (1976) 'Interpersonal communication in developing acquaintance', in G.R. Miller (ed.), *Explorations in Interpersonal Communication*. Beverly Hills, CA: Sage. pp. 127–47.

Duck, S.W. (1980) 'Personal relationships research in the 1980s: Towards an understanding of complex human sociality', *Western Journal of Speech Communication*, 44: 114–19.

Duck, S.W. (1982a) 'A topography of relationship disengagement and dissolution', in S.W. Duck (ed.), *Personal Relationships 4: Dissolving Personal Relationships*. London: Academic Press.

Duck, S.W. (ed.) (1982b) *Personal Relationships 4: Dissolving Personal Relationships*. London: Academic Press.

Duck, S.W. (1984a) 'A perspective on the repair of personal relationships: repair of what, when?', in S.W. Duck (ed.), *Personal Relationships 5: Repairing Personal Relationships*. London: Academic Press.

Duck, S.W. (ed.) (1984b) *Personal Relationships 5: Repairing Personal Relationships*. London: Academic Press.

Duck, S.W. (1988) *Relating to Others*. London: Open University Press; Monterey, CA: Brooks/ Cole.

Duck, S.W. (1989) 'Socially competent communication and relationship development', in B.H. Schneider, G. Attili, J. Nadel and R.P. Weissberg (eds), *Social Competence in Developmental Perspective* (NATO ASI Series). Amsterdam: Kluwer.

Duck, S.W. (1990) 'Relationships as unfinished business: out of the frying pan and into the 1990s', *Journal of Social and Personal Relationships*, 7: 5–28.

Duck, S.W. (ed.) with Cohen Silver, R.L. (1990) *Personal Relationships and Social Support*. Sage: London.

Duck, S.W. (1991) *Friends, for Life*. Hemel Hempstead: Harvester-Wheatsheaf. (Published in USA as *Understanding Relationships*. New York: Guilford.)

Duck, S.W. (1993) 'Preface on social context', in S.W. Duck (ed.), *Social Contexts of Relationships: Understanding Relationship Processes 3*. Newbury Park, CA: Sage. pp. ix–xiv.

Duck, S.W. (1994a) *Meaningful Relationships: Talking, Sense, and Relating*. Thousand Oaks, CA: Sage.

Duck, S.W. (1994b) 'Stratagems, spoils and a serpent's tooth: on the delights and dilemmas of personal relationships', in W. Cupach and B.H. Spitzberg (eds), *The Dark Side of Interpersonal Communication*. Hillsdale, NJ: LEA. pp. 3–24.

Duck, S.W. and Barnes, M.K. (1992) 'Disagreeing about agreement: reconciling differences about similarity', *Communication Monographs*, 59: 199–208.

Duck, S.W. and Condra, M.B. (1989) 'To be or not to be: anticipation, persuasion and retrospection in personal relationships', in R. Neimeyer and G. Neimeyer (eds), *Review of Personal Construct Theory*. Greenwich: JAI.

Duck, S.W. and Cortez, C. (1988) 'Dating choices.' Unpublished manuscript, University of Iowa.

Duck, S.W. and Craig, G. (1978) 'Personality similarity and the development of friendship', *British Journal of Sociology and Clinical Psychology*, 17: 237–42.

Duck, S.W. and Miell, D.E. (1984) 'Towards an understanding of relationship development and breakdown', in H. Tajfel, C. Fraser and J. Jaspars (eds), *The Social Dimension: European Perspectives on Social Psychology*. Cambridge: Cambridge University Press. pp. 228–49.

Duck, S.W. and Pond, K. (1989) 'Friends, Romans, countrymen, lend me your retrospections: rhetoric and reality in personal relationships', in C. Hendrick (ed.), *Close Relationships*. Newbury Park, CA: Sage. pp. 17–38.

Duck, S.W. and Sants, H.K.A. (1983) 'On the origin of the specious: are personal relationships really interpersonal states?', *Journal of Social and Clinical Psychology*, 1: 27–41.

Duck, S.W. and Wood, J.T. (eds) (1995) *Confronting Relationship Challenges*. (Vol. 5) *Understanding Relationship Processes*. Thousand Oaks, CA: Sage.

Duck, S.W., Miell, D.K. and Gaebler, H.C. (1980) 'Attraction and communication in children's interactions', in H.C. Foot, A.J. Chapman and J.R. Smith (eds), *Friendship and Social Relations in Children*. Chichester: Wiley.

Duck, S.W., Pond, K. and Leatham, G. (1991) 'The eye of the beholder revisited: insider and outsider view of relational events.' Paper presented to the Third Network Conference on Personal Relationships, Normal-Bloomington, IL, May.

Duck, S.W., Pond. K. and Leatham, G.B. (1994) 'Loneliness and the evaluation of relational events', *Journal of Social and Personal Relationships*, 11: 235–60.

Duck, S.W., West, L. and Acitelli, L.K. (1997) 'Sewing the field: the tapestry of relationships in life and research', in S.W. Duck (ed.) with K. Dindia, W. Ickes, R.M. Milardo, R.S.L. Mills and B.R. Sarason, *Handbook of Personal Relationships* (2nd edn). Chichester: Wiley. pp. 1–24.

Duck, S.W., Rutt, D.J., Hurst, M. and Strejc, H. (1991) 'Some evident truths about communication in everyday relationships: all communication is not created equal', *Human Communication Research*, 18: 228–67.

Dunkel-Schetter, C. and Skokan, L.A. (1990) 'Determinants of social support provision in personal relationships', *Journal of Social and Personal Relationships*, 7: 437–50.

Dunn, J. (1988) 'Relations among relationships', in S.W. Duck (ed.), with D.F. Hay, S.E. Hobfoll, W.J. Ickes and B.M Montgomery (eds), *Handbook of Personal Relationships*. Chichester: Wiley.

Dunn, J. (1996) 'Siblings: the first society', in N. Vanzetti and S.W. Duck (eds), *A Lifetime of Relationships*. Pacific Grove, CA: Brooks/Cole. pp. 105–24.

Duran, R. and Prusank, D.T. (1997) 'Relational themes in men's and women's popular non-fiction magazine articles', *Journal of Social and Personal Relationships*, 14: 165–89.

Eagly, A.H., Wood, W. and Chaiken, S. (1978) 'Causal inferences about communications and their effect on opinion change', *Journal of Personality and Social Psychology*, 36: 424–35.

Eiskovits, Z.C., Edelson, J.L., Guttmann, E. and Sela-Amit, M. (1991) 'Cognitive styles and socialized attitudes of men who batter', *Family Relations*, 40: 72–7.

Ellis, C. and Weinstein, E. (1986) 'Jealousy and the social psychology of emotional experience', *Journal of Social and Personal Relationships*, 3: 337–58.

Ellsworth, P.C., Carlsmith, J.M. and Henson, A. (1972) 'The stare as a stimulus to flight in human subjects: a series of field experiments', *Journal of Personality and Social Psychology*, 21: 302–11.

Engler, C.M., Saltzman, G.A., Walker, M.L. and Wolf, F.M. (1981) 'Medical student acquisition and retention of communication and interviewing skills', *Journal of Medical Education*, 56: 572–9.

Esses, V.M. and Webster, C.D. (1988) 'Physical attractiveness and the Canadian criminal code', *Journal of Applied Social Psychology*, 18: 1017–31.

Evans, K. (1983) *Advocacy at the Bar: A Beginner's Guide*. London: Financial Training Publications.

Farsad, P., Galliguez, P., Chamberlain, R. and Roghmann, K.J. (1978) 'Teaching interviewing skills to pediatric house officers', *Pediatrics*, 61: 384–8.

Fehr, B.E. (1993) 'How do I love thee? Let me consult my prototype', in Duck, S.W. (ed.), *Individuals in Relationships*. (vol. 1) *Understanding Relationships*. Newbury Park, CA: Sage.

Felmlee, D.H. (1995) 'Fatal attractions: affection and disaffection in intimate relationships', *Journal of Social and Personal Relationships*, 12: 295–311.

Festinger, L. (1954) 'A theory of social comparison processes', *Human Relations*, 7: 117–40.

Festinger, L. (1957) *A Theory of Cognitive Dissonance*. Stanford, CA: Stanford University Press.

Fincham, F.D. and Bradbury, T. (1989) 'The impact of attributions in marriage: an individual difference analysis', *Journal of Social and Personal Relationships*, 6: 69–85.

Fishbein, M. and Ajzen, I. (1972) 'Attitudes and opinions', *Annual Review of Psychology*, 23: 487–544.

Fisher, B.A. (1970) 'Decision emergence: phases in group decision making', *Speech Monographs*, 37: 53–66.

Fisher, S.W. (1996) 'The family and the individual: reciprocal influences', in N. Vanzetti and S.W. Duck (eds), *A Lifetime of Relationships*. Pacific Grove, CA: Brooks/Cole. pp. 311–35.

Fitch, K.L. (forthcoming) *An Interpersonal Ideology of Connectedness: The Practice of Relationships in Urban Colombia*. New York: Guilford.

Freedman, J.L. and Fraser, S.C. (1976) 'Compliance without pressure: the foot-in-the-door technique', *Journal of Personality and Social Psychology*, 4: 195–202.

French, D.C. and Underwood, M.K. (1996) 'Peer relations during middle childhood', in N. Vanzetti and S.W. Duck (eds), *A Lifetime of Relationships*. Pacific Grove, CA: Brooks/Cole. pp. 155–80.

Friedman, K.S. (1982) 'Nonverbal communication in medical interaction', in H.S. Friedman and M.R. DiMatteo (eds), *Interpersonal Issues in Health Care*. New York: Academic Press.

Furman, W. (1984) 'Enhancing children's peer relations and friendships', in S.W. Duck (ed.), *Personal Relationships 5: Repairing Personal Relationships*. London: Academic Press.

Furman, W., Rahe, D.F. and Hartup, W.W. (1979) 'Rehabilitation of socially withdrawn preschool children through mixed age and same age socialisation', *Child Development*, 50: 915–22.

Furstenberg, F.F., Nord, C.W., Peterson, J.L. and Zill, N. (1983) 'The life course of children of divorce: marital disruption and parental conflict', *American Sociological Review*, 48: 656–68.

Gaines, S.O. and Ickes, W. (1997) 'Relationships of cultural minorities', in J.T. Wood and S.W. Duck (eds), *Understudied Relationships: Off the Beaten Track*. (Vol. 6) *Understanding Relationship Processes*. Newbury Park, CA: Sage.

Gallup, C. (1980) 'A study to determine the effectiveness of a social skills training program in reducing the perceived loneliness of social isolation', *Dissertation Abstracts*, 41: 3424.

Garrard, G.G. and Kyriacou, C. (1985) 'Social sensitivity among young children', *Journal of Social and Personal Relationships*, 2: 123–36.

Gatewood, J.B. and Rosenwein, R. (1981) 'Interactional synchrony: genuine or spurious? A critique of recent research', *Journal of Nonverbal Behavior*, 6: 12–29.

Gelfand, D.M., Hartmann, D.P., Walder, P. and Page, B. (1973) 'Who reports shoplifters? A field experimental study', *Journal of Personality and Social Psychology*, 25: 276–85.

Giles, H. (1978) 'Linguistic differentiation in ethnic groups', in H. Tajfel (ed.), *Differentiation between Social Groups*. London: Academic Press.

Giles, H. and Powesland, P.F. (1975) *Speech Style and Social Evaluation*. London: Academic Press.

Giles, H., Taylor, D.M. and Bourhis, R.Y. (1973) 'Towards a theory of interpersonal accommodation through language use', *Language in Society*, 2: 177–92.

Glick, P. (1989) 'Remarried families, stepfamilies and stepchildren: a brief demographic analysis', *Family Relations*, 38: 24–7.

Goffman, E. (1959) *Behaviour in Public Places*. Harmondsworth: Penguin.

Goldsmith, D.J. and Baxter, L.A. (1996) 'Constituting relationships in talk: a taxonomy of speech events in social and personal relationships', *Human Communication Research*, 23: 87–114.

Goodman, R.F. and Ben Ze'ev, A. (1994) *Good Gossip*. Manhattan, KS: University of Kansas.

Gotlib, I.H. and Hooley, J.M. (1988) 'Depression and marital distress: current and future directions', in S.W. Duck (ed.), with D.F. Hay, S.E. Hobfoll, W.J. Ickes and B.M Montgomery, *Handbook of Personal Relationships*. Chichester: Wiley.

Gottlieb, B.H. (1983) 'Social support as a focus for integrative research in psychology', *American Psychologist*, 38: 278–87.

Gottlieb, B.H. (1985) 'Social support and the study of personal relationships', *Journal of Social and Personal Relationships*, 2: 351–75.

Gottlieb, B.H. (1990) 'The contingent nature of social support', in J. Eckenrode (ed.), *Social Context of Stress*. New York: Plenum.

Gottman, J.M. (1979) *Empirical Investigations of Marriage*. New York: Academic Press.

Gottman, J.M. (1989) 'The future of relationships.' Paper presented to Second Iowa International Conference on Personal Relationships, Iowa City, May.

Gottman, J.M. (1994) *What Predicts Divorce*? Hillsdale, NJ: Erlbaum.

Gottman, J.M., Markman, H. and Notarius, C. (1977) 'The topography of marital conflict: a sequential analysis of verbal and nonverbal behavior', *Journal of Marriage and the Family*, 39: 461–78.

Greenblatt, M. (1978) 'The grieving spouse', *American Journal of Psychiatry*, 135: 43–7.

Greene, J.O., O'Hair, H.D., Cody, M.J. and Yen, C. (1985) 'Planning and control of behavior during deception', *Human Communication Research*, 11: 335–64.

Gresham, F.M. and Nagle, R.J. (1980) 'Social skills training to children: responsiveness to modeling and coaching as a function of peer orientation', *Journal of Consulting and Clinical Psychology*, 48: 718–29.

Guerrero, L.K. (1997) 'Nonverbal involvement across interactions with same-sex friends, opposite sex friends and romantic partners: consistency or change?', *Journal of Social and Personal Relationships*, 14: 31–58.

Guerrero, L.K. and Andersen, P.A. (1991) 'The waxing and waning of relational intimacy: touch as a function of relational stage, gender and touch avoidance', *Journal of Social and Personal Relationships*, 8: 147–65.

Guralnick, M.J. (1976) 'The value of integrating handicapped and non-handicapped pre-school children', *American Journal of Orthopsychiatry*, 42: 236–45.

Hadar, U. (1989) 'Two types of gesture and their role in speech production', *Journal of Language and Social Psychology*, 8: 221–8.

Hagestad, G.O. and Smyer, M.A. (1982) 'Dissolving long-term relationships: patterns of divorcing in middle age', in S.W. Duck (ed.), *Personal Relationships 4: Dissolving Personal Relationships*. London: Academic Press.

Hall, E.T. (1966) *The Hidden Dimension*. New York: Doubleday/Anchor.

Hamlet, Prince (1597) 'Being and nothingness', *Journal of Danish Dilemmas*, LVII: 223–411.

Hansen, G.L. (1991) 'Jealousy: Its conceptualization, measurement and integration with family stress theory', in P. Salovey (ed.), *The Psychology of Jealousy and Envy*. New York: Guilford.

Hansson, R.O. and Jones, W.H. (1981) 'Loneliness, cooperation and conformity among American undergraduates', *Journal of Social Psychology*, 115: 103–8.

Hansson, R.O., Jones, W.H. and Fletcher, W.L. (1990) 'Troubled relationships in later life: implications for support', *Journal of Social and Personal Relationships*, 7: 451–64.

Harvey, J.H., Barnes, M.K., Carlson, H.R. and Haig, J. (1995) 'Held captive by their memories: managing grief in relationships', in S.W. Duck and J.T. Wood (eds), *Confronting Relationship Challenges*. (Vol. 5) *Understanding Relationship Processes*. Thousand Oaks, CA: Sage. pp. 181–210.

Hatfield [Walster], E.H., Aronson, V. and Abrahams, D. (1996) 'On increasing the persuasiveness of a low prestige communicator', *Journal of Experimental Social Psychology*, 2: 325–42.

Hatvany, N. and Strack, F. (1980) 'Discrediting key witnesses', *Journal of Applied Social Psychology*, 10: 490–509.

Hays, R. and DiMatteo, M.R. (1984) 'Towards a more therapeutic physician–patient relationship', in S.W. Duck (ed.), *Personal Relationships 5: Repairing Personal Relationships*. London: Academic Press.

Hazan, C. and Shaver, P.R. (1987) 'Romantic love conceptualised as an attachment process', *Journal of Personality and Social Psychology*, 52: 511–24.

Hecht, M., Marston, P.J. and Larkey, L.K. (1994) 'Love ways and relationships quality', *Journal of Social and Personal Relationships*, 11: 25–43.

Heider, F. (1944) 'Social perception and phenomenal causality', *Psychological Review*, 51: 358–74.

Heider, F. (1958) *The Psychology of Interpersonal Relations*. New York: Wiley.

Heller, K. and Rook, K.S. (1997) 'Distinguishing the theoretical functions of social ties: implications of support interventions', in S.W. Duck, K. Dindia, W. Ickes, R.M. Milardo, R.S.L. Mills and B.R. Sarason (eds), *Handbook of Personal Relationships* (2nd edn). Chichester: Wiley. pp. 649–70.

Hendrick, C. and Hendrick, S.S. (1988) 'Lovers wear rose colored glasses', *Journal of Social and Personal Relationships*, 5: 161–83.

Hendrick, C. and Hendrick, S.S. (1990) 'A relationship-specific version of the Love Attitudes Scale', *Journal of Social Behavior and Personality*, 5: 239–54.

Hendrick, S.S. and Hendrick, C. (1993) 'Lovers as friends', *Journal of Social and Personal Relationships*, 10: 459–66.

Hendrick, C., Hendrick, S., Foote, F. and Slapion-Foote, M. (1984) 'Do men and women love differently?', *Journal of Social and Personal Relationships*, 1: 177–96.

Hetherington, E.M. (1979) 'Divorce: a child's perspective', *American Psychologist*, 34: 851–8.

Hetherington, E.M., Cox, M. and Cox, R. (1982) 'Effects of divorce on parents and children', in M. Lamb (ed.), *Nontraditional Families*. Hillsdale, NJ: Erlbaum.

Hewes, D.E., Graham, M.L., Doelger, J. and Pavitt, C. (1985) '"Second-guessing": message interpretation in social networks', *Human Communication Research*, 11: 299–334.

Hinde, R.A. (1989) 'Individual characteristics and relationships.' Paper to the Second International Network Conference on Personal Relationships, Iowa City, May.

Hindelang, M.J. (1974) 'Moral evaluation of illegal behavior', *Social Problems*, 21: 370–85.

Hobfoll, S.E. (1984) 'Limitations of social support in the stress process.' Paper presented to the NATO Advances Study Seminar on Social Support, Bonas, France, July.

Hobfoll, S.E. (1988) 'Overview of community and clinical section', in S.W. Duck (ed.), with D.F. Hay, S.E. Hobfoll, W.J. Ickes and B.M. Montgomery, *Handbook of Personal Relationships*. Chichester: Wiley.

Hobfoll, S.E. and London, P. (1985) 'The relationship of self-concept and social support to emotional distress among women during war', *Journal of Social and Clinical Psychology*, 3: 231–48.

Hobfoll, S.E. and Walfisch, S. (1984) 'Coping with a threat to life: a longitudinal study of self concept, social support and psychological distress', *American Journal of Community Psychology*, 12: 87–100.

Hochschild, A.R. (1979) 'Emotion work, feeling rules and social structure', *American Journal of Sociology*, 85: 551–75.

Holmes, T.H. and Rahe, R.H. (1967) 'The social readjustment rating scale', *Journal of Psychosomatic Research*, 11: 213–18.

Homel, R., Burns, A. and Goodnow, J. (1987) 'Parental social networks and child development', *Journal of Social and Personal Relationships*, 4: 159–77.

Honeycutt, J.M. (1993) 'Memory structures for the rise and fall of personal relationships', in S.W. Duck (ed.), *Individuals in Relationships*. (Vol. 1) *Understanding Relationship Processes*. Newbury Park: Sage. pp. 60–86.

Hooley, J. and Hiller, J. (1997) 'Family relationships and major mental disorder: risk factors and preventive strategies', in S.W. Duck, K. Dindia, W. Ickes, R.M. Milardo, R.S.L. Mills and B.R. Sarason (eds) *Handbook of Personal Relationships* (2nd edn). Chichester: Wiley.

Hopper, J. (1993) 'The rhetoric of motives in divorce', *Journal of Marriage and the Family*, 55: 801–13.

Hopper, R., Knapp, M.L. and Scott, L. (1981) 'Couples' personal idioms: exploring intimate talk', *Journal of Communication*, 31: 23–33.

Hovland, C., Janis, I. and Kelley, H.H. (1953) *Communication and Persuasion*. New Haven, CT: Yale University Press.

Howells, K. (1981) 'Social relationships in violent offenders', in S.W. Duck and R. Gilmour (eds), *Personal Relationships 3: Personal Relationships in Disorder*. London and New York: Academic Press.

Hughes, G. (1991) *Swearing: A Social History of Foul Language, Oaths and Profanity in English*. Oxford: Blackwell.

Hupka, R. (1991) 'The motive for the arousal of romantic jealousy: its cultural origin', in P. Salovey (ed.), *The Psychology of Jealousy and Envy*. New York: Guilford.

Hurwitz, J.I. (1953) *Group Dynamics: Research and Theory*. New York: Bantam.

Huston, M. and Schwartz, P. (1995) 'Lesbian and gay male relationships', in J.T. Wood and S.W. Duck (eds), *Understudied Relationships: Off the Beaten Track*. (Vol. 6) *Understanding Relationship Processes*. Thousand Oaks, CA: Sage. pp. 89–121.

Huston, T.L., Surra, C., Fitzgerald, N. and Cate, R. (1981) 'From courtship to marriage: mate selection as an interpersonal process', in S.W. Duck and R. Gilmour (eds), *Personal Relationships 2: Developing Personal Relationships*. London and New York: Academic Press.

Ickes, W., Patterson, M.L., Rajecki, D.W. and Tanford, S. (1982) 'Behavioral and cognitive consequences of reciprocal versus compensatory responses to preinteraction expectancies', *Social Cognition*, 1: 160–90.

Innes, J.M. (1981) 'Social psychological approaches to the study of the induction and alleviation of stress: influences of health and illness', in G. Stephenson and J. Davis (eds), *Progress in Applied Social Psychology*. Chichester: Wiley.

James, R.M. (1959) 'Status and competence of jurors', *American Journal of Sociology*, 64: 563–70.

Janson, B.S., Ferketich, S. and Benner, P. (1993) 'Predicting the outcomes of living with asthma', *Research in Nursing and Health*, 16: 241–50.

Jarvinaan, K.A.J. (1955) 'Can ward rounds be a danger to patients with myocardial infarction?', *British Medical Journal*, 1: 318–20.

Jones, E.E. (1964) *Ingratiation: A Social Psychological Analysis.* New York: Appleton/Century/ Crofts.

Jones, R.A. (1982) 'Expectations and illness', in H.S. Friedman and M.R. DiMatteo (eds), *Interpersonal Issues in Health Care.* London and New York: Academic Press.

Jones, W.H., Cavert, C.W., Snider, R.L. and Bruce, T. (1985) 'Relational stress: an analysis of situations and events associated with loneliness', in S.W. Duck and D. Perlman (eds), *Understanding Personal Relationships.* London: Sage.

Jones, W.H., Freemon, J.E. and Goswick, R.A. (1981) 'The persistence of loneliness: self and other determinants', *Journal of Personality,* 49: 27–48.

Jones, W.H., Hansson, R.O. and Cutrona, C. (1984) 'Helping the lonely: issues of intervention with young and older adults', in S.W. Duck (ed.), *Personal Relationships 5: Repairing Personal Relationships.* London: Academic Press.

Jones, W.H., Hobbs, S.A. and Hockenbury, D. (1982) 'Loneliness and social skill deficits', *Journal of Personality and Social Psychology,* 42: 682–9.

Kane, J. (1971) 'Body buffer zones in Glaswegian prisoners.' Unpublished MA thesis, University of Glasgow.

Kaniasty, K. and Norris, F.H. (1997) 'Social support dynamics in adjustment to disasters', in S.W. Duck, K. Dindia, W. Ickes, R.M. Milardo, R.S.L. Mills and B.R. Sarason (eds), *Handbook of Personal Relationships* (2nd edn). Chichester: Wiley. pp. 595–620.

Kassin, S.M., Reddy, M.E. and Tulloch, W.F. (1990) 'Juror interpretations of ambiguous evidence: the need for cognition, presentation order and persuasion', *Law and Human Behavior,* 14: 43–55.

Kastenbaum, R. (1982) 'Dying is healthy and death a bureaucrat: our fantasy machine is alive and well', in H.S. Friedman and M.R. DiMatteo (eds), *Interpersonal Issues in Health Care.* New York: Academic Press.

Keeley, M. and Hart, A. (1994) 'Nonverbal behavior in dyadic interactions', in S.W. Duck (ed.), *Dynamics of Relationships.* (Vol. 4) *Understanding Relationships.* Thousand Oaks, CA: Sage. pp. 135–62.

Kelley, K. and Rolker-Dolinsky, B. (1987) 'The psychosexology of female initiation and dominance', in D. Perlman and S.W. Duck (eds), *Intimate Relationships.* Beverly Hills, CA: Sage.

Kelly, C., Huston, T.L. and Cate, R.M. (1985) 'Premarital relationship correlates of the erosion of satisfaction in marriage', *Journal of Social and Personal Relationships,* 2: 167–78.

Kelly, L. (1982) 'A rose by any other name is still a rose: a comparative analysis of reticence, communication apprehension, unwillingness to communicate and shyness', *Human Communication Research,* 8: 99–113.

Kelvin, P. (1977) 'Predictability, power and vulnerability in interpersonal attraction', in S.W. Duck (ed.), *Theory and Practice in Interpersonal Attraction.* London and New York: Academic Press.

Kemper, T.D. and Bologh, R.W. (1981) 'What do you get when you fall in love? Some health status effects', *Sociology of Health and Illness,* 3: 72–88.

Kendon, A. (1967) 'Some functions of gaze direction in social interaction', *Acta Psychologica,* 26: 22–63.

Kephart, W.M. (1967) 'Some correlates of romantic love', *Journal of Marriage and the Family,* 29: 470–4.

Kerckhoff, A.C. and Davis, K.E. (1962) 'Value consensus and need complementarity in mate selection', *American Sociological Review,* 27: 295–303.

Kidd, V. (1975) 'Happily ever after and other relationship styles: Advice on interpersonal relations in popular magazines, 1951–1973', *Quarterly Journal of Speech,* 61: 31–9.

King, L.A. (1993) 'Emotional expression, ambivalence over expression and marital satisfaction', *Journal of Social and Personal Relationships,* 10: 601–7.

Kitson, G.C. and Morgan, L.A. (1990) 'The multiple consequences of divorce: a decade review', *Journal of Marriage and the Family,* 52: 913–24.

Klein, R. and Johnson, M. (1997) 'Strategies of couple conflict', in S.W. Duck (ed.), with K.

Dindia, W. Ickes, R.M. Milardo, R.S.L. Mills and B.R. Sarason, *Handbook of Personal Relationships* (2nd edn). Chichester: Wiley. pp. 469–86.

Klein, R. and Milardo, R. (1993) 'Third-party influences on the development and maintenance of personal relationships', in S.W. Duck (ed.), *Social Contexts of Relationships*. (Vol. 3) *Understanding Relationship Processes*. Newbury Park, CA: Sage. pp. 55–77.

Klinger, E. (1977) *Meaning and Void: Inner Experience and the Incentives in People's Lives*. Minneapolis: University of Minnesota Press.

Knapp, M.L. and Vangelisti, A. (1994) *Interpersonal Communication and Human Relationships* (2nd edn). Boston: Allyn and Bacon.

Kovecses, Z. (1991) 'A linguist's quest for love', *Journal of Social and Personal Relationships*, 8: 77–98.

Kramer, L. and Baron, L.A. (1995) 'Intergenerational linkages: how experiences with siblings relate to parenting of siblings', *Journal of Social and Personal Relationships*, 12: 67–87.

Krauss, R.M. and Fussell, S.R. (1996) 'Social psychological models of interpersonal communication', in E.T. Higgins and A.W. Kruglanski (eds), *Social Psychology: Handbook of Basic Principles*. New York: Guilford.

Kraut, R.E. (1973) 'Effects of social labelling on giving to charity', *Journal of Experimental Social Psychology*, 9: 551–62.

Kübler-Ross, E. (1969) *On Death and Dying*. New York: Macmillan.

Kurdek, L.A. (1994) 'Conflict resolution styles in gay, lesbian, heterosexual nonparent, and heterosexual parent couples', *Journal of Marriage and the Family*, 56: 705–22.

Labov, W. (1972) 'Negative attraction and negative concord in English grammar', *Language*, 48: 773–818.

LaCrosse, M.B. (1975) 'Nonverbal behaviour and perceived counsellor attractiveness and persuasiveness', *Journal of Counselling Psychology*, 22: 563–6.

Ladd, G.W. (1981) 'Effectiveness of a social learning method for enhancing childen's social interaction and peer acceptance', *Child Development*, 52: 171–8.

Ladd, G.W. (1989) 'Towards a further understanding of peer relationships and their contributions to child development', in T.J. Berndt and G.W. Ladd (eds), *Peer Relationships in Child Development*. New York: Wiley.

Ladd, G.W., LeSieur, K. and Profilet, S. (1993) 'Direct parental influences on young children's peer relations', in S.W. Duck (ed.), *Learning about Relationships*. (Vol. 2) *Understanding Relationship Processes*. Newbury Park, CA: Sage. pp. 152–83.

La Gaipa, J.J. (1982) 'Rituals of disengagement', in S.W. Duck (ed.), *Personal Relationships 4: Dissolving Personal Relationships*. London: Academic Press.

La Gaipa, J.J. (1990) 'The negative effects of informal support systems', in S.W. Duck (ed.), with R.C. Silver, *Personal Relationships and Social Support*. London: Sage.

LaGreca, A.M. and Santogrossi, D.A. (1980) 'Social skill training with elementary school students: a behavioral group approach', *Journal of Consulting and Clinical Psychology*, 48: 220–7.

Lakoff, G. and Johnson, M. (1980) *Metaphors We Live By*. Chicago: Chicago University Press.

Lakoff, R. (1973) 'Language and women's place', *Language in Society*, 2: 45–79.

Landy, D. and Aronson, E. (1969) 'The influence of the character of the criminal and his victim on the decisions of simulated jurors', *Journal of Experimental Social Psychology*, 5: 141–52.

LaRocco, J.M., House, J.S. and French, J.R.P. Jr. (1980) 'Social support, occupational stress and health', *Journal of Health and Social Behavior*, 21: 202–18.

Larson, J.H., Crane, D.R. and Smith, C.W. (1991) 'Morning and night couples', *Journal of Marriage and Family Therapy*, 17: 53–66.

Larson, R., Csikszentmihalyi, M. and Graef, R. (1982) 'Time alone in daily experience', in L.A. Peplau and D. Perlman (eds), *Loneliness: A Sourcebook of Current Theory, Research and Therapy*. New York: Wiley-Interscience.

Latty-Mann, H. and Davis, K.E. (1996) 'Attachment theory and partner choice: preference and actuality', *Journal of Social and Personal Relationships*, 13: 5–23.

Lau, R.R., Williams, S., Williams, L.C., Ware, J.E. and Brook, R.H. (1982) 'Psychosocial problems in chronically ill children: physician concern, parent satisfaction and the validity of medical diagnosis', *Journal of Community Health*, 7: 250–61.

Lawson, J. (1996) Personal communication, 16 April.

Lea, M. and Spears, R. (1995) 'Love at first byte: relationships conducted over electronic systems', in J.T. Wood and S.W. Duck (eds), *Understudied Relationships: Off the Beaten Track.* (Vol. 6) *Understanding Relationship Processes.* Newbury Park, CA: Sage.

Leary, M.R. and Dobbins, S.E. (1983) 'Social anxiety, sexual behavior, and contraceptive use', *Journal of Personality and Social Psychology*, 47: 775–94.

Leary, M.R., Knight, P.D. and Johnson, K.A. (1987) 'Social anxiety and dyadic conversation: a verbal response analysis', *Journal of Social and Clinical Psychology*, 5: 34–50.

Leatham, G. and Duck, S.W. (1990) 'Conversations with friends and the dynamics of social support', in S.W. Duck (ed.), *Personal Relationships and Social Support.* London: Sage. pp. 1–29.

Lee, J.A. (1973) *The Colors of Love: An Exploration of the Ways of Loving.* Ontario: New Press.

Lee, L. (1984) 'Sequences in separation: a framework for investigating the endings of personal (romantic) relationships', *Journal of Social and Personal Relationships*, 1: 49–74.

Lehman, D.R. and Hemphill, K.J. (1990) 'Recipients' perception of support attempts and attributions for support attempts that fail', *Journal of Social and Personal Relationships*, 7: 563–74.

Levitt, M., Silver, M.E. and Franco, N. (1996) 'Troublesome relationships: a part of the human experience', *Journal of Social and Personal Relationships*, 13: 523–36.

Lewis, R.A. and Lin, L.W. (1996) 'Adults and their midlife parents', in N. Vanzetti and S.W. Duck (eds), *A Lifetime of Relationships.* Pacific Grove, CA: Brooks/Cole. pp. 364–82.

Lewis, R.A. and McAvoy, P. (1984) 'Improving the quality of relationships: therapeutic interventions with opiate-abusing couples', in S.W. Duck (ed.), *Personal Relationships 5: Repairing Personal Relationships.* London and New York: Academic Press.

Lin, N., Simeone, R.L., Ensel, W.M. and Kuo, W. (1979) 'Social support, stressful life events and illness: a model and an empirical test', *Journal of Health and Social Behavior*, 20: 108–19.

Lindsley, S. (1993) 'Gender influences on affective and cognitive consideration for first date initiation: an ethnographic decision tree model.' Paper presented to the Organization of Communication, Language and Gender, Tempe, AZ, October.

Linn, L.S. and DiMatteo, M.R. (1983) 'Humor and other communication: preferences in physician–patient encounters', *Medical Care*, 21: 1223–31.

Lollis, S. and Kuczynski, L. (1997) 'Beyond one hand clapping? Seeing bi-directionality in parent–child relationships', *Journal of Social and Personal Relationships*, 14: 441–61.

Lombroso, C. (1918) *Criminal Anthropology (L'Uomo Criminale).* Roma: Publicazione.

Lynch, J.J. (1987) *The Language of the Heart.* New York: Basic Books.

Lynch, J.J., Thomas, S.A., Mills, M.E., Malinow, K. and Katcher, A.H. (1974) 'The effects of human contact on cardiac arrythmia in coronary care patients', *Journal of Nervous and Mental Diseases*, 158: 88–99.

Lyons, R.F. and Meade, D. (1995) 'Painting a new face on relationships: relationship remodelling in response to chronic illness', in S.W. Duck and J.T. Wood (eds), *Confronting Relationship Challenges.* (Vol. 5) *Understanding Relationship Processes.* Thousand Oaks, CA: Sage. pp. 181–210.

Lyons, R.F., Sullivan, M.J.L. and Ritvo, P.G. (1996) *Relationships in Chronic Illness and Disability.* Thousand Oaks, CA: Sage.

Maass, A. and Kohnken, G. (1989) 'Eyewitness identification: simulating the "weapon effect"', *Law and Human Behavior*, 13: 397–408.

McCabe, S.B. and Gotlib, I.H. (1993) 'Interactions of couples with and without a depressed spouse: self report and observations of problem-solving situations', *Journal of Social and Personal Relationships*, 10: 589–99.

McCall, G.J. (1982) 'Becoming unrelated: the management of bond dissolution', in S.W. Duck (ed.), *Personal Relationships 4: Dissolving Personal Relationships.* London: Academic Press.

McCall, G.J. (1988) 'The organizational life cycle of relationships', in S.W. Duck, D.F. Hay, S.E. Hobfoll, W.J. Ickes and B.M. Montgomery (eds), *Handbook of Personal Relationships*. Chichester: Wiley. pp. 467–86.

McCarthy, B. (1983) 'Social cognition and personal relationships.' Paper to Lancaster University Relationships Research Group, November.

McGinnis, J. (1970) *The Selling of the President, 1968*. New York: Pocket Books.

Maddison, D. and Viola, A. (1968) 'The health of widows in the year after bereavement', *Journal of Psychosomatic Research*, 12: 297–306.

Malinowski, B. (1929) *The Sexual Life of Savages*. New York: Harcourt Brace.

Mallinckrodt, B. (1997) 'Interpersonal relationship processes in individual and group psychotherapy', in S.W. Duck, K. Dindia, W. Ickes, R.M. Milardo, R.S.L. Mills and B.R. Sarason (eds), *Handbook of Personal Relationships* (2nd edn). Chichester: Wiley. pp. 671–94.

Mamali, C. (1996) 'Interpersonal communication in totalitarian societies', in W. Gudykunst, S. Ting-Toomey, T. Nishida (eds), *Communication in Personal Relationships across Cultures*. Thousand Oaks, CA: Sage. pp. 217–34.

Manke, B and Plomin, R. (1997) 'Adolescent familial interactions: a genetic extension of the social relations model', *Journal of Social and Personal Relationships*, 14: 505–22.

Marangoni, C. and Ickes, W. (1989) 'Loneliness: a theoretical review with implications for measurement', *Journal of Social and Personal Relationships*, 6: 93–128.

Markman, H.J., Renick, M.J., Floyd, F., Stanley, S. and Clements, M. (1993) 'Preventing marital distress through communication and conflict management training: a 4- and 5-year follow up study', *Journal of Consulting and Clinical Psychology*, 61: 70–7.

Marston, P.J., Hecht, M. and Robers, T. (1987) '"True love ways": the subjective experience and communication of romantic love', *Journal of Social and Personal Relationships*, 4: 387–407.

Martin, T.C. and Bumpass, L. (1989) 'Recent trends in marital disruption', *Demography*, 26: 37–51.

Masciuch, S. and Kienapple, K. (1993) 'The emergence of jealousy in children 4 months to 7 years of age', *Journal of Social and Personal Relationships*, 10: 421–35.

Mayseless, O. (1991) 'Adult attachment patterns and courtship violence', *Family Relations*, 40: 21–8.

Mazur, R. (1977) 'Beyond jealousy and possessiveness', in G. Clanton and L. Smith (eds), *Jealousy*. Englewood Cliffs, NJ: Prentice Hall.

Mead, G.H. (1934) *Mind, Self, and Society* (1967 edn. edited by C.W. Morris). Chicago: CUP.

Mead, M. (1950) *Sex and Temperament in Three Primitive Societies*. New York: Mentor.

Mechanic, D. (1974) *Politics, Medicine and Social Science*. New York: Wiley.

Mechanic, D. (1980) 'The experience and reporting of common physical complaints', *Journal of Health and Social Behavior*, 21: 146–55.

Mehrabian, A. (1971) *Silent Messages*. Belmont, CA: Wadsworth.

Metts, S., Cupach, W. and Bejlovec, R.A. (1989) '"I love you too much to ever start liking you": redefining romantic relationships', *Journal of Social and Personal Relationships*, 6: 259–74.

Miell, D.E. (1984) 'Cognitive and communicative strategies in developing relationships.' Unpublished PhD thesis, University of Lancaster.

Miell, D.E. (1987) 'Remembering relationship development: constructing a context for interactions', in R. Burnett, P. McGhee and D. Clarke (eds), *Accounting for Relationships*. London: Methuen.

Miell, D.E. and Duck, S.W. (1986) 'Strategies in developing friendship', in V.J. Derlega and B.A. Winstead (eds), *Friendship and Social Interaction*. New York: Springer Verlag.

Mikulincer, M. and Segal, J. (1990) 'A multi-dimensional analysis of the experience of loneliness', *Journal of Social and Personal Relationships*, 7: 209–30.

Milardo, R.M. (1992) 'Comparative methods for delineating social networks', *Journal of Social and Personal Relationships*, 9: 447–61.

Milardo, R.M. and Allan, G.A. (1997) 'Social networks and marital relationships', in S.W.

Duck, K. Dindia, W. Ickes, R.M. Milardo, R.S.L. Mills and B.R. Sarason (eds), *Handbook of Personal Relationships* (2nd edn). Chichester: Wiley. pp. 505–22.

Milardo, R.M. and Wellman, B. (1992) 'The personal is social', *Journal of Social and Personal Relationships*, 9: 339–42.

Milardo, R.M., Johnson, M.P. and Huston, T.L. (1983) 'Developing close relationships: changing patterns of interaction between pair members and social networks', *Journal of Personality and Social Psychology*, 44: 964–76.

Miller, G.R. and Boster, F.J. (1977) 'Three images of the trial: their implications for psychological research', in D.D. Sales (ed.), *Psychology in the Legal Process*. New York: Spectrum.

Miller, G.R. and Boster, F.J. (1988) 'Persuasion in personal relationships', in S.W. Duck (ed.), with D.F. Hay, S.E. Hobfoll, W.J. Ickes and B.M. Montgomery, *Handbook of Personal Relationships*. Chichester: Wiley.

Miller, G.R. and Parks, M.R. (1982) 'Communication in dissolving relationships', in S.W. Duck (ed.), *Personal Relationships 4: Dissolving Personal Relationships*. London: Academic Press.

Miller, G.R., Mongeau, P. and Sleight, C. (1986) 'Fudging with friends and lying to lovers: deceptive communication in personal relationships', *Journal of Social and Personal Relationships*, 3: 495–512.

Miller, J.B. (1993) 'Learning from early relationship experiences', in S.W. Duck (ed.), *Learning about Relationships*. (Vol. 2) *Understanding Relationship Processes*. Newbury Park, CA: Sage. pp. 1–29.

Miller, K.I., Stiff, J.B. and Ellis, B.H. (1988) 'Communication and empathy as precursors to burnout among human service workers', *Communication Monographs*, 55: 250–65.

Miller, M.D. (1982) 'Friendship, power and the language of compliance gaining', *Journal of Language and Social Behavior*, 1: 111–22.

Miller, R.S. (1996) *Embarrassment: Poise and Peril in Everyday Life*. New York: Guilford.

Mills, R.S.L. (1997) 'Introduction to developmental psychology section', in S.W. Duck, K. Dindia, W. Ickes, R.M. Milardo, R.S.L. Mills and B.R. Sarason (eds), *Handbook of Personal Relationships* (2nd edn). Chichester: Wiley.

Milmoe, S., Rosenthal, R., Blane, H.T., Chafetz, M.L. and Wolf, I. (1967) 'The doctor's voice: postdictors of successful referral of alcoholic patients', *Journal of Abnormal Psychology*, 72: 78–84.

Mongeau, P.A. and Carey, C.M. (1996) 'Who's wooing whom II: an experimental investigation of date-initiation and expectancy violation', *Western Journal of Communication*, 60: 195–213.

Mongeau, P.A., Hale, J.L., Johnson and Hillis, J.D. (1995) 'Who's wooing whom? An investigation of female initiated dating', in P.J. Kalbfleisch (ed.), *Interpersonal Communication: Evolving Interpersonal Relationships*. Hillsdale, NJ: LEA. pp. 51–67.

Mongeau, P.A., Yeazell, M. and Hale, J.L. (1994) 'Sex difference in relational message interpretations on male- and female-initiated first dates: a research note', *Journal of Social Behavior and Personality*, 9: 731–42.

Montagu, A. (1978) *Touching*. New York: Harper and Row.

Montgomery, B.M. (1981) 'Verbal immediacy as a behavioral indicator of open communication', *Communication Quarterly*, 30: 28–34.

Montgomery, B.M. (1984) 'Behavioral characteristics predicting self and peer perception of open communication', *Communication Quarterly*, 32: 233–40.

Montgomery, B.M. (1988) 'Quality communication in personal relationships', in S.W. Duck (ed.), with D.F. Hay, S.E. Hobfoll, W.J. Ickes and B.M. Montgomery (eds), *Handbook of Personal Relationships*. Chichester: Wiley. pp. 343–62.

Montgomery, B.M. (1993) 'Relationship maintenance versus relationship change: a dialectical dilemma', *Journal of Social and Personal Relationships*, 10: 205–24.

Morgan, D.L. (1990) 'Combining the strengths of social networks, social support and personal relationships', in S.W. Duck (ed.), with R.C. Silver, *Personal Relationships and Social Support*. London: Sage.

232   *Human relationships*

Moriarty, T. (1975) 'Crime, commitment and the responsive bystander: two field experiments', *Journal of Personality and Social Psychology*, 31: 370–6.

Mortimer, J. (1983) *Clinging to the Wreckage*. Harmondsworth: Penguin.

Morton, T.L., Alexander, I. and Altman, I. (1976) 'Communication and relationship definition', in G.R. Miller (ed.), *Explorations in Interpersonal Communication*. Beverly Hills, CA: Sage.

Mowen, J.C. and Cialdini, R.B. (1980) 'On implementing the door-in-the-face compliance technique in a business context', *Journal of Marketing Research*, 17: 253–8.

Muehlenhard, C.L., Koralewski, M.A., Andrews, S.L. and Burdick, C.A. (1986) 'Verbal and nonverbal cues that convey interest in dating: two studies', *Behavior Therapy*, 17: 404–19.

Mulac, A., Studley, L.B., Wiemann, J.M. and Bradac, J. (1987) 'Male/female gaze in same-sex and mixed-sex dyads: gender-linked differences and mutual influence', *Human Communication Research*, 13: 323–43.

Newcomb, T.M. (1971) 'Dyadic balance as a source of clues about interpersonal attraction', in B.I. Murstein (ed.), *Theories of Attraction and Love*. New York: Springer.

Newell, S. and Stutman, R.K. (1988) 'The social confrontation episode', *Communication Monographs*, 55: 266–85.

Noller, P. and Gallois, C. (1988) 'Understanding and misunderstanding in marriage: sex and marital adjustment differences in structured and free interaction', in P. Noller and M.A. Fitzpatrick (eds), *Perspectives on Marital Interaction*. Clevedon and Philadelphia: Multilingual Matters.

Notarius, C. (1996) 'Marriage: will I be happy or sad?', in N. Vanzetti and S.W. Duck (eds), *A Lifetime of Relationships*. Pacific Grove, CA: Brooks/Cole.

Notarius, C. and Markman, H.J. (1993) *We Can Work It Out: Making Sense of Marital Conflict*. New York: Putnam.

O'Barr, W.M. (1982) *Linguistic Evidence: Language, Power and Strategy in the Courtroom*. New York: Academic Press.

Oden, S. and Asher, S.R. (1977) 'Coaching children in social skills for friendship making', *Child Development*, 48: 495–506.

Orbuch, T.L. (ed.) (1992) *Relationship Loss*. New York: Springer-Verlag.

Orford, J. (1976) 'A study of the personalities of excessive drinkers and their wives, using the approaches of Leary and Eysenck', *Journal of Consulting and Clinical Psychology*, 44: 534–45.

Orford, J. (1980) 'The domestic context', in M.P. Feldman and J. Orford (eds), *Psychological Problems: The Social Context*. Chichester: Wiley.

Orford, J. and O'Reilly, P. (1981) 'Disorders in the family', in S.W. Duck and R. Gilmour (eds), *Personal Relationships 3: Personal Relationships in Disorder*. London and New York: Academic Press.

Orford, J., Oppenheimer, E., Egert, S., Hensman, C. and Guthrie, S. (1976) 'The cohesiveness of alcoholism-complicated marriages and its influence on treatment outcome', *British Journal of Psychiatry*, 128: 318–49.

Orth, J.E., Stiles, W.B., Scherwitz, L. Hennrikus, D. and Vallbona, C. (1987) 'Patient exposition and provider explanation in routine interviews and hypertensive patients' blood pressure control', *Health Psychology*, 6: 29–42.

Palmer, M.T. (1990) 'Controlling conversation: turns, topics and interpersonal control', *Communication Monographs*, 56: 1–18.

Park, K.A. and Waters, E. (1988) 'Traits and relationships in developmental perspective', in S.W. Duck (ed.), with D.F. Hay, S.E. Hobfoll, W.J. Ickes and B.M. Montgomery, *Handbook of Personal Relationships*. Chichester: Wiley.

Parke, R.D. and O'Neil, R. (1997) 'The influence of significant others on learning about relationships', in S.W. Duck, K. Dindia, W. Ickes, R.M. Milardo, R.S.L. Mills and B.R. Sarason (eds), *Handbook of Personal Relationships* (2nd edn). Chichester: Wiley.

Parker, S. (1960) 'The attitudes of medical students towards their patients: an exploratory study', *Journal of Medical Education*, 35: 849–55.

Parks, M.R. and Adelman, M. (1983) 'Communication networks and the development of romantic relationships: an expansion of uncertainty reduction theory', *Human Communication Research*, 10: 55–80.

Parks, M.R. and Eggert, L.L. (1991) 'The role of social context in the dynamics of personal relationships', in W.H. Jones and D. Perlman (eds), *Advances in Personal Relationships* (vol. 2). London: Jessica Kingsley. pp. 1–34.

Parsons, T. (1951) *The Social System*. Glencoe, IL: Free Press.

Patterson, M.L. (1988) 'Functions of nonverbal behavior in close relationships', in S.W. Duck (ed.), with D.F. Hay, S.E. Hobfoll, W.J. Ickes and B.M. Montgomery, *Handbook of Personal Relationships*. Chichester: Wiley.

Patterson, M.L. (1992) 'A functional approach to nonverbal exchange', in R.S. Feldman and B. Rime (eds), *Fundamentals of Nonverbal Behaviour*. New York: Cambridge University Press.

Paykel, E.S., Emms, E.M., Fletcher, J. and Rassaby, E.S. (1980) 'Life events and social support in puerperal depression', *British Journal of Psychiatry*, 136: 339–46.

Pearson, J.C. (1996) 'Forty-forever years? Primary relationships and senior citizens', in N. Vanzetti and S.W. Duck (eds), *A Lifetime of Relationships*. Pacific Grove, CA: Brooks/Cole. pp. 383–405.

Pendleton, D. and Hasler, J. (1983) *Doctor–Patient Communication*. London: Academic Press.

Pennington, D.C. (1982) 'Witnesses and their testimony: effects of ordering on juror verdicts', *Journal of Applied Social Psychology*, 12: 318–33.

Peplau, L.A. and Perlman, D. (1982) 'Perspectives on loneliness', in L.A. Peplau and D. Perlman (eds), *Loneliness: A Sourcebook of Theory, Research and Therapy*. New York: Wiley.

Peplau, L.A., Miceli, M. and Morasch, B. (1982) 'Loneliness and self-evaluation', in L.A. Peplau and D. Perlman (eds), *Loneliness: A Sourcebook of Current Theory, Research and Therapy*. New York: Wiley.

Perlman, D., Gerson, A.C. and Spinner, B. (1978) 'Loneliness among senior citizens: an empirical report', *Essence*, 2: 239–48.

Perlman, D. and Peplau, L.A. (1981) 'Toward a social psychology of loneliness', in S.W. Duck and R. Gilmour (eds), *Personal Relationships 3: Personal Relationships in Disorder*. London and New York: Academic Press.

Perlman, D. and Serbin, R. (1984) 'A sports report: the effects of racquet matches on loneliness.' Paper to Second International Conference on Personal Relationships, Madison, WI, July.

Pettegrew, L.S. and Turkat, I.D. (1986) 'How patients communicate about their illness', *Human Communication Research*, 12: 376–94.

Pettit, G.S. and Clawson, M.A. (1996) 'Pathways to interpersonal competence: parenting and children's peer relations', in N. Vanzetti and S.W. Duck (eds), *A Lifetime of Relationships*. Pacific Grove, CA: Brooks/Cole. pp. 125–54.

Pettit, G. and Lollis, S. (1997) 'Reciprocity and bidirectionality in parent–child relationships: new approaches to the study of enduring issues', *Journal of Social and Personal Relationships*, 14: 435–40.

Pettit, G.S. and Mize, J. (1993) 'Substance and style: understanding the ways in which parents teach children about social relationships', in S.W. Duck (ed.), *Learning about Relationships*. (Vol. 2) *Understanding Relationship Processes*. Newbury Park, CA: Sage. pp. 118–51.

Petty, R.E. and Cacioppo, J.T. (1981) *Attitudes and Persuasion: Classic and Contemporary Approaches*. Dubuque, IA: W.C. Brown.

Pfeiffer, S.M. and Wong, P.T.P. (1989) 'Multidimensional jealousy', *Journal of Social and Personal Relationships*, 6: 181–96.

Phillips, D.P. (1970) 'Dying as a form of social behavior.' Unpublished PhD dissertation, Ann Arbor, MI.

Phillips, D.P. (1972) 'Deathday and birthday: an unexpected connection', in J.M. Tanur (ed.), *Statistics: A Guide to the Unknown*. San Francisco: Holden Day.

Pickering, G. (1978) 'Medicine on the brink: the dilemma of a learned profession', *Perspectives in Biology and Medicine*, Summer.

Pike, G.R. and Sillars, A.L. (1985) 'Reciprocity of marital communication', *Journal of Social and Personal Relationships*, 2: 303–24.

Pilkonis, P.A. (1977) 'The behavioral consequences of shyness', *Journal of Personality*, 45: 596–611.

Planalp, S. (1993) 'Friends' and acquaintances' conversations II: Coded differences', *Journal of Social and Personal Relationships*, 10: 339–54.

Planalp, S. and Benson, A. (1992) 'Friends' and acquaintances' conversations I: observed differences', *Journal of Social and Personal Relationships*, 9: 483–506.

Planalp, S. and Garvin-Doxas, K. (1994) 'Using mutual knowledge in conversation: friends as experts in each other', in S.W. Duck (ed.), *Dynamics of Interactions*. (Vol. 4) *Understanding Relationship Processes*. Newbury Park, CA: Sage. pp. 1–26.

Premo, B.E. and Stiles, W.B. (1983) 'Familiarity in verbal interactions of married couples versus strangers', *Journal of Social and Clinical Psychology*, 1: 209–30.

Prins, H. (1983) *Offenders, Deviants or Patients?* London: Tavistock.

Prusank, D., Duran, R. and DeLillo, D.A. (1993) 'Interpersonal relationships in women's magazines: dating and relating in the 1970s and 1980s', *Journal of Social and Personal Relationships*, 10: 307–20.

Pryor, B. and Buchanan, R.W. (1984) 'The effects of a defendant's demeanor on prior perceptions of credibility and guilt', *Journal of Communication*, 34: 92–9.

Putallaz, M. and Gottman, J.M. (1981) 'Social skills and group acceptance', in S.R. Asher and J.M. Gottman (eds), *The Development of Children's Friendship*. Cambridge: Cambridge University Press.

Putallaz, M., Costanzo, P.R. and Klein, T.P. (1993) 'Parental childhood social experiences and their effects on children's relationships', in S.W. Duck (ed.), *Learning about Relationships*. (Vol. 2) *Understanding Relationship Processes*. Newbury Park, CA: Sage. pp. 63–97.

Putallaz, M., Costanzo, P.R. and Smith, R.B. (1991) 'Maternal recollections of childhood peer relationships: implications for their children's social competence', *Journal of Social and Personal Relationships*, 8: 403–22.

Putnam, S.M., Stiles, W.B., Jacob, M.C. and James, J.A. (1988) 'Teaching the medical interview: an intervention study', *Journal of General Internal Medicine*, 3: 38–47.

Pyszcynski, T.A. and Wrightsman, L.S. (1981) 'The effects of opening statements on mock jurors' verdicts in a simulated criminal trial', *Journal of Applied Social Psychology*, 11: 301–13.

Rackham, N. and Morgan, T. (1977) *Behavior Analysis and Training*. New York: McGraw-Hill.

Radecki-Bush, C., Bush, J.P. and Jennings, J. (1988) 'Effects of jealousy threats on relationship perceptions and emotions', *Journal of Social and Personal Relationships*, 5: 285–303.

Radecki-Bush, C., Farrell, A.D. and Bush, J. (1993) 'Predicting jealous responses: the influence of adult attachment and depression in threat appraisal', *Journal of Social and Personal Relationships*, 10: 569–88.

Reis, H.T. (1986) 'Gender effects in social participation: intimacy, loneliness and the conduct of social interaction', in R. Gilmour and S.W. Duck (eds), *The Emerging Field of Personal Relationships*. Hillsdale, NJ: Erlbaum.

Reis, H.T., Nezlek, V. and Wheeler, L. (1980) 'Physical attractiveness and social interaction', *Journal of Personality and Social Psychology*, 38: 604–17.

Reiss, D., Plomin, R., and Hetherington, E.M. (1991) 'Genetics and psychiatry: an unheralded window on the environment', *American Journal of Psychiatry*, 148: 283–91.

Retzinger, S.M. (1995) 'Shame and anger in personal relationships', in S.W. Duck and J.T. Wood (eds), *Confronting Relationship Challenges*. (Vol. 5) *Understanding Relationship Processes*. Thousand Oaks, CA: Sage. pp. 22–42.

Riskin, J. and Faunce, E.E. (1972) 'An evaluative review of family interaction research', *Family Process*, 11: 365–455.

Rodin, M. (1982) 'Nonengagement, failure to engage and disengagement', in S.W. Duck (ed.), *Personal Relationships 4: Dissolving Personal Relationships*. London: Academic Press. pp. 31–50.

Rogers, R.W. (1983) 'Preventive health psychology: an interface of social and clinical psychology', *Journal of Social and Clinical Psychology*, 1: 120–7.

Rohlfing, M. (1995) '"Doesn't anybody stay in one place any more?" An exploration of the understudied phenomenon of long-distance relationships', in J.T. Wood and S.W. Duck (eds), *Understudied Relationships: Off the Beaten Track*. (Vol. 6) *Understanding Relationship Processes*. Newbury Park, CA: Sage. pp. 173–96.

Roloff, M.E., Janiszewski, C.A., McGrath, M.A., Burns, C.S. and Manrai, L.A. (1988) 'Acquiring resources from intimates: when obligation substitutes for persuasion', *Human Communication Research*, 14: 364–96.

Rook, K.S. (1988) 'Toward a more differentiated view of loneliness', in S.W. Duck (ed.), with D.F. Hay, S.E. Hobfoll, W.J. Ickes and B.M. Montgomery, *Handbook of Personal Relationships*. Chichester: Wiley.

Rook, K.S. (1990) 'Parallels in the study of social support and social strain', *Journal of Social and Clinical Psychology*, 9: 118–32.

Rook, K.S. and Pietromonaco, P. (1987) 'Close relationships: ties that heal or ties that bind?', in W.H. Jones and D. Perlman (eds), *Advances in Personal Relationships*. Greenwich: JAI.

Rubenstein, C. and Shaver, P. (1982) 'The experience of loneliness', in L.A. Peplau and D. Perlman (eds), *Loneliness: A Current Sourcebook of Theory, Research and Therapy*. New York: Wiley.

Rubin, A.M., Perse, E.M. and Powell, R.A. (1985) 'Loneliness, parasocial interactions and local TV news viewing', *Human Communication Research*, 12: 155–80.

Rubin, R.B. (1977) 'The role of context in information seeking and impression formation', *Communication Monographs*, 44: 81–90.

Rubin, Z. (1973) *Liking and Loving*. New York: Holt, Rinehart and Winston.

Rubin, Z. (1987) 'Parent–child loyalty and testimonial privilege', *Harvard Law Review*, 100: 910–29.

Rubin, Z. (1990a) Personal communication, 25 March.

Rubin, Z. (1990b) 'From love to law: a social psychologist's midlife passage', *ISSPR Bull.*, March: 3–4.

Ruehlman, L.S. and Wolchik, S.A. (1988) 'Personal goals and interpersonal support and hindrance as factors in psychological distress and well-being', *Journal of Personality and Social Psychology*, 55: 293–301.

Rutter, M. (1972) *Maternal Deprivation Reassessed*. Harmondsworth: Penguin.

Sabatelli, R. and Pearce, J. (1986) 'Exploring marital expectations', *Journal of Social and Personal Relationships*, 3: 307–22.

Saks, M.J. (1986) 'Blaming the jury', *Georgetown Law Journal*, 75: 693–711.

Saks, M.J. (1991) Personal communication, 25 March.

Salisch, M. von (1997) 'Emotional processes in children's relationships with siblings and friends', in S.W. Duck, K. Dindia, W. Ickes, R.M. Milardo, R.S.L. Mills and B.R. Sarason (eds), *Handbook of Personal Relationships* (2nd edn). Chichester: Wiley. pp. 61–80.

Sarason, B.R., Sarason, I.G. and Gurung, R.A.R. (1997) 'Close personal relationships and health outcomes: A key to the role of social support', in S.W. Duck, K. Dindia, W. Ickes, R.M. Milardo, R.S.L. Mills and B.R. Sarason (eds), *Handbook of Personal Relationships* (2nd edn). Chichester: Wiley. pp. 547–74.

Sarason, B.R., Sarason, I.G. and Pierce, G.R. (1990) *Social Support: A Transactional View*. New York: Wiley.

Sarat, A. and Felstiner, W.L.F. (1988) 'Law and social relations: vocabularies of motive in lawyer/client interaction', *Law and Society Review*, 6: 737–69.

Schachter, S. and Singer, J.E. (1962) 'Cognitive, social, and physiological determinants of emotional states', *Psychological Review*, 69: 379–99.

Scheff, T.J. and Retzinger, S.M. (1991) *Emotions and Violence: Shame-Rage in Destructive Conflicts*. Lexington, MA: Lexington Books.

Schmale, A.H. Jr. (1958) 'The relationship of separation and depression to disease', *Psychosomatic Medicine*, 20: 259–75.

Schneider, B.H., Attili, G., Nadel, J. and Weissberg, R.P. (eds) (1989) *Social Competence in Developmental Perspective* (NATO ASI Series). Amsterdam: Kluwer.

Schneider, B.H., Smith, A., Poisson, S.E. and Kwan, A.B. (1997) 'Cultural dimensions of children's peer relations', in S.W. Duck, K. Dindia, W. Ickes, R.M. Milardo, R.S.L. Mills and B.R. Sarason (eds), *Handbook of Personal Relationships* (2nd edn). Chichester: Wiley. pp. 121–46.

Schultz, N.R. Jr. and Moore, D. (1988) 'Loneliness: differences across three age levels', *Journal of Social and Personal Relationships*, 5: 275–84.

Segrin, C. (1991) 'A meta-analytic review of social skill deficits', *Communication Monographs*, 57: 292–308.

Selye, H. (1956) *The Stress of Life*. New York: McGraw-Hill.

Shanas, E., Townsend, P., Wedderburn, D., Friis, H., Milhoj, P. and Stehouwer, J. (1968) *Old People in Three Industrial Societies*. New York: Atherton.

Sharpsteen, D.J. (1993) 'Romantic jealousy as an emotion concept: a prototype analysis', *Journal of Social and Personal Relationships*, 10: 69–82.

Sharpsteen, D.J. (1995) 'The effects of relationships and self-esteem threats on the likelihood of romantic jealousy', *Journal of Social and Personal Relationships*, 12: 89–101.

Shaver, P.R. and Hazan, C. (1988) 'A biased overview of the study of love', *Journal of Social and Personal Relationships*, 5: 473–501.

Shaver, P.R., Furman, W. and Buhrmester, D. (1985) 'Transition to college: network changes, social skills and loneliness', in S.W. Duck and D. Perlman (eds), *Understanding Personal Relationships*. London: Sage.

Sher, T.G. (1996) 'Courtship and marriage: choosing a primary relationship', in N. Vanzetti and S.W. Duck (eds), *A Lifetime of Relationships*. Pacific Grove, CA: Brooks/Cole. pp. 243–64.

Shotland, R.L. and Straw, M.K. (1976) 'Bystander response to an assault: when a man attacks a woman', *Journal of Personality and Social Psychology*, 34: 990–9.

Shulz, R. (1976) 'Effects of control and predictability on the physical and psychological well-being of the institutionalized aged', *Journal of Personality and Social Psychology*, 33: 563–73.

Shuval, J.T. (1981) 'The contribution of psychological and social phenomena to an understanding of the aetiology of disease and illness', *Social Science and Medicine*, 15A: 337–42.

Shuval, J.T., Antonovsky, A. and Davies, A.M. (1973) 'Illness: a mechanism for coping with failure', *Social Science and Medicine*, 7: 259–65.

Silberfeld, M. (1978) 'Psychological symptoms and social supports', *Social Psychiatry*, 13: 11–17.

Silverstein, C. (1981) *Man to Man: Gay Couples in America*. New York: William Morrow.

Simmel, G. (1950) *The Sociology of Georg Simmel* (trans, K. Wolff). New York: Free Press.

Siperstein, G.N. and Gale, M.E. (1983) 'Improving peer relationships of "rejected" children.' Paper presented to Society for Research in Child Development, Detroit, MI, March.

Smith, A.J. (1957) 'Similarity of values and its relation to acceptance and the projection of similarity', *Journal of Psychology*, 43: 251–60.

Smith, P.K., Bowers, L., Binney, V. and Cowie, H. (1993) 'Relationships of children involved in bully/victim problems at school', in S.W. Duck (ed.), *Learning about Relationships*. (Vol. 2) *Understanding Relationship Processes*. Newbury Park, CA: Sage. pp. 184–212.

Smith, R.H. (1991) 'Envy and the sense of injustice', in P. Salovey (ed.), *The Psychology of Jealousy and Envy*. New York: Guilford.

Smith-Hanen, S. (1977) 'Effects of nonverbal behaviors on judged level of counsellor warmth and empathy', *Journal of Counselling Psychology*, 24: 87–91.

Snow, J. (1854) 'On the mode of communication of cholera.' Reprinted in *Snow on Cholera* (1936), New York: Commonwealth Fund.

Snyder, C.R. and Smith, T.W. (1982) 'Symptoms as self-handicapping strategies: the virtues of old wine in a new bottle.' Unpublished manuscript.

Sobol, M.P. and Earn, B.M. (1985) 'What causes mean: an analysis of children's interpretations of the causes of social experience', *Journal of Social and Personal Relationships*, 2: 137–50.

Solano, C.H. and Koester, N.H. (1989) 'Loneliness and communication problems: subjective anxiety or objective skills?', *Personality and Social Psychology Bulletin*, 15: 126–33.

Solano, C.H., Batten, P.G. and Parish, E.A. (1982) 'Loneliness and patterns of self-disclosure', *Journal of Personality and Social Psychology*, 43: 524–31.

Spencer, E.E. (1994) 'Transforming relationships through ordinary talk', in S.W. Duck (ed.), *Dynamics of Relationships*. (Vol. 4) *Understanding Relationship Processes*. Newbury Park, CA: Sage. pp. 58–85.

Spitzberg, B.H. (1993) 'The dialectics of (in)competence', *Journal of Social and Personal Relationships*, 10: 137–58.

Spitzberg, B.H. and Canary, D. (1985) 'Loneliness and relationally competent communication', *Journal of Social and Personal Relationships*, 2: 387–402.

Spitzberg, B.H. and Cupach, W. (1985) *Interpersonal Communication Competence*. Newbury Park: Sage.

Sprecher, S. (1987) 'The effects of self-disclosure given and received on affection for an intimate partner and stability of the relationship', *Journal of Social and Personal Relationships*, 4: 115–27.

Sprecher. S. and Duck, S.W. (1993) 'Sweet talk: the role of communication in consolidating relationship', *Personality and Social Psychology Bulletin*, 20: 391–400.

Stang, D.J. (1973) 'Effect of interaction rate on ratings of leadership and liking', *Journal of Personality and Social Psychology*, 27: 405–8.

Stein, C.H. (1993) 'Felt obligation in adult family relationships', in S.W. Duck (ed.), *Social Contexts of Relationships*. (Vol. 3) *Understanding Relationship Processes*. Thousand Oaks, CA: Sage. pp. 78–99.

Stewart, J.E. (1980) 'Defendant's attractiveness as a factor in the outcome of criminal trials: an observational study', *Journal of Applied Social Psychology*, 10: 348–61.

Stiff, J.B. and Miller, G.R. (1984) 'Deceptive behaviors and behaviors which are interpreted as deceptive: an interactive approach to the study of deception.' Paper to International Communication Association, San Francisco, May.

Stone, A.C. (1979) 'Patient compliance and the role of the expert', *Journal of Social Issues*, 35: 34–59.

Storm, C.L. (1991) 'Placing gender at the heart of the MFT Masters program', *Journal of Marriage and Family Therapy*, 17: 45–52.

Stotland, E., Zander, A. and Natsoulas, T. (1960) 'Generalization of interpersonal similarity', *Journal of Abnormal and Social Psychology*, 62: 250–6.

Strain, P.S., Shores, R.E. and Kerr, M.A. (1976) 'An experimental analysis of "spillover" effects on the social interactions of behaviorally handicapped preschool children', *Journal of Applied Behavior Analysis*, 9: 31–40.

Straus, M.A. (1985) 'Family violence.' Paper to HDFR, University of Connecticut, Storrs, April.

Straus, M.A. (1990) 'Injury and frequency of assaults and the "representative sample fallacy" in measuring wife beating and child abuse', in M.A. Straus and R.J. Gelles (eds), *Physical Violence in American Families: Risk Factors and Adaptations in 8145 Families*. New Brunswick, NJ: Transaction Books.

Straus, M.A. and Gelles, R.J. (1986) 'Societal change and change in family violence from 1975 to 1985 as revealed in two national surveys', *Journal of Marriage and the Family*, 48: 465–79.

Street, R.L. Jr. and Buller, D.B. (1988) 'Patients' characteristics affecting physician–patient nonverbal communication', *Human Communication Research*, 15: 60–90.

Strodtbeck, F.L., James, R.M. and Hawkins, C. (1957) 'Social status in jury deliberations', *American Sociological Review*, 22: 713–9.

Stroebe, W. (1980) 'Process loss in social psychology: failure to exploit?', in R. Gilmour and S.W. Duck (eds), *The Development of Social Psychology*. London: Academic Press.

Suitor, J.J. (1991) 'Marital quality and satisfaction with the division of household labor across the family life cycle', *Journal of Marriage and the Family*, 53: 221-30.

Suls, J. (1977) 'Gossip as social comparison', *Journal of Communication*, 27: 164-8.

Sunnafrank, M. (1991) 'Review of the attraction paradigm', *Communication Yearbook 14* (ed. J. Anderson). Newbury Park, CA: Sage.

Sunnafrank, M. and Miller, G.R. (1981) 'The role of initial conversations in determining attraction to similar and dissimilar strangers', *Human Communication Research*, 8: 16-25.

Teti, D.M. and Teti, L.O. (1996) 'Infant–parent relationships', in N. Vanzetti and S.W. Duck (eds), *A Lifetime of Relationships*. Pacific Grove, CA: Brooks/Cole. pp. 77-104.

Tornstam. L. (1992) 'Loneliness in marriage', *Journal of Social and Personal Relationships*, 9: 197-217.

Tracy, K., Craig, R.T., Smith, M. and Spisak, F. (1984) 'The discourse of requests: assessment of a compliance-gaining approach', *Human Communication Research*, 10: 513-38.

Trickett, E.J. and Buchanan, R.M. (1997) 'The role of personal relationships in transitions: contributions of an ecological perspective', in S.W. Duck, K. Dindia, W. Ickes, R.M. Milardo, R.S.L. Mills and B.R. Sarason (eds), *Handbook of Personal Relationships* (2nd edn). Chichester: Wiley. pp. 575-94.

Tunstall, J. (1967) *Old and Alone*. New York: Humanities Press.

Umberson, D. and Williams, C.L. (1993) 'Divorced fathers: parental role strain and psychological distress', *Journal of Family Issues*, 14: 378-400.

Valdez, A. (1996) Personal communication, 24 September.

Vangelisti, A. (1994) 'Messages that hurt', in W.R. Cupach and B.H. Spitzberg (eds), *The Dark Side of Interpersonal Communication*. New York: Guilford. pp. 53-82.

Van Lear, C.A. Jr. and Trujillo, N. (1986) 'On becoming acquainted: A longitudinal study of social judgement processes', *Journal of Social and Personal Relationships*, 3: 375-92.

Vanzetti, N. and Duck, S.W. (eds) (1996) *A Lifetime of Relationships*. Pacific Grove, CA: Brooks/Cole.

Vaux, A. (1988) *Social Support: Theory, Research, and Intervention*. New York: Praeger.

Vaux, A. (1990) 'An ecological approach to understanding and facilitating social support', *Journal of Social and Personal Relationships*, 7: 507-18.

Veroff, J., Young, A.M. and Coon, H.M. (1997) 'The early years of marriage', in S.W. Duck, K. Dindia, W. Ickes, R.M. Milardo, R.S.L. Mills and B.R. Sarason (eds), *Handbook of Personal Relationships* (2nd edn). Chichester: Wiley. pp. 431-50.

Vitkus, J. and Horowitz, L.M. (1987) 'Poor social performance of lonely people: lacking skills or adopting a role?', *Journal of Personality and Social Psychology*, 52: 1266-73.

Walker, N.M. and Hops, H. (1973) 'The use of group and individual reinforcement contigencies in the modification of social withdrawal', in L.A. Hanerlynck, L.C. Hardy and E.J. Mosh (eds), *Behavior Change: Methodology, Concept and Practice*. Champaign, IL: Research Press.

Walker, M.B. and Trimboli, A. (1989) 'Communicating affect: the rople of verbal and nonverbal content', *Journal of Language and Social Psychology*, 8: 229-48.

Walker, R.J. and Walker, M.G. (1972) *The English Legal System*. London: Butterworths.

Walster, E.H. and Walster, G.W. (1978) *A New Look at Love*. Reading, MA: Addison-Wesley.

Warner, R.M., Malloy, D., Schneider, K., Knoth, R. and Wilder, B. (1987) 'Rhythmic organization of social interaction and observer ratings of positive affect and involvement', *Journal of Nonverbal Behavior*, 11: 57-74.

Watson, O.M. and Graves, T.D. (1966) 'Quantitative research in proxemic behavior', *American Anthropologist*, 68: 971-85.

Watzlawick, P., Beavin, J. and Jackson, D. (1967) *Pragmatics of Human Communication: A Study of Interactional Patterns, Pathologies and Paradoxes*. New York: Norton.

Weber, A. (1983) 'The breakdown of relationships.' Paper to Conference on Social Interaction and Relationships, Nags Head, North Carolina, May.

Weiss, R.L. and Aved, B.M. (1978) 'Marital satisfaction and depression as predictors of physical health status', *Journal of Consulting and Clinical Psychology*, 46: 1379-84.

Weissman, M.M. (1987) 'Advances in psychiatric epidemiology: rates and risks for depression', *American Journal of Sociology*, 84: 1201–31.

Werking, K. (1997) *Just Good Friends: Cross-Sex Friendships*. New York: Guilford.

Werner, C., Altman, I., Brown, B. and Ginat, J. (1993) 'Celebrations in personal relationships: a transactional/dialectical perspective', in In S.W. Duck (ed.), *Social Contexts of Relationships*. (Vol. 3) *Understanding Relationship Processes*. Newbury Park, CA: Sage. pp. 109–38.

West, J. (1995) 'Understanding how the dynamics of ideology influence violence between intimates', in S.W. Duck and J.T. Wood (eds), *Confronting Relationship Challenges*. (Vol. 5) *Understanding Relationship Processes*. Thousand Oaks, CA: Sage. pp. 129–49.

West, L. (1994) 'The importance of what is left unsaid.' Paper to the Speech Communication Association Conference, New Orleans, LA, November.

West, L. (1996) 'Deception as a social practice.' Paper to the Annual Convention of the Speech Communication Association, San Antonio, TX, November.

West, L. and Duck, S.W. (1996) '"My sister is a pro-life lesbian tax evader": self disclosure as social commentary and impression management.' Paper presented to Speech Communication Association, November, San Diego.

West, L., Anderson, J. and Duck, S.W. (1996) 'Crossing the barriers to friendship between men and women', in J.T. Wood (ed.), *Gendered Relationships*. Mountain View, CA: Mayfield Publishing. pp. 111–27.

Weston, K. (1991) *Families We Choose*. New York: Columbia University Press.

Wheeler, L. and Nezlek, J. (1977) 'Sex difference in social participation', *Journal of Personality and Social Psychology*, 45: 943–53.

Wheeler, L., Reis, H.T. and Nezlek, J. (1983) 'Loneliness, social interaction, and sex roles', *Journal of Personality and Social Psychology*, 35: 742–54.

Wilkinson, J. and Canter, S. (1982) *Social Skills Training Manual*. Chichester: Wiley.

Winters, A. (1993) 'You shouldn't talk like that: an analysis of factors that affect the perceived inappropriateness of swearing.' Unpublished MSc thesis, Illinois State University.

Wiseman, J.P. (1986) 'Friendship: bonds and binds in a voluntary relationship', *Journal of Social and Personal Relationships*, 3: 191–211.

Wiseman, J.P. and Duck, S.W. (1995) 'Having and managing enemies: a very challenging relationship', in S.W. Duck and J.T. Wood (eds), *Relationship Challenges*. (Vol. 5) *Understanding Relationship Processes*. Thousand Oaks, CA: Sage. pp. 43–72.

Wittenberg, M.T. and Reis, H.T. (1986) 'Loneliness, social skills, and social perception', *Personality and Social Psychology Bulletin*, 12: 121–30.

Wood, J.T. (1993) 'Engendered relationships: interaction, caring, power, and responsibility in intimacy', in S.W. Duck (ed.), *Social Contexts of Relationships*. (Vol. 3) *Understanding Relationship Processes*. Newbury Park, CA: Sage. pp. 27–53.

Wood, J.T. (1995) 'Feminist scholarship and the study of relationships', *Journal of Social and Personal Relationships*, 12: 103–20.

Wood, J.T. (1997) *Communication in our Lives*. Belmont, CA: Wadsworth.

Wood, J.T. and Duck, S.W. (1995) 'Off the beaten track: new shores for relationship research', in J.T. Wood and S.W. Duck (eds), *Understudied Relationships: Off the Beaten Track*. (Vol. 6) *Understanding Relationship Processes*. Thousand Oaks, CA: Sage. pp. 1–21.

Wright, P.H. (1978) 'Toward a theory of friendship based on a conception of the self', *Human Communication Research*, 4: 196–207.

Wright, P.H. and Wright, K.D. (1995) 'Co-dependency: personality syndrome or relational process?', in S.W. Duck and J.T. Wood (eds), *Confronting Relationship Challenges*. (Vol. 5) *Understanding Relationship Processes*. Thousand Oaks, CA: Sage. pp. 109–28.

Wyler, A.R., Masuda, M. and Holmes, T.H. (1971) 'Magnitude of life events and seriousness of illness', *Psychosomatic Medicine*, 33: 115–22.

Yingling, J. (1994) 'Constituting friendship in talk and meta-talk', *Journal of Social and Personal Relationships*, 11: 411–26.

Young, J.E. (1982) 'Loneliness, depression and cognitive therapy: theory and application', in

L.A. Peplau and D. Perlman (eds), *Loneliness: a Current Sourcebook of Theory Research and Therapy*. New York: Wiley.

Zaidel, S.F. and Mehrabian, A. (1969) 'The ability to communicate and infer positive and negative attitudes facially and vocally', *Journal of Experimental Research in Personality*, 3: 233–41.

Zakahi, W.R. and Duran, R.L. (1982) 'All the lonely people: the relationship among loneliness, communicative competence and communication anxiety', *Communication Quarterly*, 30: 203–9.

Zakahi, W.R. and Duran, R.L. (1985) 'Loneliness, communicative competence and communication apprehension: extension and replication', *Communication Quarterly*, 33: 50–60.

Zietlow, P.H. and Sillars, A.L. (1988) 'Life-stage differences in communication during marital conflicts', *Journal of Social and Personal Relationships*, 5: 223–45.

Zimmer, T. (1986) 'Premarital anxieties', *Journal of Social and Personal Relationships*, 3: 149–60.

Zola, A.K. (1972) 'Studying the decision to see a doctor', in Z.J. Lipowski (ed.), *Psychological Aspects of Physical Illness*. Basel: Karger.

Zorn, T. (1995) 'Bosses and buddies: constructing and performing simultaneously hierarchical and close friendship relationships', in J.T. Wood and S.W. Duck (eds), *Understudied Relationships: Off the Beaten Track*. (Vol. 6) *Understanding Relationship Processes*. Thousand Oaks, CA: Sage. pp. 122–47.

Author Index

Subject Index